Atrocities and international accountability

DATE DUE

JUN 1 0 2008	
SEP 1 0 2008	
JUN 1 0 2009	

Atrocities and international accountability: Beyond transitional justice

Edited by Edel Hughes, William A. Schabas and Ramesh Thakur

United Nations University Press

TOKYO · NEW YORK · PARIS

The views expressed in this publication are those of the authors and do not necessarily reflect the views of the United Nations University.

United Nations University Press
United Nations University, 53-70, Jingumae 5-chome,
Shibuya-ku, Tokyo 150-8925, Japan
Tel: +81-3-3499-2811   Fax: +81-3-3406-7345
E-mail: sales@hq.unu.edu   general enquiries: press@hq.unu.edu
http://www.unu.edu

United Nations University Office at the United Nations, New York
2 United Nations Plaza, Room DC2-2062, New York, NY 10017, USA
Tel: +1-212-963-6387   Fax: +1-212-371-9454
E-mail: unuona@ony.unu.edu

United Nations University Press is the publishing division of the United Nations University.

Cover design by Sese-Paul Design

Cover photograph: UN Photo by Mathew Elavanalthoduka
UN peacekeepers effect the arrest of former Liberian President Charles Taylor at Monrovia's Roberts International Airport on his arrival from Nigeria. (29 March 2006)

Printed in India

ISBN 978-92-808-1141-4

Library of Congress Cataloging-in-Publication Data

Atrocities and international accountability : beyond transitional justice / edited by Edel Hughes, William A. Schabas and Ramesh Thakur.
    p.   cm.
 Includes bibliographical references and index.
 ISBN 978-9280811414 (pbk.)
 1. Crimes against humanity. 2. Criminal liability. 3. Atrocities. 4. Truth commissions. 5. Reconciliation—Political aspects. I. Hughes, Edel. II. Schabas, William, 1950– III. Thakur, Ramesh Chandra, 1948–
 K5301.A978   2007
 345′.0235—dc22   2007025786

Contents

Tables and figures

Contributors

Diane Marie Amann: Professor of Law at University of California, Davis. Professor Amann's scholarship examines the interaction of national, regional and international legal regimes in efforts to combat atrocity and cross-border crime. Her recent works have focused on legal responses to US policies respecting executive detention at Guantánamo and elsewhere, on the use of foreign and international law in US constitutional decision-making and on trials of deposed leaders in Iraq, Serbia and West Africa.

Peter R. Baehr: Emeritus Professor of Human Rights at Utrecht University and Leiden University and former Professor of International Relations at the University of Amsterdam. Professor Baehr is a former director of the Netherlands Institute of Human Rights and the Netherlands School of Human Rights Research.

He is a member of the Committee on Human Rights of the Netherlands Advisory Council on International Affairs.

Matthew Brubacher: Associate Analyst with the Jurisdiction, Complementarity and Cooperation Division with the Office of the Prosecutor, International Criminal Court.

Helena Cobban: Writer and internationally syndicated columnist on global affairs. Ms. Cobban has contributed a regular column to the *Christian Science Monitor* since 1990 and is a Contributing Editor of *Boston Review*, where her recent articles have included analysis on Lebanon's Hezbollah, on Hamas in Palestine and on the July 2006 war between Israel and Hezbollah.

David M. Crane: Distinguished Professor of Practice at Syracuse University College of Law and a member of the faculty of the Institute for National Security and Counterterrorism. Professor Crane was formerly Chief Prosecutor at the Special Criminal Court for Sierra Leone and served over 30 years in the federal government of the United States.

Gerald Gahima: Judge at the War Crimes Chamber of the Court of Bosnia-Herzegovina and Deputy Chief Justice of the Supreme Court of Rwanda. Mr. Gahima is a former Procurator General of Rwanda. As Procurator General he was responsible for, among other things, the prosecution of genocide and other violations of international humanitarian law arising from the 1994 genocide. Mr. Gahima is a member of the International Association of Genocide Scholars and has written abundantly on the crime.

Jorge Heine: CIGI Professor of Global Governance at Wilfrid Laurier University, and Distinguished Fellow at the Centre for International Governance Innovation in Waterloo, Ontario. A Vice-President of the International Political Science Association (IPSA), Professor Heine served previously as Ambassador of Chile to India (2003–2007) and to South Africa (1994–1999) and as a Cabinet Minister and Deputy Minister in the Chilean government.

Edel Hughes: Junior Lecturer in Law at the University of Limerick, Ireland and PhD Candidate at the Irish Centre for Human Rights, National University of Ireland, Galway.

Jeff Kingston: Director of Asian Studies at Temple University Japan. A former Fulbright Fellow, Mr. Kingston's areas of specialty include Indonesia, South-East Asian politics and contemporary Japanese history. He is the author of *Japan's Quiet Revolution: Politics, Economics and Society* and *Japan in Transformation, 1952–2000*, and also writes a regular column for the *Japan Times*.

Rama Mani: Executive Director of the International Centre for Ethnic Studies (ICES) in Colombo, Sri Lanka. Dr Mani previously served as a faculty member at the Geneva Centre for Security Policy. She is an established international practitioner and scholar, teaching and publishing on the areas of justice and human rights, conflict and peacebuilding, rule of law and the security sector and the United Nations and terrorism. From January to December 2002 she was the Senior Strategy Adviser to the Centre for Humanitarian Dialogue in Geneva, addressing issues of humanitarian policy and conflict mediation.

Jeremy Rabkin: Professor of Government at Cornell University. Professor Rabkin is a member of the board of academic advisors to the *Harvard Journal of Law and Public Policy* and publishes widely on areas of international law and sovereignty. His recent publications include *Law without Nations?* and *The Case for Sovereignty*.

Leila Nadya Sadat: Professor of Law at Washington University School of Law. Professor Sadat is a leading authority in international criminal law and human rights and a prolific scholar. She chaired the International Law Association committee on the International Criminal Court in 1995 and was also an NGO delegate to the UN Preparatory Committee and to the 1998 UN diplomatic conference in Rome at which the Court was established.

William A. Schabas: Professor of Human Rights Law and Director of the Irish Centre for Human Rights, National University of Ireland, Galway. Professor Schabas teaches and publishes in the area of international law. He is editor-in-chief of *Criminal Law Forum*, the quarterly journal of the International Society for the Reform of Criminal Law and from 2002–2004 served as a truth commissioner on Sierra Leone's Truth and Reconciliation Commission. In 2006 Professor Schabas was appointed an officer of the Order of Canada.

Michael P. Scharf: Professor of Law at Case Western Reserve University, and Director of the Frederick K. Cox International Law Centre. In 2004/05, Professor Scharf served as a member of the elite international team of experts that provided training to the judges and prosecutors of the Iraqi Special Tribunal, and in 2006 he led the first training session for the Prosecutors and Judges of the newly established UN Cambodia Genocide Tribunal. Previously Professor Scharf served in the Office of the Legal Adviser of the US Department of State.

Ramesh Thakur: Distinguished Fellow at the Centre for International Governance Innovation, and Professor of Political Science at the University of Waterloo in Canada. Professor Thakur was Vice-Rector and Senior Vice-Rector of the United Nations University (and Assistant Secretary-General of the United Nations) from 1998 to 2007. Born in India, Professor Thakur was educated in India and Canada and has held full-time academic appointments in Fiji, New Zealand and Australia and visiting appointments elsewhere. He was Professor of International Relations and Director of Asian Studies at the University of Otago in New Zealand and Professor and Head of the Peace Research Centre at the Australian National University in Canberra before joining UNU in 1998. He was a Commissioner on the International Commission on Intervention and State Sovereignty and one of the principal authors of its report *The Responsibility to Protect*. He was Senior Adviser on Reforms and Principal Writer of the UN Secretary-General's second reform report. He is the author/editor of some 30 books with the most recent being *War in Our Time: Reflections on Iraq, Terrorism and Weapons of Mass Destruction* (United Nations University Press, 2007). He also writes regularly for the national and international quality press, including the *Australian, Daily Yomiuri, Die Tageszeitung, Globe and Mail, Hindu, International Herald Tribune and Japan Times*.

Acronyms

ANC:	African National Congress
CAVR:	Commission for Reception, Truth and Reconciliation (East Timor)
CTF:	Commission of Truth and Friendship (East Timor)
DRC:	Democratic Republic of Congo
ECJ:	European Court of Justice
GDR:	German Democratic Republic
GDP:	gross domestic product
GPA:	General Peace Agreement
ICC:	International Criminal Court
ICTJ:	International Center for Transitional Justice
ICTR:	International Criminal Tribunal for Rwanda
ICTY:	International Criminal Tribunal for the former Yugoslavia
IMT:	International Military Tribunal
NGO:	non-governmental organization
OTP:	Office of the Prosecutor
PTC:	Pre-Trial Chamber
RPA:	Rwandan Patriotic Army
RPE:	Rules of Procedure and Evidence
RPF:	Rwandan Patriotic Front
RUF:	Revolutionary United Front (Sierra Leone)
SADF:	South African Defence Force
SCSL:	Special Court for Sierra Leone
SCU:	Special Crimes Unit (East Timor)
TJ:	transitional justice
TRC:	truth and reconciliation commission

1

Introduction

Edel Hughes, William A. Schabas and Ramesh Thakur

The notion that there should be some form of accountability for state-sponsored atrocities is one that is posited within discussions of the broader transitional justice framework. Its function, it is argued, is to reverse the tradition of official impunity so often prevalent in societies emerging from conflict, and perhaps deter future violators of human rights. Although the first *Human Security Report*, published in 2005, points to a decline in the number of violent conflicts,[1] the scale of those witnessed over the past two decades has been brutally evident, due in no small part to improvements in mass media communications.

Rebuilding societies where conflict has occurred is rarely a simple process but where conflict has been accompanied by gross and systematic violations of human rights the procedure becomes a good deal more fraught. Emerging societies may experience the same problems, such as a weakened economy and weakened political institutions, but where there have been widespread abuses of rights there is the additional problem of ensuring that there is some form of accountability, be it prosecutions or otherwise, for the perpetrators. Accountability, and the form it takes, may be affected by a number of issues, including the intensity of the former conflict and abuses, the current status of political institutions and societal desire for some form of acknowledgement of the past.

Inherent in the accountability process is the idea that there are a number of practical concessions that must be made. It is not always possible to punish all those responsible for human rights violations (it would, for example, have been impossible to try everyone responsible for massacres

Atrocities and international accountability: Beyond transitional justice, Hughes, Schabas and Thakur (eds), United Nations University Press, 2007, ISBN 978-92-808-1141-4

in Rwanda as the number may have been as high as 300,000), nor indeed is it always possible to punish even those who bear the greatest responsibility, as society may demand an accountability process that does not involve criminal prosecutions. Indeed the form that the accountability process may take is a much-debated subject among scholars of transitional justice. The traditional argument revolves around the peace versus justice paradigm and whether there can be justice without criminal sanctions, and accordingly peace without this form of "justice". Whereas retribution and justice are often attributed to trials, reconciliation, the argument goes, may be better achieved in the form of a truth and reconciliation commission.

The trials versus truth commission debate, however, can sometimes be usurped by the official functioning of some sort of independent inquiry. In Argentina, for example, the National Commission on Disappeared Persons was not given prosecutorial powers but had sufficient resources to complete a comprehensive investigation, culminating in a report, *Nunca Más!*, which was later relied on in the trials of some military leaders. The chapters in this collection all look in some way at how the law responds to political change in post-conflict societies and how it holds perpetrators of mass atrocity accountable. Transitional justice issues are no longer solely the preserve of individual countries; the international community through its sponsorship of prosecutions and other accountability processes has become increasingly involved in restoring order and dealing with human rights violators. This is a development that is not welcomed by all; in fact Jeremy Rabkin argues that the idea of global justice is both undesirable and unattainable; to embrace some form of international criminal justice, it is asserted, one must accept both a new understanding of international law and a new understanding of criminal justice.

If this book tells us anything about societies in transition, it is that there can be no blanket solution in terms of the form accountability is to take. As much as each conflict varies, so too do the mechanisms engaged to deal with it – legal and moral concerns must be balanced with political reality in determining the appropriate reaction to atrocities. In Chapter 2, Peter Baehr sets out the various procedures, ranging from vengeance to truth commissions, used by societies in coming to terms with the past. He identifies a major problem in dealing with the past may be that the "guilty" ones may often be those who are needed for the rebuilding of society, without whose knowledge and expertise it may be more difficult to move forward. Baehr concludes the chapter by noting the importance of giving the past some sort of official recognition, although he is sceptical about the extent to which societies can learn from past experience. The collective memory, he notes, is short.

Chapters 3 and 4 look at the timing, nature and form that transitional justice must take. Rama Mani examines some of the core questions that concern the search for justice, reconciliation and the rule of law in post-conflict societies. These include issues that must be resolved before the decision to pursue transitional justice is taken and the processes and measures of reconciliation and transitional justice embarked upon after conflict. Mani concludes that peace and justice are irrevocably inter-connected, interdependent and mutually reinforcing and can and must be pursued in tandem. Reparative justice, she asserts, underscores the requirement of a broader, more realistic framework to respond to the diverse needs in post-conflict societies. Helena Cobban looks in particular at transitional justice and conflict termination in Mozambique, Rwanda and South Africa in Chapter 4. Although the three countries underwent markedly different experiences, Cobban stresses that this does not mean that one cannot extract general lessons from them, rather it points to which kind of conflict termination and post-violence policies can make the most constructive approach to building a sustainable peace.

In Chapter 5, Jorge Heine examines some of the dilemmas of dealing with the past in new democracies and gives an insightful account of the trials of Augusto Pinochet. Heine looks at the idea of truth and recon-ciliation commissions as a compromise between blanket amnesties and special prosecutions, using the examples of Argentina, Chile and South Africa, and concludes that they are the product of the need of statesmen and politicians more generally to come to terms with the past. The theme of justice and reconciliation is explored further in the context of East Timor in Chapter 6. Jeff Kingston outlines the process of dealing with human rights abuses in East Timor and attempts at pursuing justice and holding perpetrators accountable. Kingston explains that justice in East Timor remains elusive and signs of progress toward achieving it are neg-ligible, mainly due to Indonesia and an apathetic international commu-nity. Discovery of the truth alone does not bring reconciliation in the East Timorese context and the postponement of publication of the report of the Commission of Reception, Truth and Reconciliation in December 2005 generated dismay. Kingston also considers the establishment of the Commission for Truth and Friendship in 2005 and whether this will ulti-mately provide any solace given that its establishment has been criticized as providing impunity to perpetrators and denying victims future access to justice.

If the idea that criminal punishments are necessary still dominates the transitional justice landscape, then the case of Sierra Leone presents an interesting example of the peace versus justice dichotomy, having experi-enced both a truth commission and a special court, which were held si-multaneously for a time. Whilst the truth commission concluded with the dissemination of its final report in October 2004, in Chapter 8 we are given an interesting insight into the workings of the Special Court by Prosecutor David Crane, who outlines succinctly the practical challenges of investigating and indicting those allegedly responsible for massive human rights violations. The Special Court for Sierra Leone is vested with trying those who bear the greatest responsibility for war crimes, crimes against humanity and other violations of international humanitarian law committed during the conflict in that country. The fact that not everyone responsible can be tried is central to the idea of prosecutorial discretion, which has existed in international criminal justice since the Nuremberg trials. Matthew Brubacher explores this concept in Chapter 9 and evaluates what it means in practice at the international tribunals and the International Criminal Court. Brubacher argues that whilst the International Criminal Court must maintain its independence in pursuing accountability, the jurisdictional and admissibility criteria of the Court as well as the need to obtain effective cooperation requires it to pursue a process of international consensus building.

Where prosecutions are neither possible nor desirable, alternatives may be sought. These are investigated by Gerald Gahima in Chapter 10, who looks in particular at the *gacaca* court system utilized in Rwanda following the 1994 genocide. An exploration of this alternative court system is an especially useful one, given the fact that there is also a United Nations-sponsored international criminal tribunal dealing with issues arising from the horrific events of 1994. Gahima examines the structure and jurisdiction of the gacaca system as well as the relevant procedures and penalties, and provides a critical evaluation of the system. The Rwanda tribunal and its counterpart, established to prosecute those responsible for atrocities committed in the former Yugoslavia, have naturally come under close scrutiny from the international legal community. The following two chapters deal with the vexed issue of the impartiality, or lack thereof, of international criminal judges. Diane Amann uses the term "impartiality deficit" to describe how demands for fairness and justice centre almost exclusively on victims, with scant regard to the corollary rights of alleged perpetrators. In order to achieve a justice system free of impartiality deficit, therefore, its founding charter must allude to the defence function, equal in status, resources and respect to the judicial, administrative and prosecutorial functions. Amann concludes by advocating that international criminal justice proceed alongside efforts to confront and correct errors inherent in it. In Chapter 12, William Schabas addresses the question of independence and impartiality of the judiciary in the ad hoc tribunals for the former Yugoslavia, Rwanda and Sierra Leone as well as in the International Criminal Court. The chapter analyses the independence and impartiality of judges by examining issues related to their qualifications, selection, training and conditions of service. Schabas concludes that there are structural weaknesses in the system, albeit that judicial independence and impartiality has been better protected by the International Criminal Court than by the ad hoc tribunals.

In the transitional justice arena it is perhaps fair to say that no issue provokes more division and controversy than that of amnesties. Whilst the major international non-governmental organizations and numerous legal scholars argue that amnesties are illegal under international law, if not for all crimes then at least for the most heinous, they have been used to great effect in some transitional societies, South Africa being a case in point. Because of the controversial nature of amnesties, it is often forgotten that they can allow for some measure of accountability and do not have to be mechanisms behind which perpetrators of human rights abuses can shelter with impunity. The final two contributions address the vexed issues arising from amnesty, exile and the duty to prosecute. Leila Sadat argues that the legal effect of any particular grant of amnesty or exile will be determined, in part, by the forum before which the amnesty is invoked. Michael Scharf concludes the collection of essays with a look at the contemporary debates surrounding the idea of relinquishing criminal prosecutions in the attempt to guarantee sustainable peace.

The long-held view that there should be a permanent forum where international justice would be "seen to be done" received a huge boost with the establishment of the International Criminal Court. The complex issues arising from international criminal justice and accountability for atrocity remain, however. This collection brings together contributions from some of the leading scholars in the transitional and international justice legal field. It is hoped that the theoretical analysis and pertinent case examples will be of assistance to both practitioners and scholars alike.

Note

1. A. Mack, ed. (2005) *Human Security Report* (Vancouver: The Human Security Centre: 17) states "... in terms of battle-deaths, the 1990s was the least violent decade since the end of World War II. By the beginning of the 21st century, the probability of any country being embroiled in an armed conflict was lower than at any time since the early 1950s."

2

How to come to terms with the past

Peter R. Baehr

> The truth is something that trials can acknowledge, but not something that legal processes are needed to discover.[1]

> The moral consideration ... is one of amending historical injustices.[2]

All national societies tend to remember – if not glorify – their past. National history is taught in school in order to make the young people aware of what happened to the nation in its past. It is seen as a contribution to the creation and upholding of a national identity, in addition to such symbols as the national flag, the national anthem and, in some cases, the national language – all of which should be treated with respect. This applies both to the distant past as well as to more recent events. Organizing days of remembrance is one way of emphasizing what happened in the past.[3] In the Netherlands, a small Western European country that was occupied by Nazi Germany between 1940 and 1945, "the war" is the subject of national commemoration – on the fourth of May, when a period of two minutes of silence is observed[4] in commemoration of the war dead, while the day after is celebrated by many people as a national holiday. It has been suggested by some that such celebrations tend to die out when there are no more survivors who have personal memories of what has happened. That need not be necessarily so. In the United Kingdom, for instance, to this very day, the dead of the First World War are widely commemorated on Armistice Day by people wearing paper poppies[5] on

Atrocities and international accountability: Beyond transitional justice, Hughes, Schabas and Thakur (eds), United Nations University Press, 2007, ISBN 978-92-808-1141-4

their lapels, and (mainly British) schoolchildren continue to tend war graves in France and Belgium.[6]

All this refers to the glorious past. But what about less glorious events? In the Netherlands, which tends to glorify its World War II resistance fighters, a higher percentage of its Jewish population was killed than in any other Western European country.[7] Historians have suggested that this was not only due to greater German efficiency, but also to the activities of Dutch collaborators.[8]

Such a less glorious past is of particular relevance to persons accused of having been guilty of gross violations of human rights and international humanitarian law. They have committed international crimes such as genocide; torture; cruel, inhuman and degrading treatment or punishment; disappearances; wanton killings; abductions; death in detention; rape; "ethnic cleansing"; robbery; and ill-treatment of civilians – practices with which we in this day and age have become well familiar. The question of accountability for such acts arises whenever a change of regime has occurred, either because of internal political developments or by means of international intervention: Argentina, Cambodia, Chile, Guatemala, Germany after reunification, Czechoslovakia after the fall of the Communist regime, the former Yugoslavia, South Africa after the end of apartheid, Peru, Sierra Leone – to name just a few. In some cases such persons are tried by domestic courts, in other cases international criminal tribunals are established, as with the former Yugoslavia and Rwanda. In other cases a process of "lustration" is established: a system of inspection to determine whether such persons are qualified to hold official positions under the new administration. In almost 30 countries, so-called "truth and reconciliation commissions" have been established.

In some of these cases, actual punishment of the culprits is at issue, while in others it is mainly the gathering of information about what has happened in the past. In many cases, such as that of the so-called "disappearances" in countries such as Argentina and Chile, the relatives and friends of the victims more or less knew already or at least had strong suspicions about what had happened. The famous "Mothers of the Plaza de Mayo" in Buenos Aires, who held their weekly silent demonstrations,[9] harboured little hope that they would ever see their loved ones again. But what they and others who ask for truth-finding want is official confirmation of what has happened: on the part of the government, the courts, other public officials or, for that matter, a truth and reconciliation commission. Such official confirmation may take the form of financial reparations, though full financial compensation for what has happened is in itself impossible. How could a mother who lost her son, a wife who lost her husband, be financially compensated?

The most extensive financial reparations have been paid by the German government to the victims of the Nazi-regime: *Wiedergutmachung*.[10] All in all, almost DM 100 billion have been paid out to the victims and their surviving relatives. Not all former victims were willing to accept such reparations, but what is important is that the German government in this way acknowledged its involvement in what had happened in the period 1933–1945. This in itself was more important than the actual size of the financial reparations. The term *Wiedergutmachung* ("making good again") deserves some special attention. Obviously, the Nazi crimes cannot be made good again. What has happened has happened. As Nicholas Tavuchis, in his book about apologies, has rightly observed, "An apology no matter how sincere or effective, does not and cannot *undo* what has been done."[11] What the post-World War II West German government meant, by using that term, was to do their utmost to show its distancing from what had happened in the past by its willingness to pay damages to the victims and their next of kin.

A special form of recognition of guilt that has received much attention in recent years is the offering of "apologies" for what has happened in the past.[12] This can happen in the form of an official statement by the newly created government. Thus, President Patricio Aylwin of Chile has, on behalf of the state, offered apologies to the victims of the misdeeds of the Pinochet regime and to their relatives. The United Methodist Church, a few years ago, offered its apologies for the slaughter of more than 200 Native Americans in 1864 by an army unit that was commanded by a Methodist lay preacher. The Argentine Roman Catholic Church, at the request of the Pope, had asked for forgiveness for the involvement of priests in the "dirty war" during the military dictatorship that lasted from 1976 to 1983. There is, however, always the problem of the extent of responsibility of today's governments for misdeeds committed by its predecessors. Should the present US government be held responsible for the slaughter of Native American tribes and should it apologize to their descendants? Should the Clinton administration, or the Bush administration for that matter, have apologized to the people of Viet Nam? Should the government of President Nelson Mandela have apologized to the victims of apartheid (Mandela being one of these victims himself)? When Queen Beatrix visited Indonesia in 1995, the matter of apologies came up in public discussions in the Netherlands. The Dutch government was not in favour of letting her offer apologies to the people of Indonesia as had been suggested. Apologies for what? For three hundred years of colonial domination? The bloody subjection of Aceh by Dutch troops at the beginning of the twentieth century? The military actions of 1947 and 1948? It is certain that some form of symbolic action may be more effective than the offering of formal apologies. When German Chancellor

Willy Brandt kneeled down in front of the monument for Jewish victims in Warsaw in 1970, it made a strong impression on many people all over the world.

A major problem when dealing with these matters is that the guilty ones are often persons who are also needed for the rebuilding of society. They command knowledge and expertise that is hard to do without. Sometimes, they are politically important persons who still hold important political positions and are not willing to go before a court or commission. Or they may hold information that they can use by way of blackmail against the new leaders. Moreover, there are such considerations as "we have to move on", "let bygones be bygones", "forgive and forget", "clear the decks". This explains the efforts to move from "truth" toward "reconciliation". The German sociologist Theodor Adorno has spoken in this connection of "false reconciliation": "The attitude that it would be proper for everything to be forgiven and forgotten by those who were wronged is expressed by the party that committed the injustice."[13] A precondition for any form of investigation of what has taken place in the past is that the regime that was responsible for such acts has been replaced. After all, it is not very likely that the guilty ones, as long as they are still in power, will be prepared to cooperate in such investigations. After the change of regime, a period of transition takes place during which society must decide how to deal with the past. This paper deals with alternatives to adjudication: vengeance, denial and truth and reconciliation commissions. The latter are discussed somewhat more at length.

Vengeance

A simple way of dealing with the past is vengeance or the taking of revenge.[14] During the German occupation of the Netherlands, the idea of a *Bijltjesdag* (day of reckoning) was often discussed. Such a process of unsystematic overall revenge was fortunately avoided, but there was something called "Special Criminal Procedures" (*Bijzondere Rechtspleging*), which is nowadays looked upon with somewhat mixed feelings. Under those procedures, the death penalty, which had not been practised in the Netherlands for a great number of years, was reintroduced and war 40 criminals (35 of Dutch nationality and 5 Germans) were executed.[15] The death sentence of four German war criminals was commuted to life imprisonment. Repeated calls for their release caused considerable public uproar. It took until 1989 – that is, 44 years after the war had ended – until the last two remaining prisoners were released.

Directly after the war, the heads of *Moffenmeiden*, women who had had sexual relations with German military men, were shaved and publicly exhibited. It took until the end of the 1980s before children of Dutch national-socialists dared to publish their personal post-war experiences.[16] Reading such memoirs leaves one with a sense of embarrassment about the way in which innocent children of guilty parents were treated after the war.

Acts of vengeance – however understandable against the background of the crimes that were committed – do not fit with the rule of law. If people take the law in their own hands, justice is not served but rather becomes personal revenge or ostracism. Under the rule of law, there is supposed to be an independent court whose members, while not being personally involved with the case, sift the evidence and apply general rules of evidence to individual cases. Under fair trial procedures, the accused has the right to a defence of his choice, who is given sufficient time and opportunity to examine the evidence. When a trial is no more than an act of vengeance, the system is fundamentally flawed. The secret trial of the Romanian dictator Nicolae Ceauşescu and his wife, at the end of 1989, which led to their execution, is notorious. That "trial" was in fact pure revenge. Human rights organizations such as Amnesty International, who held no sympathy whatever toward the accused, rightly protested against the unfairness of that trial. Similarly, the early genocide trials in Rwanda failed to meet elementary international standards of justice. Some defendants had no legal representation; others had lawyers without time to prepare. "The trials themselves were revenge."[17] Many people are questioning the way justice is being served on alleged terrorists imprisoned in the US naval base at Guantánamo, Cuba. It took until very recently for the US Supreme Court to rule that procedures under US law are applicable at Guantánamo.

Denial

In contrast to revenge, there are those who deny that in the past anything wrong has taken place,[18] or that, if such was the case, that the people of the present have anything to do with it. The most far-reaching are those that deny the existence of Nazi extermination camps ("Holocaust denial"). Until quite recently, such thinking could be dismissed as only that held by a few neo-Nazi freaks, but one can no longer close one's eyes to such ideas, since highly respected persons such as Abbé Pierre expressed sympathy for them.[19] In Germany, the expression of such ideas is a criminal offence, which raises of course important problems such as the limits of freedom of expression. The case of the British historian David Irving, who lost a court case in 2000, after he had accused a fellow historian, Deborah Lipstadt, of libel is a well-known one. She had described him as a shoddy historian who had suggested that the Holocaust had never taken place.[20] There are more examples of such denial.

In Japan after the Second World War, war crimes trials were held, as in Nuremberg, by an international tribunal, entirely composed of non-Japanese, dealing with the trial of individual war criminals. Different from post-war Germany, in Japan no official recognition of any form of "war guilt" has been expressed.[21] On the contrary, to the great irritation of other Asian countries, such as China and Korea, which had suffered strongly from Japanese atrocities during the war, Japanese leaders tended to deny any form of guilt or complicity with violations of humanitarian law during World War II. Repeatedly, protests were lodged against the presentation of the war in Japanese schoolbooks, which apparently showed little understanding for Japanese guilt.[22] This denial of guilt has frequently arisen in the cases of the so-called "comfort women", about 200,000 mainly Asian women who during the Japanese occupation where forced into prostitution with Japanese military men. The Japanese government has apologized for this behaviour and helped to set up a private fund to compensate the women. Most of the survivors have refused the money, saying they wanted direct compensation from the Japanese government itself. In January 1997, Japan's chief government spokesman was quoted by Japanese news media as saying that the Asian women sent to front-line brothels were simply trying to make money and were no different from Japanese prostitutes who were operating legally in Japan at the time. In early 2007, the matter came up again when the United States Congress considered a draft resolution demanding a formal apology by Japan for the wartime brothels. Prime Minister Shinzo Abe denied the charges, stating, "There is no evidence to prove there was coercion, nothing to support it". The Chinese Foreign Minister, for his part, urged Japan to accept responsibility for its use of sex slaves during World War II. The Japanese Government did not show great eagerness to do so.[23]

The situation in Communist East Germany, the German Democratic Republic (GDR), was quite different. There, the Nazi past was recognized, but dealt with as if the GDR had nothing to do with it. The communist state of peasants, workers and soldiers was founded on the ruins of the Third Reich, but any involvement with that past was systematically denied. It looked almost as if history had started anew on 7 October 1949, when Walter Ulbricht and Otto Grotewohl began to function as party leaders in the new Soviet-dominated state. That is also the reason why the GDR has never been involved in any kind of *Wiedergutmachung*. There was nothing to compensate, as all involvement with the Nazi past was systematically denied.

Later, after the demise of the GDR, the German situation offered another model for dealing with the past, with the opening of the Stasi (East German secret police) files. It gave victims of the secret police the opportunity to read about what had happened to them and who the perpetrators were.[24] However, there is also the danger that individual reputations can be tarnished without due process – a danger of witch hunting and invasion of privacy. While making information available should be judged positively, there is the danger of the improper use of such information. This is especially the case if it is accompanied by a system of "lustration", as in the former Czechoslovakia, where former government officials were denied the right to serve in the government, because of their involvement in the criticized conduct of the prior regime, without due process.

Ignoring the past comes close to denying it. For example, for many years what happened during the civil war in Spain was widely ignored. The Franco regime had of course reasons of its own not to stress the atrocities committed by its soldiers, but even after the ending of the Franco regime little was done by the Spanish government to reveal the truth. Only recently, stronger voices are heard to deal with that past. An Association for the Recovery of Historic Memory was founded that is trying to create an independent truth commission and has asked the United Nations to request that Spain open its archives to help citizens to locate the bodies of family members that were killed during the civil war and dumped in mass graves by Franco's military forces.[25] A book published in April 2004 – that is, 65 years after the civil war ended – called *The Silent Graves*, by Montse Armengou and Richard Belis, compared the killings to the Holocaust and criticized Spanish politicians and journalists for paying too little attention to the killings.[26] In September 2004, it was reported that the Spanish government had decided to rebury the Republican victims of summary executions and to rehabilitate these victims "juridically and morally". A presidential commission was set up to deal with these matters.[27]

Other governments may, on the contrary, have political reasons to keep the past alive. For instance, the Tutsi-dominated government of Rwanda has turned places where acts of genocide occurred in 1991, such as churches, where Tutsis and moderate Hutus had fled and where they were cruelly murdered, into sites of commemoration. Heaps of skulls and the belongings of the victims are put on display to remind the citizens of Rwanda of what happened in the past, perhaps in the hope that it thus may not happen again.

It should be clear from the illustrations provided above that there may be political reasons both for denying (or forgetting) as well as for revealing the past. It is thus clearly not solely a matter of keeping a straight and reliable historical record.

International adjudication

After the international tribunals of Nuremberg and Tokyo of 1946, it took until 1993 before a decision was reached to set up a comparable tribunal: the one on the former Yugoslavia, followed by that on Rwanda. Surprisingly enough, these tribunals came into being by decisions of the UN Security Council, a body whose mandate it is to look after the maintenance of international peace and security, which does not necessarily include finding ways of dealing with culprits of violations of human rights and international humanitarian law. It was mainly for political reasons that the cases of the former Yugoslavia and Rwanda were singled out for judgement. There is certainly no legal reason why human rights in these countries should be dealt with and similar events in countries such as Burundi, Cambodia, Somalia, Liberia or Zaire/Congo (to name only a few of the more notorious ones) not. Since 1948, the International Law Commission had studied the possibility of setting up a permanent international criminal court, but it took until 1994 for the Commission to submit a full, elaborate proposal, leading to the acceptance of the Statute of the International Criminal Court in 1998, which has now set up its offices in the Hague. Major powers, such as the United States, China and India have refused to become parties to the Statute. The United States has on various occasions expressed its opposition to the notion that US citizens were to be tried by the Court.[28] It has put considerable pressure on other states not to extradite US citizens to the Court. This attitude is somewhat surprising, given the fact that the mandate of the Court is of a supplementary nature; the Court may only act in the absence of action by the national courts of the state concerned.

The decision by the Security Council determined the political character of the two tribunals. Though staffed by eminent jurists of a high moral character, certain decisions remain clearly outside its mandate, for political reasons. So far it has appeared impossible to arrest two persons who have been indicted by the Yugoslavia Tribunal: the Bosnian Serb leaders Radovan Karadžić and Ratko Mladić, although allied soldiers serving with the NATO-led forces in Bosnia encounter the two of them regularly. This brings us to the general problem of peace versus justice, which has been discussed at length in the literature.[29] There is a permanent fear that pursuit of criminal prosecutions could interfere with political agreements that were necessary to end, and keep ended, both the fighting among combatants and the more numerous attacks on and abuses of civilians. This clearly diminishes the authority of the Tribunal. According to the Belgian sociologist Luc Huyse, the crucial challenge consists in finding a balance between the call for justice and the need for political prudence, "or in other words, to reconcile ethical imperatives and political constraints".[30] However, this problem has by no means been resolved. Will the pronouncements of such a tribunal be accepted? Will it, in other words, fit the sense of justice of the population concerned?

The strength of the international criminal tribunals is that they help to serve to individualize guilt. However, one may pause to wonder to what extent this is indeed an advantage, if one considers Daniel Goldhagen's thesis that most of the German people were to a greater or lesser extent involved in the extermination of the Jews.[31] Should all Germans have been punished then? Or only some of them? And by whom? One may well agree with the idea of the lowest common denominator as formulated by David Forsythe: "Perhaps the best that can be said of the Court in the light of the Dayton peace agreement is that once created the Court generated pressures that diplomats could not ignore."[32]

The activities of the criminal tribunals for the former Yugoslavia and Rwanda and the establishment of the International Criminal Court all point in one and the same direction: present and would-be perpetrators should be aware that there may come a day of reckoning in the not so distant future. The case of former Chilean dictator Augusto Pinochet shows that national courts also have become more active than in the past in prosecuting such criminals.[33]

Truth and reconciliation commissions

Truth and reconciliation commissions are a relatively new phenomenon. They appear on the scene after a change of regime, when those who have been engaged in gross violations of human rights have given up their positions of power and been replaced by another, often democratic regime. The chairman of the South African truth and reconciliation commission, Bishop Desmond Tutu, has addressed the main function of his commission as follows:

"So how important is it that the Commission addresses these scars?"

Bishop Tutu: "Absolutely crucial. You see there are some people who have tried to be very facile and let bygones be bygones: they want us to have a national amnesia. And you have to keep saying to those people that to pretend that nothing happened, to not acknowledge that something horrendous did happen to them, is to victimise the victims yet again. But even more important, experience worldwide shows that if you do not not deal with a dark past such as ours, effectively look the beast in the eye, that beast is not going to lie down quietly; it is going, as sure as anything, to come back and haunt you horrendously. We are saying we need to deal with this past as quickly as possible – acknowledge that we have a disgraceful past – then close the door on it and concentrate on the present and the future.

"This is the purpose of the Commission; it is just a small part of a process in which the whole nation must be engaged."[34]

Priscilla Hayner, who has done a major study on the subject, defines truth and reconciliation commissions as "bodies set up to investigate a past history of human rights in a particular country – which can include violations by the military of other government forces or by armed opposition forces."[35] The main objective of such commissions is to reveal the facts of human rights violations under the previous regime. They explicitly do not have the objective of adjudication, but of reconciliation after the facts have been revealed. Especially the truth commissions that were set up in Chile, after the fall of the Pinochet regime, and the one in South Africa have received a great deal of attention. Similar commissions have operated in Argentina, Chad, El Salvador, Guatemala and, most recently, Peru.

The composition of such commissions requires a great deal of care, in order to avoid the impression that they have been established with certain political objectives in mind or in order to whitewash the past. Its members must have the confidence of the public. This may or may not be stimulated by including foreign nationals in the commission, as happened, for instance, in the cases of El Salvador, Guatemala and Sierra Leone.[36] Their independence must be guaranteed. Independence, that is from the government. Therefore, José Zalaquett, who was a prominent member of the Chilean Commission, has argued that the commission should be financed by the state, not by the government: "It is important that the government secures the necessary funds before the commission begins its work. It should not reserve the right to suspend funding."[37]

Some of these commissions have considerable powers. The one in South Africa had the authority to compel witnesses to appear and to hear them under oath. It could even offer a perpetrator indemnity ("amnesty") for the human rights violations he disclosed, provided he performed them with political motives and disclosed full information on who was involved, who gave the orders, what was the objective of the action and so on. The Commission must decide whether the violation in question constituted such a political act.

The first and foremost task of the commission is to present the true facts, or rather to recognize those facts. After all, often the true facts are already well known among the people involved, but they ask for an official recognition. Hayner has called this "sanctioned fact-finding". She quotes then-director of Americas Watch, Juan Mendez: "Knowledge that is officially sanctioned, and thereby made 'part of the public cognitive scene' acquires a mysterious quality that is not there when it is 'truth'."[38]

Michelle Parlevliet has listed the following useful list of objectives to be attained by truth commissions:

- The rehabilitation of victims and the restoration of their dignity;
- The assertion of the rule of law and the building of a human rights culture;
- The legitimization of the State and its institutions;
- The establishment of an authoritative record of the past that can prevent future manipulation and distortion;
- The creation of a so-called "collective memory" that should contribute to a moral revival and provide the basis for national unity; and
- The education of the population and the deterrence of potential perpetrators.[39]

Not all of these objectives will be equally reached by each and every truth commission. It would seem that the establishment of an authoritative record of the past is common to all of them. Whether, as Parlevliet suggests, that will help to "prevent future manipulation and distortion" will depend on the particular circumstances of the case.

The recognition of the facts should help such events from occurring again in the future. It was therefore that the report of the Argentinian National Commission on Disappeared Persons was given the title *Nunca Más!* (Never Again!). Establishing a truth and reconciliation commission is often rather controversial.[40] On the one hand, there are those who prefer a policy of "forgiving and forgetting" and who are of the opinion that this process may be harmed by the establishment of a truth and reconciliation commission. Opposite to this is the idea that true forgiveness is possible only after the recognition of the facts. Also, the former perpetrators are, for obvious reasons, not very enthusiastic about the idea, unless of course it is accompanied by a process of amnesty, as in South Africa. There remains always the danger that a truth and reconciliation commission will contribute to the whitewashing of the misdeeds of a previous regime. See for example the following statement by Ntsiki Biko, widow of the slain South African anti-apartheid activist Steve Biko:

To me it is an insult [to be asked to testify before the South African Truth and Reconciliation Commission], because all that is needed is to have the perpetrators taken to a proper court of justice.... I doubt very much whether they can convince me that this Truth Commission is going to bring us reconciling: one would think of reconciling after justice, but justice must be done first.

It can never be easy. To me, really, it is just opening the wounds for nothing. Because these people are going to go to the Commission – I suppose they have applied or their names have been taken. But if they go there, are they going to tell the truth? Or are they going to lie so they will get amnesty?[41]

Another question is whether, next to members of the governing regime, the military and the police, members of the opposition should also be called to account before a truth and reconciliation commission. The relative success of the operation in South Africa can only be understood against the background of the towering presence of President Nelson Mandela, who saw to it that the truth commission received a considerable amount of public trust. This included his appointment of Bishop Desmond Tutu, who was seen as a man of great personal integrity, as chair of the commission, as well as his insistence that the misdeeds of the African National Congress were also explicitly included in the investigation. In neighbouring Namibia, the government of President Sam Nujoma has remained adamantly opposed to the whole idea of a truth and reconciliation commission. As the former leader of the South West African People's Organization, which itself was responsible for torture and disappearances during its fight for independence, he did and does not want such practices to be officially acknowledged. In contrast, in South Africa there was a powerful political consensus, created by President Mandela, for setting up such a commission; this was obviously lacking in Namibia.

If one wants to establish such a commission, a number of questions must be answered regarding the scope of its mandate, the time period to be covered, the question of whether its activities should be published, and the question of whether the names of the culprits should be made public.[42] The question must also be answered whether it should begin its activities as soon as possible after the change of regime or whether it is wiser to have some time elapse.[43] In favour of starting quickly is that public attention may wane after too much time has gone by. On the other hand, this may also be an argument to wait a little, so that emotions have cooled down and the commission can do its work in an atmosphere suitable for quiet and dispassionate analysis.

Finally, there is the important aspect of transparency of the process, which received special attention in the case of South Africa. The South African writer Antjie Krog, who has written a moving account of what happened at the South African truth commission, has made a powerful plea for openness of the process:

It is crucial to us that the Commission and its narratives be captured as fully as possible on ordinary news bulletins. Even people who do no more than listen to the news should be given a full understanding of the essence of the Commission, and hear quite a few of its stories. This means that the past has to be put into hard news gripping enough to make bulletin headlines, into reports that the bulletin-writers in Johannesburg cannot ignore. To do this we will have to use the full spectrum of hard news techniques and where necessary develop and reform them according to our needs.[44]

Conclusion

Human beings are able to commit all kinds of "inhuman" acts. This observation is true for all times and for all places.[45] What we like to call "humanitarian" is a thin layer of civilization, which is ruptured time and again. The atrocities committed by the Nazis and their accomplices and the ethnic cleansing operations in the former Yugoslavia serve to demonstrate that this observation applies also to the western world as well. These are violations of international rules of human rights and humanitarian law. Fortunately enough, after a longer or shorter period the violations always come to an end. Then the question must be faced: what next? How does one find a proper balance between the call for justice and political prudence? One thing is clear: most of the victims, their relatives and survivors, consider revelation of what has really happened of the utmost importance. This fact contains an assignment to society: to chart the past as well as possible and give it official recognition.

Two of the approaches discussed must, for obvious reasons, be rejected out of hand: acts of revenge and denial of the past. Vengeance is uncontrollable, violates the rule of law and holds no guarantee whatever that the guilty will be punished or the truth revealed. The same is true of denying the past. Offering financial reparation or other forms of compensation are at least gestures toward the victims and their relatives, and thus an official recognition of the past, which therefore is of great importance. It need not necessarily contribute toward revealing the past.

The latter objective can be served either by adjudication, whether national or international, or by the establishment of a truth and reconciliation commission. It is difficult to say which of these should be preferred. If adjudication according to the rules of fair trial is possible and the guilty ones can be caught and convicted, this should be preferred. But political circumstances do not always allow this procedure. In the absence of the proper preconditions for fair trial and in the absence of a permanent international tribunal, the establishment of a truth and reconciliation commission may be helpful. It should be added, however, that it remains for the time being an open question whether finding the "truth" will always contribute to reconciliation. Truth finding may also reveal feelings of resentment and open old wounds. In such cases "truth" and "reconciliation" do not necessarily go together. However, in the end, one has to start finding the truth first and then see whether or not it will lead to reconciliation. It should be clear that reconciliation is a long-term process for every society. It has been suggested that true reconciliation requires a focus on social justice and a concern with socio-economic conditions.[46] However, whether or not the process of reconciliation turns out to be successful, leaving war crimes unpunished is worse: it leaves the cycle of impunity unbroken. The process of truth finding and truth telling may be as important as its actual outcome.

Truth commissions tend to emphasize the role of the victims, while criminal trials focus on the perpetrators.[47] The former is a quasi-judicial process, whereas the latter is a real judicial process. In this context, it will be quite revealing to observe the further development of the process in Sierra Leone, which is one of the few countries that has experienced both a truth commission and an ad hoc criminal court.[48] It may be wise to set one's sights not too high and to be satisfied with whatever one can achieve. In this context, it is fitting to cite Michael Ignatieff, who has described the potential achievements of a truth and reconciliation commission as follows: "All that a truth commission can achieve is to reduce the number of lies that can be circulated unchallenged in public discourse.... The past is an argument and the function of truth commissions, like the function of honest historians, is simply to purify the argument, to narrow the range of permissible lies."[49]

There is reason to be somewhat sceptical about the extent to which societies are able to learn from past experience. *Nunca Más* is a noble objective, but the question remains whether it can be realized and, if so, for how long. The collective memory of society is short. Nevertheless, to try to reveal the truth is better than to do nothing at all.

Notes

1. L. E. Fletcher and H. M. Weinstein (2002) "Violence and Social Repair: Rethinking the Contribution of Justice to Reconciliation", *Human Rights Quarterly* 24(3): 589.
2. E. Barkan (2003) "Legal Settlements as a Form of Cultural Politics: A Moral and Historical Framework for the Right to Reparation", in G. Ulrich and L. Krabbe Boserup, eds, *Human Rights in Development Yearbook 2001: Reparations: Redressing Past Wrongs*, London: Kluwer Law International, p. 407.
3. See M. Minow (1998) *Between Vengeance and Forgiveness*, Boston: Beacon Press, p. 143.
4. After considerable debate it was decided to include the people who died in the colonial war in Indonesia (1945–1949), the war in Korea (1950–1953) and eventually all war dead. More recently, children of Moroccan immigrants committed some disturbances on that day, as they felt that commemorating Jewish victims of the Second World War was akin to expressing support for the state of Israel.
5. After the poet John Macrae's famous lines: "In Flanders fields the poppies blow/ Between the crosses, row on row."

6. Nowadays, there are continuous debates in both France and Belgium whether these graves should still be maintained or be turned into building sites.
7. Of the prewar 140,000 Jews, only some 20,000 survived the war.
8. J. Presser (1969) *The Destruction of the Dutch Jews*, New York: EP Dutton.
9. See I. Guest (1990) *Behind the Disappearances: Argentina's Dirty War against Human Rights and the United Nations*, Philadelphia: University of Pennsylvania Press, pp. 52 ff.
10. See E. Barkan (2000) *The Guilt of Nations: Restitution and Negotiating Historical Injustices*, Baltimore: The Johns Hopkins University Press, pp. 3–29; and K. J. Partsch (1992) "The Federal Republic of Germany", in T. van Boven, C. Flinterman, F. Grünfeld and I. Westendorp, eds, "Seminar on the Right to Restitutions, Compensation and Rehabilitation for Victims of Gross Violations of Human Rights and Fundamental Freedoms, 11–15 March 1992", SIM Special (SIM Utrecht), No. 12, pp. 130–145 at 132. "The uniqueness of the case was that, for the first time, a perpetrator paid compensation to the victims without being forced to do so by the victors in the war" (Barkan, p. 411 n. 2).
11. N. Tavuchis (1991) *Mea Culpa: A Sociology of Apology and Reconciliation*, Stanford, Calif.: Stanford University Press, p. 5.
12. See R. L. Brooks (1999) *When Sorry Isn't Enough: The Controversy over Apologies and Reparations for Human Injustice*, New York: New York University Press; M. Gibney and E. Rokstrom (2001) "The Status of State Apologies", *Human Rights Quarterly* 23: 911–939; and J. Torpey, ed. (2003) *Politics and the Past: On Repairing Historical Injustices*, Lanham, Md.: Rowman and Littlefield.
13. T. Adorno as cited in Michael Ignatieff (1996) "Articles of Faith", *Index on Censorship* 25(5): 110–122 at 112.
14. Minow, *Between Vengeance and Forgiveness*, pp. 10–14.
15. Since 1983, the Dutch Constitution contains an article (114) that states "The death penalty cannot be imposed."
16. See for example D. Blaauwendraad-Doorduijn (1989) *Niemandsland* (*No Man's Land*), Amsterdam: Ambo; H. Visser (1989) *Het Verleden Voorbij* (*Beyond the Past*), Sliedrecht: Merweboek; and S. van der Zee (1997) *Potgieterlaan 7: Een Herinnering* (*Potgieterlaan 7: A Memory*), Amsterdam: Prometheus.
17. Minow, *Between Vengeance and Forgiveness*, p. 124.
18. See the writings by Stanley Cohen about the ways in which governments can and do deny violations of human rights: "Government Responses to Human Rights Reports: Claims, Denials, and Counterclaims", (1996) *Human Rights Quarterly* 18: 517–543 and *States of Denial: Knowing about Atrocities and Suffering of Others* (2001) Malden, Mass.: Blackwell.
19. In France, the Gayssot act was adopted, which penalizes the denial of Nazi war crimes. This act was considered by the UN Human Rights Committee, with reference to the case involved, not to be a violation of freedom of expression (CCPR/C/58/D/550/1993, 16 December 1996, p. 15). A Dutch Minister of Justice, several years ago, expressed her opposition to such legislation: "One cannot outlaw the expression of nonsense." In December 2006, an international conference was held in Tehran, organized by the Iranian government, which convened persons who denied or questioned whether the Holocaust had actually taken place ("Holocaust Conference Draws Skeptics to Iran", *International Herald Tribune*, 12 December 2006). In a contrary development, the German government took the initiative to make denial of the Holocaust punishable by prison sentences throughout the 27 member states of the European Union ("Berlin Seeks to Bar Holocaust Denial in EU", *International Herald Tribune*, 13/14 January 2007).
20. D. Lipstadt (1993) *Denying the Holocaust: The Growing Assault on Truth and Memory*, New York: Free Press. See also "Historian Called Pro-Hitler Loses Libel Suit", *International Herald Tribune*, 12 April 2000.

21. See A. Cairns (2003) "Coming to Terms with the Past", in J. Torpey, ed., *Politics and the Past: On Repairing Historical Injustices*, Lanham, Md.: Rowman & Littlefield, pp. 63–90, who reviews I. Chang (1998) *The Rape of Nanking: The Forgotten Holocaust of World War II*, New York: Penguin Books.
22. See L. Hein (2003) "War Compensation: Claims against the Japanese Government and Japanese Corporations for War Crimes," in Torpey, *Politics and the Past*, pp. 127–147.
23. "Abe Denies Wartime Brothel Charge" (2007) *International Herald Tribune*, 3/4 March; "China Asks Japan to Admit Past Sex Slavery" (2007) *International Herald Tribune*, 7 March.
24. Minow, *Between Vengeance and Forgiveness*, p. 127.
25. "Spain Begins to Examine the Terror that Spawned Franco" (2002) *International Herald Tribune*, 12 November. In Russia, a team of researchers from the human rights organization Memorial has unearthed 50 trenches containing the skeletons of what may be thousands of people executed by Stalin's secret police (see "As Its Stalinist Past is Exhumed, Russia Turns Away" (2002) *International Herald Tribune*, 21 October).
26. "A Demand for Light on Spain's Dark Past" (2004) *International Herald Tribune* 26–27 June.
27. "Spanje Graaft Doden Franco Op" ("Spain Digs Up Franco Dead") (2004) *NRC Handelsblad* (Rotterdam), 10 September.
28. See D. Forsythe (2002) "The US and International Criminal Justice", *Human Rights Quarterly* 24: 974–991; and J. Mayersfeld (2003) "Who Shall Be Judge? The United States, the International Criminal Court, and the Global Enforcement of Human Rights", *Human Rights Quarterly* 25: 91–129.
29. See for example J. Laber and I. Nizich (1994) "The War Crimes Tribunal for the former Yugoslavia: Problems and Prospects" *Fletcher Forum* 18: 8–9; and D. P. Forsythe (1994) "Politics and the International Tribunal for the former Yugoslavia", *Criminal Law Forum* 5: 415 ff. Forsythe quotes the former US diplomat Morris Abrams as follows: "It is a very tough call whether to point the finger or try to negotiate with people. As a lawyer or as a politician or as a statesman, I would also like to stop the slaughter, bring it to a halt. You have two things that are in real conflict here ... I don't know the proper mix." See further P. Akhavan (1996) "The Yugoslav Tribunal at a Crossroads: The Dayton Peace Agreements and Beyond", *Human Rights Quarterly* 18: 267–274; and D. P. Forsythe (1997) "International Criminal Courts: A Political View", *Netherlands Quarterly of Human Rights* 15(11).
30. L. Huyse (1995) "Justice after Transition: On the Choices Successor Elites Make in Dealing with the Past", in Albert J. Jongman, ed., *Contemporary Genocides: Causes, Cases, Consequences*, Lieden: PIOOM, pp. 187–214 at 196.
31. D. J. Goldhagen (1997) *Hitler's Willing Executioners: Ordinary Germans and the Holocaust*, London: Abacus.
32. Forsythe, "The US and International Criminal Justice", 13.
33. Although, on account of his supposed poor state of health, Pinochet escaped extradition from Britain to Spain and was allowed to return to Chile in early March 2000, his detention and subsequent house arrest for almost sixteen months have carried a powerful message to other former perpetrators of human rights violations.
34. "Interview with Desmond Tutu" (1996) *Index on Censorship* 25(5): 38–43 at 39.
35. P. B. Hayner (1994) "Fifteen Truth Commissions – 1974 to 1994: A Comparative Study" *Human Rights Quarterly* 16: 600, and *Unspeakable Truths: Confronting State Terror and Atrocity* (2001), New York: Routledge.
36. Respectively, Thomas Buergenthal, a US citizen; Christian Tomuschat, a German citizen; and William Schabas, a Canadian citizen.

37. *Truth Commissions: An Interdisciplinary Discussion Held at Harvard Law School in May 1996* (1997) Cambridge, Mass.: Harvard Law School Human Rights Program, p. 50.
38. Hayner, "Fifteen Truth Commissions", 607.
39. M. Parlevliet (1998) "Considering Truth: Dealing with a Legacy of Gross Human Rights Violations", *Netherlands Quarterly of Human Rights* 16: 141–174.
40. On a more philosophical level, the question can be asked whether there is such a thing as one and only one "truth". See Parlevliet, "Considering Truth".
41. "Interview with Ntsiki Biko" (1996) *Index on Censorship* 25(5): 67–68.
42. Cf. D. Bronkhorst (1995) *Truth and Reconciliation: Obstacles and Opportunities for Human Rights*, Amsterdam: Amnesty International, pp. 26–27.
43. Minow, *Between Vengeance and Forgiveness*, p. 134.
44. A. Krog (1998) *Country of My Skull*, Johannesburg: Random House, p. 31.
45. Therefore Rhoda Howard-Hassmann was right when she claimed that torture was not "inhuman". See R. Howard (1992) "Dignity, Community and Human Rights", in A. An-Na'im, ed., *Human Rights in Cross-Cultural Perspectives: A Quest for Consensus*, Philadelphia: University of Pennsylvania Press, pp. 81–102 at 89.
46. See Parlevliet, "Considering Truth", p. 172.
47. This division leaves out the usually largest group: that of the (passive) bystanders. See Fred Grünfeld's inaugural address: "Vroegtijdig Optreden van Omstanders ter Voorkoming van Oorlogen en Schendingen van de Rechten van de Mens" (Early Action of Bystanders to Prevent Wars and Violations of Human Rights) (2003) Utrecht University. See also Minow, *Between Vengeance and Forgiveness*, pp. 74–79.
48. See W. A. Schabas (2003) "The Relationship between Truth Commissions and International Courts: The Case of Sierra Leone", *Human Rights Quarterly* 25: 1035–1066.
49. Ignatieff, "Articles of Faith", 113.

3

Does power trump morality? Reconciliation or transitional justice?

Rama Mani

Introduction

This chapter addresses some of the core questions that lie at the heart of the search for justice, reconciliation and the rule of law in the aftermath of conflict. The first section consists of a brief examination of the vexed issues that must be debated and resolved before the very decision is taken to pursue transitional justice (TJ) and to design and implement a transitional-justice policy. These are questions about the timing of transitional-justice measures and the ripeness of the situation for such justice and about achieving the problematic balance between politics and ethics. It also raises the question of what kind of justice we wish to pursue and the remit and scope of this justice. It underscores the need for a broader definition of justice that includes the social and distributive and the legal or rule of law dimensions.

The second section turns its attention to the processes and measures of reconciliation and transitional justice embarked upon after conflict. Starting from an understanding of the original intent and current standing of reconciliation, some of the problems of pursuing reconciliation through TJ are explored. The chapter examines why, paradoxically, transitional-justice measures may often fail to deliver the kind of reconciliation sought after conflict. It then seeks to make some practical recommendations for future practice, structured around the concept of reparative justice.

Atrocities and international accountability: Beyond transitional justice, Hughes, Schabas and Thakur (eds), United Nations University Press, 2007, ISBN 978-92-808-1141-4

Timing and ripeness: Remarrying peace with justice

Here I address three key questions briefly: first, does power always trump morality and law, that is, will political "pragmatism" always win over the moral and legal argument to pursue transitional justice, and, therefore, will peace and justice always be in tension? Second, is it always politics that is paramount, or are there other factors in the tension between peace and justice? And third, is transitional justice a matter of timing, and when is the best time to implement it?

Does power trump morality?

There is an age-old tension between the political reality of ending costly conflict and bringing violators to justice.[1] While, on the one hand, there is the imperative of ending war's abuses or removing brutal dictators as soon as possible by getting warlords to the negotiating table and offering them sweeteners; on the other hand there are the moral and legal requirements and the public demands to bring them to justice. Today, the former political imperative seems all the more pressing because conflict is so brutal in human terms and devastating in material terms that there is urgent pressure to terminate conflict in order to save lives and limit damage. Furthermore, the violence and insecurity that continues long after conflict and the continuing military power and weaponry in possession of warlords mean that the threat of a return to hostilities is very real. This is no empty threat but a reality, as experienced with Jonas Savimbi in Angola, with Charles Taylor in Liberia and with Afghan warlords associated with the US-led coalition in Afghanistan.

Nevertheless, offering war criminals political power ensures that this new "peaceful" dispensation will be discredited in public eyes and seen as illegitimate if old war criminals continue to enjoy power with impunity. It is impossible to build an independent and fair rule of law and obtain security and legitimate governance in such conditions. The population will lack trust and confidence in leaders who are the very persons that abused them during war. This was the clear opinion of the majority of the population in Afghanistan following the forced departure of the Taliban, when warlords allied with the Coalition forces were given governorships and Ministries as compensation for their alliance.[2] Offering a safe exit, such as exile in a third country in exchange for relinquishing power, as with Charles Taylor of Liberia and Bertrand Aristide in Haiti, is not ideal either because such charismatic and powerful leaders continue to manipulate the political situation even from afar. The population remains gripped by uninterrupted fear of a violent return and reversal of peace, and continued public distrust and a climate of fear persist. In many cases, groups that have pressured for justice against violators undergo a last minute *volte-face* during peace negotiations and adopt a policy of total or conditional amnesty. This was the case with the South West Africa People's Organization in Namibia, the Hun Sen government in Cambodia and the rebel Guatemalan National Revolutionary Unity movement.

Trends today are ambivalent. On the one hand, we have an unprecedented situation with three heads of state and one senior genocide leader undergoing or likely to undergo trial: Slobodan Milošević, Saddam Hussein, Augusto Pinochet and possibly Khieu Sampan. Yet, Charles Taylor's free exit and the lack of justice measures in certain recent transitions, as in East Timor and Afghanistan, suggest a continuing accommodation of political power and a negation of both law and public demands for justice.

Economic motives alongside political ones

The trends noted above would suggest that politics often if not always trumps ethics. However, this may not be the whole answer: Economic rationales have a larger role to play than is publicly acknowledged. While political motives for the tension between peace and justice appear paramount, there are often other tacit factors and motivations, primarily economic, behind such a *volte-face* in the rhetoric and policy of parties to a conflict or the reluctance to pursue war criminals. In many countries where TJ was not pursued or was "softened", this decision was not only politically but also economically motivated. More specifically, the intent was to avoid a displacement of economic resources through emigration of the economic élite and to appease international investors and the financial community. While such policies are presented by the political leadership as being in the interest of "national unity" or "national reconciliation" – which are indeed real and legitimate motives – an economic motive of stability, growth and investment is often underlying or even predominant. This was the case in Namibia, Mozambique and South Africa.[3]

Unfortunately, sometimes the economic causes of conflict are overlooked in the eagerness to satisfy international donors and the demands of the global economy. For example, much needed land reform and economic redistribution is not undertaken in societies emerging from conflict, for fear of creating economic destabilization and scaring off investors. However, ignoring these continued grievances that underlied the war for too long could lead to a backlash later on. In some cases, it could also become a factor that is open to manipulation and exploitation by political forces, leading to conflict, as in Zimbabwe.

These economic factors underlying the decision to pursue or ignore justice claims are even more important today as the issue is not just about economic inequality and exclusion but about gross economic crimes and war economies. The exploitation of natural and precious resources in the Democratic Republic of Congo by a host of national, regional and international interests is a vivid case in point. These entrenched war economies often persist well after conflict is resolved and lead to criminal violence and organized crime in the volatile post-conflict environment.[4] There is a pressing need in this context not only for political accountability but also for accountability of internal and international actors for economic crimes and war economies.

Is timing of the essence?

There is no doubt that the timing of transitional justice can determine its success. However, history and experience since 1945 teaches only one lesson about timing: that it is entirely unpredictable and case-specific, or *sui generis*. In Latin American transitions from dictatorship, which took place primarily during the 1980s, it is only now, two decades later, that some measure of justice is being pursued against Pinochet and Argentine generals who benefited from an amnesty at the time of transition.[5]

In some cases, there is no doubt that justice has to be pursued in the immediate aftermath and cannot be postponed. This was the case in Rwanda, due to the sheer enormity of the crimes committed there, and in Sierra Leone. In some cases, as in Cambodia, all early attempts, including by international actors, met with failure in the immediate aftermath of the Khmer Rouge bloodbath, due to insurmountable political obstacles and lack of political will. However, now, as Khmer Rouge veterans die of old age, the United Nations is continuing to pursue painstaking negotiations with the Cambodian leadership to establish a hybrid trial within Cambodia, three decades after the deadly events.

Notwithstanding the uncertainty and unpredictability of the time factor, only one thing is certain: the pulse of the public. In the chaotic aftermath of divisive conflict, "public opinion" will not be a uniform, homogenous, consensual single answer that is easy to uncover. Inevitably, there will be wide differences in opinion among different sectors of the local population, particularly on the extent, scope and type of justice desired, and several will insist on pursuing no accountability at all. However elusive, in all cases, there is a discernible, perceptible groundswell of public opinion that is audible to those who care to pay careful attention without leaping to conclusions or making sweeping generalizations.

It is not easy to conduct the kind of thorough investigations necessary to establish the thrust and diverse directions of local opinion in situations where great insecurity continues after conflict. Yet, there are almost always ways and means, especially through local civic networks, to identify this pulse and its direction(s). In Afghanistan, despite persistent insecurity and lack of access to many areas, the Afghan Independent Human Rights Commission conducted thorough investigations and consultations across the country on the subject of transitional justice.[6]

This groundswell of domestic opinion either demands justice – as in Sierra Leone – or aches for reconciliation that is not retributive – as in Mozambique. In some cases, this throbbing pulse of public opinion is so overwhelming that to ignore it and try to do away with transitional justice for political or economic reasons is to compromise the process of peace-building itself. While a violent backlash must be averted, tolerating the impunity of warlords and war criminals is not a guarantor of security either. Furthermore, crimes against humanity, war crimes and genocide should never be seen to be tolerated or condoned by the United Nations as this erodes the hard-won gains of international and human rights law.[7]

This does not imply that the most confrontational and divisive means of transitional justice be adopted immediately in the name of pursuing justice. Rather, it suggests that a sagacious, timely and contextually appropriate use of the right mix of justice measures be undertaken to ensure that some measure of justice, peace and reconciliation could ensue, rather than derailing the process entirely. It is, in effect, a call for an inclusive, flexible, sensitive, survivor-oriented form of reparative justice, rather than one-shot, politically-charged and emotive single mechanisms, i.e., either truth and reconciliation commissions (TRCs) or trials alone, as will be elaborated later.

Can peace and justice cohabit, or is tension between them inevitable?

Often, the clash between pursuing peace and justice is presumed to be inevitable. However, the answer to this question depends largely on what we mean by "peace" and what we mean by "justice". If peace is taken to mean only a cessation of hostilities, and if justice is taken to mean only formal legal measures such as prosecution of all responsible, then it is likely that the two will clash. In the heat of battle and during tense negotiations, peace and justice are often reduced to these limited meanings. It is often the fear of warlords about their personal future, and the fear of third party mediators that negotiations will collapse if warlords are pressured, that leads to this tension between the two. However, if we are intent on pursuing lasting peace and deeper and broader justice, it becomes clear that the two are inseparable and interdependent and cannot be addressed in isolation. If justice is taken in its full expression to encompass not only the rectification of violations but also legal justice, or the rule of law, and social justice, or the fair and equitable distribution of economic, political and social resources, power and opportunities within society, then this clash is neither inevitable nor insurmountable.

Unfortunately, this may not lead necessarily to less resistance to a policy pursuing a broader vision of justice than to a more narrowly defined version of justice that highlights prosecution, for example. A case in point is the El Salvador government's utter refusal in early years to comply with rule of law reforms recommended by the international Truth Commission, despite its binding commitments under the peace agreement. The same could be said of Guatemala's stubborn recalcitrance on security sector reform.[8] Likewise, El Salvador's government's willingness to make surprising concessions on human rights was matched by utter unwillingness to concede any ground on economic reforms and redistribution of wealth, which had been the principal original cause of war.[9]

However, this broader approach to justice and the concern with peace beyond the cessation of hostilities opens a new array of options for negotiating the way out of the traditional tension between "peace" and "justice" narrowly conceived, as also for dealing with the problems of timing raised above. When there is a concurrence between palpable local opinion, political powers and international actors that traditional transitional justice in terms of trials and truth commissions cannot feasibly be conducted in the immediate aftermath of conflict, there is still room to begin immediately with other justice reforms in the rule of law and social justice arenas. These reforms will create the conducive space for accountability issues to be addressed later when the timing is more suitable. Particularly important at this stage are reforms of the rule of law, to overturn impunity, to hold all actors including political leaders equal before the law, to hold the state to account, and to develop the capacity within an independent judiciary to provide fair trial to its war criminals over time. Also important at this stage are security sector reforms: civilianizing and democratizing the all-powerful military, demilitarizing society and reintegrating ex-combatant populations. Most important – though least often undertaken – are social and economic reforms that will begin to redress the grievances and feelings of exclusion and marginalization of certain groups of the population that led to the conflict in the first place. This alone will recreate an inclusive political community where all are treated as equal and given a fair share of opportunities and resources. This inclusive political community is the touchstone of reconciliation and a lasting and just peace.

Reconciliation or transitional justice?

In this section, we turn our attention to the actual questions of reconciliation and transitional justice.[10] This section examines the meaning of reconciliation and the mechanisms, intent and consequences of transitional justice. Thereafter, it puts forward an alternative approach of reparative justice that would more appropriately fulfil the multiple and diverse needs of post-conflict societies seeking to transit from a violent past to a peaceful future.

Understanding the meaning and intent of reconciliation

The definition and meaning of reconciliation merits re-clarification despite the increasing use of the term. It is not apparent that there is clarity about its meaning or original intent and whether current practices, particularly of transitional justice, actually fulfil or forward the aims of reconciliation.

The complexity of "reconciliation" is understandable given the many meanings and contexts in which the term is used, its manifold dimensions and implications. In dictionary terms, reconciliation has three meanings: first, reconciling differences; second, resignation or acceptance; and third, restoring relationships after estrangement or conflict. All three are relevant in post-conflict contexts but convey entirely different meanings and intent.

If attention is given to the aspect of restoring relationships after estrangement or conflict, even here, there are two primary and distinct levels: individual reconciliation and national reconciliation. The two would require entirely different processes and approaches, and it is not guaranteed that promoting one would automatically lead to the other. While the emphasis in politically driven post-conflict processes is laid on national reconciliation, this does not bring about individual reconciliation and may even run counter to it. Yet, national unity and reconciliation are entirely dependent on individuals within society feeling reconciled with each other and with the new state authorities and institutions, as well as being able to reinvest their trust in the state.

Reconciliation creates ambiguity due to its diverse dimensions. For many, it is a theological concept, as used for example by Archbishop Desmond Tutu in the South African Truth and Reconciliation Commission. For conflict resolution practitioners, it is a psychological and social concept concerning rebuilding fractured relationships.[11] One author identifies four separate dimensions of reconciliation: psychological, theological, cultural and political.[12]

Another conundrum for the policymaker and practitioner operating in a post-conflict setting is whether reconciliation is understood as the "end" to be achieved or as the "process" through which it is achieved. The frequent rhetoric is "it is both a process and an outcome". Even more confounding for the pragmatic time-constrained practitioner, it is a process that is deemed to require a long time and whose timing cannot be determined, forced or paced.[13] A shorthand definition of the term that seeks to eschew these various areas of confusion is proposed in the International Institute for Democracy and Electoral Assistance *Reconciliation Handbook*: "it is a process through which a society moves from a divided past to a shared future".[14]

The fundamental nexus to transitional justice and to post-conflict peacebuilding is this *bridging function* between past and future. This feature at once links and separates transitional justice and reconciliation: both seek to make this bridge. The former is weighted more heavily in the past as its main locus is resolving the burden of past violations; the latter is weighted more heavily in the future as its main locus is making normal life possible in the future.

This brief examination of the ambiguous term reconciliation brings to light the critical question we have to answer here: does transitional justice as currently practised enable this bridge to be crossed from past to future? Does it facilitate the central intention of reconciliation, which is to rebuild fractured relationships, whether between individuals, between individuals and their national institutions or at the level of national institutions and entities? Experience to date would seem to suggest that it does not, for the reasons examined below.

Can transitional justice deliver reconciliation?

The field of transitional justice has come a long way, especially since the end of the Cold War, building on the earlier experiences with transitions from dictatorships in Latin America and from authoritarianism in Central and Eastern Europe. Transitional justice has now become a household term in the lexicon and practice of post-conflict peacebuilding and raises little confusion about its intent or mechanisms. While its mechanisms were earlier largely confined to trials and truth commissions, now it is generally understood to include (a) a range of different kinds of trials – international, hybrid and national, (b) different kinds of truth commissions, (c) non-legal measures such as vetting and (d) institutional reform.[15] Some also acknowledge a wider range of measures such as commemoration, acknowledgement, reparation, restitution and education to be within transitional justice's scope.[16]

Despite acknowledgement of this broad scope, in international practice and in public understanding, the main mechanisms continue to be trials and, with increasing frequency, truth commissions. These are considered to be ubiquitously good, or at least so clearly well intentioned and morally and legally soundly grounded that it is presumed by proponents that their outcome cannot but be positive. However, there is now a body of evidence that suggests some caution, as well as a need to look more closely at the way in which TJ is conducted and what its unforeseen consequences might be. More specifically, for our purposes, it leads to questions as to whether transitional-justice measures can or do lead to reconciliation and inclusion after the division and exclusion created by violent conflict.

The shortfalls of trials

For several decades, despite the precedent-setting Nuremberg and Tokyo trials after World War II, impunity seemed to be the standard response to war crimes and crimes against humanity committed in most wars.[17] In recent years, this trend has finally changed, and a new wind of accountability through trials seems to be sweeping past at least some countries emerging from conflict. The ad hoc international tribunals for the former Yugoslavia and Rwanda and more recent innovations of hybrid tribunals in Sierra Leone and, potentially, in Cambodia have accompanied more traditional national trials.

Notwithstanding this much-needed and long-awaited swing from impunity to accountability, questions about the efficacy of trials in promoting reconciliation after conflict have been raised for some time now.[18] While a full discussion of each of these shortcomings is not possible here, enumerated succinctly, these include: the problems of political will; the danger of a backlash and relapse into violence; the adversarial and confrontational nature of trials, which exacerbates hostility and reifies divisions between victim and offender; the further victimization of victims through cross-examination; the destruction of evidence in conflicts; the difficulty of finding and providing evidence in chaotic post-conflict environments that will stand up in a court of law; the weakness or outright destruction or corruption of the judiciary and non-existence or paucity of lawyers to provide fair trial; the difficulty of providing adequate witness protection; the corruption or weakness of law enforcement officials to apprehend suspects; and the need for a functioning penal system to keep suspects in safe custody under decent conditions. The recent experiences in Sierra Leone and East Timor and the difficulties in Cambodia in even establishing a hybrid tribunal – despite decades of sustained efforts by the United Nations, international diplomats and human rights advocates – expose some of these difficulties.[19]

Additionally, there is the troubling question of financing trials, amidst all the other financial demands of post-conflict reconstruction.

The International Criminal Tribunal for the former Yugoslavia and the International Criminal Tribunal for Rwanda have cost an average of US$100 million a year over the last several years while locally run hybrid trials are not that much cheaper at an estimated US$100 million for three years for Sierra Leone and the proposed Cambodian trial.[20]

Each of the problems listed above merits serious attention. Over and above them, however, there is a more troubling question that besets trials and which so far has drawn little debate or discussion in transitional-justice and peacebuilding circles: that of punishment itself. Notwithstanding the many trials of prominent war criminals, including former heads of state, the questions are: even if trials are successfully conducted, what kind of punishment will be proportionate and fitting to the crimes? And how and where will these sentences be carried out? The only part of this broad and vexed debate that has been played out is that over death sentences. This debate was provoked by the ideological clash that arose between Rwanda's insistence on the death penalty for *génocidaires* in its national trials and the United Nations's opposition to the death penalty as applied to the International Criminal Tribunal. However, even if the UN standard against the death penalty is upheld, this does not resolve the problem of how to mete out "just desserts" to war criminals. On a practical and logistical level, some countries have come forward on an ad hoc basis to propose their prison facilities and services in certain cases. This, however, only addresses the logistical and practical angle, but not the philosophical and moral questions that lie at the heart of rectificatory justice and punishment theories.

There has thus been little debate or discussion in the international transitional-justice and peacebuilding community about the question that philosophers, criminal psychologists and prison reformers have spent centuries debating: why punish and how to punish? Aristotle, Kant, Hegel and innumerable other philosophers have debated alternative rationales for punishment: whether utilitarian, that is, for the overall good of society; retributive; duty-based; or, more recently, alternative or informal, for example, through community or restorative justice.[21]

In terms of *why* to punish, today, despite all the well-intentioned moral indignation about impunity and its consequences for fragile societies, there is neither clarity nor consensus on whether we wish to punish Saddam Hussein or Slobodan Milošević to reform them, to make them repent, to deter future war criminals, for the broader national or planetary good or simply because we feel a deontological Kantian imperative to do so because they "are evil" or "did wrong". Furthermore, in terms of *how* to punish, we are well aware of the deep crisis in prison systems in leading democracies, notably the United States, the United Kingdom and France, despite significant penal reform movements in places like Wales,

Scotland and Canada. Leading contemporary philosophers and penal reformers acknowledge ruefully that all available rationales, methods and
types of punishment practised in our societies today are deeply unsatisfactory. Furthermore, they note that the social systems in which we live
are themselves responsible, due to the marginalization and exclusion
they cause, for creating the conditions for violent crime.[22] As legal philosopher R. A. Duff puts it, "there is no course of action available to us
that is completely justifiable or free from moral wrong". He concludes,
"the radical imperfection not only of our existing legal institutions but
also of our own moral capacities ... should induce a salubrious humility
and restraint in our treatment of, and our attitudes towards, those who
break the law".[23]

If this is the state of affairs in developed long-established legal systems,
we can imagine how much more troubled the situation is in post-conflict
countries with devastated judicial systems. In international tribunals, the
bitter complaint from locals, as in the Rwandan case, has been that suspected war criminals were living better lives in their UN-standard prisons
than the victims back home – hardly conducive to reconciliation between
them. This bitterness will be all the deeper once these people are tried
and their guilt proven beyond reasonable doubt, yet sentenced in the relative "luxury" of Western or international prisons.

The outstanding conundrum of why and how to punish will continue
to plague us, however successful prosecutions might be. Alternatives
such as non-custodial sentences or community service have been experimented with in Rwanda and elsewhere. Such appropriate alternative
forms of punishment that might be more socially constructive and might
help rebuild fractured societal relations should be pursued further if the
option of trials is to serve as a means of reconciliation and societal regeneration.

The Achilles' heel of truth commissions

Truth commissions have been strongly supported as an alternative mechanism, to compensate for all the failings or weaknesses of trials noted
above. They now have a long and well-documented history, with each
truth commission generating a veritable library of research and analysis
into its every aspect and its comparative advantages and disadvantages
over previous attempts.[24] Truth commissions certainly seem to gain in
popularity with every passing year, with commissions springing up not
only in recently concluded conflicts but also long-concluded transitions
like Peru's. However, the chinks in the armour are also beginning to be
revealed through these years of enquiry. The leading scholar of truth
commissions, Priscilla Hayner, is also their most candid critic.[25] Whatever its assets, she asserts that if certain critical pre-conditions are not

met, a truth commission will be unable to fulfil its mandate and, more-over, the high expectations it elicits. And a poorly executed truth com-mission may be worse than no truth commission at all as the opportunity for justice will be lost and is unlikely to be repeated. These pre-conditions include a broad and clear mandate; political support during and after the enquiry, including political will and a commitment to carry through reforms and recommendations; sufficient resources; and full access.

In the conditions that prevail after conflict and given the frequent hos-tility of political and military élites toward truth commissions, it is rare that these pre-conditions are fully met. The greatest failing has been that even when truth commissions have been able to do remarkable work de-spite serious political and financial constraints, there has simply not been the political will to carry through reforms, and international pressure has not been present or sufficient. This was true of Haiti's truth commission, whose report was ignored by the very President Aristide who had insti-tuted the commission on his return to Haiti in 1994. It was also largely true of the internationally lauded reports of the commissions in El Salva-dor and Guatemala, where the government and ruling élite circumvented the reports' recommendations. What many see as the most positive long-term legacy of truth commissions – their recommended institutional and structural reforms – is often still-born due to this lack of political will to enact the reforms.

The most concrete and vaunted asset of truth commissions is their pur-ported contribution to reconciliation. This is why most truth commissions since South Africa's have also incorporated "reconciliation" in their title. The reason offered is that truth is seen to be a fundamental and central component of reconciliation. However, this is open to dispute. First, it is debatable whether a TRC's version of the truth will be acceptable to all sections of society. Indeed, questions have been raised as to whether a "single" truth should be favoured or if in fact multiple truths should be allowed to surface. If a TRC tries to present these multiple truths, it will only confuse people and become the object of controversy; yet if it fails to do so, it will be dismissed by those who do not see "their" truth re-flected in the report.

The more specific question is whether truth does indeed promote reconciliation. The answer unfortunately is not a clear affirmative or negative, but rather the unhelpful "it depends". While several have expe-rienced or documented the vaunted "cathartic" effect of expressing long-suppressed loss and grief to a truth commission, and thus having their pain vindicated in a more public way, for many others it has fuelled the desire for revenge. As sociologist Mahmood Mamdani observed in South Africa, for many, TRCs simply lay bare the extent of the egregious impunity granted to violators by exposing their violations in full detail for public consumption.[26] The desire to forgive and reconcile with one's enemy or wrongdoer is individual and cannot be preached or imposed. Therefore, the reconciliatory effect of truth commissions cannot be either predicted or presumed.

Even if the truth could be considered to be cathartic and reconciliatory, this would depend on the extent to which both the process of accumulating and distilling the truth and the process of dissemination and consumption of the truth, through the report thereafter, are broad, inclusive and participatory of the wider population and especially victims. Yet, while some commissions, like South Africa's TRC, were very broad in their reach during inquiries and dissemination, this has not been true of each commission. Often, either due to deliberately restricted mandates, like with Guatemala's Truth Commission (TC), or due to the lack of access or funds, like with Haiti's, outreach to, and participation of, the local population is limited and the dissemination of reports has been erratic and incomplete. For example, Haiti's TC report was not distributed at all, while the lauded El Salvador report had only limited dissemination. The Sierra Leone TRC made a specific, strong recommendation in its report for deep and wide dissemination to ensure it would have these broader effects. However, given earlier difficulties with financing the TRC's work, it remains to be seen whether sufficient funding will be secured to ensure this potential benefit of reconciliation through its dissemination.

The desire to know the full truth is not and cannot be presumed to be ubiquitous. In Mozambique, there simply was not this desire to remember. The greater public urge was to forgive and move on. In Rwanda, despite the huge emphasis on retributive justice through trials, there has not been a deep desire, at least on the part of the victimized Tutsi population, to make a faithful and full accounting of the historical truth. It has been noted that history has not been taught in Rwanda since 1994. Apparently, "truth" is not the commodity being sought in Rwanda despite the heavy emphasis in political discourse about national reconciliation.[27]

It is important not to overload a single official mechanism with so many demands and expect it to produce reconciliation. In some ways, TRCs have been victims of their own success by generating such high and unrealistic expectations. It is perhaps misleading to include "reconciliation" in the title of truth commissions as it overcharges and "ups the ante" on these bodies to deliver far more than just the truth. This was the Achilles' heel of the TRC in South Africa, which was expected to deliver the miracle of reconciliation at all levels for every one. Though it is without doubt the most significant and "successful" experiment so far, the very definition of "success" is being debated, and there is huge divergence among different South Africans on its outcome and reconciliatory impact.[28] In conclusion, a linear correlation between truth and reconciliation cannot simply be presumed.

Transitional justice: Mechanisms that divide more than they (re-)unite

The intent here is not to discredit the gains of these mechanisms, particularly in restoring some measure of justice and dignity to victims. Most important, the need for countering impunity and restoring accountability must not be underestimated and is central to restoring security in the aftermath of conflict. To the extent that transitional-justice measures, especially trials, further accountability and signal to war criminals and warlords that their days of impunity are numbered, they are essential for security and longer term peace. Here, however, we are looking more specifically at the impact of transitional-justice measures as currently pursued on reconciliation and the regeneration of an inclusive political community after conflict, and here the evidence is more mixed.

The two primary transitional-justice mechanisms and processes, that is, trials and TRCs, have the inadvertent side-effect of being divisive, although their stated or aspired-to outcome is to reconcile. Trials sharpen the divide between perpetrators and victims, while focusing on the guilt of perpetrators. They alienate perpetrators by putting them on the defensive, but they also alienate victims through the harrowing cross-examination procedure. Furthermore, they alienate the vast majority of the society's population that suffered through conflict but is left outside the courtroom. Truth commissions seek to bridge this divide by focusing more on silenced victims. But in doing so, they again alienate perpetrators. And rarely do they raise the role and participation of those who were beneficiaries of the system or mere bystanders to evil, again alienating a vast part of the population.

Neither trials nor truth commissions can aspire to meet the goals of either individual or national/societal reconciliation for two reasons: first, they *divide rather than unite* victims and perpetrators; second, they *exclude rather than include* bystanders, beneficiaries and populations structurally and indirectly rather than directly affected by war. They fail to move from the divided past of perpetrators versus victims to a united future of all survivors of conflict, whatever their past role. Reconciliation can stem only from a form of justice that is inclusive and uniting rather than exclusive and dividing; that is survivor-oriented rather than slanted toward either perpetrator or victim; that is permanent and incremental rather than transitional, that is, by implication, temporal and incomplete.

The concept of "reparative justice" is proposed as a response to the complex and shifting realities of societies torn apart by conflict and the varied and often contradictory claims for justice that arise therein. It recognizes that categories such as "victim" or "perpetrator" are fluid in situations of dynamic conflict and can change over time. Victims can and do become aggressors and often have been in the past, just as former perpetrators may become victimized: Rwanda, the former Yugoslavia and Israel being cases in point. As noted by Marie Smyth on Northern Ireland, "The acquisition of the status of victim becomes an institutionalised way of escaping guilt, shame or responsibility".[29] She also notes that victims often become political tools used by politicians to gain moral authority.[30] All individuals living in a society after conflict must be included in the form of justice pursued and must be treated in common with "survivors" of conflict, while taking into due consideration their different roles in the past.

Reparative justice is "survivors' justice" rather than "victors' justice" or "victims' justice". As truth commissioners have found in South Africa, Sierra Leone and elsewhere, despite the trauma they have undergone, many victims prefer to be identified as "survivors", to connote that they are not passive beings who lack agency and the capacity to act. They wish to be identified in a forward-looking, active way. As one woman testified to the South African TRC, "I resent being called a victim; I have a choice in the matter. I am a survivor."[31]

Mahmood Mamdani notes, "Only social justice that underlines the empathy between a community of survivors can lay the foundation of a new political community based on consent".[32] The concept of "reparative justice" rather than transitional justice provides this, and its application could pave the way toward reconciliation with justice and peace. As I have elaborated the conceptual sources and main features of reparative justice elsewhere at length,[33] here I allude only to its main practical characteristics as relevant to this discussion.

Reparative justice is a broader, flexible and sensitive concept drawing its dual origin from both the legal practice and the psychological concept of reparation. In law, "Reparation must, as far as possible, wipe out all the consequences of the illegal act and re-establish the situation which would, in all probability, have existed if that act had not been committed".[34] In psychology, the concept of reparation was developed by Freud's disciple, the famous psychoanalyst Melanie Klein. "In Klein, guilt stimulates attempts at reconciliation with the object: 'The urge to undo or repair this harm results from the feeling that the subject has caused it, i.e., from guilt. The reparative tendency can, therefore, be considered as a consequence of guilt.'"[35] Thus, reparation encompasses both the legal harm and the psychological harm suffered during conflict and recognizes and responds to the need to address both of these dimensions.

Reparative justice validates the full range of rights identified in the United Nations' draft "Basic Principles and Guidelines on the Right to a Remedy and Reparation for Victims of Violations of International Human Rights and Humanitarian Law". This document defines victims' right to remedy as follows:

> Remedies for violation of international human rights and humanitarian law include the victims' right to:
>
> 1. Access justice;
> 2. Reparation for harm suffered;
> 3. Access the factual information concerning the violation.[36]

However, rather than treating them as passive, reparative justice helps victims regain agency as survivors and build a "bridge" toward their future, and it seeks to reintegrate them actively into society.

While enshrining victims' rights, reparative justice does not focus only on victims to the exclusion of other groups, as truth commissions tend to do. Nor does it focus on perpetrators exclusively, as trials do. Rather, it extends to all parts of society. It includes neglected economic categories, such as beneficiaries, and neglected structural categories, such as those suffering systemic injustice, that is, discrimination, in seeking therefore to address or redress not only the direct abuses perpetrated in conflict but also its social, economic and cultural consequences and ramifications.

Several other concepts have become popular in the ongoing debate, of which transformative justice and restorative justice are perhaps the most established. Both these concepts are worthy additions to the field and are backed by an extensive, rich and valuable literature and an emerging field of practice. However, a clear and personal preference is expressed here semantically for the term "reparative justice", without seeking to contradict or undermine the parallel and complementary notions of transformative or restorative justice, whose aims and approaches are largely similar to those described here. This is because reparative justice puts the emphasis on "reparation", that is, repair, which is realistic and modest but honest. This is a more realistic choice of term in a post-conflict situation than "restoration" or "transformation". It acknowledges the real harm committed and suffered and recognizes that this harm may never be fully restored or transformed. However, it makes a committed attempt to repair the harm done, recognizing that the scars may always remain.

This concept of reparative justice provided here is not an attempt to replace or "overthrow" transitional justice. Rather, it seeks to provide a broader conceptual and contextual framework for the mechanisms and processes currently described by the generic term "transitional justice". This exposition seeks to describe and delineate an alternative, broader and more flexible concept that may be more applicable to the post-conflict context than the current more thin term of transitional justice, which is descriptive rather than analytical and lacks these contextual notions and conceptual underpinnings.

Conclusion: Reconciliation and lasting peace through reparative justice

We concluded earlier that peace and justice were not in opposition or contradiction if taken in their full meaning to represent more than simply the cessation of hostilities, on the one hand, and retributive justice through trials, on the other. Rather, taken in their full broad sense, peace and justice are irrevocably interconnected, interdependent and mutually reinforcing and can and must be pursued in tandem. Reconciliation, notwithstanding its multiple meanings, represents a bridge between peace and justice, between past and future. Reparative justice as presented here provides a path toward reconciliation that eschews the exclusive triumph of either politics or morality and avoids the pitfalls of transitional-justice mechanisms.

Reparative justice would not discard current practices of transitional justice and seek to reinvent the wheel by spewing forth a new series of justice mechanisms and processes. Reparative justice in practice would include all existing methods of transitional justice, including trials and TCs. It would also, and importantly, reinvigorate broader social practices of commemoration, healing, education, meaningful apologies, acknowledgement and restitution. Importantly, it would insist upon reparation, which is now the neglected element of transitional justice in most situations. The International Criminal Court's championing of reparation and victims' rights would provide a lead in this respect. Reparative justice would explore the ignored debate on punishment, and it would undertake punishment in wider community-defined and socially beneficial ways, in addition to incarceration. It would return attention to the neglected dimensions of trauma and healing. It would try to find ways to elicit, and give expression to, meaningful apologies backed by commemorative action by political leaders.

In conclusion, reparative justice provides a broad conceptual framework and a practical, applicable matrix for achieving reconciliation and laying the foundation for the regeneration of an inclusive political community after the violent divisions of conflict. It underscores the requirement of a broader, more realistic reparative framework to respond to the diverse and often overlooked needs in most post-conflict societies. In this reparative approach, transitional-justice mechanisms would be pursued in alignment with this wider requirement of reconciliation between, and inclusion of, all survivors of conflict to achieve a more durable and stable peace.

Notes

1. N. Kritz (1995) *Transitional Justice*, Washington, D.C.: United States Institute for Peace.
2. R. Mani (2002) *Beyond Retribution: Seeking Justice in the Shadows of War*, Cambridge: Polity Press.
3. Ibid., chapter 5.
4. M. Pugh and N. Cooper (2004) *War Economies in a Regional Context: Challenges of Transformation*, Boulder, Colo.: Lynne Reinner.
5. Kritz, *Transitional Justice*.
6. Afghan Independent Human Rights Commission (2005) *A Call for Justice*, available from http://www.aihrc.org.
7. S. R. Ratner and J. L. Bischoff, eds (2003) *International War Crimes Trials: Making a Difference?* Proceedings of an International Conference at the University of Texas School of Law, Austin, Texas, 6–7 November, Austin: University of Texas.
8. Mani, *Beyond Retribution*.
9. Ibid.
10. This section draws substantially on a previously published article by the author, "Rebuilding an Inclusive Political Community After War", (2005) *Security Dialogue* 36(4): 511–526.
11. See J. P. Lederach (1997) *Building Peace: Sustainable Reconciliation on Divided Societies*, Washington, D.C.: United States Institute for Peace; and H. Miall, O. Ramsbotham and T. Woodhouse (1999) *Contemporary Conflict Resolution*, Cambridge: Cambridge University Press.
12. I. Furtado de Mendonça (2004) "Searching for Reconciliation in a Post Complex Political Emergency Scenario", Paper presented at the Fifth Pan-European International Relations Conference, The Hague, 9–11 September.
13. D. Bloomfield, T. Barnes and L. Huyse, eds (2003) *Reconciliation after Violent Conflict: A Handbook*, Stockholm: International Institute for Democracy and Electoral Assistance.
14. Ibid., p. 12.
15. Kritz, *Transitional Justice*.
16. See M. Minow (1998) *Between Vengeance and Forgiveness*, Boston: Beacon Press; and Mani, *Beyond Retribution*.
17. For further discussion see R. Thakur and P. Malcontent, eds (2005) *From Sovereign Impunity to International Accountability*, Tokyo: United Nations University Press; and A. Neier (1998) *War Crimes: Brutality, Genocide, Terror, and the Struggle for Justice*, New York: Random House.
18. Mani, *Beyond Retribution*, pp. 89–101; and Minow, *Between Vengeance and Forgiveness*, pp. 25–51.

19. See Human Rights Watch (2004) "Bringing Justice: The Special Court for Sierra Leone", September, New York; Open Society Justice Initiative and Coalition for International Justice (2004) "Unfulfilled Promises: Achieving Justice for Crimes against Humanity in East Timor", New York; and A. Sipress (2004) "Khmer Rouge Trials Stalled by Political Deadlock", *Washington Post*, 5 May.
20. "Quatre dictateurs en process: La justice enfin?" (2005) *Courier International*, 13 January.
21. See R. Mani (2000) "Restoring Justice in the Aftermath of Conflict: Bridging the Gap between Theory and Practice", in T. Coates, ed., *International Justice*, Aldershot, England: Ashgate, pp. 264–299; and W. Cragg (1992) *The Practice of Punishment: Towards a Theory of Restorative Justice*, London: Routledge.
22. See Cragg, *Practice of Punishment*; and R. A. Duff (1986) *Trials and Punishment*, Cambridge: Cambridge University Press.
23. Duff, *Trials and Punishment*, p. 298.
24. For interesting perspectives on this subject, see J. Crandall (2004) "Truth Commissions in Guatemala and Peru: Perpetual Impunity and Transitional Justice Compared", *Peace, Conflict and Development* 4: 1–19; I. Hovland (2003) "Macro/Micro Dynamics in South Africa: Why the Reconciliation Process Will Not Reduce Violence", *Journal of Peacebuilding and Development* 1(2): 6–20; and C. O. Lerche (2000) "Truth Commissions and National Reconciliation: Some Reflections on Theory and Practice", *Peace and Conflict Studies* 7: 1–20.
25. P. Hayner (2002) *Unspeakable Truths: Facing the Challenge of Truth Commissions*, London: Routledge.
26. M. Mamdani (1996) "Reconciliation without Justice", *South African Review of Books*, 46: 3–5.
27. E. Zorbas (2004) "Reconciliation in Post-Genocide Rwanda", *African Journal of Legal Studies* 1(1): 29–52.
28. T. A. Borer (2001) "Reconciliation in South Africa: Defining Success", Occasional Paper #20:OP:1, Notre Dame, Ind.: Kroc Institute; K. Lombard (2003) "Revisiting Reconciliation: The People's View", Rondebosch, South Africa: Institute for Justice and Reconciliation.
29. M. Smyth (2000) "Putting the Past in Its Place: Issues of Victimhood and Reconciliation in Northern Ireland's Peace Process", in N. Biggar, ed., *Burying the Past*, Washington, D.C.: Georgetown University Press, pp. 125–153, at pp. 126–127.
30. Ibid., pp. 141–146.
31. Jeannette Fourie, cited in A. Krog (1998) *Country of My Skull*, Johannesburg: Random House, p. 230.
32. M. Mamdani (2000) "The Truth According to the TRC", in I. Amadiume and A. An-Naim, eds, *The Politics of Memory: Truth, Healing and Social Justice*, London: Zed Books, pp. 182–183.
33. Mani, "Restoring Justice", pp. 173–178.
34. D. J. Harris (1991) *Cases and Materials on International Law*, 4th ed., London: Sweet & Maxwell, citing Chorzow Factory Case (Indemnity) (Merits), *Germany v. Poland* (1928).
35. S. Forster and D. Carveth (1999) "Christianity, A Kleinian Perspective", *Canadian Journal of Psychoanalysis/Revue Canadienne de Psychanalyse* 7(2): 187–218, citing M. Klein (1948) "The Theory of Anxiety and Guilt" in *Envy and Gratitude and Other Works, 1946–1963*, London: Hogarth Press.
36. "United Nations Basic Principles on the Right to a Remedy and Reparation for Victims of Violations of International Human Rights and Humanitarian Law" (revised), UN Document E/CN.4/2005/59, UN Commission on Human Rights.

4

Transitional justice and conflict termination: Mozambique, Rwanda and South Africa assessed

Helena Cobban

In the short period between October 1992 and July 1994, Mozambique, South Africa and Rwanda all made significant attempts to end deep-rooted and violent inter-group conflicts that had been marked by the commission of serious atrocities. At the time, each country's leadership adopted a distinct and different approach to the challenge of dealing with the legacies of the recent atrocities; now, some 12 years later, it is possible to go back and assess the effectiveness of those approaches. As I have undertaken this task, I have looked in particular at the ability of these three countries in the years since those conflict-termination attempts to escape from the climate of conflict itself, as well as to achieve key tasks in the good-governance agenda such as could be expected to make any collapse back into violent inter-group conflict far less likely in the future. One of my major underlying assumptions throughout has been that the vast majority of acts of atrocity are committed in situations of violent inter-group (that is, political) conflict, whether this is confined within one nation's boundaries or transcends them. This assumption seems borne out by both observation and common sense. It is also strongly enshrined in the underpinning of modern-day "atrocities law", which grew, after all, out of the body of law known as the "laws of war".

The three countries studied all went through markedly different experiences as they moved to and through their moments of hoped-for conflict termination in 1992 to 1994. This means that making direct comparisons among their experiences and drawing out general lessons therefrom are tasks that need to be done with great care. Nevertheless, the

Atrocities and international accountability: Beyond transitional justice, Hughes, Schabas and Thakur (eds), United Nations University Press, 2007, ISBN 978-92-808-1141-4

fact of these differences need not deter us from undertaking the tasks at hand. Indeed, many of these differences can themselves helpfully suggest which kinds of post-violence policies – as well as which means of conflict termination – can be expected to make the most constructive contribution to long-term peacebuilding and thus to the general wellbeing of citizens of countries wracked by atrocious violence.

Comparing the burdens of conflict and atrocity

The kinds of atrocities with which this study is concerned – nowadays generally understood as war crimes, crimes against humanity and genocide – are acts that are nearly always associated with significant political conflict. I have traced and sought to understand the political context of atrocity perpetration in the countries studied, as well as the nature of the atrocities themselves.

Regarding the political context of atrocity commission, in Rwanda, the conflict between Hutu-power extremists and those Tutsis and Hutus who challenged their views had continued at some level for more than 30 years (and the Hutu-Tutsi cleavage was exploited and exacerbated by the Belgian colonial regime prior to 1959, as well). The atrocities of 1994 occurred in the more immediate political context of the war between the returning, armed exiles of the Rwandan Patriotic Front (mainly Tutsis) and the Hutu-dominated government that had ravaged much of north-western Rwanda since 1990. There was little direct involvement by outsiders in that war, though Rwanda remained vulnerable to many strong influences from Uganda, France and other outside actors.

In South Africa, the conflict between African nationalists and the country's white colonial regime had lasted 350 years and taken many forms, though by the second half of the twentieth century most of the internal opposition to the minority regime was not armed. In 1973, the General Assembly determined that South Africa's apartheid system itself constituted a crime against humanity. In 1976/77 and again from 1985 on, there were serious upturns in the anti-apartheid movement inside the country and in the very violent measures that the government adopted in response. From the late 1980s on, the apartheid regime also successfully enrolled the South African Zulu party Inkatha in fighting against the African National Congress (ANC). There was very little involvement by outsiders in the conflict in South Africa.

In Mozambique, the armed conflict between the Frelimo government and the Renamo insurgents started in the late 1970s and was almost purely political. It had some regional and ethnic dimensions but these were relatively insignificant. There was significant involvement by white

Rhodesia and then South Africa in launching and sustaining Renamo's anti-government insurgency.

Regarding the profiles of the atrocities committed during these conflicts, the three countries' experiences were similarly divergent. In Rwanda, starting in early April 1994, the paroxysm of extreme violence in which the Hutu-extremist militias killed between 800,000 and one million people – Tutsis and pro-coexistence Hutus – lasted for only 100 days. The organizers of the genocide had aimed for and won a high level of popular participation in this violence from the Hutu communities. There was also some retaliatory violence against Hutus at and after the end of the 100-day genocide.

In South Africa, the regime used massive administrative violence and significant direct physical violence against its opponents for 350 years, and the levels of this violence were ratcheted up in the years after the "Soweto Uprising" of 1976. The regime's African nationalist challengers pursued their goals mainly by using tactics of mass organizing (which included some violent coercion of fellow blacks viewed as collaborators); they also undertook some small armed operations against regime-linked targets, some of which killed or harmed non-combatants.

In Mozambique, Renamo used a large amount of extremely atrocious violence over a period of 15 years in an attempt to terrorize communities into cooperation or acquiescence. The Frelimo government generally tried to abide by the laws of war, but it also committed some excesses, including the use of "villagization" programmes and other coercive methods that starved some communities of food and other basic needs.

Finally, at the time that the three countries attempted to end these conflicts in 1992 to 1994, they faced widely varying situations of basic demography and socio-economics. Of these differences, the most distinctive was that between South Africa's relatively larger population and high per-capita GDP, in comparison with the much lower figures registered in both spheres by Rwanda and Mozambique.[1] Table 4.1 summarizes some of the basic facts about the three countries at the time of conflict termination.

Ending the conflicts

The ways that the three countries' conflicts were terminated diverged markedly. The most evident difference in this regard was that in Rwanda, the conflict that ravaged the country in 1994 was ended through the military victory won by the Rwandan Patriotic Front (RPF) while in both South Africa and Mozambique the conflicts were ended through lengthy

Table 4.1 Basic country data at time of conflict termination, 1992–1994

	Rwanda	South Africa	Mozambique
Population: size, 1992[a]	7.4 million	38.8 million	14.7 million
Estimated population mix	85% Hutus, 14% Tutsis, 1% Twa	77% black, in 12 or so language groups; 11% white, in two language groups; 11% "coloured" and Indians[b]	nearly all black Africans in around 24 language groups
Real GDP per capita (PPP$)	352 (1994)[c]	4,291 (1994)[c]	380 (1992)[d]
Basic strategic geography	a small, landlocked country in a region dominated by the chronic instability of neighbouring behemoth Zaire (DRC)	a large country, able to dominate or influence many neighbouring states	a large, sprawling country that has always faced much pressure from South Africa and other neighbours

[a] All population sizes in this row are from *Human Development Report 1995*, New York: UN Development Programme, Table 16, pp. 186–187.
[b] These were roughly the proportions existing in 2001.
[c] *Human Development Report 1997*, New York: UN Development Programme, Table 1, pp. 147–148.
[d] *Human Development Report 1995*, Table 2, p. 159.

negotiations among the contending parties. Both of those negotiation processes lasted roughly four years. In the course of them, the relationship between the contesting parties moved from one of extreme distrust marked by the frequent voicing of charges that the other party was "not even a legitimate interlocutor", through a phase of wary intention-testing, to a situation of conditional cooperation marked by agreement on the ground rules for further reciprocal engagement on non-violent, purely political terms and the eschewal of further violence. In South Africa, these negotiations were conducted purely among the concerned national-level parties. In Mozambique, outsiders played a larger role: the original mediation had been undertaken by national-level church leaders who later brought in mediators from elsewhere (Sant'Egidio); and these mediators in turn brought in the Italian government and the

United Nations. Finally, as the Mozambique peace talks neared their conclusion, the United Nations's role in underpinning the peace agreement became quite significant. In Rwanda, meanwhile, outside actors played almost no direct role in the RPF's attainment of its military victory in June/July 1994. But as the RPF's government struggled to rebuild the country after the genocide, the role of outside aid donors became very large indeed.

There were significant differences among the states of the three countries' national infrastructures at the time of conflict termination. In 1994, South Africa had a relatively highly developed physical infrastructure that had been little dented by the conflict (except in some parts of KwaZulu-Natal). The country's socio-political infrastructure, which included many of the institutions of a functioning – though until 1994, strictly segregated – democracy, likewise remained largely in place. One consequence of this was that the new South African government could express a "threat" to prosecute perpetrators of earlier atrocities that had some degree of credibility with those individuals – though not, as it turned out, very much.

In Rwanda, the country had had a fairly well developed physical infrastructure prior to the genocide. That infrastructure was then badly damaged by the violence of spring and summer, 1994; but Rwanda's socio-political infrastructure suffered far, far more from the violence. Its cadres of experienced administrators were shattered first by the genocide and then by the mass exodus of Hutus that followed. Equally importantly, basic social trust among Rwandans had also been shattered, and this affected all the country's institutions without exception.

In Mozambique, the physical infrastructure, which was still very underdeveloped at the time of independence in 1975, received further blows during the years of civil strife and almost did not exist by late 1992. Many millions of Mozambicans had been displaced by the fighting and were near starvation; millions of acres of arable land were contaminated with land mines; a large proportion of the country's already poor stock of roads, bridges, schoolhouses and health posts had been destroyed. But Mozambique's socio-political infrastructure proved much more resilient; some of the key pre-colonial underpinnings of its society managed to survive the decades of liberation war and civil war.

The content of the peace differed greatly among the three countries, depending mainly on the means used to end the conflict. Since conflict termination had not been the subject of any negotiation at all in Rwanda, the government that took power there in July 1994 was under no contractual obligation whatever to take the kinds of "peacebuilding steps" – holding elections, offering amnesties, demobilizing former fighters – to which the post-conflict governments of South Africa and Mozambique were, by contrast, obligated, as shown in Table 4.2.

The post-conflict era

It was within the context of these broader peacebuilding efforts that the three post-conflict governments chose policies to deal specifically with the legacies of the conflict-era atrocities. In this regard, it was Mozambique whose path was most markedly different from those of the other two. The post-General Peace Agreement (GPA) government in Maputo had already enacted a blanket amnesty for all civil-war-era political violence; that amnesty resonated widely in a national culture that placed a lot of emphasis on forgiveness, social reintegration and "not dwelling on the hurts of the past". Additionally, there were many evident infrastructural constraints on the country's ability to undertake any form of "accountability" project that would require the processing of individual cases in any significant numbers. The government therefore made no attempt to enact any kind of an "individual accountability" project; and nor did it undertake any memorialization efforts with respect to the civil-war-era atrocities. It received wide public support for those decisions – then, and through today.

By contrast, both Rwanda and South Africa did try to pursue policies based on the concept of "individual accountability" and the processing of individual cases in significant numbers, though this approach took a very different form in each place. In Rwanda, the initial stress at both the national and international levels was on prosecutions in regular criminal courts of all suspected *génocidaires*. At the national level, in 1996 the parliament adopted legislation that established special Genocide Courts to try cases related to the 1994 genocide, as such. (Meanwhile, the government notably refrained from launching equally vigorous prosecutions against those from the pro-RPF side who were accused of committing the other two kinds of generally recognized atrocities – war crimes and crimes against humanity – but not of committing genocide.) At the international level, at the end of 1994 the Security Council established the International Criminal Tribunal for Rwanda (ICTR), headquartered in Arusha, Tanzania. The ICTR operated with procedures that mirrored those of its sister-court for the former Yugoslavia (ICTY), and like the ICTY it has tried cases of genocide, war crimes and crimes against humanity. The ICTR's judges and prosecutors saw its role as being to try the highest ringleaders and organizers of the atrocities of 1994. By 2005 it had issued indictments against some 60 individuals; but these notably did not include any pro-RPF individuals and it looked very unlikely that any such indictments would be issued. The ICTR is scheduled to finish its work in 2008, 14 years after the genocide.

At the national level the sheer administrative unmanageability of the strict insistence on prosecuting all suspected génocidaires became clear

Table 4.2 Content of the peace

	Rwanda	South Africa	Mozambique
Elections?	The RPF was under no obligation to hold elections.	Democratization and the holding of elections formed a central pillar of the peace agreement.	Democratization and elections were mandated by the 1992 General Peace Agreement (GPA).
Amnesties?	The RPF regime was under no obligation to amnesty anyone.	The new regime was obligated by the Interim Constitution to amnesty those who had committed politically motivated violence during apartheid.	As one of its commitments under the GPA, the Frelimo government enacted a blanket amnesty for all civil-war-era violence.
Demobilization/reintegration efforts; cost of these; and who paid	The RPF regime was not obligated to demobilize, and did not. Nor did the Hutu extremists disarm: their military regrouped in refugee camps around Rwanda. The government pursued the Hutu militias into Zaire/DRC and exported its conflict there.	As part of the transition agreements, c. 35,000 freedom fighters and c. 101,000 members of the apartheid-era military were integrated into a new national army. Later, c. 7,200 freedom fighters, and c. 12,500 former SADF members were demobilized. The government paid 168 m Rand (c. US$21 m) through these programs.[a]	The GPA mandated a broad demobilization of former fighters from both sides and their re-integration into civilian life. Fighters not demobilized were integrated into a new national army. Some 93,000 former fighters were demobilized at a cost of c. US$100 m. Of that, 11% came from the government and the rest from international donors.[b]

Other significant efforts at peacebuilding or social transformation

- The government ordered nationals to self-identify only as "Rwandans" and erase the concepts of "Hutu", "Tutsi", and "Twa".
- Relatively large amounts of external aid flowed into Rwanda after 1994.
- By the early 2000s some faith groups were undertaking grassroots reconciliation projects, with some success.

- The entire cultural content of "South African-ness" was transformed to reflect the ANC's intentionally non-racial, multi-cultural view of the country. This was reflected in language policies, the new Constitution, etc.
- Some attempts were made by the ANC governments to redistribute land and other forms of wealth in a non-coercive way and to equalize opportunity for all citizens.

- Opinion leaders like the *curandeiros/as*, other cultural figures and the country's churches and mosques all worked hard to implement grassroots community-rebuilding and social healing efforts.
- Relatively large amounts of external aid flowed into the country in the decade after the GPA.

[a] P. Batchelor, J. Cock and P. Mackenzie (n.d.) "Conversion in South Africa in the 1990s: Defence Downsizing and Human Development Challenges", available from http://www.bicc.de/publications/briefs/brief18/brief18.pdf.
[b] Iraê Baptista Lundin, Martinho Chachina, António Gaspar, Habiba Guebuza and Guilherma Mbilana (2000) " 'Reducing Costs through an Expensive Exercise': The Impact of Demobilization in Mozambique", in K. Kingma (ed.) *Demobilisation in Sub-Saharan Africa: The Development and Security Impacts*, Basingstoke: Macmillan Press, pp. 186, 187.

within a few years; and by 1998/99 the government dominated by Paul Kagame started moving (very slowly) to establish the new (neotraditional) "*gacaca* courts" to handle the majority of these cases.[2] The gacaca courts finally started operating in March 2005, almost 11 years after the genocide. Early views of their achievements were mixed, and in September 2005 it was still far too early to make any settled assessment of their work: they were still, very conservatively, expected to take an additional three to five years to get through their caseload. (Regarding memorialization, the Rwandan government has invested heavily in preserving and refurbishing the sites of several large genocide-era massacres, and in maintaining them as prominent public memorials; it also started sponsoring a month of nationwide genocide commemoration in April each year.)

In South Africa, the Truth and Reconciliation Commission (TRC) was established primarily to process the amnesties previously promised to the apartheid-era security bosses, but its procedures were designed also to provide dignity, a voice and valuable public acknowledgement to victims and to establish a full historical record of the "gross human rights violations" of the apartheid era. The TRC's work proved noticeably speedier than the mechanisms used by, and with respect to, Rwanda. It started its work in late 1995; the main part of its work was finished in October 1998, but the Amnesty Committee continued through August 2002 – just over eight years after the country's landmark 1994 elections. Only a handful of TRC-related cases still dangled after 2002. Regarding memorialization, the government made some, fairly half-hearted, efforts in this regard but it saw its main priority in the cultural sphere as being to implement a series of much broader language, renaming and re-education projects that would transform the entire cultural content of what it meant to be a "South African".

The direct outcomes and achievements of these post-atrocity policies differed widely. In Rwanda, the total number of genocide suspects, each of whose cases had to be considered individually, rose swiftly in the mid-1990s to above 140,000. By 2004, the regular national court system had completed the processing of only around 1,000 of these cases. By then, many of those suspected only of "lower level" crimes related to the genocide had been released, and their cases transferred to the gacaca courts. However, once the gacaca courts started working they themselves generated – through their encouragement of full confessions – new cases in which additional suspects would need to have their actions formally investigated, too. Inside Rwanda, the case-processing, in general, continued to be chaotic even 11 years after the genocide. Regarding the budget for the gacaca courts, one September 2003 report estimated that the whole, multi-year gacaca project would cost around US$75.5 million, with nearly all of this sum expected to be met from foreign donors.[3] (For resolving 140,000 cases, this would result in a per-case cost of US$540.)

As for the ICTR, in its first ten years of operation the court had completed the first-instance trials of only 23 suspects (and the appeals in several of these cases were still outstanding). The ICTR's budgets are hard to figure out accurately because some foreign governments gave a lot of support to it in the form of "special" supplementary and in-kind aid. But by 2004, the ICTR had evidently consumed more than US$1 billion of international funds, giving a per-case processing cost of more than US$43.5 million.

In South Africa, throughout the total, seven-year life of both the main TRC and its Amnesty Committee (1995 to 2002), the TRC accepted 21,000 victim statements, processed 7,116 amnesty applications and produced a seminal seven-volume report of the gross rights violations of the apartheid era. Its main budget for the years 1995 to 2000 totalled 244 million rand (c. US$30.5 million).[4] This was all met from the national budget, though some foreign donors gave small amounts of in-kind aid for supplemental programs. It is hard to give a good picture of the proportions of TRC spending that went into each of its areas of activity. But if we were to say that the whole of that US$30.5 million of TRC spending went only into processing the cases of suspected rights abusers (which was, after all, the most lawyer-heavy and therefore expensive portion of its budget), then we could say that the per-case processing cost for each of those cases came to around US$4,290 – that is, one ten-thousandth part of the ICTR's per-case processing cost.[5]

Outcomes

Some 10 to 12 years after the ending of these atrocity-laden conflicts it is possible to assess the broad socio-political outcomes attained by these societies as a result of the mix of policies – including the atrocity-response policies – pursued by their governments in the post-conflict era. Regarding the situation in Rwanda, long-time Rwanda-affairs analyst René Lemarchand noted at the end of 2004 that the country enjoyed a high level of general stability. But he added, "What lies at the heart of the country's stability [is] the ever present threat of repression. The Tutsi-dominated state has successfully eliminated all forms of organized political opposition."[6] In late 2003, Rwanda held its first multi-party elections since 1993. They were widely judged to be neither free nor fair.

At the international level, meanwhile, Rwanda's RPF government continued to pursue a highly militarized and often escalatory policy inside the neighbouring Democratic Republic of Congo (DRC). In December

2004 it launched a new, very destructive military incursion there that blatantly flouted its previous commitments.[7]

In South Africa, democratic elections that were judged free and fair were held at both the national and the provincial level in 1994, 1999 and 2004. In November 2003, the Cape Town-based Institute for Justice and Reconciliation reported that 83 per cent of all South Africans – including 67 per cent of the country's whites – agreed that, "It is desirable to create one united South African nation out of all the different groups who live in this country."[8] In contrast to the record of the country's apartheid-era governments, South Africa's democratic governments launched no military expeditions against any other countries.

In Mozambique, national elections that were judged generally free and fair were held in 1994, 1999 and 2004. A first round of local elections held in 1998 had many problems, but local elections held in 2003 were judged to be free and fair. At the end of 2004, Swisspeace analyst Elísio Macamo wrote of the latest national elections that, "Compared to the previous two [national] elections, there were fewer events of a violent or hostile nature ... both Renamo and Frelimo appear to have decided to moderate the tone of their campaigns." He did note that turnout at that poll was low – estimated at 36 to 43 per cent. But he also noted that political tensions inside the country had been eased by the recent adoption – by a two-thirds majority in parliament – of significant constitutional changes, including the introduction of the right of parliament to impeach a president.[9] Like democratic South Africa, post-GPA Mozambique had launched no military expeditions against any of its neighbours.

The main dimensions of the socio-political outcomes in the three countries 10 to 12 years after their conflict-termination attempts can be summarized as in Table 4.3.

What, finally, do we know about the satisfaction of the primary stakeholders in the policies adopted by their respective national governments (and, in Rwanda's case, that adopted by the United Nations) to deal with the legacies of the earlier atrocities? In South Africa, in late 2000, 68.2 per cent of all citizens, including 76 per cent of black South Africans, said they approved strongly or somewhat of the TRC's performance.[10] In Rwanda, a February 2002 survey found that only 29.2 per cent of the Rwandan respondents expressed any degree of approval of the ICTR's record, while 56.5 per cent expressed some approval of the work of the national-level courts.[11] Regarding the gacaca courts, it was still too early in early 2005 to measure Rwandans' "satisfaction" with their work, but low rates of participation in the pilot gacacas indicated a low popular investment in the project's success and/or low expectations regarding its achievements. In Mozambique, though there was no survey data to rely on, my own clear observations during research trips in 2001 and 2003 were that there was still a very high level of general satisfaction in the "amnesty, reconciliation and rebuilding" approach that the government adopted in 1992.

Restoring peacemaking

The American legal scholar Diane Orentlicher has written a lot about what she calls the "duty to prosecute" the perpetrators of atrocities. She, British attorney Geoffrey Robertson and other legal thinkers working in prosperous and settled western countries have strongly contested the notion that offering amnesties during peace negotiations may bring something of value to men and women living in societies mired in atrocity-laden inter-group conflict. These influential scholars have argued that the risk that such amnesties will foster a "climate of impunity" and thus allow the continued commission of atrocities, or their resumption after a brief hiatus, is so great that no peace that is won through the granting of amnesties can be considered valuable – or, indeed, secure – at all. The evidence I have gathered challenges those arguments. In particular, the experiences of South Africa and Mozambique in the 10 to 12 years after each country's conflict termination attempt of the early 1990s show clearly that an amnesty-reliant peace agreement does not always foster a "climate of impunity". On the contrary, such a peace agreement can, if well crafted, mark a clear turning point between the conflict-riven and impunity-plagued climate of the past and a new, much more peaceable social climate in which human rights protection can finally be guaranteed and the basic norms of the rule of law – including the ending of impunity for all persons, however powerful – can be respected. (It is worth restating very forcefully here that in situations of classic warfare or other grave inter-group conflict none of the human rights of civilians in the territories affected, including rights as basic as those to life or the physical integrity of persons, can ever be assured. In conflict zones, indeed, the entire panoply of human rights articulated in the Universal Declaration on Human Rights and its attendant Covenants are under constant threat. This simple fact about warfare seems to have eluded too many western-based rights activists in recent years.)

Meanwhile, the experience of Rwanda since 1994 stands in stark contrast to those of Mozambique and South Africa. It indicates that pursuing a rigorously interpreted "duty to prosecute" can all too easily perpetuate existing social and political cleavages and maintain a situation in which fundamental human rights continue to be denied and threatened on a massive scale.

Travelling in Mozambique in 2001 and 2003 I heard over and over,

Table 4.3 Broad socio-political outcomes, as of 2004/05

	Rwanda	South Africa	Mozambique
Democracy well institutionalized?	No	Yes	Apparently, yes
Movement on Freedom House indicators, 1994–2004.[a] (1 is most free; 7 is least free. The first rating is for "political rights"; the second for "civil liberties".)	1994: 6 ; 5 2004: 6 ; 5 Total movement: 0 points	1994: 5 ; 4 2004: 1 ; 2 Total positive movement: 6 points	1994: 6 ; 5 2004: 3 ; 4 Total positive movement: 4 points
Human Development Index ratings, 1990 and 2002[b]	HDI figures for: 1990 – 0.351 2002 – 0.431	HDI figures for: 1990 – 0.729 2002 – 0.666	HDI figures for: 1990 – 0.310 2002 – 0.354
Movement on size of military forces, 1993 → 2003[c]	c. 5.2K → 51K Soldiers per 1,000 population: c. 0.65 → 6.30	67.5K → 55.7K Soldiers per 1,000 population: 1.75 → 1.25	50K → 8.2K Soldiers per 1,000 population: 2.91 → 0.45
Status of political and other violence, 2004	Overt, Rwanda-linked political violence continued in 2004, but mainly outside the country. Administrative and repressive violence continued to be widespread inside Rwanda.	Political violence persisted at a high rate after 1994 in KwaZulu-Natal, but it abated there in the late 1990s. A high rate of non-political crime persisted nation-wide, including a 2000 murder rate of 51 murders per 100,000 people.	Levels of political violence were low but not zero after the conclusion of the GPA. Levels of violent crime were fairly high in the early 2000s, but not nearly as high as in South Africa.

Other factors affecting the above			
	• An estimated 7.6% of the population was living with HIV at the end of 2003.[d] • Rwanda continued to intervene militarily in DRC. • It received relatively generous international aid through at least 2002.	• An estimated 13.7% of the population was living with HIV at the end of 2003. • S. Africa had one of the highest levels of economic inequality in the world.	• An estimated 7.6% of the population was living with HIV at the end of 2003. • Two very serious floods and IMF-imposed economic adjustment all impeded national development. • It received relatively generous international aid (though in wildly varying amounts) through at least 2002.

[a] Freedom House country ratings available from http://www.freedomhouse.org/ratings/index.htm.

[b] The Human Development Index (HDI) is an index of human wellbeing developed by the UN Development Programme. It is compiled on a scale of 0 to 1.000 from weighted components derived from national figures for GDP per capita, life expectancy and educational levels. In 2001, the country with the highest HDI score was Norway, with 0.944. The figures presented here are from the *Human Development Report 2004*, New York: UNDP, Statistical Table 2, "Human Development Index Trends".

[c] Force size figures from the relevant annual volumes of International Institute for Strategic Studies' *The Military Balance*, London: IISS.

[d] The figures for HIV infection rates are taken from the raw UNAIDS numbers, available from http://www.unaids.org/bangkok2004/GAR2004_html/GAR2004_14_en.htm, divided by each country's population figures.

from people in many different sections of society, expressions of great satisfaction with the peace agreement that the political leaders had concluded in 1992, and horror at the thought that anything might happen to reignite the cleavages of the war years. To them, the post-1992 peace most evidently was its own dividend. They all seemed to value highly the fact that the continuing disagreements between their political leaders could now be addressed through parliamentary mechanisms rather than armed conflict (though I did hear from some Mozambicans the same kind of criticisms of the pretensions and alleged corruptibility of their politicians that one hears from citizens of many other democratic countries). The principles of the rule of law seemed to be broadly respected and generally implemented in Mozambique.[12] The major problem that groups such as Amnesty International and Penal Reform International noted with respect to rights observance in Mozambique in the early years of the 21st century had much more to do with the continued impoverishment of the society, and the accompanying lack in government institutions, like prisons, of even the most basic tools needed to do an acceptable job, than with the existence of a "climate of impunity" or the absence of the rule of law.

Visiting South Africa, also in 2001 and 2003, I found a similarly palpable (though slightly less universal) sense of relief that the long-running conflict over human inequality in the country had finally been resolved in 1993/94. In South Africa, as in Mozambique, a number of important rights-protection issues remained to be worked on 10 years after the transition. These issues were particularly in the realm of assuring the basic economic and social rights of all citizens, and in the prevention of police brutality.[13] Meanwhile, as noted in Table 4.3, the records kept by Freedom House showed that in South Africa, as in Mozambique, the aggregated ratings of the country's political rights and civil liberties had registered a significant improvement between 1994 and 2004: by a total of six points (out of a possible seven) in the case of South Africa, and by four points (out of a possible nine) in Mozambique. In Rwanda, meanwhile, the Freedom House ratings showed no change at all between 1994 and 2004: they remained mired near the bottom of the charts and earned the organization's summary judgment that the country was still "not free".

When I visited Rwanda in 2002 all of the Rwandans whom I met were unanimous in expressing relief that their country was no longer living in the maelstrom of violence that had beset it in 1994. But many Rwandans still seemed extremely fearful – either of a recurrence of violence broadly similar to that which erupted in 1994, or of the eruption of some other form of atrocity-laden mayhem.[14] Meanwhile, in a situation in which President Kagame had significantly consolidated the RPF's hold over all of the country's institutions, the norms of the rule of law were not even on their way to being respected there. In 2005, Human Rights Watch noted that,

> In 2004, the RPF further reinforced its control by attacking civil society organizations, churches, and schools for supposedly disseminating 'genocidal ideology.' Authorities arrested dozens of persons accused of this crime.
>
> Judicial authorities carried out a sham trial of a former president and seven others, but few other trials. Tens of thousands of persons remained jailed on accusations of genocide, some of them detained more than ten years....
>
> In the course of reforming the judicial system, authorities obliged judges and judicial personnel, more than five hundred of them, to resign. Fewer than one hundred were re-appointed to positions in the new system. During [2004] nearly half the 106 mayors were also obliged to resign.[15]

With Kagame's RPF still able to manipulate, undermine and control all of the country's national institutions at will, the climate of impunity reigned supreme.

An insistence on pursuing a "duty" to prosecute therefore seemed not to have helped Rwanda to escape from impunity and establish a general respect for the rule of law. Meanwhile, the two countries that had used amnesties in 1993/94 ended up with much more significant improvements in their assurance of and general respect for the rule of law![16] Clearly the paradigm posited by Orentlicher, Robertson and others needs considerable re-examination. I submit that what is wrong with their model is that it is fundamentally apolitical. By focusing narrowly on only the "technical-legal" aspect of the challenges faced by societies struggling to emerge from deep-seated inter-group conflict, their approach neglects the broader political context within which decisions to prosecute or not to prosecute are always taken. Specifically, it ignores the overarching need in such societies for an intentional politics of peacemaking and longer-term peacebuilding.

Prosecutions, opportunity costs and peacebuilding

How can launching (or refraining from launching) criminal prosecutions of alleged perpetrators of atrocities affect the processes of peacemaking and peacebuilding? It can do so in a number of ways, at the levels of both politics and economics. Politically, the offering of amnesties is often, as in Mozambique or South Africa, the only way that a negotiated transition out of a deep-seated conflict can be effected. This price is often – in many countries around the world today, as in Abraham Lincoln's United States – seen as one that is worth paying in the broader interest of conflict termination. Secondly, and more broadly, amnesties can often be part of a process of broadening political inclusion. For example, in both South Africa and Mozambique, the existing political conflicts were prolonged so long as the parties in power used the language – and practice – of criminalization to try to exclude their opponents from exerting any political influence. (In South Africa, the government excoriated its opponents by dubbing all opponents "terrorists", with whom negotiation was impossible. In Mozambique, the government called Renamo's people "nothing but armed bandits", and similarly refused to negotiate with them.) Once these governments were persuaded of the need to negotiate, they had to end the exclusionary, marginalizing policies they had previously maintained against their opponents. Foreswearing the language and practice of criminalization was a big part of that. In Mozambique, the offering of blanket amnesties for wartime wrongdoing flowed directly from that. In South Africa, the amnesty offer was the result of the political bargain the ANC leaders made with the South African Defence Force security chiefs on the eve of the April 1994 election.

In Rwanda, by contrast, the fact that even 10 and more years after the end of the genocide large numbers of genocide-related cases continued to be tried – in the Rwandan regular courts, the gacaca courts and the ICTR – meant that a considerable amount of public and media attention was still being focused on the precise and painful details of those 13 weeks of genocide. The relatively few survivors of the genocide found it almost impossible – throughout those 10 crucial post-genocide years, and for many foreseeable years into the future – to escape from the repeated retraumatizations occasioned by the need to relive and re-describe their traumas in different judicial settings throughout that period. In addition, the one-sided (anti-Hutu) nature of the proceedings pursued by both the ICTR and the Rwandan government had a strong effect in keeping the Tutsi-Hutu cleavage alive inside Rwanda, despite the best efforts of the Kagame government to claim that this cleavage no longer existed.

When the Security Council established the ICTR, as when it established the ICTY, its members expressed the sincere hope that the work of these courts could "contribute to national reconciliation" within the territories that their work covered. However, the veteran Balkan-affairs analyst Tim Judah reported after a late-2003 visit to Serbia, Croatia and Bosnia that in those three countries, "I met virtually no one who believed that the tribunal was helping to reconcile people."[17] (Since the ICTY has launched "equal opportunity" prosecutions against ethnic Serbs, Croats and Bosniaks, this indicates that it might be the sheer length of the ICTR's proceedings, rather than its one-sided nature, that has had the greatest negative effect on reconciliation inside the country. The Nuremberg trials were also, in their day, extremely one-sided. But they were completed with admirable speed – just eleven months to try all 22 top Nazi leaders! They were, moreover, embedded in the Western Allies' broader project of the economic and political rebuilding of West Germany on a democratic basis. They thus did not lead to any lasting anti-Allied sentiment amongst most Germans.)

In 2000–2002, Harvey Weinstein and Eric Stover and other colleagues from the University of California, Berkeley, conducted considerable surveys and other research into the effects that the two ad hoc tribunals – the ICTY and ICTR – and Rwanda's national-level courts had had on national reconciliation in the countries concerned. Weinstein and Stover concluded that, "Our studies suggest that there is no direct link between criminal trials (international, national, and local/traditional) and reconciliation, although it is possible this could change over time. In fact, we found criminal trials – and especially those of local perpetrators – often divided multi-ethnic communities by causing further suspicion and fear. Survivors rarely, if ever, connected retributive justice with reconciliation."[18] The aspiration that the Security Council expressed when it established the ICTR (and ICTY) a decade earlier, that these courts would somehow contribute to national reconciliation, has not been fulfilled.

While Judah, Stover and Weinstein report that there is no positive link between the work of the United Nations (and the Rwandan national) courts and reconciliation it is also, I believe, possible to make the stronger case that – certainly in Rwanda – the work of these courts may well have had a considerable negative effect on the prospects of reconciliation. This is the case not only because of the political effects described above, but also because of the opportunity costs incurred by the courts at the economic level. Criminal prosecutions can easily become an incredibly expensive project.

Concerning the Rwandan government's plans to prosecute all genocide suspects in the national courts, we can note that for a large portion of the decade after the end of the genocide the government was holding more than 100,000 untried genocide suspects (out of a national population of some 8 million people) in its prisons and lock-ups. Given that nearly all of these were people of breadwinning age, many with numerous dependents, the deleterious effects on the country's economy of their incarceration at government expense and their separation from normal productive labour become clearer. Regarding the gacaca courts, these have also started to impose heavy manpower costs on the country's localities, since all adult citizens are supposed to devote one day of unpaid labour per week to their participation in the gacacas, for as long as they continue their work. (This is in addition to the traditional day of *umuganda* – unpaid community service – and, for most Rwandans, one day off for church.)

But it is in the case of the ICTR that the economic costs of pursuing a very robust prosecutorial strategy become more visible and more staggering. Based on the figures given earlier, the per-case cash cost of pursuing various different kinds of policy toward suspected former perpetrators of violence can be roughly calculated as in Table 4.4.

It was not just the per-case cost at the ICTR that seemed wildly disproportionate; the global cost of establishing and running the court – over $1 billion by the end of 2004 – was a sum that, had it been differently used, could have made a substantial difference to the long-term economic and social wellbeing of any one of a number of very vulnerable, very low-income countries, including Rwanda. For example, the entire amount of overseas aid invested in Rwanda's 8.3 million people in 2002 was US$356.1 million, and the amount invested in the DRC's 51 million even more deeply impoverished and violence-wracked people was US$806.7 million. How much more stabilization and how much less human misery might the citizens of Rwanda and the DRC have known if the ICTR's budgets for the preceding years had been spent in supporting economic and social stabilization programmes in one or both of those countries, instead? But the very high financial opportunity costs involved in, in effect, taking $1 billion out of the available international aid budget and pouring it into sustaining an extremely high-cost and low-efficiency international court in Arusha have seldom been mentioned in the flood of articles in Western publications about the court's "jurisprudential breakthroughs".[19]

Meanwhile, study after study of the needs and preferences of people living in post-conflict, post-atrocity societies shows that economic and social stabilization has been absolutely their main priority. In Rwanda, an opinion survey conducted in June 2000 showed that "Poverty/economic hardship" was the social problem most frequently identified by respondents – 81.9 per cent of them.[20] Eric Stover and Harvey Weinstein summarized the results of the research they organized in Rwanda, Bosnia and Croatia in 2000–2002 by noting, "Our informants told us that jobs, food, adequate and secure housing, good schooling for their children, and peace and security were their major priorities."[21] My own respon-

Table 4.4 Per-case cost of different policies

Each case completed at the ICTR	US$43,500,000
Each amnesty application at South Africa's TRC	US$4,290
Each case in Rwanda's gacaca courts (projected)	US$540
Mozambique: each former fighter demobilized/reintegrated	US$1,075
South Africa: each former fighter demobilized/reintegrated	US$1,066

dents in Rwanda, South Africa and Mozambique all stressed the central-
ity of economic stabilization to the success of post-conflict peacebuilding
in their countries. (There is a strong resonance here with the record of
peacebuilding efforts in post-World War II Europe and Japan.)

Meanwhile, it is clear that in the early years of the twenty-first century
a high proportion of the atrocities being committed in different countries
around the world occur in the context of conflicts pursued within some of
the world's most deeply impoverished nations. In many of those countries, including those sometimes referred to as "failed states", there is an
apparent vicious circle at work in which grave conflict wrecks the social
and physical infrastructure needed to sustain livelihoods, and the dashing
of the expectations of many people – especially young people – that they
might be able to find a sustainable livelihood in the civilian world then
just continues to fuel the conflict and all its attendant lawlessness. The
goal, for everyone who wants to maximize the wellbeing of citizens of
those stricken areas, must be to help them find a way to escape from
that vicious cycle. Very often, ancient indigenous cultures have resources
to do this that are woefully under-recognized by members of western-
based policy elites. For example, in Mozambique the cultural resources
safeguarded by the country's traditional healers played a significant role
in sustaining the country's citizens throughout their long years of disaster;
and once the General Peace Agreement had been concluded in 1992, the
practices of forgiveness and community-wide healing embodied in the
country's indigenous traditions (and also its Christian and Muslim institutions) helped to rebuild shattered communities throughout the land.

Now, in the era of the (very expensive) International Criminal Court
(ICC), will such amnesty-based indigenous practices of forgiveness and
community reintegration still be allowed to proceed? One key indicator
will be to see what comes of the judicial investigation into the atrocities
committed in the civil war inside northern Uganda. This "situation" was
referred to ICC Chief Prosecutor Luis Moreno-Ocampo by Ugandan
President Yoweri Museveni in January 2004. Moreno-Ocampo began
studying the situation and in late July opened a formal judicial investigation into it – such as can, under the mixed civil law/common law procedure according to which the ICC works, be expected to result in the
issuing of a number of indictments. Inside northern Uganda, however,
many community leaders had a very different idea of what needed to be
done to end the commission of atrocities there. As *New York Times*
reporter Marc Lacey wrote,

> Some war victims are urging the international court to back off. They say the
> local people will suffer if the rebel command feels cornered. They recommend
> giving forgiveness more of a chance, using an age-old ceremony involving raw

eggs. "When we talk of arrest warrants it sounds so simple," said David Onen Acana II, the chief of the Acholi, the dominant tribe in the war-riven north.... "But an arrest warrant doesn't mean the war will end."[22]

In March 2005, Acana led a high-level delegation of northern Uganda community leaders to the Hague, where they discussed their concerns with Moreno-Ocampo. At the end of the meeting, the prosecutor issued a statement, in which he said,

I am mindful of traditional justice and reconciliation processes and sensitive to the leaders' efforts to promote dialogue between different actors in order to achieve peace.... I also recognize the vital role to be played by national and local leaders to achieve peace, justice and reconciliation. We agreed on the importance of continuing this dialogue in pursuit of the common goal of ending violence.[23]

A month later, Acana led an even larger delegation to the ICC headquarters. This time, unlike in March, the two sides reached agreement on a joint statement. It read in part:

The Lango; Acholi; Iteso and Madi community leaders and the Prosecutor of the International Criminal Court have agreed to work together as part of a common effort to achieve justice and reconciliation, the rebuilding of communities and an end to violence in Northern Uganda.... In working towards an end to violence, all parties agreed to continue to integrate the dialogue for peace, the ICC and traditional justice and reconciliation processes.[24]

The work of the ICC prosecutor was thus emerging as one focusing considerably more on the diplomacy of peacemaking than that of most prosecutors. Indeed, in the Rome Treaty, Article 53, part 2 specifically allows that, "upon investigation, the Prosecutor [may] conclude that there is not a sufficient basis for a prosecution because ... (c) A prosecution is not in the interests of justice, taking into account all the circumstances". In addition to the prosecutor being allowed some discretion in his work as noted there, the treaty also allowed the UN Security Council to request the deferral of an ICC investigation or prosecution, provided it did so under a resolution adopted under Chapter VII of the UN Charter; and Article 16 stipulates that when faced with such a request the court must totally halt any work on the relevant investigations or prosecutions.

As of September 2005, Moreno-Ocampo had still not launched any prosecutions. There thus seemed to be a good chance that northern Uganda's traditional, non-punitive methods of conflict resolution would be given a chance to work. Human rights activists everywhere should rejoice.

Notes

1. In South Africa, the raw GDP figures masked extremely serious inequalities between the incomes and wealth enjoyed by the country's white and its non-white (especially black) communities.
2. The most serious genocide cases – those in "Category 1" – would still be tried in the regular courts.
3. Penal Reform International (2003) *Research on the Gacaca*, London: Penal Reform International, p. 68, available from http://www.penalreform.org/download/Gacaca/september2003.pdf.
4. Summed from the separate "Expenditure" line items given in each of the annual budgets presented in Vols. 1 and 6 of the *Truth and Reconciliation Commission of South Africa Report* (1998) Cape Town: Truth and Reconciliation Commission and Department of Justice.
5. Of course, if we say (quite realistically) that only a portion of the TRC's US$30.5 million budget was used to process the cases of perpetrators of violence then the estimated per-case processing cost would be correspondingly lower.
6. Analysis by René Lemarchand in Swisspeace (2004) "FAST Early Warning System Report for Rwanda", available from http://www.swisspeace.org/uploads/FAST/updates/Rwanda%20Update%204_2004%20final.pdf, pp. 3, 5.
7. Ibid., p. 6.
8. K. Lombard (2004) "Opportunities and Obstacles: The State of Reconciliation", Report of the Second Round of the SA Reconciliation Barometer Survey, Cape Town: Institute for Justice and Reconciliation, p. 29. The percentage of whites expressing support for the statement had climbed by nearly 10 percentage points between April and November 2003.
9. Analysis by Elísio Macamo in Swisspeace (2004) "FAST Early Warning System Report for Mozambique", available from http://www.swisspeace.org/uploads/FAST/updates/MOZ_Update_4_2004.pdf, pp. 3, 4.
10. J. L. Gibson and H. Macdonald (2001) *Truth – Yes, Reconciliation – Maybe: South Africans Judge the Truth and Reconciliation Process*, Rondebosch, South Africa: Institute for Justice and Reconciliation, p. 19.
11. Figures for "approve" and "strongly approve" aggregated from Table 10.4, line 1, and Table 10.5, line 1, in Timothy Longman, Phuong Pham and Harvey M. Weinstein (2004) "Connecting Justice to Human Experience: Attitudes toward Accountability and Reconciliation in Rwanda", in E. Stover and H. M. Weinstein, eds, *My Neighbor, My Enemy: Justice and Community in the Aftermath of Mass Atrocity*, Cambridge: Cambridge University Press, pp. 214, 216.
12. For example, in November 2000 a noted local journalist was murdered while researching a story about large-scale fraud at a state-run bank; but in 2003 two businessmen and a former manager of the bank were convicted for having contracted the killing, and three other men for having carried it out; all received lengthy prison terms. Amnesty International (2004) "Mozambique", in *Report 2004*, available from http://web.amnesty.org/report2004/moz-summary-eng.
13. For example, Human Rights Watch reported about South Africa that, "From April 2003 to March 2004 ... a statutory oversight body received reports of 383 deaths in police custody". Human Rights Watch (2005) "South Africa", in *World Report 2005*, available from http://hrw.org/english/docs/2005/01/13/safric9886.htm. The report judged that, "While it is encouraging that the reporting mechanism is in place, the increasing number of deaths, particularly in police custody, is worrying."
14. The general fearfulness inside Rwanda was most likely also fuelled in part by the sense

that many Rwandans have that their tiny country is very vulnerable to violent influences from its neighbours, particularly from massive and violence-wracked DRC. But the Rwandan government seemed trapped in a classic "security dilemma" with respect to the DRC: the escalatory actions that it repeatedly undertook within DRC with the stated aim of increasing Rwanda's security only ended up, time and again, increasing the overall insecurity of the entire region, including their own country.

15. Human Rights Watch (2005) "Rwanda", in *World Report 2005*; available from http:// hrw.org/english/docs/2005/01/13/rwanda9860.htm.
16. It is also true that in a number of cases, amnesty-reliant peace agreements have failed, and the countries concerned have been plunged back into conflict, lawlessness and the commission of atrocities. But the failure in those cases represented a failure of the peace-making diplomacy at a broader, political level rather than being related to the offers of amnesties per se.
17. T. Judah (2004) "The Fog of Justice", *New York Review of Books* 51(1), January. Judah also expressed his own judgment: "I don't believe that the Hague Tribunal is the only, or even a major, reason for the collapse of the reformist government that led Serbia since 2000, but it has contributed to it."
18. E. Stover and H. M. Weinstein, eds (2004) *My Neighbor, My Enemy: Justice and Community in the Aftermath of Mass Atrocity*, Cambridge: Cambridge University Press, p. 323.
19. I realize that the ideal would be for all the world's rich countries to live up to their commitments and actually increase the proportion of their GDP that they devote to international development aid to the promised 0.7 per cent. But especially while most rich countries remain very far from meeting that goal, the diversion of so much international aid to sustaining a court system whose primary financial beneficiaries are highly-paid international lawyers rather than the people in the impoverished and war-torn communities seems very questionable.
20. National University of Rwanda Centre for Conflict Management (2000) *Les Juridictions Gacaca et les Processus de Réconciliation Nationale*, Kigali: Editions de l'Université National du Rwanda, p. 106. The next most frequently named problem was "insecurity", named by 20.8 per cent of respondents. Some respondents described more than one of the eight identified problems as "major". The figures for all eight items totalled 152.5 per cent.
21. Stover and Weinstein, *My Neighbor, My Enemy*, p. 325.
22. M. Lacey (2005) "Atrocity Victims in Uganda Choose to Forgive", *New York Times*, 18 April. The community reintegration rituals described by Lacey had many features in common with those I learned about in Mozambique.
23. International Criminal Court (2005) "Statements by ICC Chief Prosecutor and the Visiting Delegation of Acholi Leaders from Northern Uganda", ICC-OTP 2005.042-EN, The Hague: ICC, 18 March, available from http://www.icc-cpi.int/press/pressreleases/ 96.html.
24. International Criminal Court (2005) "Joint Statement by ICC Chief Prosecutor and the Visiting Delegation of Lango, Acholi, Iteso and Madi Community Leaders from Northern Uganda", ICC-OTP-20050416. 047-EN, The Hague: ICC, 16 April, available from http://www.icc-cpi.int/press/pressreleases/102.html.

5

All the truth but only some justice? Dilemmas of dealing with the past in new democracies

Jorge Heine

> Without truth and acknowledgement, reconciliation is not possible.
> José Zalaquett[1]

How do newly established democracies come to terms with the human rights violations that are such a prominent feature of the dictatorships that preceded them?[2] How does a democratic dispensation deal with an evil past? Although we have had representative democracies (or polyarchies, in Robert Dahl's expression)[3] for a little over two centuries now, the established practice, whenever such regime changes took place, was either to engage in "victor's justice" *tout court*, or simply "let bygones be bygones", with the deposed dictator taking the next plane to some off-shore paradise to enjoy his ill-gotten riches, and his acolytes either following him or quickly adapting to the new political dispensation.

It is only over the past 60 years or so, starting with Germany and Japan after the Second World War, that attempts have been made to deal with past wrongdoings in any systematic fashion, and this is especially true of the past 30 years, during what Samuel P. Huntington has referred to as the "Third Wave" of democratization, which started in the mid-seventies with the Portuguese "Carnation Revolution".[4]

Recent developments in *ex parte* Pinochet

Two of the most emblematic transitions of the nineties were the South African and the Chilean.[5] To illustrate the very real and ongoing

Atrocities and international accountability: Beyond transitional justice, Hughes, Schabas and Thakur (eds), United Nations University Press, 2007, ISBN 978-92-808-1141-4

statecraft dilemmas the management of these processes entail, it is useful to examine developments in the trials and tribulations of the former dictator, General Augusto Pinochet, as this throws light on the very delicate and fine balancing act democratic leaders must accomplish in order to come to terms with the past.[6]

In February 2005, Judge Juan Guzmán, then a member of Santiago's Court of Appeals, and in many ways the man who almost single-handedly brought General Pinochet to court in Chile after the latter's arrest in a London clinic, indicted two former Home Affairs ministers of the military government, Air Force General Enrique Montero and Army General César Benavides. The reasoning was that, given their positions and responsibilities, they must have been aware what was being done by Chile's infamous secret police, the Directorate of National Intelligence, in the killings, "disappearances" and extensive torture practices of the regime's political opponents. Both were promptly arrested, albeit subsequently released on bail.

Contrary to what is normally thought abroad, much progress has been made in Chile not only in uncovering the truth about what happened in those dark days of dictatorship, but also in meting out a measure of justice. Some 40 military personnel (including, perhaps for the first time anywhere, the former head of the secret police, General Manuel Contreras) have served time behind bars for crimes committed in those years, and another 250 are facing trials. The latter, of course, include General Pinochet himself, whose lawyers are handling some 200 criminal lawsuits against him, and who is now in even greater difficulties after US$27 million in secret bank accounts under his name were uncovered by a US Senate investigation.

In indicting Generals Montero and Benavides, Judge Guzmán actually raised the political stakes, going one step further. Guzmán's reasoning in this case was not based on specific evidence that linked each of the former Pinochet ministers to any human rights violations, but, rather, on the assumption that, given their responsibilities as Home Ministers (in Chile, the Cabinet's most senior members, and traditionally in charge of law and order and the national police) they must have known what was going on at a time of high levels of repression and when, at any one time, tens of thousands were being imprisoned and mistreated, or worse, for their political views.

In a country where, even today, sixteen years after Pinochet handed over power, the heads of the two main opposition parties are men who served in high-level positions in the military government, this was seen as the opening of a Pandora's box. If ministers of the military regime could be indicted on such assumptions, where would you draw the line in the future? Was anybody who worked for that government criminally liable?

Other former Home Affairs ministers of the General became especially nervous, including then-Senator Sergio Fernández, who made a public statement to the effect that he was ready, "as he had always been" to take on his "political responsibility" for his duties as Cabinet minister, but that he did not see why he should be criminally liable for any human rights violations, particularly since the security services did not report to him, and he had no way of knowing what they were doing.

Under the circumstances, the then-Home Affairs minister, José Miguel Insulza, responded by way of a newspaper article in which he reiterated the established government policy:[7]

1. In matters pertaining to events occurring during the military regime, a clear-cut distinction between criminal and political responsibility is made, in the understanding that political responsibilities will not be prosecuted.
2. A second principle has been to consistently pursue truth and justice in matters of past human rights violations, including the commissioning of various reports and the payment of compensation for those killed, disappeared, tortured and exiled.
3. Justice is administered only by the courts.
4. Criminal liability is individual and specific. No trials of institutions, or of individuals because they are part of them, can take place.

Still, this did not preclude at least one Socialist party MP, Sergio Aguiló, from suing Fernández for his involvement in Aguiló's arrest, imprisonment and torture.

The nature of the problem

This excursion into the saga of Judge Guzmán and its repercussions illustrates the very real (and current) challenges faced by democratic regimes even decades after the initial transition from authoritarianism, and the futility of pretending they do not exist in the hope that doing so will make them go away. They will not, and the only way to deal with them is to confront them. What does this involve? The democratization wave that started in southern Europe in the mid-1980s (in Portugal, Spain and Greece), moved on to Latin America and East Asia and Central and Eastern Europe in the 1980s and early 1990s, and southern Africa in the early 1990s. This has become one of the (if not *the*) most significant political trends in world affairs.[8] How to manage these transitions from dictatorial rule to more participatory forms of government rapidly became one of the central challenges faced by political leaders throughout much of the developing world. The fact that, in many cases, this process involved multiple and overlapping transitions (in both the political and the economic sphere, as largely closed economies open up) made them particularly complex and challenging.

In terms of the political transitions, many analysts distinguish between at least three phases:

1. The *abertura*, or opening, in which the old regime, often under severe pressure from below (a mobilized civil society) and/or abroad (such as in the case of the international boycott against the apartheid regime in South Africa) starts to liberalize, allowing greater manoeuvring room to the opposition and democratic forces.

2. The *transition* per se, that is, the actual process whereby the *ancien regime*, realizing the irreversible nature of the political change, and under varying circumstances such as military defeat or the death of the dictator, or a negotiated compromise, hands power over to the democratic opposition.

3. The *consolidation* of the newly established democratic regime, in which the danger of an authoritarian regression gradually recedes, the newly crafted institutions take hold and democracy takes root.[9]

Despite the smooth and seamless progression these categories and this scheme seemingly entail, there is, of course, nothing automatic or preordained about it. Democratization will often proceed in fits and starts, there is an escalation effect (Namibia's rather smooth decolonization in 1990 had a positive impact on South Africa's white regime and population, which realized that black rule in southern Africa did not necessarily mean chaos) and there is nothing guaranteed about it all. But these features, in turn, highlight the key role played by the leadership of the newly elected ruling coalition in the management of it all.

Under the many conditions that affect this process will be the *type* of transition that took place, and whether it entailed a *ruptura* (a total break with the *ancien regime*), such as took place with the Sandinista victory in Nicaragua in 1979 or the military defeat and humiliation of the dictatorship (as happened with the Greek colonels in 1973 or the Argentinean *junta* in the Malvinas/Falklands in 1982), or whether it was a *pacted* transition.[10] In the latter, and given a relative equilibrium of forces, both sides (the leaders of the outgoing regime and those of the democratic opposition) realize they would be better off avoiding what can potentially degenerate into a bloody civil war, and thus reach an agreement designed to give certain guarantees to the members of the *ancien regime* and establish a more or less even playing field for the next phase.

Paradoxically, many observers have noted that it is out of such pacted transitions, in which the democratic forces quite self-consciously limit their own margin of manoeuvre, that consolidation is more likely to emerge. The vertigo of close-to-absolute power that can arise out of the total collapse of the previous regime can leave the new coalition with the heady feeling that they can "start from a blank slate" and this is often the source of much trouble, political conflict and polarization.

Yet there is little doubt that, in addition to the many tasks of institution-building, reshaping foreign relations, paying back the country's "social debt" and otherwise giving a new impetus to economic growth, one of the key challenges facing the newly installed democratic regime is what to do about the human rights violations committed by its predecessor.

The choice is by no means an easy one. On the one hand, there is so much to do on so many fronts that the last thing the new leaders may want is to "frontload" their own political agenda. If, as is often the case, the possibility of authoritarian regression is very much there, this only compounds the problem. Is it worth sliding back to the dark days of dictatorship for the mere sake of revisiting and reopening old wounds, about which nothing much can be done anyway?

On the other hand, the very legitimacy of the incoming coalition will often be based on their moral superiority over the outgoing elites. It was the new order's denunciation of those human rights violations that contributed so much to depleting the political capital of the *ancien regime* and impelled them to the opposition frontlines. To do nothing about them now that they are safely ensconced in office would seem to many the height of cynicism. Moreover, the pressure from the relatives of the dead and "disappeared" will not abate, and may make for further radicalization and polarization.

Whatever the case, the problem cannot be ignored, and governments have dealt with it in different ways. One way has been to pass an amnesty law that effectively pardons all human rights violations committed under the previous regime, thus "sweeping them under the rug". Another, very different approach, has been to set up special courts to try the top rung of the leadership of the outgoing regime, largely on the model of the Nuremberg and Tokyo trials after World War II. Yet, the unsatisfactory results of both of these approaches have been instrumental in the development of a third option – that of the Truth Commission, or TRC (for Truth and Reconciliation Commission).

TRCs as a middle way between blanket amnesties and special prosecutions

TRCs are officially appointed (although usually independent) bodies tasked with investigating human rights violations during a specific period (often that of the previous authoritarian regime). Their powers vary, but they are generally made up of respected personalities who are supposed to produce within a specified time period (ideally not more than six months to two years) a report that documents those violations for the record and establishes a factual truth about what actually happened. They are not tribunals, and they may be formed by nationals (the general rule), foreign citizens (in cases where nationals dare not tread) or both.

They are not necessarily incompatible with pre-existing amnesty provisions (the Chilean military regime passed one such self-amnesty law in 1978), nor do they preclude subsequent prosecutions by the courts, but they have increasingly emerged as the policy tool of choice for new democracies eager to heal the wounds of the body politic, in the understanding that "there is no tomorrow without yesterday".[11]

Argentina's TRC (headed by noted novelist Ernesto Sábato) produced a report, suggestively titled *Nunca Más!* (Never Again!), which became a national bestseller. Since then, twenty-four countries in Europe, Asia, Africa and Latin America have established such commissions, with varying degrees of success. One can disagree about their impact, but it is difficult to dispute the fact that they are considered an attractive option. The United Nations Development Programme, with offices in some 140 countries, is actively considering the funding of TRCs as part of its regular nation-building programs.

Since the end of the Cold War, and given the rise in internal conflicts and civil wars, there has been a growing need to bring reconciliation to post-conflict societies, and TRCs have emerged as one of the critical tools in the policy kit of peacebuilders. In political science over the past two decades "transitology" (i.e., the study of the transitions from authoritarianism to democracy) has been one of the fastest growing subfields within Comparative Politics.[12] Since the mid-1990s the study of "transitional justice", in some ways itself a subfield of "transitology", has also seen a veritable explosion, with new institutes being set up to study the subject and a steady stream of monographs, symposia volumes and journal articles being published on its many facets and dimensions.[13] The study of transitional justice is of a much more interdisciplinary nature, and one in which (in addition to politics) the law, sociology, psychology, anthropology and religious studies, among other disciplines, blend into a seamless web.

The reasons for this sudden eruption of "truth-commissioning" are complex, but they reflect both the changing nature of the international system and the increasing significance of human rights within it. The end of the Cold War, of course, has meant that superpowers are less concerned with protecting "their own" tyrants and their record as a way of avoiding giving an advantage to "the other side". Globalization, on the other hand, and its expression in both the information technology and the telecommunications revolutions, has led to a much quicker spread of information and awareness in international public opinion about human rights violations, something that goes a long way toward explaining developments in Kosovo in 1999, as European public opinion was simply not ready to accept "another Bosnia".

Within the human rights field itself, TRCs reflect in many ways a "coming of age" of the struggle for such rights.[14] It has been pointed out that the field has gone through three distinct stages; first, in the immediate post–World War II period, with the establishment of the United Nations, the drafting of the Universal Declaration of Human Rights and the establishment of international human rights law and humanitarian law with governments and international organizations as key players. A second phase emerged in the 1970s, as non-governmental, citizen organizations (NGOs) such as Amnesty International took centre stage in the struggle to defend human rights on a worldwide basis, and became increasingly effective in it, even as they were joined by other like-minded NGOs such as Human Rights Watch. Finally, the 1990s saw the coming together of both governmental and citizen initiatives in bodies like TRCs – officially established, but manned by independent citizens, often internationally funded, but whose main purpose is to give post-hoc "voice to those without voice", that is, to the victims and relatives of the victims of those who suffered the most under authoritarian rule and need to "regain their feet" in the new democratic dispensation.

Why not simply move on, and let bygones be bygones, thus letting "sleeping dogs lie"? The conditions for successfully setting up TRCs – and there is some evidence now to be able to make some tentative generalizations – are not always present.[15] Many observers agree with the proposition that they are most appropriate after a significant regime change, in which major human rights violations were committed primarily by one side, and when there is still a certain balance between the democratizing forces and those of the outgoing coalition. Under such circumstances, and when there is often some dispute about what actually happened under the *ancien regime*, the need to have a common national narrative about those facts is especially acute if a nation is ever to overcome those past divisions and forge a solid, prosperous future.

The parallel has been made with the needs of patients suffering from post-traumatic stress disorder. People who have undergone major traumas in their lives often find themselves disoriented and in acute need of "telling their story" to someone who will take it seriously and is able to help them overcome those symptoms. It should not be surprising to realize that individuals who lost their loved ones and/or were themselves submitted to torture, and were even then publicly denounced as "subversives" or "enemies of the state" should suffer from all sorts of psychological (often, of course, also physical) difficulties that demand attention.

For a wife whose husband was taken by the security forces and then made to "disappear" (as was often the established practice in many Latin American countries), then to be told that no such thing happened, but that he had instead simply left her for another woman and gone abroad ("absconded with a blonde" was a favourite phrase) was, needless to say, to add insult to injury. The notion that such tragic situations could simply be ignored or papered over is, of course, difficult to sustain, and that is precisely the purpose of TRCs.

Beyond individual grief and the imperative to overcome it, however, looms a larger issue, one to which José Zalaquett has referred as the "cathartic function" of TRCs. This means that, after the collective trauma of repressive dictatorships, nations need a moment of "rebirth" or "regeneration" of their sense of identity and being, one that provides a clean break with that oppressive past and thus provides them with the necessary impetus to forge ahead and build a better future. If done properly, TRCs can perform that function very well, and the experience of the South African TRC, to which we shall return, which in its two-and-a-half years of existence (1995–1998), and under the able leadership of Archbishop Desmond Tutu and its vice-chair, Alex Boraine, engaged in one of the most extraordinary exercises in national soul-searching perhaps ever undertaken, remains a prime example of that. The public hearings held during these years, often in churches, with strong religious undertones and amply covered in the media, made the country come to terms with the legacy of apartheid in a way that perhaps no other mechanism could have.[16]

If the *process* of the TRC is an important part of its contribution to national reconciliation, so is the final *product*, as a rule a report that summarizes the findings of the Commission, puts them into a proper context and otherwise makes the facts of human rights violations, such as they were uncovered by the Commissioners and staff, available to the public.

The Chilean TRC and its aftermath

The Chilean experience is widely considered to be one of the most successful, despite its many limitations. Upon taking office on 11 March 1990, Chilean President Patricio Aylwin found himself in a curious predicament, one perhaps not faced by any other head of state before him. His predecessor, General Augusto Pinochet had kept, to shield himself from any eventual litigation and through his own, tailor-made Constitution, the position of Commander-in-Chief of the Chilean Army for an eight-year term.[17] The notion of a dictator who had exercised almost unbridled power for 17 years that would now stand guard as head of a highly autonomous Army over the succeeding democratic government was not exactly one that enhanced the sense of self-assurance of Chile's newly elected leaders, and many warned President Aylwin to tread carefully, since the military were ready to engage in some "sabre-rattling" if they were to feel threatened in any way.

Yet, and much to his credit, Aylwin took on as one of his first tasks the creation and official launch of a Truth and Reconciliation Commission. A lawyer and professor of administrative law, who had been a Senator and seven-time president of the Christian Democratic party (long Chile's largest party) and one of the opposition leaders who had been involved in the last-minute negotiations to forestall the 11 September 1973 coup against President Salvador Allende, Aylwin saw his main task as one of securing a successful transition, for which a TRC would be critical. Both the instrument itself and the *modus operandi* that he devised for it reflected both his centrist, moderate leanings, very much in tune with Chile's political climate at the time, and his legal training and background.[18]

A key element in his consideration was the experience of two neighbouring countries, Argentina and Uruguay, which had undergone similar periods of dictatorial rule in the 1970s and 1980s, but had dealt very differently with their respective pasts. In some ways, Chile had the advantages of late democratization – if it is possible to state such a thing – as it was the last country in South America to return to democratic rule. Uruguay had passed a blanket amnesty law that evoked considerable opposition and even led to a subsequent referendum designed to abrogate it. Argentina, in addition to its own TRC, had also set up a special tribunal to prosecute the members of the military *junta*, and had in fact convicted and imprisoned them. Yet, a number of military uprisings only a few years later pressed President Raul Alfonsín into revoking their sentences and letting the generals go.

Against this background, and especially given the rather special position in which the Chilean Armed Forces found themselves, not only had they not lost a war – as their counterparts across the Andes had in 1982 in the Falklands/Malvinas, thus leaving their national prestige and standing at rock bottom levels – but they had effected an orderly transfer of power according to the military regime's own constitutional stipulations and had left a growing economy in place. Aylwin took a different course.

The great advantage of the TRC approach was that it meant taking action on one of the most significant issues facing Chile at the time, but doing so in a non-confrontational manner. And this was true not only of the TRC in itself, but also of the specific shape it took in Chile. It was highly balanced (four of the eight Commissioners had supported the military regime – one of them, Gonzalo Vial, had even served as Education

Minister – and four had opposed it; seven of them were lawyers); it had a very limited mandate (to inquire solely into human rights violations that ended in death); it had no subpoena powers (as it was created by executive decree, since it was unlikely that a Parliament with nine Pinochet-appointed Senators would approve legislation on the subject); its proceedings were to be held *in camera*, thus excluding public hearings; and it was given a bare six months to file its report.

With a professional staff of 60 and an austere budget,[19] it quickly took up its duties, in which it was immensely helped by the fact that in Chile many of the human rights violations had already been carefully and methodically documented by various NGOs, most prominently the Catholic Church-affiliated Vicaría de la Solidaridad.[20] In the end, even if somewhat hampered by its limitations (with no obligation to testify, no active-duty military officers did so, although several retired officers did) the Commission went about its work rather quietly, asked for a three-month extension to produce its report, and ended up producing a massive, three-volume document in February 1991. A month later, the report was presented to the nation by a visibly distraught President Aylwin, who publicly asked for forgiveness for the crimes committed by state agents (although he himself bore no responsibility for them) meticulously documented in the so-called Rettig report (after the chair of the Commission, former Senator Raúl Rettig).

The report indicated that some 3,200 people had been killed and/or forcibly made to "disappear" by the security forces between 11 September 1973 and 10 March 1990 (the period of the military government); it listed their names, and gave the details as to how they came about their fate, as well as the Armed Forces units responsible. It did not, however, give the names of the presumed culprits, although some of that information had been made available. It was, in many ways, a victim-oriented, rather than a culprit-driven, undertaking. Although no lump-sum reparation payments were considered, pensions and scholarships to the relatives of the victims were recommended, tasks to be taken up by a follow-up Reparations Commission.

Needless to say, the Armed Forces strongly objected to the report – albeit mostly on matters of interpretation and context rather than on any factual grounds. One of the immediate effects of the report (none of whose facts has been successfully challenged to this day) was to change the national discourse on the subject – talk of the "so-called disappeared" or "presumed detained-disappeared", gave way to straightforward references to the "disappeared".

Yet, ultimately, the national debate that was supposed to have been triggered by the TRC report was nipped in the bud by the 31 March 1991 assassination of Senator Jaime Guzmán, a close confidante of General Pinochet and one of the main drafters of the 1980 Constitution that rules Chile to this day. Apparently undertaken by left-wing extremists, its very occurrence was given as proof that repression of such elements under the military had actually been necessary to save the country from "communism" and revolutionary violence.

South Africa's TRC: Setting a new standard

Just three years later, with the election of Nelson Mandela to the South African presidency, the country of Oliver Tambo faced a predicament not dissimilar to Chile's. Apartheid had left deep wounds in the South African psyche and body politic, wounds that desperately needed healing. Nelson Mandela was determined to bring about national and racial reconciliation, very much in the spirit of the African National Congress Charter. Yet, this could not be done under false pretences. How to go about it?

Professor Kader Asmal, one of South Africa's leading legal minds, and later Water Affairs Minister in Nelson Mandela's Cabinet (1994–1999) and Education Minister in President Thabo Mbeki's first term (1999–2004), was the first to suggest, as early as 1992, that South Africa should have a close look at the Latin American TRCs, especially Chile's, and seriously consider setting one up to come to terms with the legacy of apartheid.[21] A number of seminars, with the participation of one of the Commissioners and a driving force behind the Chilean TRC, José Zalaquett, as well as with by-then-former Chilean President Patricio Aylwin, took place in February and July 1994, putting the issue of the creation of a TRC in South Africa squarely on the agenda. This was taken on with special zeal and verve by Justice Minister Dullah Omar.

By then the Chilean TRC was widely considered to have "set the standard" for such Commissions, and it was a significant source of inspiration and information for South Africans. Yet, characteristically, the latter went about setting their own such body in a much more systematic and thorough fashion, casting a wide net in their search for other relevant experiences, bringing in civil society and even opening a national dialogue of sorts as to the precise nature the TRC should take (this process, which lasted some 16 months, alone took longer than the whole period of existence of its Chilean counterpart, from inception to the delivery of the report).

Not surprisingly, the net result, while keeping the same name, was a much more ambitious and powerful body. To start with, it was a statutory body, approved by Parliament, with all that entails. It also had subpoena powers, making it possible to force relevant parties to testify before it.

Intriguingly, and innovatively, it was also invested with the power of amnesty. To elicit relevant information about human rights violations from 1960 to 1994 (the period covered by its mandate), it could dangle the "carrot" of full amnesty, under appropriate conditions, for those who came forward. The "stick" was that those who did not come forward could later be prosecuted *sine die*. Moreover, it was authorized to hold public hearings, something that no other TRC had done before. This raised some concerns about the dangers of "grandstanding" in front of the television cameras this could entail.

Accordingly, it was also a much larger body than anything that had been seen until then, with seventeen Commissioners, a staff of 400, offices in Cape Town, Johannesburg and Port Elizabeth and a generous budget, sourced both nationally and internationally. In marked contrast to the Chilean TRC, there were relatively few lawyers, but many priests. Nobel Peace Prize winner Archbishop Desmond Tutu, the Anglican prelate for South Africa, was appointed as chair, giving it instant credibility, and Alex Boraine, a theologian and former Democratic party MP, one of the driving forces behind the whole endeavour, as vice-chair.

The very process of setting up the South African TRC had taken so long, the parliamentary debates had been so extensive and the expectations had been raised so high that many observers, including this writer, had serious apprehensions if not outright misgivings about how the whole thing would play out. The strong religious undertones in what were, after all, matters of state, were not particularly reassuring either.

For two and a half years, the South African TRC went about its business, taking the country by storm. Public hearings were held all over the country, from churches surrounded by the skyscrapers of Johannesburg to the spaces under big trees in villages in KwaZulu-Natal. Many hearings were covered live by radio and television, and the lead item on many newscasts would often be provided by the TRC. A large number of women testified, and many said it was the first chance they had to tell their side of the story. For much of this period, the TRC was *the* national story, and emblematic stories of the apartheid era that captured not only South African but also world attention, like those of Steve Biko and, toward the end of the hearings, Amy Biehl, allowed South Africans to once again come to terms with their past.

After all this veritable national catharsis, the massive report itself, released in October 1998, was almost an afterthought. In the case of South Africa, the TRC process itself became much more important than the report; that is, the *process was the product*. This was very different from the Chilean case, in which the low-key, behind-closed-doors work of the TRC had meant that much of the onus of the impact of the Commission's work fell on the report itself – a national debate on which was then precluded by the assassination of Senator Guzmán a month after the report's release. Although it started from the "baseline" provided by Chile's TRC in 1994, South Africans took it much farther, effectively setting a new standard for TRCs worldwide, and one that also generated a considerable literature, much of it written by TRC members themselves, but some also by outsiders.[22]

On TRCs and politics

The considerable "success" of the South African TRC contributed also to the growing popularity of them worldwide. Among others, East Timor, Nigeria and Peru have established them subsequently. Departing from the Latin American practice of having only *in camera* hearings, Peru adopted the public hearings approach to "dealing with the past", with fruitful results.

As was to be expected, TRCs do not command universal approval. From the Right, they are often criticized as thinly veiled attempts at witch-hunting, whereas from the Left they are sometimes disparaged as nothing more than "whitewashing": the South African TRC report was criticized both by the National Party and the African National Congress. Not surprisingly, there is also now a "revisionist" school, which questions many aspects of the functioning of TRCs.[23] Other scholars have called for greater rigour in the assessment of TRCs and draw attention to the relative "incestuousness" of the field of transitional justice, in which the roles of practitioner, theorist and commentator are often difficult to disentangle, making objective, quantitative evaluations difficult to undertake.[24] TRCs are neither panaceas nor magic wands that by themselves can heal deeply divided societies. Quite a few of them have failed abysmally in their assigned task, in some cases not even turning in a report of their findings, presumably their main duty. In the end, TRCs, with all their limitations but also with all their virtues, are the product of the need of statesmen and politicians more generally to come to terms with an imperfect world as best they can.

As has been pointed out, Max Weber once wrote about two very different approaches to the exercise of the craft of politics, one based on the "ethics of conviction" and another on the "ethics of responsibility". For the first, what matters is "to do the right thing", no matter what the cost or the consequences. "What is right is right", and if the cost is civil war, a *coup d'état* or the breakdown of democracy, so be it. *Après moi, le déluge*. The mass appeal of such an approach is considerable, and history is replete with leaders who followed it. Intellectually, it is very attractive, since it seems to be based on high principles and uncontaminated with the "give and take" and compromise of political management. Yet, the "ethics of responsibility" advocated by Weber, that is, measuring the consequences of one's actions and acting accordingly, rather than plunging head on into whatever seems to be the "politically correct" thing to do, would in the end seem to be the wiser course. It is, of course, very important "to do the right thing" but if, like shouting "fire!" in a crowded theatre, that may lead to the deaths of hundreds or thousands of people, it may be advisable to think twice before doing so and considering alternatives courses of action, including one more moderate.

Chile and South Africa represented two of the most emblematic transitions of the 1990s. In establishing TRCs, and in giving them the sort of mandate that they gave them, their distinguished leaders – Patricio Aylwin in Chile and Nelson Mandela in South Africa – chose a middle-course between the extremes of blanket amnesty and Nuremberg-style tribunals to deal with the human rights violations of the past. They received their share of criticism from both sides of the political spectrum for doing so, and in neither country has the book on past human rights violations been closed. But, in the end, most observers would agree that both societies are better off for the leaders' chosen courses. It is not a mere coincidence that both countries are today among the most politically stable and economically prosperous in their respective regions, despite their highly divided and polarized recent pasts.

Notes

1. José Zalaquett (1997) "Why Deal with the Past?" in Alex Boraine, Janet Levy and Ronel Scheffer, eds, *Dealing with the Past: Truth and Reconciliation in South Africa*, 2nd ed., Cape Town: IDASA, p. 13. I am indebted to José Zalaquett, a friend of many years, from whom I have learned much about the increasingly complex and wide-ranging field of transitional justice, of which he, a former president of Amnesty International, a UNESCO Human Rights Prize winner and now president of the Inter American Human Rights Commission, is one of the foremost practitioners and theorists.
2. This is a revised version of a text under the same title delivered as the Sixth Oliver Tambo Lecture at Delhi University, New Delhi, on 22 March 2005.
3. Robert Dahl (1967) *Polyarchy: Participation and Opposition*, New Haven, Conn.: Yale University Press.
4. Samuel P. Huntington (1991) *The Third Wave: Democratization in the Late Twentieth Century*, Norman, Okla.: University of Oklahoma Press.
5. On both, the literature is extensive. On Chile, see Paul Drake and Ivan Jaksic, eds (1991) *The Struggle for Democracy in Chile*, Lincoln, Neb.: University of Nebraska Press; and, by the same editors, *El modelo chileno: Democracia y desarrollo en los noventa* (1999) Santiago: LOM. On South Africa, see Timothy Sisk (1996) *Democratization in South Africa*, Princeton, N.J.: Princeton University Press; and Patti Waldmeir (1997) *Anatomy of a Miracle*, New York: Viking.

6. The Pinochet case in itself, by setting the extraordinary precedent of a former head of state arrested abroad for human rights violations in his own country, has also generated an enormous bibliography, in many languages. For some of the sources in English, see Madeleine Davis, ed. (2003) *The Pinochet Case: Origins, Progress, Implications*, London: Institute of Latin American Studies, University of London; Ariel Dorfman (2002) *Exorcising Terror: The Incredible Unending Trial of General Augusto Pinochet*, New York: Seven Stories Press; Peter Kornbluh (2003) *The Pinochet File: A Declassified Dossier on Atrocity and Accountability*, New York: New Press; Geoffrey Robertson (2000) *Crimes against Humanity: The Struggle for Global Justice*, New York: New Press; and José Zalaquett (2001) *The Pinochet Case: International and Domestic Implications*, Toronto: University of Toronto Faculty of Law, 2001. See also the documentary film by Patricio Guzmán, *The Pinochet Case* (2001).

7. José Miguel Insulza (2005) "Responsabilidad política y acciones judiciales", *La Segunda*, 7 March. For a defence of Fernández, see the piece by another former Home Affairs minister under General Pinochet, Carlos Cáceres (2005) "Responsabilidades políticas y penales", *El Mercurio*, 13 March.

8. The classic source on the subject, although based only on the Latin American and Southern European cases, is Guillermo O'Donnell, Philippe Schmitter and Laurence Whitehead, eds (1986) *Transitions from Authoritarian Rule*, Baltimore: The Johns Hopkins University Press. See also Ursula van Beek, ed. (2005) *Democracy under Construction: Patterns from Four Continents*, Leverkusen, Germany: Barbara Budrich.

9. On consolidation, see Juan Linz and Alfred Stepan (1996) *Problems of Democratic Transition and Consolidation*, Baltimore: The Johns Hopkins University Press. On institutional crafting, see my "Institutional Engineering in New Democracies" in van Beek, *Democracy under Construction*.

10. The concept of "pacted transitions" was developed by Terry Karl. See her chapter on Venezuela in O'Donnell et al., *Transitions from Authoritarian Rule*.

11. This expression was used by Chilean President Ricardo Lagos in setting up a Commission on Political Imprisonment and Torture (the so-called Valech Commission) in 2003 to investigate these types of human rights violations under the 1973–1990 military regime. The Commission delivered its report in October 2004, and President Lagos made it public on 28 November of that year. See *Informe de la Comisión Nacional sobre prisión política y tortura*, Santiago: Ministry of the Interior. For an English-version summary of the report, see *Report of the National Commission on Political Detention and Torture* (2005) Santiago: Ministry of the Interior.

12. Even leading to the founding of academic journals exclusively devoted to that subject, such as the *Journal of Democracy*, published by The Johns Hopkins University Press, and *Democratization*, published in England by Taylor & Francis.

13. Two of these institutes are the International Center for Transitional Justice, based in New York, and the Institute for Justice and Reconciliation, headquartered in Cape Town. Former participants in the South African TRC, like the vice-chair, Alex Boraine, and the director of research, Charles Villa-Vicencio have been especially active in transitional justice scholarship, and were in fact the respective founders of each of these institutes. For their own books on the South African TRC, see Alex Boraine (2000) *A Country Unmasked: Inside South Africa's Truth and Reconciliation Commission*, Cape Town: Oxford University Press; and Charles Villa-Vicencio and Wilhelm Verwoerd, eds (2000) *Looking Back/Reaching Forward: Reflections on the Truth and Reconciliation Commission of South Africa*, Cape Town: University of Cape Town Press. For Boraine's recent reflections on the field, see his paper "Transitional Justice as an Emerging Field" (2004), delivered at the International Development Research Centre-sponsored

symposium "Repairing the Past: Reparations and Transitions to Democracy", Ottawa, Canada, 11 March.

14. Henry J. Steiner and Philip Alston (1996) *International Human Rights in Context: Law, Politics, Morals*, Oxford: Clarendon Press.

15. Some of the key scholarly sources on the subject are: Neil Kritz, ed. (1995) *Transitional Justice: How Emerging Democracies Reckon with Former Regimes*, Washington, D.C.: United States Institute of Peace (3 volumes); Priscilla Hayner (2001) *Unspeakable Truths: Confronting State Terror and Atrocity*, New York: Routledge; and Robert Rotberg and Dennis Thompson, eds (2000) *Truth versus Justice: The Morality of Truth Commissions*, Princeton, N.J.: Princeton University Press.

16. Having attended many of these hearings in Pretoria, Johannesburg and Cape Town, this writer had the chance to personally observe this extraordinary exercise. See my article, "Truth Commission Is Safely across Minefield" (1998) *Sunday Independent*, Johannesburg, 2 August. Perhaps the most compelling narrative of the TRC can be found in Antjie Krog (1998) *Country of My Skull*, Johannesburg: Random House. Krog, a poet and a reporter for the South African Broadcasting Service covered the TRC for the latter. The book was made into a film, *In My Country* (2005), by John Boorman.

17. On Pinochet, see Pamela Constable and Arturo Valenzuela (1991) *A Nation of Enemies: Chile under Pinochet*, New York: Norton; and, especially, Carlos Huneeus (2000) *El régimen de Pinochet*, Santiago: Sudamericana.

18. For Aylwin's reflections on Chile's transition to democracy, see his *El reencuentro de los demócratas: Del golpe al triunfo del No* (1998) Santiago: Grupo Zeta, Ediciones B.

19. The total budget for the Chilean TRC reached US$1 million. That of the South African TRC, with a much broader and complex mandate, was US$35 million. Compared to the cost of the Special Tribunals for the former Yugoslavia and for Rwanda, whose costs to the present have been estimated to exceed US$1 billion, these are modest amounts indeed.

20. The report was so well received that it was quickly translated into English and published by a university press in the United States. See *Report of the Chilean Truth and Reconciliation Commission* (1993) Notre Dame, Ind.: University of Notre Dame Press.

21. See Kader Asmal, Louise Asmal and Ronald Suresh Roberts (1997) *Reconciliation through Truth: A Reckoning of Apartheid's Criminal Governance*, Cape Town: David Philip.

22. A recent survey of the literature on the South African TRC listed 437 items. Annelies Verdoolage (n.d.) "The Debate on Truth and Reconciliation: A Survey of the Literature on the South African Truth and Reconciliation Commission", Ghent, Belgium: Ghent University.

23. Charles T. Call (2004) "Is Transitional Justice Really Just?" *Brown Journal of World Affairs* 11(1) (Summer–Fall): 101–113.

24. Eric Brahm (2004) "Getting to the Bottom of the Truth: Evaluating the Contribution of Truth Commissions to Post-Conflict Societies", paper prepared for the 20th Annual Conference of the Wisconsin Institute for Peace and Conflict Studies, "Challenges and Paths to Justice", Marquette University, Milwaukee, Wisconsin, 6–8 October.

6

East Timor's search for justice, reconciliation and dignity

Jeff Kingston

Written laws are like spiders' webs; they will catch, it is true, the weak and poor, but would be torn in pieces by the rich and powerful.
Anarchis, sixth century BC

The outbreak of violence in East Timor in 2006 and the return of international peacekeepers was a powerful reminder that the government remains vulnerable and that a descent into political chaos is far more than a distant rumor. For a society just emerging from a prolonged nightmare, the bloody clashes demonstrate just how tenuous peace is and how dependent East Timor remains on international support. These events suggest that the hasty downsizing of the UN mission in 2002, after only two years of nation building, and withdrawal of UN peacekeepers in 2005 was premature and that many urgent tasks of nation building remain unfinished. The eruption of gun battles on the streets of Dili, coinciding with the fourth anniversary of independence, powerfully evokes the legacies of Indonesian repression, the unfulfilled yearnings of the East Timorese and the international community's responsibility. Widespread corruption and the authoritarian tendencies of the ruling party threaten a fragile democracy. Reconciliation has become an even more pressing, and difficult, priority.

East Timor has been plagued by violence that erupted at the end of April 2006. These clashes claimed 37 lives and left 155,000 homeless. Former Prime Minister Mari Alkatiri is widely blamed for mismanaging a grievance by soldiers into a full-blown crisis. Protests by dismissed

Atrocities and international accountability: Beyond transitional justice, Hughes, Schabas and Thakur (eds), *United Nations University Press, 2007, ISBN 978-92-808-1141-4*

soldiers escalated into conflict within and between the military and police forces, and sparked widespread looting and arson by roaming gangs of young men who have found little to cheer since the nation became independent in 2002. Unemployment and poverty are a fuse waiting to be lit.

The new Prime Minister is Dr. José Ramos-Horta, a Nobel Peace Prize laureate. He is an affable, accomplished and charismatic diplomat who was handed recently one of the biggest challenges of his life. On 10 July he became this young nation's second prime minister amidst high expectations that he can restore political stability, reconstitute the security forces, promote development, eradicate corruption and revive public faith in this fledgling democracy. Although conditions remain bleak in East Timor, he is widely viewed as the best man for promoting reconciliation and restoring hope. At considerable personal risk, he crisscrossed this island during the height of the violence to negotiate with rebel groups, reassure the public, stop looting and stem unrest. This is the sort of brave and engaged leadership that is needed. In addition to accepting mission impossible, he put aside his personal ambitions by withdrawing his name from the shortlist of candidates vying to succeed UN Secretary-General Kofi Annan.

In his inauguration speech, PM Ramos-Horta made clear that his priorities are restoring stability based on the rule of law, re-housing refugees and giving the public reasons to regain faith in the government. He candidly spoke of the government's failures: "We failed in the area of internal security, we failed in the dialogue with the people, we stand accused of insensitivity and arrogance, and corruption started to invade institutions of the state."[1] In his nine-month term before elections, he promised that there would be no "excuses for inertia", and that he would lead, "the fight against poverty. We are going to use existing money to dignify the human being, give them hope, give them food, clothing and give them a roof."

The swearing in ceremony under tarpaulins in the ruins of an administrative building was a stark reminder of the lingering scars of prolonged oppression under Indonesian rule. The collective trauma remains vivid and the challenges of nation building enormous. There is a consensus that the recent violence is symptomatic of a more fundamental problem. PM Ramos-Horta noted that it is impossible to make a small business viable in two years, let alone a nation. Fast tracking the process of nation building is, as we see, a short cut toward creating a faltering state.

East Timor and the international community are now facing steep repair bills for the quick fixes and expedient compromise approach to nation building that prevailed under UN auspices. Recently, the United Nations compiled a needs assessment, and an expanded mission of large scope and long duration is expected. The nation's military and police forces desperately need to be reconstituted, a huge undertaking requiring considerable time and resources. This means that the 2,500 international peacekeepers currently deployed, mostly from Australia, will play a critical role for some time.

It is worth recalling that East Timor is only beginning the process of coming to grips with the horrible experience precipitated by Indonesia's invasion of 7 December 1975. For 24 years, East Timor was occupied by Indonesia, a time when an estimated one-third of the population – nearly 200,000 people – died from conflict-related causes. In 1999 the Indonesian government agreed to allow the United Nations to administer a referendum permitting the East Timorese to choose between independence and continued rule by Jakarta. Despite widespread voter intimidation by militia groups backed by Indonesian security forces, almost all of East Timor's eligible voters cast ballots, and nearly 80 per cent chose independence. This result was announced on 3 September 1999, sparking a widely predicted rampage by Indonesia's militia groups, which claimed over 1,000 lives and involving countless rapes and beatings, destruction of some 80 per cent of all buildings and the forced exodus of one quarter of the population to Indonesian-controlled West Timor. On 20 September, under UN auspices, an Australian force was dispatched to restore law and order.[2]

From October 1999 until May 2002, the United Nations governed East Timor while preparing it for independence. This was an ambitious challenge amidst unfavorable circumstances. East Timor had been reduced to "ground zero" and an array of government institutions was created from scratch, under a tight timetable.[3]

Given the systematic infringement on human rights under Indonesian rule, and the especially spiteful and brutal denouement unleashed by Indonesian-backed militia groups, there was an understandable international concern about pursuing justice and holding perpetrators accountable.

The United Nations and the Indonesian Human Rights Commission produced reports recommending the establishment of an ad hoc international tribunal to prosecute the perpetrators.[4] The United Nations, however, ignored these recommendations and instead accepted the promises of the Indonesian government that those responsible for the outrages would be held accountable.[5] These promises have not been kept. Since then, East Timorese with wavering international support have been pursuing justice with scant success.

International justice is under fire because it has been elusive, time consuming and expensive. Helena Cobban succinctly states the case against international tribunals, raising important questions about whether such courts facilitate peace, justice and human rights, and if they deter future war crimes.[6] This essay examines East Timor's experience, focusing on why attempts at justice have failed and why the leadership favors reconciliation over retribution despite popular preference for accountability.

Experimenting with justice

UN attempts to build a functioning judiciary in East Timor were hampered from the outset by insufficient resources and the dire need for capacity building.[7] Due to Indonesia's scorched earth policies, the pre-existing legal infrastructure had been destroyed and there were no experienced lawyers or judges to serve in a new justice system. Ground zero, thus, meant a rule of law vacuum that severely compromised efforts toward transitional justice.

A fair and effective judicial system is a priority for post-conflict nations because it is important to restore the rule of law, rebuild trust, promote accountability and prevent resort to extra-judicial retribution. However, what everyone agrees needs to be done did not happen in East Timor because of insufficient resources and political will.[8]

In this context, how could justice be achieved in East Timor? Given the expense and slow course of justice associated with the international tribunals in Yugoslavia and Rwanda, there is no support within the UN Security Council to create similar bodies in other post-conflict societies.[9] Summarizing widespread scepticism about these courts, Helena Cobban writes, "Criminal tribunals in places such as Rwanda and the former Yugoslavia were supposed to bring justice to oppressed peoples. Instead, they have squandered billions of dollars, failed to advance human rights, and ignored the wishes of the victims they claim to represent. It's time to abandon the false hope of international justice."[10]

In response to such criticisms, the United Nations developed hybrid tribunals that would share judicial functions between the United Nations and the national government.[11] These tribunals combine UN authority, funding, resources, judges and prosecutors with local participation, creating a process that is potentially more meaningful to the victims, less politically divisive and more effective in capacity building. However, East Timor's hybrid tribunal never realized this potential.

This is principally due to Indonesia's failure to cooperate with extradition requests or assist in investigating crimes. In addition, there was insufficient financial support. For example, the UN budget for the hybrid tribunal in East Timor amounted to US$6.3 million in 2001, compared to US$178 million for the International Criminal Tribunal for Rwanda and US$223 million for the International Criminal Tribunal for the former Yugoslavia in 2002/03.[12]

Aside from not holding those most responsible for the crimes accountable, the hybrid tribunal also failed to provide minimum standards of due process in the cases that it did try. In general, defenders did not get fair trials or competent defense and, now that the tribunal has been shut down, prospects for appeals are uncertain.

The experiment in East Timor has undermined the United Nations's reputation; the sense of outrage at crimes against humanity that propelled support for justice at any cost was superseded by a penurious approach that casts doubt on the entire enterprise.[13] Is such tainted justice worth pursuing? If those most responsible for these crimes are not held accountable and only those from the lower echelons are prosecuted without competent defense, what messages are being sent and what lessons learned? This sorry state of affairs has stoked justified and widespread scepticism about pursuing justice in the courts and undermined efforts to restore respect for the rule of law. The Jakarta sham trials have further eroded trust in the courts as a means to achieve justice. There, the theater of justice has facilitated a whitewashing of the military's role in orchestrating and carrying out crimes against humanity. And the Indonesian government has flouted its agreements with the United Nations with impunity, confident that in the post–11 September world pressures to pursue accountability are trumped by desires to cultivate Jakarta as a moderate Islamic ally in the war on terror. Consequently, this promising experiment in promoting the rule of law and transitional justice never had a chance, doomed by shifting political realities.

Justice on trial

The verdict on justice for East Timor is one of disappointment. The East Timorese have demanded accountability and are frustrated that the international community has not helped them to achieve it.[14] The main obstacle to accountability is Indonesia, aided and abetted by an international community that seeks its assistance in the war on terror.[15] Calls for an international tribunal are not welcome in the United Nations and thus, left to their own devices, East Timor's leaders have opted for reconciliation and restorative justice while advocating good governance and alleviating pressing socio-economic needs.[16]

As the initial international outrage over Indonesia's rampage in 1999 has faded, so too has political and financial backing for mechanisms of justice to hold ranking perpetrators accountable. Indonesia's high-ranking officers and their goons are evading justice because there has been insufficient political will in Indonesia to hold them accountable. The ad hoc tribunal established by Jakarta did conduct trials and there were some convictions, but all but one of these convictions have been overturned on appeal. Not only did the big fish get away, even the designated scapegoats have walked.

On 20 May 2005, when the United Nations pulled the plug on the hybrid tribunal, it sent a clear message that in the pursuit of justice East Timor is on its own.

Truth and consequences?

> We are charged to unearth the truth of our dark past, to lay the ghosts of our past, so that they will not return to haunt us.
> Bishop Desmond Tutu

East Timor's 924,000 citizens are finding that the truth does not set them free or promote justice and reconciliation. The final report published by East Timor's Commission for Reception, Truth and Reconciliation (CAVR is the commonly used Portuguese acronym) at the end of 2005 estimates that there were as many as 200,000 conflict-related deaths during Indonesia's brutal occupation between 1975 and 1999.[17] Responsibility for this carnage, in addition to widespread torture and rape, rests largely with the Indonesian military.

Citing credible and extensive evidence that planning for and knowledge of the post-referendum scorched earth campaign in 1999 extended to the highest echelons of the Indonesian military, the CAVR report calls for reparations and judicial proceedings.

Jill Jolliffe, an Australian journalist who has covered East Timor since the mid-1970s, understands the need for justice expressed by those who testified to the CAVR, saying, "There has been no rule of law in East Timor for the life of an entire generation. It is important to restore peoples' faith in the rule of law by pursuing justice."[18] In her view, the victims have not been served by the discredited efforts toward justice and accountability described above but it is not too late to redeem the process through an international tribunal.

East Timor President Xanana Gusmão criticizes the CAVR report for embracing what he terms "grandiose idealism" and for the insistence on prosecution, retribution and reparations.[19] He believes that rigorous prosecution may perpetuate cleavages and place human rights and peace at risk. He also maintains that it is not possible for the government to pursue justice given the absence of international support for such an endeavor. Dwelling on this agonizing past carries the risk of finding reasons in old grievances for renewed violence. In his view, the priority must be on a process of reconciliation and healing the wounds of a traumatized society.

Prime Minister José Ramos-Horta shares President Gusmão's emphasis on reconciliation. He rhetorically asked me, at a time when he was serving as Foreign Minister, "Why didn't the UN establish a tribunal here back in 1999 when they had 7,000 PKO [peacekeeping operation troops] here who could have arrested the culprits in West Timor? There is not much we can do to bring Indonesians to trial by ourselves. This isn't only pragmatism. I sincerely believe that Indonesia is making progress on democratic reforms and strengthening the rule of law. However this takes a long time and the situation is fragile. SBY [Indonesian President Susilo Bambang Yudhoyono] is weak and does not fully control the military and can't challenge them in this way without risking that his opponents would gang up on him. It is important that we do not destabilize the slow process of democratization in Indonesia because it is our best guarantee. They have shown the courage to accept our independence. Knowing that the situation is so difficult and that the UN Security Council doesn't want an International Tribunal it doesn't make sense for us to pursue it."[20]

Eduardo Gonzalez, Senior Associate at the International Center for Transitional Justice (ICTJ), observes, "The geopolitical setting has changed dramatically since 9/11. Now Indonesia is a valued ally in the global war on terror. Because of that there is little inclination in the international community to press Indonesia hard on what happened in 1999. Sadly, such geopolitical considerations create double standards of justice."[21] Unlike East Timor's leaders, he strongly supports prosecution of perpetrators, arguing that the failure to do so erodes the quality of independence and democracy in East Timor.[22]

Although highly critical of attempts to secure international justice, Helena Cobban correctly insists that it is important to listen to the survivors of atrocities and address their concerns rather than imposing international agendas. In East Timor, the people have made their wishes clear both in front of the truth commission and in media polls – they want formal prosecution of those suspected of serious crimes against humanity.

President Gusmão thinks this is unwise and told me that he is inspired by the example of South Africa where amnesty was exchanged for truth. Truth commissions may facilitate impunity but they do guard against collective amnesia. Moreover, they can induce a healing catharsis, but only if the testimonies are forthright and accepted by the victims as a credible account of what they experienced.

The CAVR report represents a start, giving voice to the victims and establishing a historical record for this horrible epoch. However, it is an incomplete record because those most responsible for orchestrating the atrocities have not yet testified.

Commission of Truth and Friendship

In an attempt to get Indonesian perpetrators to add their testimony to the record, the Commission of Truth and Friendship (CTF) was launched in the summer of 2005. There is widespread concern among East Timorese that the CTF emphasizes reaching closure, has no judicial mandate and only ensures impunity for ranking perpetrators.

The President favours getting at the truth of what happened, granting amnesty where appropriate and turning the page on this dark chapter. In contrast, the Catholic Church, civil society organizations and many victims emphasize breaking the cycle of impunity and prosecuting those responsible for committing crimes.

The Catholic Church in East Timor held a workshop on 10 December 2005 that pilloried the CTF because it was established without public consultation and offers scant prospects of truth or justice for the victims. One organizer told me that the CTF is a doomed effort to promote collective amnesia.[23] It is seen as a deeply flawed process aimed at burying the past and heading off recourse to justice. I was told that only the Indonesian generals who committed crimes welcome the CTF.

There are also concerns that the CTF's terms of reference are inadequate. Unlike the process in South Africa where there were very specific criteria for granting amnesty – in the end, a relatively small number of applications was approved – the CTF criteria are vague and permit a wide range of discretion. In the court of public opinion, the CTF lacks credibility and seems more likely to fan antagonisms than improve bilateral relations or promote reconciliation.

The President counters that Indonesia should be given another chance to come clean, doubts that amnesty will be granted for serious crimes and emphasizes that the CTF does not prejudice any future judicial initiatives. He takes a long-term view, arguing that progress in seeking justice and accountability for crimes committed by Germany and Japan is an ongoing process and not yet fully resolved. In his view, the time is not yet ripe for formal legal justice, but this could change depending on the international community. In the meantime, he says that it is his duty to promote reconciliation and devote scarce resources to the more pressing needs of the Timorese that are all too evident.

Father Martinho Gusmao, the Director of the Justice and Peace Commission in the Catholic Diocese of Bacau told me, "There is no need for reconciliation between Indonesian and Timorese people, we have no problems. The problem is that Indonesian security forces committed crimes here and they need to be held accountable. This is also part of the process of building democracy here. We need to see that nobody is above the law, and the victims in our country need to see that the victimizers – whoever they are – are prosecuted. Amnesty is meaningless and will not promote reconciliation, only resentment. Victims want their day in court."[24]

He condemns the CTF as "just a cosmetic exercise" that won't lead to the truth. He termed it a "Commission of Forgetfulness" that seeks to bypass justice. In his view, "Amnesty without confession and taking responsibility is meaningless. Forgiveness without accountability is illogical."[25] In his opinion, the CTF is a political exercise that is not relevant to the real process of reconciliation that occurs at the grassroots level.

Reverend Agustinho de Vasconselos, a Presbyterian who served as a commissioner on CAVR, contends that in dealing with crimes against humanity an international tribunal is needed, arguing that such problems cannot be resolved bilaterally through the CTF.[26] He points out that the CTF lacks international legal standing to handle such serious crimes. He admits that the CAVR commissioners know that the international community opposes an international tribunal, but says that their guiding principle has been, "No reconciliation without justice". However, he raises the question of what constitutes justice and points out that the needs and demands of the victims vary. "We have lots of victims' statements requesting a tribunal but others ask for help with housing, medical care, education, et cetera. There are many paths to justice."

As of October 2006, the CTF has succeeded neither in gathering testimony from those most responsible for the most serious crimes nor in digging out the truth about the events in 1999. Therefore, it is hard to imagine that it will quell public demands for justice. The wounds are too fresh and the pain remains poignant for the victims and survivors. There is no enthusiasm for closure and no point in rushing the healing process.

Judicial romanticism and realpolitik

Ramesh Thakur, regarding East Timor, refers to the concept of judicial romanticism. This involves the problem of overestimating the capacity of courts to resolve issues of justice and accountability and taking a purely judicial approach to transitional justice. He argues that the insistence on formal legal justice by civil society activists and the international community risks preempting the prerogatives of elected political leaders, a sensitive issue in East Timor where the government's attempts to balance justice and reconciliation has drawn heated criticism.

Regarding "judicial romanticism", Thakur writes that it is, "the idea of always looking to courts for a solution to every problem. In the commitment to justice at any price, the romanticists discount political and diplomatic alternatives. Not everyone in South Africa was happy with the amnesty granted to some apartheid-era criminals by the Truth and Reconciliation Commission. Some in Britain would like to see IRA terrorists brought to book even at the cost of imperiling the peace accords. And we see it within East Timor in calls for no compromise with the murderers of 1999.

"Romanticism turns into judicial colonialism with demands that the political and diplomatic decisions made by democratically elected governments of other countries be subordinated to 'international' judicial processes that reflect the values of the most dominant countries of the day. It is based in moral imperialism: Our values are so manifestly superior to theirs that we have the right to impose it on them."[27]

This concept of judicial romanticism is implicit in President Gusmão's use of "grandiose idealism" in describing the CAVR report. He says that the time is not ripe for seeking what he calls "formal justice", arguing that the people are better served by the government concentrating its meager resources on achieving economic and social justice and consolidating peace. Cultivating a working relationship with Indonesia is a priority for East Timor both in terms of its security and economic interests. Seeking justice now without any international backing and political cover could imperil bilateral relations. The President is well aware of public yearning for justice, but argues that it is not the most pressing concern for people living in impoverished villages without electricity, clean water, decent housing or medical care. He also is concerned that the pursuit of justice will lead to a destabilizing settling of scores among Timorese while Indonesian perpetrators remain beyond the reach of prosecutors.

Gusmão's dilemma is being caught between high public expectations for justice and accountability, and insufficient international support to make this happen. Indeed, the United Nations has grown increasingly ambivalent about promoting international justice and more circumspect in its ambitions to pursue accountability. As the failures and costs mount, the United Nations advocates shifting responsibility and implementation to national authorities.[28] This is especially problematic in war-ravaged societies where the capacity to administer justice is clearly inadequate and the "need" for convictions overshadows impartiality and due process.

Gusmão's pro-reconciliation views have drawn criticism from various domestic and international civil society organizations that fear he is betraying justice. Is justice postponed justice betrayed? Do ongoing reconciliation efforts preclude future initiatives?

Gusmão pointedly draws attention to traumatized nations such as South Africa and Mozambique that have gained a measure of social stability by treading softly on the question of justice. He also cites the examples of Pinochet, ongoing Nazi hunting and Sino-Japanese disputes to suggest that postponing justice need not preclude justice. It is clear that at the moment, he does not see the pursuit of justice as a viable option because international support is lacking. He is acting in what he believes to be the national interest now, but this does not mean his successors won't have other options. Clearly, he does not oppose pursuing such options at some later date.

Thakur sees "hope for a permanent reduction in the phenomenon of impunity. In 1990, a tyrant would have been reasonably confident of escaping international accountability for any atrocities. Today, there is no guarantee of prosecution and accountability, but not a single brutish ruler can be confident of escaping international justice. The certainty of impunity is gone. Fifteen years is a very short time in the broad sweep of history for such a dramatic transformation of the international criminal landscape."[29]

Perhaps, but there are those who argue that such dramatic gains have been achieved precisely because principle has trumped pragmatism. Professor Yozo Yokota, one of the UN experts who prepared the 2005 report on East Timor cited above, understands the concept of judicial romanticism as a critique of human rights activists who assert their agenda with disregard for prevailing political realities.[30] Such critics, he explains, complain that the activists feel a self-congratulatory satisfaction by insisting on justice and invoking international laws and principles whether or not it is pragmatic or a viable course of action. These critics advocate a judicial pragmatism that is rooted in political reality and national self-interest. Rigorously applying such constraints, he argues, would necessarily limit reform, accountability and further improvements in international criminal justice.

The problem with judicial pragmatism is that powerful perpetrators will understand that they need not be worried about accountability. This approach thus condones a continued cocoon of impunity for those from influential countries and reserves justice for those who are not. In Yokota's opinion, it is idealistic challenges to prevailing political realties and the pervasive disregard for human rights that have promoted greater accountability. He also dismisses the issues of judicial or moral colonialism, arguing that in calling for accountability, the Commission of Experts voiced the justified and explicit demands of the East Timorese.[31]

According to Joseph Nevins, the cost of realpolitik for the international community in East Timor is the high-profile reneging on promises, fleeing from commitments and betrayal of principles – in short, the acceptance of a double standard that ensures scant accountability for those who victimize the relatively weak.[32] In the space of five years the international community has swung from outraged condemnation of Indonesia and demands for justice to averting its eyes for the "common good"; participating in the war on terror exonerates sins past.

As for judicial colonialism, the evident desire of East Timorese for accountability indicates that this is a homegrown yearning and not a question of standards and practices imposed from without. According to Augustus Vasconselos, a CAVR Commissioner and Presbyterian Minister, the 8,000 witnesses who testified expressed a strong desire for justice.[33] He sees this as a normal human desire rather than the agenda of civil society organizations or a reflection of judicial colonialism. Suggestions to the contrary are, in his view, condescending to the Timorese and the appeal they made in *Chega!* In his view, retributive justice is not the answer for all victims and other avenues beyond judicial processes are necessary, but it remains important for many victims still coming to terms with their agonizing experiences.

Professor Yokota expresses disappointment that the Secretary General and the Security Council have effectively buried the report he and his colleagues submitted in mid-2005 largely due to realpolitik. He still thinks it is possible and advisable to revive the hybrid tribunals and still hopes that the dictates of justice will ultimately prevail, and soon. Speaking for many in the activist community, he asserts that justice postponed is justice lost.[34]

Yokota, along with Eduardo Gonzalez of the ICTJ, both assert that the United States has lobbied on Indonesia's behalf to dissuade the Security Council from acting on the Commission's recommendations. Aside from losing Indonesian assistance in the war on terrorism, there is an additional geo-strategic concern that pressing accountability for human rights violations might push Indonesia toward China as has happened with Myanmar.

Regaining dignity

We have to see what we can do, not what we wish to do. Now we need reconciliation and we have to think of socio-economic rather than formal justice. That is our priority.

Xanana Gusmão, 16 December 2005

Our mission was to establish accountability in order to deepen and strengthen the prospects for peace, democracy, the rule of law and human rights in our new nation.

Chega! (CAVR report), December 2005

These statements frame the ongoing debate in East Timor. Justice or reconciliation? Principles or pragmatism? Accountability or impunity? These are the major questions facing the international community and the people of East Timor as they cope with the trauma of Indonesia's brutal occupation and departure. In realizing justice, reconciliation and democracy the United Nations reminds us that there is a virtue in a sensible sequencing of these processes and in finding a middle ground.[35] Given that East Timor's 24-year struggle for independence is an object lesson in the value and rewards of idealism in the face of impossible odds, some critics are baffled by the government's pragmatism in its pursuit of justice.

President Gusmão is making a calculated gamble. He seeks to draw a line under the past and postpone a reckoning in favor of reconciliation and recovery in his war-ravaged nation. He hopes the people will follow him. For him, the potential of independence cannot be realized by trying perpetrators in a courtroom, especially when there are so many more pressing problems. The complex political calculus of the President's choice involves, inter alia, weighing the costs and benefits of pursuing justice at a time when East Timor is poorly prepared to do so, the international community is indifferent and Indonesia remains recalcitrant, unrepentant and unencumbered by international pressures. He sees no benefit in antagonizing dangerous neighbors with quixotic gestures that are bound to fail and likely to boomerang.

The CTF process may indeed be a dead-end, but at least East Timor can say it gave the Indonesians a second chance to make up for the sham trials. If Indonesia fails to deliver yet again, they can blame only themselves while East Timor can gain credit for acting in good faith with patience.

President Gusmão is risking his substantial political capital in defying public opinion on justice. Like Nelson Mandela, he wants to shape public expectations and steer them away from retribution and toward peaceful and democratic development. He is demonstrating leadership and prodding the people to embrace reconciliation. Few doubt that this revered and charismatic national hero can sway public opinion. He emphasizes that reconciliation also means reintegrating Timorese who committed crimes while serving Indonesian interests. This tricky process has gone better than anyone expected and owes a great deal to his emphasis on healing. This remains a difficult process in many local communities and does not involve those guilty of serious crimes, but does mark a step forward out of the nightmare.

East Timor's demonstration of reasonableness is a significant confidence-building measure and an important step toward influencing hostile Indonesian attitudes toward its tiny neighbor. Especially in light of Jakarta's recent success in negotiating a deal with separatist rebels in Aceh that preserves Indonesian territorial integrity, there are widespread regrets, and recriminations, about East Timor's independence. While the threat of renewed hostilities with Indonesia may well be exaggerated, fence mending with Indonesia and mollifying the Indonesian military could pay dividends. There is no shortage of potential bilateral rifts.

Whether or not justice postponed is justice lost remains to be seen. The Church and civil society organizations will continue to give a voice to the victims and lobby for justice. They are keeping the issue of accountability alive and preserving an option important for many traumatized victims. While national leaders follow the dictates of realpolitik, and embrace alternative forms of justice, other actors usefully promote what the leaders cannot. In this sense, there is a symbiotic relationship between the state and civil society/international organizations. Leaders can consolidate peace and build trust while such organizations maintain pressure for retributive and restorative justice.[36]

These parallel efforts contribute to what could be a gradual, incremental and often sputtering process of accountability and reconciliation. Understandably, victims will be disappointed by what portends to be a frustratingly slow and fitful process, but total satisfaction for them is impossible. Modest satisfaction entails recognition of their suffering, acceptance of responsibility by Indonesia, clear signs of contrition and atonement, and cultivating a common historical memory of what happened in East Timor in the final quarter of the twentieth century.

Reconciliation is difficult because the aggressor nation must humble itself by acknowledging wrongdoing and demonstrating sincere contrition in ways that confront national pride and identity.[37] Germany demonstrates this is possible and beneficial, Japan that it is difficult, but decidedly problematic if neglected. The onus is on Indonesia; reconciliation will depend on its political choices and actions. However, the East Timorese must also be ready to accept meaningful, symbolic gestures of responsibility and atonement that will fall short of a full reckoning.[38] Reconciliation thus also requires the wronged nation to act with restraint such that the victimizing nation can atone while retaining its dignity.

Ultimately, the ongoing failure of justice in East Timor and the recent violence serve as an indictment of the international community and bestow a responsibility to facilitate both reconciliation and justice. As elsewhere around the world, those who bear the greatest responsibility for human rights violations are the least likely to face accountability. This is not an encouraging basis for reconciliation and unlikely to address even the most modest needs of victims. It is important to recognize that it is not too late – the evidence has been gathered and is available – and that the window of opportunity remains open.[39] Targeted prosecution of those who orchestrated excesses can send a powerful message to perpetrators and victims. A collective shrug of the shoulders is equally eloquent.

Helena Cobban dismisses efforts at international justice as a "false hope", and certainly East Timorese know all too well what it is like to be forsaken, but they patiently await a reckoning. Why not? For 24 years these people nurtured a "false hope" against the odds and in the end managed to prevail over pragmatism and power. Perhaps these initial efforts at reconciliation will serve as a confidence-building measure, facilitating reciprocal gestures. As both nations consolidate democracy and the rule of law, the basis for such a reckoning may improve. This trend merits sustained and generous international support.[40] The failures of justice in East Timor are obstacles to reconciliation among a people hungry for justice and do not justify abandoning efforts to get it right. Regaining dignity for Indonesia and the East Timorese hangs in the balance.

Notes

1. Prime Minister José Ramos-Horta Inauguration Speech, 10 July 2006. Available from http://www.parasindonesia.com/news_read.php?gid=211 (last accessed 10 March 2007).
2. Geoffrey Robinson (2003) *East Timor 1999: Crimes against Humanity*, Geneva: Office of the United Nations High Commissioner for Human Rights.
3. The circumstances of ground zero are assessed in Joseph Nevins (2005) *A Not So Distant Horror: Mass Violence in East Timor*, Ithaca, N.Y.: Cornell University Press.
4. These reports are available from http://www.jsmp.minihub.org/Resources.htm (last visited 31 May 2006).
5. This UN preference for nationally led, domestically based judicial processes is espoused in Report of the Secretary-General (2004), "The Rule of Law and Transitional Justice in Conflict and Post-Conflict Societies" (23 August) S/2004/616*.
6. Helena Cobban (2006) "International Courts", *Foreign Policy*, March/April: 22–28.
7. See Hansjörg Strohmeyer (2001) "Collapse and Reconstruction of a Judicial System: The United Nations Missions in Kosovo and East Timor", *American Journal of International Law* 95(1): 46–63; and Hansjörg Strohmeyer (2001) "Policing the Peace: Post-Conflict Judicial System Reconstruction in East Timor", *University of New South Wales Law Journal* 24(1): 171–182.
8. The problems plaguing the Serious Crimes Unit (SCU) and the Special Panels charged with investigating and prosecuting violations are examined by one of the first prosecutors in the SCU: Suzannah Linton (2001) "Cambodia, East Timor and Sierra Leone: Experiments in International Justice", *Criminal Law Forum* 12: 185–246; and Suzannah

Linton (2002) "New Approaches to International Justice in Cambodia and East Timor", *International Review of the Red Cross* 84(845): 93–119. Also see Simon Chesterman (2002) "Justice under International Administration: Kosovo, East Timor and Afghanistan", report of the Transitional Administrations Project, New York: International Peace Academy.

9. Report of the Secretary-General, "The Rule of Law and Transitional Justice".
10. Helena Cobban, "International Courts".
11. Suzanne Katzenstein (2003) "Hybrid Tribunals: Searching for Justice in East Timor", *Harvard Human Rights Journal* 16: 245–278.
12. As of November 2005, the International Criminal Court for Rwanda had spent a total of US$1 billion while handing down a mere 25 judgements.
13. For a scathing assessment, see David Cohen (2002) "Seeking Justice on the Cheap: Is the East Timor Tribunal Really a Model for the Future?" *Asia Pacific Issues* 61, August.
14. For a summary of the testimony of 8,000 East Timorese witnesses who testified before the nation's truth commission and strong recommendations favouring accountability, see *Chega!: The Report of the Commission for Reception, Truth and Reconciliation in Timor-Leste (CAVR)* Dili: CAVR, 2005, available from http://etan.org/news/2006/cavr.html (last accessed 29 May 2006).
15. US Secretary of State Condoleeza Rice announced a strategic partnership with and expanded military assistance to Indonesia during a visit in March 2006. She also urged Indonesia to sign a treaty with the United States that would exempt each country's citizens from extradition for prosecution by the International Criminal Court. Neither the United States nor Indonesia have ratified the treaty establishing the court.
16. Recent violence was sparked by troops dismissed over various disputes, but the rioting and looting reflect wider grievances and disappointment among the people that the realities of independence have fallen short of expectations, especially in terms of living standards.
17. CAVR, *Chega!*
18. Interview with Jill Jolliffe, 17 December 2005.
19. Interview with President Xanana Gusmão, 16 December 2005. All quotes and attributions draw from this interview.
20. Interview with Foreign Minister José Ramos-Horta, 13 December 2005.
21. Interview with Eduardo Gonzalez, 28 December 2005.
22. In Bacau I spoke with a man on 22 December 2006 who echoed these remarks, asking, "If we don't pursue justice for what these people did to us, how can we be sure the government won't do the same to us?"
23. Interview with Father Martinho Gusmao, Director of the Justice and Peace Commission of Bacau, 17 December 2005.
24. Ibid.
25. Ibid.
26. Interview with Reverend Agustinho de Vasconselos, 17 December 2005.
27. Ramesh, Thakur (2005) "Tyrants under the Gun: The Reduction of Impunity", *Japan Times*, November 10. Also see Ramesh Thakur and Peter Malcontent, eds (2004) *From Sovereign Impunity to International Accountability: The Search for Justice*, Tokyo: United Nations University Press, pp. 284–289.
28. Report of the Secretary-General, "The Rule of Law and Transitional Justice".
29. Thakur, "Tyrants under the Gun".
30. Interview with Yozo Yokota, 25 January 2006.
31. Everyone I met in East Timor in December 2005, with the exception of government leaders, strongly supported an international tribunal, expressing frustration that the United Nations abandoned the process.

32. Nevins, *A Not So Distant Horror*, p. 202.
33. Interview with Reverend Augustus Vasconselos, 17 December 2005.
34. See for example, Judicial System Monitoring Programme (2005) "Submission to the United Nations's Commission of Experts", Dili, East Timor: JSMP, April 6; JSMP (2005) "Justice for Victims Still Elusive", press release, Dili, East Timor: JSMP, May 24; Megan Hirst and Howard Varney (2005) "Justice Abandoned? An Assessment of the Serious Crimes Process in East Timor", New York: International Center for Transitional Justice; "Commission of Truth and Friendship Brings Neither" (2005) *La'o Hamutuk Bulletin* 6(3), August, available from http://www.laohamutuk.org/Bulletin/2005/Aug/, last accessed 10 March 2007.
35. Report of the Secretary-General, "The Rule of Law and Transitional Justice".
36. On the role of civil society organizations in the reconciliation process, see Lily Gardner Feldman (2005) "The Role of Non-State Actors in Germany's Foreign Policy of Reconciliation: Catalysts, Complements, Conduits, or Competitors?" unpublished manuscript, Baltimore, Md.: American Institute for Contemporary German Studies, The Johns Hopkins University.
37. For further discussion of reconciliation issues, see: Jane W. Yamazaki (2005) *Japanese Apologies for World War II: A Rhetorical Study*, London: Routledge; Sven Saaler, (2005) *Politics, Memory and Public Opinion: The History Textbook Controversy and Japanese Society*, Munich: German Institute for Japanese Studies; and Andrew Horvat, (2004) "Overcoming the Negative Legacy of the Past: Why Europe Is a Positive Example for East Asia", *Brown Journal of World Affairs* 11(1): 137–148.
38. In this context, to facilitate reconciliation there is a "need" for high profile convictions of Indonesian perpetrators. The United Nations suggests a targeting of prosecutions focusing on those most responsible for the most serious crimes. Report of the Secretary-General, "The Rule of Law and Transitional Justice".
39. During the looting at the end of May 2006, government offices were ransacked. Attorney General Longuinhos Monteiro said that looters succeeded in breaking into the Serious Crimes Unit archive and files concerning all of the most prominent Indonesians implicated in the 1999 massacres, including General Wiranto, were stolen. Christopher Torchia (2006) "East Timor President Moves to Curb Unrest", Associated Press, May 31. On 17 July 2006 a senior government advisor assured me that the archive and files are intact and that only some computers from the office remain missing. In a 16 December 2006 interview, Patrick Walsh, Advisor to the Post-CAVR Technical Secretariat, told me that all of the files had been returned in exchange for a refrigerator.
40. Charles Call argues that international justice can be redeemed and is essential to a stable and just global order. Charles T. Call (2004) "The Future of Transitional Justice", *Brown Journal of World Affairs* 11(1): 101–113.

7

No substitute for sovereignty: Why international criminal justice has a bleak future – and deserves it

Jeremy Rabkin

Perhaps no aspect of American foreign policy in recent years has been so widely dismaying to traditional friends and allies of the United States as America's opposition to the International Criminal Court (ICC). Of course, the war against Saddam Hussein, in the spring of 2003, aroused more intense passions for a time. But after Saddam was ousted, no government urged that he be returned to power. Meanwhile, Australia and Britain and half the governments in the European Union actually endorsed the resort to war in 2003. Yet even these US partners in the second Gulf War continued to deplore the US refusal to embrace the ICC.

In fact, the American position was not quite as isolated as it appeared from Europe. Russia and China also remained aloof from the ICC, constituting (with the United States) a clear majority of permanent members on the UN Security Council. Major regional powers such as India and Pakistan, Japan and Indonesia also remained aloof, along with dozens of other, smaller nations. A majority of the world's nations – representing a clear majority of the world's population – remained uncommitted to the ICC at the end of 2004.

Still, the extent of opposition or scepticism about the project testifies, in a way, to the political appeal of the idea behind it. An international project, aspiring to universality, does not usually get beyond initial discussions if the world's foremost military power, and so many other powers, decline to support it. As it is, proponents of the ICC can argue, with some truth, that even the United States and other powers that have been sceptical of the ICC were, some years earlier, willing to support

Atrocities and international accountability: Beyond transitional justice, Hughes, Schabas and Thakur (eds), United Nations University Press, 2007, ISBN 978-92-808-1141-4

international tribunals for the former Yugoslavia and for Rwanda, thus indicating at least some general sympathy for the background idea. Proponents of the ICC therefore express hope that, in time, the United States and other sceptical powers will finally come around to embracing the ICC.

It is easy to see the appeal of the underlying idea. If justice is good, than more justice is better and universal justice might seem to be best of all. Without global institutions to ensure minimal standards of justice – at least for the most terrible atrocities – the worst offences will remain unpunished and perpetrators will be tempted to proceed to new outrages, threatening not only the security of their own peoples but the peace of their regions. To challenge this vision almost seems to require sceptics to embrace injustice or at least to affirm that it is acceptable for terrible crimes to remain unpunished.

Hard as it is, the challenge is worth making – or rather, it is worth spelling out. I do not think anything like global justice will ever be attainable. But I think the argument against it is not simply the "realist" claim, that nations are too selfish or too jealous of other nations to submit to international controls. Rather, the civilized world has for many centuries agreed on a moral barrier to the demand for universal justice. That barrier is summed up in the word "sovereignty". And the argument for sovereignty is, at least in part, a moral argument.

Of course, talk about "the civilized world", though a standard feature of nineteenth century treatises on international law, now leaves many people quite uncomfortable. There are good reasons for this, as well as bad reasons. In the past century, European nations, including some regarded as among the most civilized, participated in crimes beyond the imagination of any barbarian. The determination to resist a recurrence of such terrible crimes is understandable and even praiseworthy.

But if we have learned to distrust even the governments of civilized peoples, we have no more reason than the people of previous ages to think that a universal authority – claiming to speak for all the different peoples of the world – will be more trustworthy. We have no more reason to think that force can be entrusted to one body, claiming to act for all peoples in the world. And we have no more reason to think that justice can be achieved without force. So we have, after all, as much reason to respect the principle of sovereignty as did previous generations. Given the horrors perpetrated in recent generations by nations that disdained the principle of sovereignty, we have rather more reason to embrace that principle. And if sovereignty means anything, it means very sharp limits to any serious notion of international criminal justice.

In what follows I will argue, first, that nothing in previous history could serve as precedent for the projects set in motion in this area during the

1990s. So, far from building on past practice, the efforts at genuine international criminal justice in that decade proceeded by disregarding all earlier notions about the limits of international legal authority. Second, whatever the hopes of that very hopeful decade, we have since learned that the end of the Cold War, even the collapse of the Soviet Union, did not produce an end to the underlying challenges of international relations. So the world still cannot dispense with sovereignty as the basic, organizing principle in international affairs. Third, even if internal strife or extreme human rights abuses within particular countries may justify international responses, it will rarely be a serious or promising response to send international prosecutors to restore decent government. Fourth, the practical objections to international criminal justice are not merely regrettable complications to an otherwise inspiring ideal. Even as a theory, the notion of justice to which international criminal tribunals appeal is quite unsatisfactory. At some level, it is altogether repellent.

Flight from history

The association between criminal justice and sovereign authority is very old. It is, in fact, at least as old as the idea of sovereignty itself. Jean Bodin's great treatise, *Six Livres de la République*, generally taken to be the first systematic elucidation of sovereign authority, was first published (in French) in 1576. Bodin was already quite emphatic that the enforcement of criminal justice is one of the special prerogatives of sovereignty. Nor did Bodin claim to be setting out a novel theory at the time. He depicted sovereignty as a well-recognized principle of his time and treated the highest elements of criminal justice – the power to add or remove criminal prohibitions and penalties from the law, the power to determine final appeals, the power to grant reprieves or pardons – as "marques" or indicators of where true sovereignty resided.[1]

The idea seems to have been well-rooted by the sixteenth century, even while modern ideas of statehood or nationhood were still in their infancy. To find a genuine precedent for the extension of criminal jurisdiction to the world at large, one must go back to 1533, when the Spanish conquistador Francisco Pizarro organized a trial of the Inca king Atahualpa – and then carried out the resulting death sentence – for committing murder and adultery before the arrival of the Spaniards in Peru. Even this early instance of something that looks like an assertion of universal jurisdiction, however, was viewed as discreditable, even by Spanish writers of the immediately following generation.[2] The most distinguished Spanish legal commentators, such as the Jesuit Francisco Suárez, writing at the very beginning of the seventeenth century, did not endorse such grandiose claims of Spanish jurisdiction to punish wrong-doing throughout the world – let alone endorse the notion that all governments could claim such universal jurisdiction.[3]

Many commentators in recent decades have claimed that the historic treatment of piracy is a precedent for contemporary claims of universal jurisdiction. At least since the seventeenth century, pirates were regarded as *hostis humani generis* ("enemies of mankind") and subject, as such, to punishment by all nations. Commentators thus argue that in allowing nations to assert universal jurisdiction for the punishment of modern enemies of mankind, such as perpetrators of mass murder or organizers of systematic torture, the world would simply be extending a well-established practice. This argument may inspire contemporary human rights advocates, but it is not well-grounded. Certainly, it is not well-grounded in history.

Pirates were not regarded as enemies of mankind because armed robbery on the high seas was viewed as the most heinous offence. They were enemies of all mankind because they did not even respect the laws of their home nations. But since they plied their trade in the no-man's-land of the high seas and did not dare to return to their home nations, they could not easily be punished by their home governments. Their own governments were quite content to let them be punished by any power able to seize them, especially when (as was usually the case) they were seized on the high seas.

Far from being regarded as an unpardonable offence, sea-borne robbery was routinely authorized by governments prior to the mid-nineteenth century. The framers of the US Constitution thought it prudent to grant Congress the power to authorize such attacks on enemy shipping with "letters of marque". In the international law of the day, such official licenses exempted the holders from charges of piracy, even if the raiding ship was privately operated (as a "privateer", authorized to keep some of the cargo seized from enemy ships), even if the raider's crew were subsequently seized by naval forces of the enemy nation whose ocean commerce they had been seizing. The essence of piracy was not that it was contrary to international morality but that it was not authorized by any government.[4] Even when governments abandoned the authorization of private raiders, naval seizures of enemy cargoes – or their outright destruction at sea – remained a standard instrument of war and a quite important military factor in the two world wars of the twentieth century. As it happens, the United States declined to subscribe to the 1855 convention that sought to outlaw privateering and has never officially endorsed it.[5]

There were, to be sure, other restrictions on the conduct of war, both at sea and on land, the violation of which was subject to punishment. But even someone guilty of breaking the customary rules – as by executing prisoners who had surrendered – was not subject to punishment by all other nations. If captured by the victimized nation, the perpetrator might be subject to its military justice. More often, the victimized nation might demand that the home army of the perpetrator should punish perpetrators. But such demands were hard to enforce between nations already at war and were not often insisted upon as conditions of peace, where the belligerents were otherwise disposed to make peace. So, despite all the passions stirred by the long wars against Napoleon Bonaparte, the victorious allies did not think to organize war crimes tribunals. Napoleon himself remained in British custody (or at least, under British supervision in his remote island exile) for more than a decade after his defeat at Waterloo, but the British did not subject him or any of his marshals or generals to formal trials.

After the First World War, the victorious Allies demanded trials of German war criminals but were content to leave these trials to German officials. They did not give serious thought to organizing an international criminal tribunal to pursue such trials, even at a time when they were organizing the League of Nations. The so-called Permanent Court of International Justice, the judicial organ of the League, was restricted in its jurisdiction to the traditional domain of international arbitration, the assessment of claims by one state against another – and then only with the consent of both states. The International Court of Justice, established with the United Nations in 1945, was organized on the same lines. Nobody imagined that either of these international courts could impose criminal justice on individual human defendants.

The International Military Tribunal (IMT), organized at Nuremberg after the Second World War, is often taken to be the most pertinent precedent for contemporary ventures in international criminal justice. The Nuremberg tribunal was indeed established to impose criminal justice on individuals. Nearly half the original defendants were hanged pursuant to sentences handed down by the tribunal.

But if this were criminal justice, it was not in any real sense international justice. The four occupying powers in Germany organized the tribunal on their own initiative, without consulting any other nations.[6] The status of the tribunal was emphasized in its very first ruling. When German defence lawyers moved for the inclusion of judges from neutral powers, to accord with the traditional practice in international arbitration, the judges dismissed the motion out of hand. The IMT, the judges explained, was an instrument of the new sovereign power in Germany, which had reverted to the occupying powers upon the unconditional surrender of the Nazi state. The terms of the tribunal made no provision for judging crimes that might have been committed by Allied nations. The prosecutors, accountable to their home governments, would not have considered such charges, in any case. After the initial trials of some two dozen defendants before the four-power tribunal, each of the occupying powers simply organized its own tribunals in its own occupation zone and proceeded to impose justice on thousands of war criminals unilaterally.

It is true that some commentators at the time hoped the Nuremberg trials would prove a precedent for a more encompassing scheme of international criminal justice. The Convention on the Prevention and Punishment of the Crime of Genocide, endorsed by the UN General Assembly in 1948, makes vague reference to an international tribunal that might be subsequently established. For decades thereafter, the International Commission of Jurists – an advisory body of legal scholars – debated various proposals. All seem to have assumed that the jurisdiction of a permanent international criminal tribunal would be established by the consent of a defendant's home state to each particular prosecution. But all such plans had no serious prospects while the world remained so divided by the Cold War between the superpowers.

The prospects began to change only in the early 1990s, after the collapse of the Soviet Union. In Yugoslavia, the collapse of communism brought a disintegration of the multi-ethnic nation into separate national states, the largest of which, Serbia and Croatia, then sponsored ethnic militias to carve territory from multi-ethnic Bosnia. The UN Security Council responded, in 1993, by establishing a special International Criminal Tribunal for the former Yugoslavia (ICTY). It was the first international criminal tribunal since Nuremberg and, properly speaking, the first ever.

Unlike the Nuremberg tribunal, the ICTY not only owed its existence to a fully international body, but also was organized on fully international terms. The decision to prosecute would be left to an independent prosecutor, not accountable to any particular government. The Security Council adopted the same model a year later, when it established a special tribunal to punish perpetrators of genocide in Rwanda. Only four years thereafter, a 1998 United Nations-sponsored conference in Rome drew up detailed plans for a permanent, free-standing International Criminal Court.

Almost immediately thereafter, new theories of international justice were put into practice when a Spanish judge demanded the arrest of Augusto Pinochet, former president of Chile, for crimes committed after the military coup that had brought him to power 25 years earlier. Pinochet, who had travelled to Britain on a diplomatic passport, was arrested by British police while recovering from back surgery in a British hospital. Pinochet spent the next year and a half in an unsuccessful battle to defeat the Spanish arrest warrant as an improper interference with Chilean sovereignty. Over the objections of the Chilean government, the House of Lords finally determined that the Convention against Torture had, without explicitly saying so, established a right of all signatories to try former heads of state from all other signatory states, for violating its general prohibitions. The British Home Secretary then allowed Pinochet to return to Chile, ostensibly because he was too feeble to stand trial. But human rights advocates celebrated the ruling of the House of Lords as a milestone in the evolution of international law – which it certainly was. As with the ICC and the special tribunals for Yugoslavia and Rwanda, the assertion of universal jurisdiction in the Pinochet case had no substantial precedent over the previous five centuries.

The best that can be said for these innovations is that they were launched in an era when many people genuinely believed the world had entered an entirely new era. It was, after all, an era in which a book speculating about "the end of history" became a best seller and a worldwide topic of discussion. But it should have been obvious, even in the 1990s, that the ending of the Cold War did not mean that all international conflicts had ended or that all the world had become a single, global polity.

The persistence of international relations

The attempted prosecution of Pinochet was widely applauded, at least in western Europe. There was no real precedent for the trial of a former head of state in another country for offences committed in his own country against his own nationals. But the groundbreaking character of the prosecution simply stoked enthusiasm for the venture. Before Pinochet's return to Chile, several European countries offered to host a Pinochet trial, if Spain had second thoughts. The European Parliament passed a resolution encouraging such offers. The trial would prove that dictators no longer enjoyed immunity for their crimes.

But Pinochet was a very minor figure in the horrors of the twentieth century. When Pinochet agreed to step down, in 1991, the new democratic government organized a Commission on Truth and Reconciliation to clarify the record of his dictatorship. That Commission concluded that the Pinochet government was responsible for some 3,000 extra-judicial killings. Almost all of the victims were adult males associated with leftist opposition forces and almost all were killed in the first two years after the 1973 coup, when the new military government still feared violent resistance. The crimes of Pinochet barely register against the scale of mass murder perpetrated by a Hitler or a Stalin.

True, there had been justice, of some sort, for many top officials of the Nazi regime. What about the victims of Stalin, who numbered in the millions? There was no possibility, of course, that Soviet crimes could be prosecuted at Nuremberg. The Soviet government would never have agreed to participate in a tribunal that exposed Russians as well as Germans to prosecution. For that matter, the other participants – the Americans, the British and the French – would not have agreed to expose their own wartime policies to an international tribunal. There were many reasons for this resistance on the part of the western powers, not the least of which was the recognition that, even if their misdeeds paled beside those of the Soviet Union, they had relied upon Soviet assistance to defeat Nazi Germany and still hoped for Soviet cooperation in the postwar world.

The enthusiasts for the Pinochet prosecution often talked as if the world had left behind all need for such moral compromises. Power politics would no longer restrain the moral imperative for justice. It was not enough to ease dictators out of power, as Pinochet had been eased from power. It was not enough to achieve transitions to more democratic and law-bound governments for the future, as had happened in so many countries in Latin America during the same period when Chile made its transition. Human rights activists insisted that those guilty of terrible abuses must be personally held to account.

And what of those who perpetrated vast crimes on behalf of Stalin or his less murderous but still quite brutal successors? While the communist regime remained in power, such prosecutions were unthinkable in the Soviet Union. Even after the collapse of the Soviet Union, the new regime in Russia did not pursue justice for past atrocities. It did not even organize a truth commission to document the precise details of the terrible crimes committed under the communists. Europeans, who were so insistent on justice for victims of Pinochet, made no effort to demand justice for the millions of victims of the Soviet government.

It was not that European governments were unwilling to make any demands on the successor government in Russia. In the early 1990s, Russia sought to join the Council of Europe and take part in its monitoring of compliance with the European Convention on Human Rights. The existing members of the Council pressed for a number of reforms, such as the abolition of capital punishment in Russia. They made no effort at all, however, to urge accountability for the crimes of the communist regime. Nor does this passivity seem to have aroused any controversy among human rights activists. For Russia, the past could be left in the past.

What was true of Russia was also true of China. European governments urged liberalizing reforms in China, as did the United States. There was no serious demand that China bring to justice those responsible for terrible atrocities during earlier periods of communist rule. The government of China made no effort at all to make an accounting for such crimes, let alone bring perpetrators to justice. Even human rights advocates, demanding much more extensive reform in China, did not demand a full accounting for past crimes.

Why such different treatment of Russia and China, compared with Chile? A number of factors may have influenced attitudes. But surely the overriding difference was that Russia and China remained large and important countries. Western governments were anxious to bury Cold War tensions and cultivate friendly and cooperative relations with these countries for the future. In Russia and China, there were good grounds to hope that future governments would not repeat the horrors inflicted on their own peoples by their predecessors. But relations between the new governments and the rest of the world remained uncertain. Precisely because the foreign policies of new governments in China and Russia remained uncertain, there was a prevailing eagerness not to stir unnecessary disputes. Justice for past victims in these countries was among the very lowest priorities. In this respect, the world of the 1990s was not, after all, so removed from the difficult tradeoffs in justice that western powers had accepted in 1945.

Only by tacitly exempting Russia and China could one pretend, as so many people tried to do in the 1990s, that the world was now ready for a scheme of universal justice. But it should have been obvious that these were not the only exceptions required. Demands for reliable, universal justice would impose unacceptable strain on many other aspects of international relations.

Within three years after the attempted prosecution of Pinochet, Belgian prosecutors, working on a similar program of universal jurisdiction for extreme human rights offences, announced that they would begin proceedings against Ariel Sharon for the killing of Palestinian refugees during the Israeli invasion of Lebanon in 1982. Sharon, who had been Defence Minister in 1982, had, in the meantime, become Prime Minister. It was, in a way, quite logical to say that if former officials should be held accountable, those who had remained in office or ascended to higher offices should be even more open to prosecution. After all, officials still in office had the opportunity to do more harm. But at the very time Belgian prosecutors sought to hold Sharon to account, the European Union was pressing for a renewal of peace negotiations between Israel and the Palestinian Authority. How could the European Union expect to play a role in peace negotiations when a pending prosecution would prevent the Israeli prime minister from setting foot in Brussels, both the European Union capital and the site of the attempted prosecution?

Sharon was blamed for not exerting himself to prevent a massacre of Palestinians which was actually perpetrated not by Israeli forces under his direct command but by Lebanese Christian militias, cooperating at the time with the Israeli Defense Forces. By that standard, Yasser Arafat and other top leaders of the Palestinian Authority could all be blamed for decades of terrorism, culminating in the wave of suicide bomb attacks unleashed on Israel starting in the summer of 2000. Whatever their personal involvement in particular terror attacks, Arafat and his top aides had not seriously exerted themselves to prevent or punish such atrocities. Still, if there were ever going to be peace, there would have to be painful compromises on both sides. Would it help to move the parties toward peace – or help to maintain a fragile peace – to insist that leaders on both sides (or on either side) would still have to be punished?

There is no easy way of separating demands for criminal accountability from other demands that are typically entangled in international conflicts. Both sides usually believe that they are fighting on behalf of just claims – for territory or security or sovereign rights – which the opposing side has wrongly denied them. It is not easy to see how demands for criminal justice regarding particular perpetrators can be separated from other demands or war aims. If conflicts are settled by compromise, it is hard to see why there should not be compromise in this area, too. At the very least, it is hard to see why it is sensible to insist that some sort of amnesty or waiver of criminal accountability may never be part of the negotiations. But it can only be part of the negotiations if jurisdiction is, to begin with, limited to the immediate parties. The whole point of universal jurisdiction is that any third country can intervene, with its own prosecution, whenever it chooses to do so.

Perhaps universal jurisdiction will not be much invoked in the future. Belgian prosecutors went far to discrediting the idea of universal jurisdiction when they moved from investigating complaints against Sharon to investigating complaints against President George H. W. Bush and his Secretary of Defence, Richard Cheney, for supposed abuses committed during the 1991 war against Iraq. It was a particularly ill-timed initiative in 2002, when President Bush's son, George W. Bush, had succeeded him in the White House, with Cheney as his Vice President. The United States responded by threatening to seek the relocation of NATO headquarters from Brussels, if US officials were to be subject to Belgian subpoenas whenever they attended NATO meetings. The Belgian government quickly persuaded its parliament to rescind claims to universal jurisdiction in Belgian criminal law.

But in some ways, the theory behind universal jurisdiction had already been institutionalized in the new international criminal tribunals. The charters of the Yugoslav and Rwandan tribunals, like the statute of the ICC, presuppose that justice must go forward. They make no explicit provision for amnesty or pardon, let alone for political considerations for withholding prosecution in particular circumstances.

From the standpoint of international relations, these tribunals risk many serious problems. The history of the Yugoslav and Rwandan tribunals vividly illustrates one of the problems, which might be termed the "moral hazard" of treating gestures as serious responses. Insurance analysts use this phrase to describe the common tendency to ignore continuing dangers, once one has purchased an insurance policy – so that, for example, people often become more careless about piling flammable items in a building that has fire insurance. The tendency has obvious counterparts in international affairs. Governments routinely delude themselves into thinking that, because they have signed a treaty, they no longer need to worry about defence preparations for threats they might face if the treaty breaks down. The problem of moral hazard is particularly great when governments are not all that concerned about the ultimate threat – because, let us say, it involves a fire in someone else's house. Even if one is concerned about human rights, perhaps especially if one is concerned about human rights, one must acknowledge the possibility that, in a particular case, mass atrocities can be stopped only by outside forces. Establishing an international tribunal is a way of avoiding recourse to force. For the victims, however, it is not an adequate substitute for outside force.

In Rwanda, the United Nations stood by while some 800,000 people were massacred. Actually, the United Nations did not simply remain inert. Rather, the Security Council stirred itself to order the withdrawal of existing peacekeeping forces so that they would not be entangled in the conflict. So, the United Nations effectively denied whatever protection it might have offered the victims – which might well have been considerable – at the outset of the genocide. The Security Council moved to intervene only after a force of Tutsi rebels, sponsored by neighbouring countries, had overthrown the genocidal Hutu government and put a stop to the slaughters. Then the United Nations hastily established a tribunal to punish perpetrators of the genocide. It would not send troops, but was prepared to send lawyers. They were not, of course, much compensation for the failure to send troops.

In the Balkans, too, sending lawyers became a substitute for sending troops, or at least for sending serious military forces when they were seriously needed. The most notorious massacre, the killing of some 8,000 Muslims in Srebrenica, took place after the establishment of the ICTY. The UN peacekeeping forces, which were charged with protecting civilians, remained utterly passive while Serb militias forced their way into the city and took Muslim males out to be executed. It is probably not mere coincidence that these UN troops were supplied by the Netherlands. The Dutch do not seem to have imagined that they might be called on to risk the lives of their own troops to protect Bosnian civilians. After all, they were already hosting the ICTY in the Hague. What is certain is that the Dutch government, proud of its contribution to the extension of international law, did not make any serious effort to prepare its troops to engage in actual combat when innocents could be protected only by fighting back.

The point is not simply that there is much hypocrisy in international affairs. The more important point is that establishing criminal tribunals is no substitute for serious responses. The novelty of these tribunals is precisely that, for the first time in history, criminal jurisdiction was asserted by courts that were not organs of actual governments. That is, these tribunals were not backed by armed force, as the organs of every government are backed by police and military forces. No government in the world would claim that it did not need police because it had set up judges and prosecutors to deter criminals with the mere moral authority of law. That is literally what the Yugoslav tribunal was asked to do. No one had any right to be surprised that the court did not establish peace and justice. It could not even get its hands on many of those it indicted, since it had no police of its own to capture them. International troops in the region, charged with peacekeeping responsibilities, did not want to threaten cease-fire agreements by chasing after popular local leaders who happened to be subject to indictment by that faraway tribunal in the Hague. Some governments contributing troops seemed to have other sorts of diplomatic distractions.[7]

If anything, the existence of the ICTY creates perverse incentives for nations that have contributed peacekeeping troops. The charter does not provide jurisdiction on the basis of nationality, much less on the basis of actual consent to prosecutions by the home country of the defendant. Rather, the Security Council decided that anyone operating in the territory of the former Yugoslavia should be subject to the ICTY's scrutiny. There is no liability for failing to take action – so nobody seemed to think the shameful dereliction of Dutch commanders should generate a prosecution. But there is liability for acting with excessive force. And the decision on whether force has been excessive would be left to the prosecutor and judges in the Hague – hundreds of miles from the scene of conflict and much further than that, perhaps, from the moral dilemmas facing actual commanders operating in that territory.

The problem was dodged by the ICTY following the NATO war against Serbia on behalf of the persecuted Albanian minority in Kosovo. NATO chose to fight its war by bombing from the air. There were civilian casualties in Belgrade. The ICTY went through the motions of questioning NATO commanders before concluding that no prosecution was warranted. Perhaps a prosecutor appointed by the Security Council, where NATO members hold three of the five permanent seats, was bound to be especially solicitous of NATO campaign tactics. But it is fair to wonder whether the prosecutor's authority would have been more acceptable even if more insulated from politics. Rules of war have never previously been enforced by independent monitors.[8] There is a bit too much at stake.

The ICC threatens to make the problem more pervasive and enduring. Following the war against Saddam Hussein in 2003, lawyers in Europe urged the ICC Prosecutor to undertake investigations of British tactics, some of which may have violated rules in the ICC Statute. There was, of course, much bitterness about the war, because it was not authorized by the Security Council and because its principal justification – that Saddam was violating his obligations and threatening other nations by stockpiling weapons of mass destruction – seemed much more questionable when no such weapons were subsequently found in Iraq.

Still, the premise of the ICC is that in a war between a western democracy and a monstrous tyranny, the ICC Prosecutor would adhere scrupulously to the rules. In this case, since Hussein had (predictably) declined to endorse the ICC Statute, while Britain had actually done so, only British commanders or government officials would be exposed to prosecution. Those who presided over Hussein's torture centres or mass killing sites were exempt from ICC investigation. In the aftermath of the war, respectable bodies of European jurists actually did urge the ICC Prosecutor to commence proceedings against British commanders and officials for improper war tactics in Iraq.[9]

Perhaps the threat of prosecution would not deter a western country from undertaking military operations it thought absolutely necessary. But what about interventions that do not really contribute to the security of the intervening powers? In the summer of 2004, the US Secretary of State went so far as to invoke the word "genocide" in regard to massacres in the Darfur region of Sudan. Agreement that terrible things were happening in Sudan did not prompt any country to offer troops to protect the victims. But will it be easier to mobilize support for such interventions if, in addition to other risks, the intervening forces have to worry about the second-guessing of their tactics by international lawyers in the Hague?

The United States had raised this issue two years earlier. It urged the Security Council to make an exception from ICC jurisdiction for international peacekeeping forces. The Security Council declined to do more than suspend the ICC's investigative authority for a year at a time, as the ICC Statute itself authorizes. To do anything more, European ambassadors insisted, would undermine the moral authority of the ICC. By 2003, the Council was not even prepared to continue the one-year deferrals. International humanitarian interventions, even when authorized by the United Nations, must be exposed to the ICC, just as much as any other activities under the ICC's jurisdiction.

The posture makes sense only if one thinks that upholding the moral authority of the ICC is more important than advancing the goals the ICC was supposed to serve – such as deterring or stopping the most murderous practices by the most abusive governments. Of course, there is disagreement in the world about which governments are most abusive. Mere body counts do not settle the matter. If it did, the United Nations might have been more reluctant to rely on sanctions against Iraq, when sanctions imposed far more civilian fatalities (according to estimates accepted by the United Nations) than resulted from the 2003 war, which Secretary-General Kofi Annan insisted on decrying as "illegal". For good reasons and bad reasons, other considerations necessarily enter into international disputes, beyond the most abstract calculation of likely death tolls from one course or another.

But in a world where there is still conflict – not to mention murderous oppression within nations – it is very strange to suggest that a court, operating in abstraction from strategic or diplomatic calculation, not to mention in abstraction from force, can make the proper determinations about where and when and how much to invoke its prosecutorial authority. If such judgments involve too many diplomatic subtleties to be left to statisticians or economists, totalling up "costs" on each side, why suppose that they can be safely left to mere lawyers, juggling mere legal abstractions?

Yet the architects of the ICC Statute actually did aspire to establish a court that could render impartial judgments in apportioning blame for international conflicts. The opening section stipulates that the Court will have jurisdiction not only over genocide, war crimes and crimes against humanity but also over the crime of "aggression" – that is, wrongful resort to war. The Rome Conference imagined that the most sovereign of sovereign prerogatives, the decision to take a nation to war, could be constrained by standing rules that would be interpreted and enforced by a detached cadre of international civil servants in the Hague. Presumably, the idea was to stigmatize aggressors in order to deter resort to aggression.

The ambition might seem to be a logical extension of the Nuremberg indictments, where Nazi leaders were tried for this crime ("conspiracy to commit aggressive war"). But the Nuremberg tribunal was authorized to invoke this charge only against the defeated Germans. The terms of the Nuremberg charter relieved the tribunal from the awkwardness of examining the unprovoked Soviet attack against Finland in 1939. Stalin seemed to have decided upon a pre-emptive invasion of Finland, from fear that the Finns would otherwise endanger the Soviet Union by allying with Germany – which they did indeed do, when the Germans turned on the Soviet Union in 1941. At the time, the League of Nations condemned the Soviet attack on Finland but in 1940 members of the League were too preoccupied with the existing war with Germany to contemplate any sort of military response to the Soviet action. The ICC would, in principle, be licensed to make such judgements without regard to political context.

One could say, in a similar way, that the ICC's jurisdiction over "aggression" was a logical extension of the UN Charter's underlying concern to preserve peace by restraining aggression. But again, the association is misleading. The Charter authorized the Security Council only to make binding determinations about particular threats to peace. And the Charter scheme provided that no resolution of the Council could be adopted if any one of the five great powers, the five permanent members, opposed it. What the framers of the UN Charter were unwilling to submit even to a majority of great powers on the Council, with all their combined military strength for enforcing Council determinations, the ICC Statute proposes to entrust to a handful of independent international officials in the Hague, operating with no military or police backup at all.

But the Rome conference found that, having embarked on this scheme, it could not actually agree on a definition of "aggression". That is, the conference could not even agree on the most general characterization of the difference between improper "aggression" and legitimate acts of self-defence. The conference was not willing to abandon its vision of a court that would bring peace to the world by the mere say-so of judges. Instead, it simply bracketed the provisions on "aggression" and announced that the necessary definitions would be supplied at some future time by the nations that had already ratified the Statute in the meantime.

There may have been a technical reason for this reticence. The provisions defining genocide were adopted from existing provisions in the 1948 Convention on the Prevention and Punishment of the Crime of Genocide. Provisions on war crimes and crimes against humanity were taken over, in the main, from language in the 1976 Additional Protocol I to the Geneva Conventions of 1949. The Rome conference was not troubled by the fact that these treaties did not actually describe the subsequent conduct of nations – neither in their response to mass slaughter in other countries nor in their own tactics in war. It did not faze the Rome conference that none of the permanent members of the Security Council had actually ratified the Additional Protocol at the time of the conference (Britain and France did so only after the conference, while Russia, China and the United States still have not done so). It was enough that other nations had given formal assent to these treaties, so they could be treated – at least in the legalistic reckoning of lawyers – as "international standards". There was no comparable document offering specifications of the crime of "aggression", so given their usual legalistic approaches to standards, the Rome conference had little material with which to work.

This technical difficulty may, in itself, have reflected the underlying problem. The world could not agree on definitions for "aggression" even in a nominal or formalistic or fundamentally non-binding treaty like the Geneva Protocol. The reticence of the Geneva conference probably reflected, in turn, the recognition of most national delegations that when one comes to such ultimate questions, there is not much hope that nations will be bound by rules. Certainly this was the traditional attitude of statesmen and commentators toward international arbitration. Treaties could insist that many questions be submitted to arbitration but it would be futile to try to impose arbitration in disputes touching fundamental questions of national security. Accordingly, neither the Covenant of the League of Nations nor the UN Charter made provision for mandatory international arbitration of disputes.

But the ICC Statute suggested this was merely a matter of time. Questions on which even democratic nations had been prepared to send men to their deaths could now be decided by merely consulting a set of standing rules – as soon as the parties to the Rome Statute agreed on the wording of those rules. And when these rules were in place, the Court would punish anyone who ordered armies into action in violation of these rules. The highest prerogative of sovereignty could then be transferred to international civil servants.

Or could they, really? Perhaps the parties to the ICC will find it much harder to agree on such rules than the existing text implies. Perhaps a Court entrusted with these rules will find it even harder to enforce them. Perhaps this aspect of the project is merely a gesture. If it could work, it would mean that the ultimate attributes of world government – ultimate control over the deployment of force in the world – had been delegated to a handful of lawyers in the Netherlands. So perhaps the Rome Statute, in contemplating future ICC jurisdiction over "aggression", was simply a gesture of piety – a ceremonial bow to a vision that inspires many commentators, but which few governments will ever take quite seriously.

Yet perhaps it is wrong to treat the uncompleted provisions in the ICC Statute as mere gestures. The same sort of piety may be necessary to sustain those provisions of the Statute which are supposed to be already in effect. If decisions about ultimate resort to war are too momentous for sovereign states to entrust to bystanders in the Hague, why should nations let these same bystanders determine what tactics they may use when they do go to war? If one takes the completed provisions of the Rome Statute at face value, they imply that the conduct of war has no connection with the tactics used by the opposing side, just as they have no connection with the actual strategic implications of any particular tactic. An attacking army must never, for example, direct attacks against churches or mosques or hospitals – even if the defending army violates traditional rules by using these sites as hiding places for snipers. An attacking army must never mount a siege of a civilian population centre, even if a successful siege would put an end to the enemy's overall capacity or will to resist. Taken at face value, the Rome Statute suggests that some practices, even very traditional military practices, must now be seen as unlawful, regardless of other circumstances, if that is how lawyers come to view them. There is a binding legal obligation to refrain from such practices – even if such restraints are not observed by the opposing forces, even if such restraints risk more casualties in a longer war, even if such restraints risk ultimate defeat for the nation that accepts them. As the Rome Statute envisions such contests, it is more important to fight fairly than to win – or to win at acceptable cost. It is a compelling vision for sporting contests. It is not very credible that nations will feel this way about war.

It is more realistic to think that bystanders may embrace this view of war – when they do remain bystanders. Those not engaged in a war may feel it is more important to fight fair than to win. Their refusal to join the war may be already a sign that they do not care strongly about the actual outcome but perhaps it is simply a sign that they do not have military resources to offer. In practice, the rules of the ICC offer the chance for non-fighting nations to pass judgment on the tactics employed by nations that may actually have to engage in combat operations. It is not obvious why this arrangement should appeal to fighting nations. So, nations that can imagine themselves at war (Russia, China, India, Pakistan, Japan, Israel, Egypt, the United States, etc.) have refused to submit themselves to the judgments of the ICC.

The calculus may look different for nations that rely on others for their security – as most European nations relied on the United States for their protection for so long. Nations that rely on others for security often find it convenient to abandon their own defence preparations, as most European countries did in the last decades of the Cold War and, even more so, afterwards. If all they have to contribute to potential security partners is advice, they are apt to find that their advice is not taken too seriously. The ICC is a way for bystanders, who contribute only advice, to insist that their opinions be heeded by those nations still equipped to fight wars.

But it still requires an astonishing leap of faith to suppose that those nations that actually do the fighting will agree to be bound by the judgments of those who sit on the sidelines, offering only impartial advice. It only made sense for European enthusiasts during that happy period when Europeans imagined they would never again feel threatened by outside forces – so their relations with the United States could be subordinated to "international law". It was to be expected that, even when the majority of European governments endorsed the American-led war against Saddam Hussein in 2003, only Britain was able to provide significant numbers of troops. Most Europeans had decided they could be adequately protected by "international law".

National reconciliation – by foreign lawyers?

It may be that the parties to the Rome Statute will never be able to agree on actual definitions for the crime of "aggression". It may be that this reserved provision of the ICC Statute will never come into effect. Perhaps the stated intention to extend the ICC's jurisdiction to all international conflicts will remain a distant hope, always receding over the horizon, as new complications impress actual governments with the actual difficulties involved in implementing this vision.

The more substantial hope, many people think, is that international justice will provide a useful service for societies trying to recover from internal abuses, especially from the most severe or brutal governmental abuses. That is the main argument advanced by one of the most widely acclaimed recent books on international criminal justice, the aptly titled *Stay the Hand of Vengeance* by Canadian political scientist Gary Bass.[10]

At first glance, this seems far less grandiose and absurd than the idea that civil servants at the Hague will be referees for all future wars between states. Cannot international judges at least supplement international election monitors by providing some sort of backstop to efforts at corrective justice in transition regimes? But the idea is actually far less plausible than it may at first appear. Indictments are not likely to have much effect on reigning tyrants, since they will not turn themselves in for trial. International tribunals, without forces of their own to apprehend the worst perpetrators of abuse, without even the resources to impose any sort of sanction beyond the indictment, must rely on cooperation. That means, in the immediately affected country, they must deal with a government that is somewhat inclined to cooperate. That means, in practice, that international justice will come into play only when the tyranny has been replaced by a more decent government.

But how do decent governments come to power? One way is through rebellion, which often requires a prolonged struggle – itself a sort of war, even if a civil war. Sometimes the threat to pursue rebellion or civil war is enough to pressure a tyrant to open negotiations for reform or transition to a new government. In either case, there may not be such great difference between domestic conflict and international conflict. As international conflicts are often settled by compromise, so domestic conflicts are often settled by compromise. Even when conflict is settled by the victory of one side, the victor often finds incentives to make conciliatory gestures in order to strengthen the peace. The same is true in domestic conflicts. Just as international conflicts have rarely in the past been followed by international war crimes tribunals, the usual practice after the demise of a hated tyranny within a country has been some form of compromise.

Almost every country that made a transition from dictatorship to some more democratic government in the 1980s and early 1990s tried to conciliate adherents of the previous regime by providing broad amnesty for past misdeeds. This was true in Eastern Europe, when decades of communist brutality ended. It was true in Latin America when military dictatorships were replaced by democratic governments. It was even true in South Africa, where the white minority government gave way to a government based on full multiracial democracy. In South Africa, as in many other places, amnesty was accepted by rebels (or opponents) of the old government as the price for cooperation in a peaceful transition. In all cases, new governments were concerned to rally broad support and avoid reopening old wounds. Many countries established truth commissions to investigate and publicize the actual record of abuses under the old governments and provide at least public acknowledgement to the victims. There were very few prosecutions and many versions of amnesty, official and unofficial.

One of the most notable facts about the ICC is that it makes no provision for amnesty or pardon. In this it follows the charters for the ad hoc tribunals for the former Yugoslavia and for Rwanda. We do not yet know how prosecutors will actually deal with amnesties approved by new democracies but the ICC Statute virtually flaunts its determination to establish a higher form of justice than national states can sustain on their own. More than five years after South Africa's peaceful transition from apartheid to multiracial democracy – by coupling reform with amnesty and a truth commission – the drafters of the ICC Statute thought it proper to include, among unpardonable crimes, the resort to "apartheid". It could not affect the settlement in South Africa, since the Statute does not have retroactive reach. But it was a way of signalling that the ICC would not accept compromise. It would be more principled than the people who actually had fought and won the struggle against apartheid in South Africa and achieved a multiracial democracy without further violence.

Human rights activists have argued that, even with truth commissions, amnesty provisions or other devices for "forgetting" past abuses (the literal meaning of "amnesty") are a danger for the future, leaving the sense of injustice to continue rankling or the perception of impunity to encourage new crimes. But given the actual historical record, it is strange that anyone should pretend to know how much justice is required to heal a society. After the Second World War, the victorious Allies organized more extensive trials of German war criminals than any society has done on its own. Was this effort a success? Barely four years after this effort began, as soon, in fact, as Germans were allowed to elect a new government of their own in the western occupation zones, the new Bundestag clamoured for amnesty and a repeal of the war crimes prosecution program – on the ground that it had been so excessive that it was discrediting the notion of justice. The prosecution was indeed scaled back by the western Allies in order to conciliate German opinion at a time when German cooperation seemed vital in the gathering confrontation with the Soviet bloc in the east.

In Japan, the United States helped to secure Japanese surrender by promising not to interfere with the Emperor, and subsequent war crimes tribunals did not touch the Emperor. As in Germany, this was a political decision. Perhaps it was mistaken. The Japanese have not fully acknowledged their wartime offences. But then, Germans have also come to view themselves as victims in the Second World War – victims of a common European tragedy, as German leaders now say – more than uniquely guilty perpetrators. On the other hand, there has been no resurgence of fascist sentiment in Germany and no resurgence of militarist or imperialist sentiment in Japan.

The enthusiasm of contemporary Europeans for assuring full justice is not based on an accurate recollection of what happened after the war. Certainly, it does not reflect the decisions of their own governments, which, in all countries occupied by Germany, decided after the war to make token gestures of retribution against prominent collaborators but no extensive investigations into the true scale of wartime betrayals. Substituting a few show trials for a genuine accounting, most European countries launched a mythical history in which almost everyone had really resisted German-directed atrocities. Nobody bothered to inquire how such very small German police units had managed to round up hundreds of thousands of people for murder camps, if they had not received extensive assistance from local police and bureaucracies. French officials directly involved in genocide in France were found decades later to have resumed high-level careers in the French bureaucracy.

Whether or not the minimal gestures by post-war European governments were sound policy, no one can say that Europeans have reverted to racism – or at least to the murderous intensity of racism they displayed in the 1940s. Certainly democracy and civil liberty have been more secure in post-war Europe than they were in earlier times. During the Second World War, Europeans perpetrated more systematic horror than almost any nations now likely to be judged by the ICC. It is, to say the least, not obvious from the historical record why Europeans now demand a more impartial accounting from other nations than they demanded from themselves in the aftermath of the Second World War.

The fundamental problem with international justice is not that it is too severe, however. The absence of provision for amnesty or pardon is merely symptomatic of a wider problem. The underlying problem is the indifference of the relevant international justice schemes to hard political choices in the affected countries.

The experience in Rwanda is particularly revealing. Simple numbers tell the heart of the story. Some 800,000 Tutsi civilians were slaughtered in an orchestrated campaign of genocide. Five years after the United Nations established its special tribunal, it had still not convicted a single person for the crime; ten years later, it had convicted a mere twenty perpetrators.[11] Those actually convicted, moreover, were not always those most responsible for mass killings. The prosecutors selected a number of cases to establish new precedents, to prove, for example, that sexual humiliation should be regarded as a war crime even if it did not result in direct physical injury or even involve direct physical contact.[12]

A poor country, still recovering from the devastation of civil conflict and full-scale war, Rwanda could not, of course, provide comfortable or efficient support for an international institution. But the international tribunal avoided this problem by conducting its trials in neighbouring Tanzania. This meant that such justice as the tribunal provided would not be readily accessible to people in Rwanda – all the more so as the common language of Tanzania is English, while Rwanda is (apart from native languages) Francophone. Operating out of Arusha, Tanzania, made things more comfortable for UN officials. It does not seem to have done anything to speed the proceedings. It did not help things that the same prosecutor was in charge of the legal efforts in Arusha and the otherwise unrelated prosecution efforts of the Hague-based tribunal for the former Yugoslavia. Even when the UN Secretary-General insisted on appointing a separate chief prosecutor for Rwanda, the pace of activity in Arusha remained torpid.

The Security Council finally became so impatient with the dragging pace of proceedings that it demanded, in a resolution passed in August 2003, that the Rwandan tribunal (along with the comparably slow-paced companion tribunal for Yugoslavia) should plan on finishing all its trials by 2008. The international prosecutor for Rwanda subsequently announced that more than forty individuals it had been holding for possible future trials were actually "medium to low level participants" in the genocide, who could properly be transferred to "national jurisdictions" (that is, presumably, the Rwandan government) for less elaborate trials.[13]

Meanwhile, it turned out that extended trials afforded lucrative remuneration for UN-funded defence lawyers. So a number of foreign lawyers induced defendants to select them as official defence counsel by agreeing to split legal fees with the defendant or his family.[14] When the International Criminal Tribunal for Rwanda (ICTR) did turn to perpetrators of the most horrible crimes, then, it not only shielded them from quick justice but made them beneficiaries of international funding.

And no one was executed – at least not by the ICTR. By the terms of the tribunal's charter, the death penalty had been ruled out. At the time the tribunal was established, a majority of permanent members on the Security Council still provided for capital punishment in their own criminal justice systems, as many other respectable nations, such as Japan, still did (and do). But European governments and human rights organizations had become strongly opposed to capital punishment by the 1990s.

In the aftermath of the Second World War, European governments were content to single out only a few collaborators for public trials, but these trials often produced capital sentences. Precisely because they were not prepared to examine the full scope of their own contribution to the wartime genocide, European governments pursued exemplary executions to prove that, at least in some abstract moral sense, Europeans did take these crimes seriously. What had been acceptable punishment for those who assisted in mass murder in Europe, however, was now unacceptable for perpetrators of mass murder in Africa.

All in all, the ICTR did not give the impression to Rwandans that the United Nations was very concerned about winning their respect. The ICTR has, in fact, been the subject of persistent protest in Rwanda.[15] Five years after the tribunal was organized, the government of Rwanda was so exasperated with the conduct of the tribunal that it refused to provide a visa for the chief prosecutor of the ICTR to visit the country supposed to be tribunal's special concern.

The Balkan tribunal also became entangled in procedural refinements and has not compiled a much better record than that of the Rwandan tribunal. There was a similar pattern of delay, similar questions about priorities and similar concerns about justice at a distance, answering to its own bureaucratic imperatives.[16] The Security Council was, accordingly, no more sympathetic to pleas for more time from the Yugoslav tribunal than from its counterpart in Rwanda. The most celebrated trial, often cited as a sign of the tribunal's great achievement, has been the trial of former Serbian president Slobodan Milošević. But the Milošević trial actually reinforces doubts about the tribunal's effectiveness.

Milošević was indicted in the spring of 1999, in the midst of a NATO-led war on Serbia. The war was not authorized by the Security Council and was controversial in many countries, even in Europe. The timing of the indictment made it easy for Milošević to claim that he was the victim of a political manoeuvre – all the more so because the prosecutor who filed the indictment was a prominent jurist in a NATO nation, who was soon after honoured by her home government with an appointment to its Supreme Court. Eighteen months later, Milošević was forced from power when the Serbian military refused to support his efforts to disregard the electoral success of the Serbian opposition. But the new president, a former law professor, argued that extraditing Milošević to the Hague would violate Serbian law and this position was endorsed by the Serbian Supreme Court. When foreign governments (including the United States) insisted that the new Serbian democracy would forfeit outside financial assistance if it did not extradite Milošević to the Hague, the Serbian prime minister disregarded the objections of the Serbian president, court and members of his own cabinet to arrange a hand-over of Milošević in the spring of 2001.

The trial was still dragging on almost four years later, amidst complaints from western journalists that the prosecutors were not even making a very compelling case.[17] In the meantime, the prime minister who arranged the midnight delivery of Milošević was assassinated – apparently at the behest of conspirators in the Serbian military who feared further extraditions. The trial gave Milošević a platform to defend his past policies and stir nationalist feeling in Serbia. At the next elections, Milošević's party gained seats in the Serbian parliament – with one set aside for Milošević, himself. Rather than strengthening Serbia's path to democracy, the trial seems to have deepened old wounds and exacerbated political divisions.

Regardless of its impact on Serbia, the trial ground on and on and on. At Nuremberg, representatives of the Allied powers had agreed on indictments in June of 1945, commenced the formal trial three months later and finished the entire proceeding, down to the rejection of appeals and the carrying out of death sentences, within another twelve months. Even this was considered too long at the time and home governments seem to have pressured prosecutors to speed up the proceedings at the end. Some national governments proceeded with much more speed. In France, for example, the trial of Pierre Laval, the minister who designed and implemented French wartime collaboration with the Nazis, lasted a mere four days. The former prime minister was then executed the following week.

National governments in the aftermath of World War II were quite focused on the political effects of trials on European opinion. Whatever else one might say of the ICTY, it was not focused on Serbian opinion. Perhaps it was focused on justice. But for whose benefit? The ultimate objection to international criminal justice is that it does not even seem to be concerned with this fundamental political question. It is, in a way, premised on the notion that such questions need never arise.

Not even appealing in principle

To embrace international criminal justice, one must accept not only a new understanding of international law but a new understanding of criminal justice. For many centuries, the administration of criminal justice was thought to be the exclusive responsibility of sovereign governments – indeed, a defining attribute of sovereignty. At the bottom of this traditional view was the assumption that criminal justice is inherently connected with wider responsibilities of government. To separate criminal justice from wider governing authority, one must look at criminal justice in a different way. It is highly questionable whether it is a better way.

The absence of any provision for pardon or amnesty is a good illustration of this shift in perspective. Every country with a serious legal system makes some provision for overriding the normal legal system with a scheme for granting pardons. The power to grant pardons (or commutations of sentences) is usually vested in the executive. Legislatures usually have some parallel capacity to enact general amnesties. These powers are entrusted to political or politically accountable officials because the ultimate decision is assumed to reflect judgment and discretion rather than fixed rules. The whole point is to authorize exceptions from the normal rules when circumstances seem to justify exceptions.

Neither the ad hoc tribunals for Yugoslavia and Rwanda, nor the new ICC, make any provision for pardon. To acknowledge such a power in these institutions, it would be necessary to acknowledge that they do exercise some form of political authority. But why should individuals appointed by the UN Security Council or by a random list of governments participating in the ICC be entrusted with such political discretion? Would they make their decisions with an eye to the benefit of the particular nation most affected – the home state of victims, for example, or the home state of perpetrators? But it is not easy to explain why lawyers operating in the Hague are equipped to judge what is in the best interests of affected countries. Neither the judges of the various tribunals nor the prosecutorial staffs have been selected for the sake of their expertise in the politics or culture (or even the language) of the affected nations. Legal service in the Hague does not necessarily provide opportunities for acquiring such background mid-career.

The ad hoc tribunals were imposed without the consent of the affected nations and are not in any way accountable to national governments in these countries. No one has any good reason to think that those staffing these tribunals will have special insight into the best interests of the affected nations. With over 100 nations now eligible in principle to have their nationals prosecuted by the ICC, it is hopeless to imagine that the staff of the ICC will have special understanding of all these nations or even a large number of them. Perhaps the courts are supposed to serve the best interests of humanity as a whole? But what does that really mean? How does legal training equip lawyers in the Hague to judge the best interests of humanity?

All these insoluble challenges can be readily evaded if one simply refuses to ask whose interests are served by these institutions. The international courts will enforce the relevant international law. There is no political choice to make, because the international rule of law overrides political choice. The law is the law and must be enforced.

There is a political tradition behind this outlook. The Prussian philosopher Immanuel Kant insisted that adherence to formal rules was the essence of morality – and quite consistently with this philosophy, he argued that pardons were always improper. Kant's motto, *fiat justitia, pereat mundus* ("Let justice be done, even if the world perish"), was suitably globalist but not exactly humanitarian. Kant's strictures against compromise or exceptions were not so much animated by a demand for love of others or sacrifice on behalf of others. It is more accurate to say that the Kantian identification of moral duty with abstract rules was meant to efface any distinction between oneself and others – to establish, as Kant himself explained, the standard of conduct for an abstract "rational being" rather than an actual human being, living out his destiny in this world in a particular human body with a particular human soul.[18]

Kant was the first great philosopher whose intellectual efforts were financed, through his entire career, by a regular salary, supplied by a government ministry. Kant's sponsors in the Prussian state were, in their way, patrons of science and learning – at least, of approved sorts of science and learning, since the Prussian state was not exactly committed to free inquiry. Prussian authorities were also great patrons of administrative order and standardization – in a word, of bureaucracy. And the Kantian ethic has, at least, much in common with the bureaucratic ethic, with the notion that adherence to the rules is the highest duty, for the official and even for the citizen.

It hardly needs saying that this ethic could lend itself to very sinister ends. The most common defence offered by German war criminals, after the Second World War, was that, whatever horrors they may have perpetrated, they were "only following orders". Those who invoked this defence were not pleading that they were too frightened to resist but rather claiming – in a way that seemed honourable in their understanding – that they had acted from adherence to duty. At his trial in Jerusalem, Adolf Eichmann not only repeated this well-worn defence but explicitly invoked Kant's authority in explaining that he was bound to do his duty and not let his personal feelings interfere with his work. Judges at his trial (who happened to be trained at German universities before the war) demanded that the defendant explain how his actions could possibly have been consistent with "Kantian" morality. No less a philosophic authority than Hannah Arendt, who was present at the trial, acknowledged that Eichmann gave a reasonably competent summary of Kant's doctrine.[19]

Advocates of international criminal justice will certainly deny that their project has anything at all in common with such a demented extreme of legalism – of the doctrine that following rules is a good in itself. But the prosecutors in contemporary international tribunals regularly defend their decisions by claiming that they have no other criterion for decision except what the rules command. One must presume that they do mean to be taken seriously when they say such things. The claim, of course, is quite ludicrous. Even the ad hoc tribunals for Yugoslavia and Rwanda lack the resources to pursue more than a tiny fraction of those perpetrators who would, by consulting the rules alone, be eligible for prosecution. When it comes to the International Criminal Court, the disproportion between possible assertions of jurisdiction and actual resources for prosecutions is staggeringly vast. With a hundred countries subject to the court's jurisdiction, with the definitions of relevant "crimes" so detailed that routine abuses in almost every country's prison system might qualify for prosecution, each year will bring hundreds, perhaps even thousands of cases eligible for prosecution. The ICC Prosecutor has announced that his staff will actually attempt less than a dozen prosecutions in the Court's first five years.

On what basis, then, do prosecutors in international tribunals exercise their inevitable discretion to focus on a few cases and disregard the rest? It is absurd to claim that these decisions rest entirely on legal analysis of what the rules require. Yet international prosecutors cannot say that they exercise political judgment to determine which cases would be most beneficial to pursue. The prosecutors have no particular qualifications to determine what would be in the best interest of the states most affected by prosecutions. They have no particular qualifications to determine which prosecutions would best serve the interests of international stability or peaceful future relations among the largest number of states in the international community. Certainly there is no requirement that prosecutors and their staffs have any background in diplomacy, international relations, comparative politics or actual government service. The one thing the ICC Statute specifies is that the prosecutor should have some background in criminal law – as if "criminal law" were a universal science, essentially the same in all nations.

It may be more plausible to insist that the actual judges in international tribunals will attend only to the rules. But the claim is plausible only in comparison with the utter absurdity of the claim for prosecutors. The judges operate with a set of rules that are largely drawn from international treaties. Whatever patina of respectability this may give to the rules, however, it does not supply them with a well-established case law. Precisely because international criminal courts are such an innovation, the treaties they invoke do not have much history as actual criminal law standards. Even if one believes judges may, over time, be constrained in their decisions by the accumulating precedent of case law, there is not much precedent for international criminal courts to work with. And the judges do not, in fact, all come from countries where judicial precedent is an accepted authority for criminal courts. The procedure followed by these courts is an improvised synthesis of common law and civil law systems, something unique to the settings of these courts. Even the most conscientious and legalistic judge will often face decisions where there is little guidance from pre-existing rules, precedents or traditions. The judges are supposed to be experts in "criminal law" – again assumed to be an abstract, universal science.

There are many reasons to doubt that this view of criminal law is widely accepted. Among other things, one might notice no country currently appoints foreign judges to its own criminal courts. Many countries are prepared to entrust managerial responsibilities to gifted foreigners. The current head of the London transit system, for example, is an American. If criminal justice were simply a matter of abstract expertise, like managing a transit service, one would expect distinguished jurists from countries rich in legal experience – such as the United States – to be recruited to national courts in countries with less extensive experience in this field. But it never happens. Indeed, in an era when international agreements sponsor cross-border traffic in specialized services, as well as raw materials and manufactured goods, most countries still maintain considerable restrictions on legal services, even when it comes to appearing as defence counsel in the courts of another country.

The structure of international criminal courts really assures only one thing – that prosecutors and judges will have no direct connection to the countries most affected by their decisions (except in unusual cases). So, if the authority of international prosecutors and judges can't be justified by the empty pretence that they are merely following rules, it must fall back on the claim that they are, at any rate, not influenced by political concerns. They may not be bound by pre-existing rules in every decision they make, but at least they might be thought of as impartial. Of course, that was the real point of Kant's insistence on rigid adherence to rules. Any deviation from the rules might be motivated by self-interest or some personal passion. The international tribunals exalt the notion of impartiality without the actual legal constraint supposed to assure it.

It may seem another empty pretence. Judges and prosecutors are likely to be influenced by the preferences of their home countries, where they have launched their careers and may expect to resume such careers – if their own governments approve of their performance at the Hague. Even when a government is not directly affected by an international prosecution, it may have preferences or expectations about the proper outcome, depending on its own foreign policy aims. (Were the abuses at Abu Ghraib prison a deplorable exception or a sign of systematic American disregard for human rights? Nationals of countries most opposed to the American war might see the question rather differently from nationals of countries more generally sympathetic to the American effort.) In any case, the personnel of an international tribunal always have some interest in protecting or promoting the prestige of their institution, which may often influence their sense of whether it is proper to go forward with an unpopular prosecution or refrain from action when media outlets in powerful countries demand "justice".

Still, as questionable as it is likely to be in practice, the international tribunals do seem to rest on this premise – that impartiality is a good in itself. Otherwise, it is hard to understand why an outside tribunal is empowered to second-guess the decisions of a national government. In the extreme case, the national government may determine that amnesty will best serve the interests of that country. But the ICC is empowered to disregard this judgment – presumably in the interest of humanity at large. The ICC's one claim to better decision-making is that it is not affected by political pressures in the most effected country. One can, with only a bit of legal training, smile at the naive presumption that judges are really bound by nothing more than "the law". One cannot get past the insistent premise of the ICC that impartiality is a good in itself.

But why is it a good? Of course, it is advantageous in many ways to separate law from immediate political pressures or merely partisan sympathies. That is why every country with a serious legal system tries to insulate judges from immediate political pressures. But in the United States, a country with rather more experience with the rule of law than most participants in the ICC – and a much longer and more honourable experience of protecting human rights than almost any country in Europe – it is accepted that prosecutors exercise political judgment. In most US states, prosecutors are directly elected by voters, and even the federal

prosecutors are appointed by the president and must expect to be replaced when a new president (particularly a new president of a different
party) assumes office. In most American states, even judges are elected
for limited terms and in some states are subject to recall by special voter
initiatives. Even appointments to federal courts, where judges have life
tenure, are often the occasions for partisan contention, blocking confirmation of a judge who strikes the majority of senators as having questionable views.

Europeans are more comfortable with the pretence that judges and
even prosecutors can be seen as absolutely impartial servants of the state.
But even Europeans, with their authoritarian and statist traditions, do
not pretend that appointments to the highest judicial or legal posts can
be severed from political judgments of politically accountable cabinet
members or parliamentarians. As one moves higher up in the system,
the claims of political discretion have more weight even in European nations. And no country, even in legalistic, bureaucratic Europe, actually
fails to make provision for a pardon power or amnesty power, vested
entirely in the hands of political organs.

In practice, it is an astonishing innovation to claim that the ultimate
legal authority should reside in the authority with most claim to "impartiality" – with whatever content one chooses to pour into that amorphous
category. It is not merely an innovation in institutional practice but in political philosophy. It is, of course, contrary to any previous understanding
of democracy. It says that the highest and most important determinations
of the state – those dealing with justice – can, in principle, be entirely removed from any sort of accountability to the electorate of that state.
True, no modern democracy entrusts its justice system to citizen assem-
blies or even popular referenda. But even indirect means of accountability are lost in the international criminal justice scheme. The improvised,
haphazard interventions of the international court then demand to be accorded higher authority than decisions of national governments, even
those with long proven records of respect for law and justice.

Democracy is not well established in most countries. Even in Europe
it has proven quite fragile and elected governments have been quite willing to cede authority to supranational institutions. Still, the more telling
point is that the exaltation of "impartiality" is not merely contrary to
the liberal democratic ideals of countries, such as the United States,
that have preserved democracy for much longer periods. The exaltation
of "impartiality" is also contrary to the long history of natural law teaching nurtured and sustained by Catholic thinkers since medieval times. In
the older version of natural law, the law was seen as the guardian or
instrument of the common good. It was taken for granted, by Thomas
Aquinas in the thirteenth century, as by Francisco Suárez in the seven-

teenth century or Jacques Maritain in the twentieth century, that different nations inevitably will have different legal systems because what can be seen as the "common good" in one nation may reasonably be seen as not serving the "common good" of a different political community, which faces different circumstances with different traditions.

One may well believe that there is a higher law that rightfully claims a higher moral authority than the positive law that happens to have been enacted in any particular state. One may believe the version of the argument advanced by followers of Thomas Aquinas or the version advanced by followers of John Locke or Thomas Jefferson. But what makes this belief credible is the understanding that the higher law – whether one calls it natural law or natural rights or human rights – is not something that can be reduced to minute specifications, binding in all circumstances. Whether in the medieval natural law tradition or in the modern liberal tradition, the state was always seen as the necessary instrument of justice – precisely to give precision and reliable enforcement to law, in the here and now. In the alternative understanding, which seems to be the premise of international criminal law, it is enough for an international authority to pronounce the law for everyone to accept it. In this view, the higher law is a law for obedient slaves or programmable robots, not a law for human beings, endowed with reason and perception and the free will to follow different understandings.

The argument for entrusting the ICTY with the trial of Milošević or the ICTR with the trial of chief perpetrators of the Rwandan genocide is that only such tribunals will have "credibility". If the trials drag on and do not please the people in the affected countries, they still have more "legitimacy". Why? Because the legal technicians say so.

The claim is silly, but also revealing. In the United States, with a long established legal system, it is taken for granted that trials and trial results may remain controversial. Americans do not imagine that public scepticism can be answered by pointing to the credentials of the judges or the prosecutors or the architects of the relevant rules of criminal procedure. In the end, the justice administered by the state will not be perfect justice. Certainly, it cannot be expected that all citizens will see it that way. One does not even hope for such a thing, because it would imply that most citizens had lost their capacity to think – or think critically – and simply remained in awe of state authorities. God provides perfect justice. No state should aspire to be trusted, let alone venerated, as the ultimate Author of Justice.

The international tribunals, which have less reason to claim reliable justice, nonetheless have no fall-back except some claim to perfection. In a national state, one can argue that rulings must be accepted because the alternative is chaos. The alternative to the rule of international criminal courts is not chaos but the world as it has been for centuries – a world with many deficiencies, to be sure, but habitable for those with the discipline to maintain free and lawful government in their own countries. What to do about countries that have failed to master this political discipline is a serious question but sending judges and lawyers to tame them – or rather, messages from judges and lawyers in the Hague – is not a serious answer.

There is much to be said for the idea that all nations are bound by some higher authority, which rightly inhibits them from attempting everything they might otherwise be capable of doing. But there is, as has been noticed, much disagreement about the source of this authority – whether it is, for example, vouchsafed to us by Christian or by Islamic revelation or by the reasoning of the Stoics and the Church or by the Enlightenment and the eighteenth century revolutions. It is not visionary to hope that international dialogue may help to widen consensus. But it is likely that such consensus would never be so detailed and precise as the definition of crimes in the ICC Statute.

It is necessary for a functioning legal system to have precision. At least, it must have more precision than the conclusions of philosophers or religious visionaries, when it comes to precise definitions of precise crimes. That is why, until recently, it was always assumed that criminal justice required a state. It does not demonstrate the contrary that the UN Security Council or a conference in Rome can draw up detailed specifications for crimes when there is no capacity at the international level to enforce them, in any reliable sort of way, and no disposition, in reality, even to act as if international prosecutors deserved the same respect as actual authorities in actual states.

It is probably enough to say that the vision behind international justice is not realistic. But we should also acknowledge that it is not, even as an ideal, particularly appealing. It is, at some level, a vision of authority that is – like the Kantian philosophy and its various extensions in twentieth century Europe – not designed for human beings. Older and sounder political philosophies recognized that human beings may not always be entirely rational, at least as a philosopher might assess rationality. But they also recognized that human beings have a natural tendency to be political. No earlier political philosophy imagined that justice could be entirely separated from the common good of the particular community seeking to establish justice.

The philosophy that seems to animate contemporary visions of international criminal justice starts with a presumption that the highest justice, the most reliable justice, is that which is most removed from the common good of any particular political community. This philosophy may appeal to Europeans, because it echoes traditional authoritarian impulses. Perhaps it developed stronger appeal after the Second World War, as Europeans sought to ensure against a recurrence of their own worst political impulses by placing more and more political authority in the hands of technical experts, guiding a new, transnational "construction". It may be true, as some commentators claim, that Europeans support international criminal justice because they are now determined to safeguard the world at large from horrors that Europeans carried to the most systematic extreme in the twentieth century. But if guilt over past crimes does haunt Europeans, they seem, at least, very determined to abstract from the difference between countries that perpetrated such horrors (or collaborated in these crimes) and those countries with the strength and resolve to defeat the perpetrators of such crimes. On the premise of international criminal justice, all countries are potentially guilty, all stand in need of international correction and only those entities incapable of fighting or enforcing anything can be fully trusted – namely, the impartial legal staffs in the Netherlands.

It should not be surprising that many countries continue to reject this vision. Not all countries have the same need to escape from their own history. Not all countries have the same capacity to deny evident realities. Not all countries are so easily seduced by empty abstractions. If the world is not likely to accept the ongoing guidance of countries that have a better history, that indicates not that all countries must submit to common authority, but that each country should be left to come to terms with its own understanding of justice, given its own experience. That is what sovereignty offers. If it is sometimes necessary to make exceptions, as for humanitarian intervention against the most extreme abuses, the exceptions should still be seen as exceptional. The point of the International Criminal Court is to present the exceptions as somehow normal, because, after all, draped in the trappings of legality. The premise again is that all countries are in need of outside correction, because all countries may be partial to their own understandings and the highest and most reliable understanding is the most impartial – the most removed from any concrete experience, any concrete understanding, any concern for concrete consequences.

There is nothing in this vision that can appeal to Americans. There is very little in it that should appeal to any country that still has self-respect as an independent nation. The best that can be said for most countries that have embraced this project is that they do not really believe in it for themselves, but assume that it will be focused entirely on lesser nations, standing more in need of correction. The saddest thing about the project is that many countries that view it in this light actually believe they have done something valuable for the benefit of others – those others who need only outside lawyers to set them straight.

Notes

1. J. Bodin (1576) *Six Livres de la République*, Paris: Du Puys, vol. 1, p. 10.
2. For a detailed account of this episode, see W. H. Prescott (1960) *History of the Conquest of Peru* (reprinted with *History of the Conquest of Mexico*), New York: Modern Library, pp. 972–976, followed by reports of Spanish criticism of the action, starting shortly afterwards, pp. 979–981. The same nineteenth century author took pains, in recounting the trial and execution of the Aztec king, Montezuma, to show that the charge laid by conquistadors in that case – perfidy after previous surrender – "was justified by the law of nations", pp. 347–351, with citations to Pufendorf and Vattel, p. 350 n. 25.
3. F. Suarez (1612, 1944) "De Fide", in J. B. Scott, ed., *Selections from Three Works of Francisco Suarez, S.J.*, Oxford: Clarendon, limiting enforcement obligations of Christian kings to their own territories.
4. E. Kontorovich (2004) "The Piracy Analogy: Modern Universal Jurisdiction's Hollow Foundation", *Harvard International Law Journal* 45(183): 183–237, demonstrates the point with an impressive survey from actual cases on piracy.
5. J. E. Thomson (1994) *Mercenaries, Pirates, and Sovereigns: State-Building and Extra-Territorial Violence in Early Modern Europe*, Princeton, N.J.: Princeton University Press.
6. I have developed the decidedly non-international quality of the Nuremberg proceedings in a separate article. J. Rabkin (1999) "Nuremberg Misremembered", *SAIS Review* 19(81).
7. N. Barnett (2003) "Catch Me if You Can", *Spectator*, London, 6 September, reports activities of French military officials warning Serb suspects about impending arrests by NATO forces – evidently to advance unique French goals in the region. But, as the same author concedes, "even without French help, the Hague [that is, the ICTY] is quite capable of not catching [prominent figures such as] Radovan Karadžić on its own."
8. When the International Committee of the Red Cross offered to monitor bombing damage to civilian centres, by both German and British raids, British Prime Minister Winston Churchill dismissed the offer out of hand, arguing that the Red Cross would not be reliably impartial and in any case would simply impede British war strategy, which by then was almost entirely dependant on bombing raids on Germany. M. Gilbert (1983) *Winston S. Churchill: Finest Hour*, Boston: Houghton Mifflin, vol. 4, p. 832 n. 1.
9. E. MacAskill (2004) "UK Should Face Court for Crimes in Iraq, Say Jurists", *Guardian*, London, 21 January.
10. Gary Bass (2000) *Stay the Hand of Vengeance*, Princeton, N.J.: Princeton University Press.
11. The Annual Report of the International Criminal Tribunal for Rwanda (ICTR) for 2004 reports that, as of 30 June 2004, the tribunal had convicted 20 persons and acquitted three others. Another 19 trials were underway, with 6 more scheduled for the near future. See United Nations Security Council (2004) "Report of the International Tribunal for the Prosecution of Persons Responsible for Genocide and Other Serious Violations of International Humanitarian Law Committed in the Territory of Rwanda and Rwandan Citizens Responsible for Genocide and Other Such Violations Committed in the Territory of Neighbouring States Between 1 January and 31 December 1994", UN Doc A/59/183-S/2004/601, 27 July, New York: United Nations (ICTR Annual Report 2004).
12. If such precedent-setting efforts were a bid for mention in casebooks, they achieved their goal. See H. Steiner and P. Alston (2000) *International Human Rights in Context*, 2nd ed., Oxford: Oxford University Press, pp. 1187–1188, on cases designed to establish that "sexual violence" may "include acts which do not involve ... physical contact" and that "coercive circumstances need not be evidenced by a show of physical force" –

entirely plausible claims for a domestic legal system but not, one might think, of highest priority for prosecutors faced with an actual pattern of mass murder that had consumed 800,000 lives.

13. The Annual Report for 2004 indicates that 41 "individuals" had been identified over the preceding year as not requiring trial by the ICTR. It also reports the tribunal's intention to complete 65 to 70 trials overall by 2008 – that is, at least twice as many in the five years following the Security Council's imposition of a deadline as in the entire previous decade. Apparently the planned trials do not include 33 "suspects" or actual "indictees" not in the ICTR's custody. ICTR Annual Report 2004.

14. US House of Representatives Committee on International Relations, *UN Criminal Tribunals for Rwanda and the former Yugoslavia* (28 February 2002) 107th Congress (Pierre-Richard Prosper, Ambassador-at-Large for War Crimes Issues, responding to questioning from Representative Jo Ann Davis). The same hearing also includes discussion of procedural irregularities, such as prosecutors withholding exculpatory evidence (testimony of Larry Hammond, former attorney in the US Department of Justice).

15. See R. Sezibera (2002) "The Only Way to Bring Justice to Rwanda", *Washington Post*, Washington, D.C., 7 April, noting that national courts in Rwanda, with one-tenth of the funding supplied to the international tribunal, had rendered judgements in more than 5,000 cases, while the international tribunal was still struggling through its first dozen cases. Gary Bass notes that Rwandan national courts had handed down over 100 death sentences and a comparable number of sentences of life imprisonment in a period in which the international tribunal had not managed to conclude a single trial. "No one," he concludes, "should have expected the Rwandans to be as unconcerned about the punishment of the genocide as the UN was" (*Stay the Hand of Vengeance*, pp. 307–308). For an extended survey of complaints about the operations of the ICTR, see H. Nichols (2002) "U.N. Court Makes Legal Mischief", *Insight*, Washington, D.C., 23 December, concluding, "It's clear the lawyers and judges of the ICTR like the idea of working on behalf of humanity rather than something as trifling or temporal as a country such as Rwanda and its 800,000 dead."

16. The ICTY reported that, as of 14 October 2004, it had launched 86 indictments – but only 36 "judgments" (some of which involved procedural appeals rather than actual convictions). In its Annual Report for 2003, the tribunal reported that it was still pursuing 42 indictments, covering 74 individuals – but 18 of these individuals were still "at large" (that is, not yet apprehended), with more than half of the indictments in these cases (involving 10 individuals) already more than five years old. United Nations Security Council (2003) "Report of the International Tribunal for the Prosecution of Persons Responsible for Serious Violations of International Humanitarian Law Committed in the Territory of the Former Yugoslavia Since 1991", UN Doc A/58/297-S/2003/829, 20 August. These figures cover only "public" indictments. Sealed indictments are not reported – except when the tribunal decides to "unseal" them. More individuals have probably been indicted without being apprehended, since the tribunal does not hold prisoners in secret. How many indicted perpetrators are still "at large" is therefore not something that can be known, with precision, from public record. Among those still at large in the fall of 2004 were the chief organizers of the 1994 Srebrenica massacres.

17. See J. Laughland (2004) "Let Slobbo Speak for Himself", *Spectator*, London, 10 July; and C. Stephen (2004) "War Crimes Muddle", *Prospect*, London, 24 June. Laughland treats the problems of the Milošević trial as symptomatic of corruption in international institutions. Stephen concludes his criticism with a plea for the International Criminal Court as "the only alternative to America making up international law as it goes along." He treats the problems of the ICTY as illustrating "what happens when a court is left

too long to its own devices" – though he does not explain which (or whose) "devices" would provide better guidance for the ICC.

18. I. Kant (1965) "The Right to Punish", in J. Ladd, ed., *The Metaphysical Elements of Justice*, Indianapolis, Ind.: Bobbs-Merrill, p. 100: "The law concerning punishment is a categorical imperative and woe to him who rummages around in the winding paths of a theory of happiness looking for some advantage to be gained by releasing the criminal from punishment or by reducing the amount of it."

19. H. Arendt (1977) *Eichmann in Jerusalem*, New York: Penguin, pp. 135–138.

8

Dancing with the devil: Prosecuting West Africa's warlords – current lessons learned and challenges

David M. Crane

It was a warm day in March 2003. As a part of our town-hall program begun in September of 2002, I was in Makeni listening to my clients tell me what the conflict in Sierra Leone was all about; how the Court and my office, the Office of the Prosecutor, were doing from their point of view; and to answer any and all questions posed by the assembled citizens in the hall, the number of whom was estimated at around 300, not an uncommon turnout for these events. During the course of the meeting a young woman, holding a child, stood up waiting to ask a question or make a comment. After answering the question at hand I turned to her to allow her to speak. This young Sierra Leonean woman was missing a large part of her face, her burn scars radiated down her shoulder, chest and arms. Blinded by her horrific injuries and through cracked lips she whispered, "The rebels did this to me; do something about what they have done here".

The Special Court for Sierra Leone is a recognized hybrid international war crimes tribunal set up by the United Nations on behalf of the international community and the Republic of Sierra Leone to try those who bear the greatest responsibility for war crimes, crimes against humanity and other violations of international humanitarian law during the decade-long conflict in Sierra Leone in the 1990's. This bold new experiment in international criminal law initially began after Sierra Leone asked the United Nations to consider setting up a tribunal to investigate and prosecute individuals responsible for the atrocities committed in that lush tropical country. In August of 2000 the United Nations Security

Atrocities and international accountability: Beyond transitional justice, Hughes, Schabas and Thakur (eds), United Nations University Press, 2007, ISBN 978-92-808-1141-4

Council authorized the Secretary-General to explore the possibilities of setting up a tribunal.

In January of 2002, the UN Undersecretary General for Legal Affairs, Hans Corell, and the Attorney General of Sierra Leone at the time, Solomon Berewa, signed an international treaty creating the Special Court for Sierra Leone. Subsequently, the Republic of Sierra Leone passed the appropriate legislation ratifying that treaty. The next generation of international war crimes tribunals was born. In April, the Secretary-General appointed me to be the Prosecutor and Robin Vincent the Acting Registrar. Early that summer, Sierra Leone nominated Desmond De Silva to be the Deputy Prosecutor; he was subsequently confirmed in the fall.

The Registrar and an advance team from my office arrived in Sierra Leone in July, followed by myself on 6 August 2002. We began our investigations two weeks later, on 19 August, with a team of Sierra Leonean and international investigators. We have not stopped. Since then we have issued 13 indictments. Two indictees have since died, one by natural causes and the other murdered by Charles Taylor in May of 2003. Of the 11 outstanding indictments, 10 are in custody in various joint trials and only one remains at large. All of the major players in this conflict are accounted for and the trials began just 22 months after our arrival in the summer of 2002. These trials will most likely end in 2007.

The Special Court of Sierra Leone has four organs, the Office of the Prosecutor, the Office of the Registrar, the Chambers and the Defense Office. The Chambers consist of two trial chambers and an appellate chamber. The trial chambers are a mix of two international judges and one Sierra Leonean-nominated judge per chamber and the appellate chamber has five judges: three from the international community and two from Sierra Leone. The Court sits in Freetown, Sierra Leone.

What this paper will address are the key lessons learned from my perspective as the Prosecutor. Additionally, I will address the challenges faced as we investigated, indicted and prepared our cases for trial. It is hoped that these practical points outlined below will capture for interested readers and practitioners the multilayered complexities faced in prosecuting the warlords of West Africa.

What are the lessons learned so far?

As the year 2000 began, the world was becoming frustrated by the enormous costs of international justice. When Sierra Leone requested assistance in setting up a tribunal, the UN Secretary-General and the Security Council began to consider various ways international justice could be administered fairly, efficiently and effectively. The Special Court is the result, and I believe the international community got it right.

The mandate for the Court is achievable

Political events spawn all international war crimes tribunals, and these are inherently creatures of political compromise. The particular compromise that created the Special Court resulted in a mandate to try those "who bear the greatest responsibility" for war crimes, crimes against humanity and other serious violations of international humanitarian law. The operative word is "greatest". It is this adjective that makes the work of the Court achievable in a manageable period of time. By inserting this word, the number of potential indictees that could be indicted is less than two dozen. Change the word to "most" responsible and the number of indictees rises dramatically to 50 to 100 persons, with a minimum of ten years needed to fairly try them. Drop the adjective before responsibility and the number is unmanageable, the time indefinite. The purpose of the Court ceases to be a way to sustain peace, but a hindrance to any peace. The country or region would never be able to put the conflict and the resulting horrific crimes behind them. The wounds would never heal.

The time frame for the Court to do its work is realistic

The reason any tribunal should exist is to seek justice for the victims, their families and the society as a whole. A tribunal with an indefinite life span frustrates the expectations of that society and its citizens. The concept that the rule of law is more powerful than the rule of the gun is watered down and the foundations for a sustainable peace, a respect for the law, weakened.

It is certainly my opinion that no investigation or trial of war criminals should last more than three to five years. It is essential that the purpose of the Court be clearly understood by its staff and the citizens they serve. In our case, that purpose is to seek justice for the people of Sierra Leone. For them to have a chance to move on with their lives, to reconcile, and to heal from the trauma of conflict, three to five years is the right target.

However, where authorities obstruct the work of a tribunal and shelter its indictees, artificial deadlines should not shut down a tribunal and allow obstructionists to out-wait the rule of law. This was a significant problem with the international community's reluctance to turn over one indictee, Charles Taylor, until March 2006, three years after I signed his indictment on 3 March 2003.

Place the tribunal at the scene of the crimes

Because the Court is for and about the people of Sierra Leone, the location of the Court must be in Sierra Leone. That is where we are. It allows the people to see justice begin, work and end right before their very eyes in a time frame that causes less trauma to the society at large. Of course, being on location brings with it very real concerns such as security, health and availability of support, among other issues. Despite those challenges, the benefits far outweigh the risks. A devastated country needs to rebuild an infrastructure to carry it forward. The cornerstone to that building process is the rule of law. A distant and seemingly impersonal tribunal has a greater challenge to demonstrate this concept. The ability of the citizens within the region to feel a sense of justice and closure is severely tested. Politically, the existence of the Court can become a liability. The transition from conflict to sustainable peace becomes difficult.

Our experience of living in the middle of the crime scene allows for a better focus, ease in investigation and a more complete understanding of the pain and suffering of the populace. Freetown, Sierra Leone, is a hard place to live and work, but it is the right place for the Court to do its work.

An outreach and a legacy program are two keys to success

Early on in assembling my overall strategic plan for the Office of the Prosecutor, I factored in a town-hall concept where I would go out and listen to the people of Sierra Leone tell me what happened in their country. Eventually I would turn this and the outreach aspect of the strategy over to the Registry, which has a robust program headed by a Sierra Leonean and a dedicated staff.

During the first four months, our goal was to visit every district and every major town within that district. We accomplished this task just before Christmas of 2002. The town-hall concept continued during my three years in Sierra Leone. I visited my clients regularly to report to them on how the Court and my office were doing.

Though planned and developed well in advance, a typical event is a day-long affair. An outreach team arrived a day prior to talk to various chiefs and elders and to brief them on the next day's events. They usually were present and ran the program. The day of the event, the outreach team set up the venue and briefed the audience in general on the program and talked to them about the Special Court in general. I arrived and, after brief remarks, opened up the floor for comments and questions. It is in these settings that the citizens got to meet their prosecutor and allowed their prosecutor to understand in some small way the horror of the past conflict. My focus was never on the indictees but on the Court, the process and the organization of the Court. The central themes generally were that the rule of law is more powerful than the rule of the gun, no one is above the law and that the law is fair. After I left there was sometimes more discussion with the outreach team.

Additionally, our legacy program has been in existence since the beginning. As stated above, the Court is for and about the people of Sierra Leone. We need to leave to them not just the newly built complex just off Jomo Kenyatta Road in Freetown, but a cadre of trained and dedicated Court personnel to carry on the hard work after we depart. The Court works closely with the Sierra Leonean Bar Association, non-governmental organizations and other civil society organizations to develop creative projects that local and international organizations can sponsor in helping to rebuild a devastated judiciary. In many ways, the legacy program means that the Court will never leave Sierra Leone.

A truth commission is necessary for a sustainable peace

Over the past several years it has been shown that a truth commission and a war crimes tribunal can exist side by side, working on their respective mandates. It has become quite clear that in order to have a sustainable peace you have to have both truth and justice. We found that having a truth commission concurrent to the investigations and indictments of war criminals allows the citizenry to tell their story officially to the truth commission. The likelihood that citizens will actually testify before the Court was remote. I considered the Truth and Reconciliation Commission (TRC) in Sierra Leone a key partner in calming and assuring the citizens of the country that the complete story would be told and that truth and justice would prevail.

One of the important aspects of this professional co-existence was our decision immediately upon arrival in Sierra Leone that we would not use any information that was given or submitted to the TRC in our criminal investigation. I encouraged the people of Sierra Leone to go and talk to the TRC to tell their important stories. This they did in the thousands to include perpetrators who even confessed to crimes in an act of reconciliation.

A public defence office is essential for proper management and support of the defence teams

The citizens of Sierra Leone must understand that the law is fair. There must be an equality of arms between the prosecution and the defence teams. Early on in the development of the Court, Robin Vincent, our Registrar, conceived an innovative plan to model the defence on a public defender's office. The purpose of this was to appropriately manage the various defence teams and to ensure that they have adequate means by which to defend an indictee. The Principal Defender ensures that there is consistency in this support. On behalf of the Registrar, the Principal

Defender also manages the contracts for the various attorneys appointed to represent an indigent indictee.

A tribunal can tap unsuspected resources

While international war crimes tribunals at times can face difficulties in garnering material support, they can also look beyond obvious sources of assistance. Our office has done this, particularly through tapping into the deep support our work has enjoyed in academic circles.

In June 2002, before I even arrived in Freetown, we created the Academic Consortium, which consists of law schools from around the world enlisted to provide my office with legal research. Specifically, the Consortium has provided thousands of pages of legal research to our Appellate Section. This assistance from some of the world's best law schools was pivotal in helping my attorneys weigh their arguments in complicated jurisdictional matters heard by the Court's Appeals Chamber. These thorny issues included:

- whether an amnesty granted during peace negotiations applies to those charged by an international war crimes tribunal with violations of international humanitarian law;
- whether an international war crimes tribunal can be created outside of Chapter 7 of the UN Charter;
- when forcible recruitment of child soldiers crystallized as a crime under international humanitarian law; and
- whether a head of state is immune from prosecution before an international tribunal; among other key issues of international criminal justice.

For high-quality research on these issues and others, we had to pay nothing. For the law schools, their students' interaction with a war crimes tribunal on cutting-edge legal issues has been more than enough reward. Schools have eagerly sought to take part in this program, and we have even had to turn away some top law schools.

Challenges in prosecuting West African warlords

Despite the successes apparently achieved thus far, and the lessons learned, there are many challenges to prosecuting these warlords in West Africa. The overwhelming challenge is indifference to the plight of West Africa.

International indifference: The dark corners

All too often in places where the light of the law never shines – the dark corners – a horror erupts that shocks the international community. This condition is spawned by indifference bred by lack of understanding for or care about the region concerned. As in Rwanda, the international community, overtaxed and burdened with other challenges to peace and security, turned away from West Africa and shone that light elsewhere. The result of this decades-long lack of care was chaos and the resultant commitment of serious international crimes.

This indifference continues and challenges the Special Court politically and financially. Initially, the Special Court was to have been financed purely through voluntary contributions from UN member states. We received enough voluntary funding to last one and a half years, but then the political will to donate to a war crimes tribunal waned. Now the Special Court has had to return to the United Nations to receive assessed funds to help make up the shortfall. West Africa simply is not important to a jaded world suffering through the agony of a confused and uncertain future in Iraq. This focus has completely put West Africa back into its dark corner, war crimes tribunal and all.

Reaching out to the region: Communication

There is no mass media in Sierra Leone. In and around Freetown are several local newspapers, various radio stations, and one television station. The rest of the population's access to news and information is limited. The BBC radio program "Focus on Africa" is the principal way most Sierra Leoneans receive news.

It is imperative that a tribunal make its hearings and trials available and open to the public. With limited capacity internally to build such a capability, the tribunal is left to whatever the local communications infrastructure can bear.

Thus, an outreach program becomes important as it allows teams of workers from the Court, the Prosecutor, the Registrar and the Defense Office to go "up country" and report on the progress of the court proceedings and answer questions.

Geographic distance and location

Though properly placed within the scene of the crime, the remoteness of West Africa to the rest of the world and poor infrastructure within the region has taxed the ability of my office to support our investigators. Travel into and within West Africa is difficult at best and certainly not reliable. It is impossible to quickly move about to meet or react to situations requiring immediate attention. Movement is measured in days or weeks, not hours. It is also expensive. In many cases, travel to Europe and then back to Africa is the most efficient and effective way to ensure timely travel within the region.

Time

For political reasons, the lifespan of the Special Court was set initially at around three years. Though certainly possible to achieve the vast majority of the work, this timeframe does not leave a great deal of room for mistakes, calculated risks, missteps or obstruction. Time was the sword over all our heads and all decisions are measured with time in mind. This objective yardstick in the subjective world of the legal process certainly produces stress. Careful planning becomes essential in all that is done from prosecutorial strategy, support and travel, as well as whom to indict, when and on what charges. The Special Court is obsessed with time. It is important to note, however, that at the end of the day the rules of procedure and evidence, as well as our statute, govern the eventual decision as it relates to the fundamental rights of the accused and the proper representation of the victims by the Prosecutor.

Security

Part and parcel to living and working in Sierra Leone is the most important challenge of all: the security of the people and places affiliated with the Special Court. This includes witnesses and their families. My first consideration when developing overall general strategy was the security of my staff. I wanted them to have a safe place to live and to work. Presently they do.

With victims, perpetrators and witnesses living together throughout the country, security became problematic. Everyone is at risk, and that risk has increased with the start of trials. Early on in the life of the Court, security was a theory, but over time we have developed a considerable ability to protect ourselves. Coupled with the fact that we have a very supportive police force, the Court has many assets to draw upon if the risk or threat changes for the worse. In some capacity, peacekeepers will remain in Sierra Leone for the life of the Court.

Mandate enforcement

Created by international treaty at the behest of the UN Security Council, the Special Court was not created through Chapter 7 of the UN Charter. Thus, there is no Chapter 7 enforcement mandate. During the initial drafting of the statute it was considered to be unnecessary. In large part that is still the case; however, getting various states to assist in enforcing various court orders presented a challenge as well. Though most states have supported the Court in various bilateral agreements related to witness relocation and protection and sentence enforcement, requesting compliance with an arrest warrant for some indictees resulted in a political standoff. The outcome was uncertain and the credibility of the Court and the international community's commitment to ending impunity was at stake. Through patience and consistent diplomatic and political pressure, maintained largely by the Office of the Prosecutor, the former president of Liberia, Charles Taylor, was handed over for a fair trial in March 2006. He currently awaits trial by the Special Court for Sierra Leone in the Hague, in a courtroom leased to the Special Court by the International Criminal Court. It is anticipated that the trial will begin in January 2007.

Conclusion

The new hybrid international war crimes tribunal in West Africa, called the Special Court for Sierra Leone, is essentially showing the international community that international justice can be fairly, efficiently and effectively delivered to a war-torn part of the world in a way that allows the people to see that the rule of law is more powerful than the rule of the gun. The keys to success are an achievable mandate and a realistic time frame in which to accomplish the mandate, with the tribunal located in the place where the crimes took place. From that flows a better understanding by the citizenry of the legal process, that no one is above the law and that the law is fair.

The challenges this bold new experiment faces are manageable and can be overcome with proper leadership, management and financial and political support. Of all the challenges, international indifference and obstruction are the most serious of them all.

Impunity must not be allowed to exist in the twenty-first century. We must learn from the horrors of the past century. Mankind is better than that. War criminals and those who commit crimes against humanity must be held accountable before the law. There can be no exceptions.

9

The development of prosecutorial discretion in international criminal courts

Matthew Brubacher

The establishment of international criminal courts is a testament to the growing will of the international community to hold persons accountable for committing serious crimes. The creation of the International Criminal Court (ICC) as the first permanent international criminal court is just the latest effort to strengthen international law enforcement. While all international criminal courts build on one another's jurisprudence and practice, each court is a discrete international organization founded upon a specific constituent instrument created for a specific situation. The ICC, as a permanent court, is the first international criminal court created to address a variety of contexts. As each context has its own particularities, which cannot necessarily be foreseen, the ICC Statute contains jurisdictional and admissibility criteria that require the Prosecutor to consider an array of interests in both the investigative and prosecution stages.

Due to the nature of the crimes over which the ICC has jurisdiction, the Court will operate largely in ongoing conflicts where a host of other national and international initiatives are also working to address needs and find solutions. While the ICC must maintain its independence in pursuing its mandate to hold persons accountable, this paper will argue that the jurisdictional and admissibility criteria of the ICC, as well as the need to obtain effective cooperation, require the ICC to pursue a process of consultation and a sufficient degree of international consensus-building in order to forge the necessary degree of support to be effective. This paper will assess the unique jurisdictional and admissibility criteria of the ICC Statute, particularly the complementarity regime and the inter-

Atrocities and international accountability: Beyond transitional justice, Hughes, Schabas and Thakur (eds), United Nations University Press, 2007, ISBN 978-92-808-1141-4

ests of justice, and compare these provisions to the statutes of the International Tribunal for the former Yugoslavia (ICTY) and the Special Court for Sierra Leone (SCSL). Before evaluating the statutory criteria of the ICC as well as the policies being developed by the ICC Office of the Prosecutor (ICC-OTP), the paper will first explore the purposes of prosecutorial discretion and the trigger mechanisms that may initiate an investigation by the Prosecutor.

The purpose of prosecutorial discretion

Since the time of the Nuremberg Tribunals, the ability of the prosecutor to determine whom to prosecute and when has been a central element of every international criminal court.[1] This power was explicitly included in the *ex officio* powers of the ICTY[2] and the SCSL.[3] In the ICC, prosecutorial discretion is implied as the Statute uses the non-compulsory language of "may" instead of "shall" in reference to the decision to initiate an investigation.[4]

There are numerous reasons why prosecutorial discretion is included within the legal regimes of international criminal courts. Firstly, by virtue of the nature of crimes over which international criminal courts are established, the courts will always be established either within or in the wake of widespread armed conflict and have jurisdiction over potentially thousands of cases.[5] As the trial of every potential offence by the court is a practical impossibility, prosecutors must be able to select those who are to be investigated in order that the system ensures that resources are directed toward the right investigations.[6]

As stated by former ICTY Prosecutor Louise Arbour,

> An immediate distinction can be seen between the work of these Tribunals and a domestic criminal justice system because a domestic prosecutor is never really seriously called upon to be selective in the prosecution of serious crimes. Crimes are committed, they are reported, investigated, charges are brought, and the prosecutors prosecute all major crimes where the evidence permits. By contrast, in the work of the international Tribunals, the prosecutor has to be highly selective before committing resources to investigate or prosecute.[7]

The need for selectivity was particularly pronounced in the SCSL, particularly as the Court was originally created with an anticipated life span of three years.[8]

Although the permanent nature of the ICC reduces the time pressures faced by the SCSL, capacity limitations remain, particularly as the ICC has global jurisdiction and, consequently, a potentially high number of cases. The magnitude of potential situations is already indicated by the fact that, in less than three years, the OTP has received a UN Security Council referral,[9] three state referrals and some 1,400 communications concerning possible cases.[10] Obligating the Prosecutor to launch investigations into all of these situations would be a practical impossibility. Instead, the Prosecutor is expected to be judicious in the selection of cases.[11]

The need to restrict the number of cases contributed to the creation of a general policy among international criminal courts to focus on those most responsible for committing the most serious crimes. Soon after the creation of the ICTY, former Chief Prosecutor Richard Goldstone stated that the policy of the ICTY was to focus on those who are in senior positions of authority and are the most responsible for the crimes.[12] This policy of focusing on those most responsible was explicitly included in the SCSL Statute, where Article 1 provides the Prosecutor the "power to prosecute persons bearing the greatest responsibility".[13] Although not explicitly stated in the ICC Statute, the multiple references to "exercise jurisdiction over persons for the most serious crimes of international concern",[14] as well as the references to the "gravity of the crime",[15] informed the decision of the ICC-OTP to focus on those most responsible for committing crimes. As stated in a draft ICC-OTP policy paper, "As a general rule, the Office of the Prosecutor should focus its investigation and prosecutorial efforts and resources on those who bear the greatest responsibility, such as the leaders of the State or organisation allegedly responsible for those crimes".[16]

Another reason for including prosecutorial discretion is that it provides the prosecutor with the independence and insulation from external influences to give effect to the rule of law.[17] As international criminal courts are created to provide accountability for all persons, including government officials, it would be contradictory to allow these same individuals the ability to determine when to allow and disallow the Court to initiate an investigation.[18] Only through the independent exercise of prosecutorial discretion will international criminal courts, including the ICC, be able to hold all persons accountable regardless of their position or the political interests of states.[19]

Trigger mechanisms

As at the ICTY and SCSL, the Prosecutor of the ICC is responsible for receiving *notitia criminis* ("referrals and any substantiated information on crimes"), which will trigger an investigation.[20] However, unlike the ad hoc tribunals where no explicit preference was given to the source of *notitia criminis*,[21] the ICC Statute provides three sources, which some commentators believe are arranged in a hierarchy that implicitly favours those received by governments.[22]

The three so-called "trigger mechanisms" include a referral by the UN Security Council, a state or any other source.[23] The confidence in government referrals is evidenced by the fact that a referral made by a state[24] or by the Security Council when acting under Chapter 7 of the UN Charter[25] is not subject to the same procedural safeguards as investigations launched by the Prosecutor *proprio motu*,[26] and can be processed more expeditiously.[27] While all investigations, regardless of the trigger mechanism, begin only after a preliminary investigation by the Prosecutor determines that a *prima facie* case exists,[28] the Prosecutor must seek Pre-Trial Chamber (PTC) authorization before launching a formal investigation *proprio motu*.[29] The procedural safeguard requiring PTC authorization ensures that, in the absence of state backing, the Prosecutor will have the judicial backing of the Court.[30]

Although there is a different procedure within the Statute to facilitate action by the Prosecutor for state referrals, communications from other sources are important, as they provide the Prosecutor not only with the option of launching an investigation *proprio motu* but provide information and an ability to engage national authorities in encouraging cooperation. This ability to constructively engage with states prior to a referral was practiced by the ICC-OTP during the preliminary analysis of the Democratic Republic of Congo (DRC). In this situation, the Prosecutor announced his interest in investigating the situation in the Ituri Province and invited the support and cooperation of the government of the DRC.[31] After a period of engagement, the Government of the DRC decided to refer the situation to the ICC, thereby strengthening the cooperative relationship of the ICC-OTP with the national authorities.[32]

Invigorating the principle of complementarity

Unlike the ICTY[33] and SCSL,[34] which have primacy over national courts, the ICC-OTP must defer to genuine national proceedings.[35] The complementarity regime under the ICC Statute allows states the first chance to exercise jurisdiction.[36] States have the ability to challenge the admissibility of a case once the Prosecutor provides notice of his intention to investigate.[37] This regime was unknown in previous international courts and could be viewed as an impediment to the ability of the ICC to operate effectively. However, the ICC-OTP is transforming this limitation into a proactive strategy to close the impunity gap.

The impunity gap refers to the fact that international courts will prosecute only a limited number of those responsible for committing crimes, leaving the majority of lesser offenders unaccountable. This gap is particularly acute for the ICC, as the 2005 Budget for the ICC provides funding for full investigations into only three situations[38] and even within these situations the Prosecutor will conduct a very focused investigation.[39] To address this limitation, the ICC-OTP is developing a policy of "positive complementarity" that emphasizes the responsibility of national authorities, as the primary law enforcers, to hold individuals accountable.[40]

The legal regime that enables "positive complementarity" derives from the duty of the Prosecutor to evaluate information provided on alleged crimes[41] and assess whether national proceedings are or have already investigated these allegations.[42] During this preliminary analysis, the Prosecutor has the ability to seek additional information from other sources in order to determine whether to initiate a formal investigation.[43] If national proceedings exist, the Prosecutor must defer to those systems but is required to monitor whether the investigations and prosecutions are genuine.[44] Rather than compete for jurisdiction, the complementarity regime allows the Prosecutor to encourage national authorities to proceed with domestic proceedings.

The policy being developed by the ICC-OTP to encourage genuine national proceedings involves an interchange between developing partnerships with the national authorities and vigilance over their performance.[45] In terms of partnership, the ICC-OTP could provide assistance in information, investigative and forensic expertise and training to national authorities in order to improve their capacity to investigate. Similarly, the ICC-OTP could use its networks to encourage other international organizations and non-governmental organizations to become involved in increasing the capacity of national authorities.

At the same time, the ICC-OTP retains the ability to review its decision to launch an investigation in light of new facts, including indications that the national authorities are unable or unwilling to genuinely investigate the accused.[46] This ability to review the genuineness of national proceedings and re-examine a decision on whether to initiate an investigation provides the ICC-OTP with the independence and vigilance necessary to give momentum to its partnership with national authorities.

The policy of positive complementarity also has the potential to create the ability for the ICC-OTP to work with judicial and quasi judicial processes capable of holding persons accountable and furthering national reconciliation processes. As stated in the UN Secretary General's report on the rule of law and transitional justice,

> We must learn as well to eschew one-size-fits-all formulas and the importation of foreign models, and, instead, base our support on national assessments, national participation and national needs and aspirations.[47]

The ICC must avoid being perceived as imposing the law from high above without an appreciation for local legal and cultural traditions.[48] Although there are limitations as to the extent to which national or local proceedings such as truth commissions can constitute genuine national proceedings as required in the ICC complementarity regime,[49] such mechanisms can work to close the impunity gap in a manner more appropriate to the local context and should be encouraged.

Increased sensitization of the OTP-ICC to contextual factors

The statutes of the ICC and of the ICTY and SCSL all provide a mandate to prosecute those persons most responsible for committing serious crimes. However, the ICC Statute provides greater reference than previous international criminal courts to specific elements that require the Prosecutor to take contextual matters into consideration. In the ICTY Statute, there are no explicit qualifications to the exercise of prosecutorial discretion beyond the territorial and temporal limitations. Rather, the ICTY Statute provides a clear mandate to the Prosecutor to investigate and prosecute persons responsible for serious violations of international humanitarian law.[50]

Under this mandate, former ICTY Chief Prosecutor Richard Goldstone adopted a policy of indicting those who are the most responsible for crimes "without regard to political considerations or consequences".[51] This policy was reiterated by Goldstone's successor, Louise Arbour, when she stated, "It is unacceptable for any court to be at the mercy of outside interests".[52] Given the clear mandate provided in the ICTY Statute and given the Court's Chapter 7 authority obligating all states to comply with its decisions, this policy is understandable.

The prosecutorial mandate articulated in the SCSL Statute is similar to that of the ICTY in its unqualified emphasis on holding the most responsible accountable. Article 1 provides the Prosecutor with the "power to prosecute persons bearing the greatest responsibility".[53] Given this mandate, Prosecutor David Crane adopted a policy similar to that of the ICTY in pursuing investigations and arrests despite their political consequences. In the Prosecutor's opening statement for the trial of the Revolutionary United Front leaders, Crane emphasizes the gravity of the crimes above other considerations: "Despite the obvious political dimension to this conflict, these trials, this trial, are about crimes; and these individuals are indicted for those crimes, the most grievous of acts that a person can be charged with by mankind – war crimes and crimes against humanity."[54]

However, unlike the ICTY Statute, whose authors appear to have assumed that the operation of the international tribunal would contribute to peace,[55] the Statute for the SCSL explicitly emphasizes the importance of prosecuting "leaders who, in committing such crimes, have threatened the establishment of and implementation of the peace process in Sierra Leone".[56] While this provision does not require the Prosecutor to target those leaders who threaten the peace process in Sierra Leone, the reference does reflect the intention of the court to play a positive role in the implementation of the national peace process, including focusing on those leaders who may disrupt the stability of that country.

The SCSL Statute also provided limited reference to the interests of victims. Article 15 states that "[in] the prosecution of juvenile offenders, the Prosecutor shall ensure that the child-rehabilitation programme is not placed at risk and that, where appropriate, resort should be had to alternative truth and reconciliation mechanisms, to the extent of their availability".[57] Although this provision is limited to only juvenile offenders, ensuring that child combatants are provided with special protection was important to the larger victim community, given the high number of children forcibly conscripted into the conflict.[58]

This emphasis on the need to contribute to furthering efforts to achieve peace and serve the interests of victims was given increased effect in the ICC Statute. Article 53 provides that in assessing whether a reasonable basis exists to launch an investigation or prosecution, the Prosecutor must take account of the interests of justice, which include the gravity of the crime, the interests of victims and the circumstances of the accused.[59] Given the wide range and unforeseen complexities in which the ICC would operate these contextual elements requires the Prosecutor to balance a range of competing interests in the pursuit of justice.

Victim participation

Public prosecutors have a general obligation to consider the views and concerns of victims when personal interests of victims are affected.[60] The ICC Statute complies with this obligation by directing the ICC-OTP to take the interests of victims into consideration when deciding to initiate an investigation or prosecution.[61] In fact, this consideration may be taken continually throughout the investigative process. Taking the "interests of victims" into account is given increased effect by the ability of victims to make representations before the PTC when the personal interests of victims are affected at a stage in the proceeding determined appropriate by the Court.[62]

As the term "proceedings" is not clearly defined in this provision and as the Court has not had an opportunity to provide guidance on this issue, victim representatives could theoretically make representations before the commencement of a trial that would allow them to make submissions on questions of jurisdiction and admissibility.[63] Given this ability and given that the definition of victims is relatively wide,[64] the Chambers appears to have a wide degree of discretion to allow victims' legal representatives to make applications on matters traditionally within the remit of Prosecutorial discretion.

Interests of justice

As public servants, prosecutors of international criminal courts represent the interests of the entire international community. According to UN guidelines, international prosecutors have an obligation to protect the public interest, act with objectivity, take account of the circumstances of the suspect and the victim and pay attention to all relevant circumstances.[65] While public policy interests are applicable to all international courts,[66] the ICC Statute identifies specific elements of public policy by including in Article 53 the element of "interests of justice" into determinations as to whether to proceed with an investigation or prosecution. The wording of Article 53 posits the interests of justice as an element that may in exceptional circumstances counter the presumption of proceeding with criminal proceedings after finding a reasonable basis:

> Taking into account the gravity of the crime and the interests of victims, there are nonetheless substantial reasons to believe that an investigation would not serve the interests of justice.[67]

The wording of Article 53(1)(c), places the gravity of the crime and interests of victims in a manner that appears to favour decisions to launch investigations. This construction was likely due to the assumption that victims generally desire redress for harm suffered. Article 53(2), however, does not place the interests of victims and the gravity of crimes in opposition to the "interests of justice" but constructs them as part of a non-exhaustive list of elements to be taken into consideration in making determinations on whether to proceed.[68] The difference in construction, however, is unlikely to be of great significance, particularly given that both determinations contain similar elements and both are made only after a positive determination to proceed has been taken.

The content of the "interests of justice" is a matter of debate, with some authors arguing that the definition should include considerations as broad as the possible effect of criminal proceedings on peace and stability[69] while others, particularly from the human rights community, argue for a more restrictive interpretation.[70] Those that argue for a more limited scope of the criteria argue that it must be interpreted in light of the object and purpose of the statute, which in the ICC Statute is oriented toward permanently reducing impunity.[71] The more limited scope may be further evidenced by the use of the "interests of justice" in Articles 55(2)(c), 65(4), and 67(1)(d), all of which restrict the use of interests of justice to matters regarding the rights of the accused or victims as affected in the course of an investigation or trial.

While the construction of Article 53 suggests that the interests of justice may only in exceptional circumstances displace the presumption in favour of prosecutions, its inclusion does require the Prosecutor to conduct a type of balancing test between the need to pursue accountability and other countervailing facts and circumstances particular to the situation or case in question that may result in a reason not to proceed.

As victims' interests may include an interest to avoid the pursuit of justice undermining the safety of themselves or their community, the Prosecutor may take contextual matters of peace and security into account. However, it would be misleading to equate the interests of justice with the interests of peace. Were a situation to arise whereby ICC involvement directly threatens peace and stability, the authors of the Statute included Article 16, which allows the Security Council to defer an investigation or prosecution for one year by issuing a Chapter 7 resolution. The insertion of this provision is significant as the mandate and capacities of this body are more capable in resolving conflicts between peace, justice and security than is a judicial body such as the ICC.

That said, the insertion of the interests of justice does require the Prosecutor to assess the contextual ramifications of an intervention into a situation. With global jurisdiction over crimes of international concern and with a mandate to pursue those persons in positions of leadership,[72] the political effects of investigations and prosecutions will be significant, particularly given the fact that the temporal limitation and the policy of investigating the gravest crimes will orient the ICC to opening investigations involving ongoing armed conflicts.[73]

Proceeding with prosecutions in the midst of an ongoing conflict may complicate situations if those indicted are political leaders who have public support or are seen as key personalities in a possible negotiated settlement.[74] As stated by one observer of the preparatory conference on the drafting of the ICC Statute, "No peace without justice yes but in rare cases justice might need to be deferred for a while in order to ensure the adoption of a peace settlement".[75] It should be noted that any decision not to proceed based solely on the "interest of justice" is reviewable by the Chambers and any such decision can be reviewed on the basis of additional information.[76]

The impact of an investigation and prosecution on regional stability will also affect the effectiveness of an investigation as states are unlikely to support activities of the Court that undermine security. While state parties and international organizations with which the ICC has agreements have an obligation to ensure that ICC decisions, including issuing warrants, are given effect,[77] the Court will need steadfast support going beyond the narrow legal obligations of the Statute.

Need for state cooperation

With no policing power or enforcement agencies and little ability to seize evidentiary material, the ICC-OTP is highly dependent on cooperation, particularly the cooperation of national authorities. As stated by the ICTY, "In the final analysis, the International Tribunal may discharge its functions only if it can count on the *bona fide* assistance and cooperation of sovereign States".[78] As with other international criminal courts, the effectiveness of the ICC depends on its ability to solicit the cooperation of governmental and non-governmental organizations.[79] To acquire this cooperation requires not only an application of rules but also an effort to synchronize state interests in pursuing a particular course of action that furthers the strategic interests of the Court. Although still in its early stages of development, the policy of ICC-OTP Prosecutor Luis Moreno-Ocampo reflects the range of diverse interests that need to be taken into consideration. In the draft policy paper, the OTP states: "It is clear in the first place that no investigation can be initiated without having careful regard to all circumstances prevailing in the country or region concerned, including the nature and state of the conflict and any intervention by the international community".[80]

To ensure that these contextual matters are taken into consideration and that cooperative links are systematically developed, the OTP created a division specifically to address these issues. The Jurisdiction, Cooperation and Complementarity Division is new to international criminal courts, but was considered necessary given the unique jurisdictional and admissibility provisions and the need to forge cooperative links with a diverse range of state parties, non-state parties, non-governmental organizations and international organizations.[81]

The need to evaluate factors such as the interests of justice, as well as the need to maintain the cooperation of national and international authorities, requires the Prosecutor to act in coordination with other bodies to a greater degree than the other international criminal courts. The ICC does not have the established support of national authorities as did the SCSL, nor does it have the support of the United States, who provided a quarter of the budget for the SCSL[82] and was a main financial backer of and enforcer for the ICTY.[83] Rather, the ICC must engage with willing actors in order to forge a sufficient degree of support to proceed forward.[84] To do this, the ICC-OTP must engage in a wide consultative process with national and international actors in order to assess the situation, the effect of ICC intervention on the dynamics of the conflict and the prospects for forging effective cooperation. Through this consultative process, the ICC-OTP can create the relationships necessary to acquire cooperation with the relevant actors to the region. This process may also contribute to the ICC-OTP harmonizing its intervention with the array of other local and international initiatives working to address a particular conflict. As stated in a recent report by the UN Secretary-General, by recognizing the political context and working to synchronize efforts and generate sufficient consensus, justice can be integrated as a component of conflict resolution as well as of the transition to a post-conflict situation.[85]

Finding the balance

International criminal courts are established to hold those most responsible for committing the gravest crimes to account. However, in situations of ongoing armed conflict, the tension between obtaining justice and seeking a political settlement must be managed responsibly. Maintaining the balance between these two interests is one of the greatest challenges confronting the establishment of a credible international justice system. Although international prosecutors must act judiciously to uphold international law, there can be no oversimplification of the complexities in which the Court operates or its impact on conflicts.[86] While the absoluteness of rules must be maintained, a degree of flexibility in enforcing those rules is necessary to maximize the positive impact of the respective actors and pursue justice in a manner that prevents further victimization.

The experience of previous international criminal courts demonstrates that the pursuit of justice must be tempered to some extent by the realities of the context in which the courts operate.[87] Just as peace and security are expressly interdependent in the UN Charter, the interests of justice and peace are also inextricably interrelated.[88] Maintaining a balance between the two is complex and priorities need to be adjusted with time.[89] As stated by Richard Goldstone after his term as ICTY Prosecutor, for lasting peace to emerge "an appropriate balance" has to be found in each context between justice and reconciliation.[90] International criminal courts cannot be parties to a negotiated settlement but can contribute to reducing crime and re-establishing the rule of law. However, the dynamics of every situation are different and what works to temper one armed conflict may inflame another.

While prosecutors from previous international tribunals had a limited statutory ability to take matters of peace and stability into consideration, the array of interests identified in the ICC Statute obligate the Prosecutor to exercise a higher degree of sensitivity to these matters. The ICC-OTP cannot be viewed as blind or obstructive toward efforts to achieve peace and security, as to do so could expose the local population to increased insecurity – a result that would challenge the long-term integrity of the ICC and may result in the withdrawal of cooperation, which could ultimately make the Court ineffective.

Advocates and practitioners alike must realize that justice is merely one aspect of the multifaceted approach needed to secure enduring peace in a transitional society.[91] Developing an adequate response to conflict and post-conflict situations depends on a high level of coordination between non-governmental organizations, governments and international organizations.[92] While international prosecutors must maintain independence in the exercise of their discretion, their effectiveness will ultimately be dependent on the degree of cooperation that they receive and their ability to synchronize their activities with other actors. This dependence is not wholly "unhealthy" as presented by Arbour,[93] as it requires international criminal courts to operate in coordination with, rather than in opposition to, international efforts to address conflicts.

Notes

1. While the discretion of the Chief Prosecutors in the International Military Tribunals of Nuremberg and Tokyo were subject to the guiding principles of selection agreed upon by the Allies, the Charter for both the Nuremberg and Tokyo Tribunals provided that the Chief Prosecutors were responsible for the "final designation of major war criminals to be tried by the Tribunal". Charter of the International Military Tribunal (8 August 1945), art. 14(b) and Charter of the International Military Tribunal of the Far East (19 January 1946), art. 8(a). See also T. Taylor (1992) *The Anatomy of the Nuremberg Trials*, New York: Knopf, p. 40.
2. Statute of the International Criminal Tribunal for the former Yugoslavia (25 May 1993), S/RES/827 (ICTY Statute), art. 18(1).
3. Statute of the Special Court for Sierra Leone (16 January 2002) (SCSL Statute), arts 1(1), 15(1).
4. Rome Statute for the International Criminal Court (adopted 17 July 1998, entered into force 1 July 2002), UN Doc A/Conf. 183/9 (ICC Statute), arts 13, 53, 54.
5. Though there were thousands of possible suspects, only 24 were actually indicted by the Chief Prosecutors in the Nuremberg Tribunal and only 28 in the Tokyo Tribunal. M. Bergsmo, C. Cisse and C. Staker (2000) "The Prosecutors of the International Tribunals: The Cases of the Nuremberg and Tokyo Tribunals, the ICTY and ICTR, and the ICC Compared", in L. Arbour, A. Eser, K. Ambos and A. Sanders, eds, *The*

Prosecutor of a Permanent International Criminal Court, Freiburg im Breisgau: Edition Luscrim, p. 123.

6. United Nations Economic and Social Council (1997) "The Administration of Justice and the Human Rights of Detainees", E/CN.4/SUB.2/1997/20 [48].

7. L. Arbour (1997) "Progress and Challenges in International Criminal Justice", *Fordham International Law Journal* 21: 531–535.

8. According to Article 6 of the SCSL Statute, the Court may receive voluntary funding from states. As a result, the SCSL has had difficulty obtaining sufficient funding. See Human Rights First, "The Special Court for Sierra Leone", available from http://www.humanrightsfirst.org/international_justice/w_context/w_cont_04.htm.

9. On 31 March 2005, the Security Council referred the situation of Darfur to the ICC. See UN Security Council Resolution 1593 (31 March 2005), UN Doc S/RES/1593.

10. ICC-OTP (2005) "Prosecutor Receives Referral Concerning Central African Republic", press release, The Hague: ICC-OTP, 7 January; ICC-OTP (2004) "Prosecutor Receives Referral of the Situation in the Democratic Republic of Congo", press release, The Hague: ICC-OTP, 19 April; ICC-OTP (2004) "President of Uganda Refers Situation Concerning the Lord's Resistance Army (LRA) to the ICC", press release, The Hague: ICC-OTP, 29 January.

11. M. Caianiello and G. Illuminati (2001) "From the International Criminal Tribunal for the former Yugoslavia to the International Criminal Court", *North Carolina Journal of International Law & Commercial Regulation* 26: 407.

12. R. Goldstone, quoted in P. Williams and M. Scharf (2002) *Peace with Justice? War Crimes and Accountability in the former Yugoslavia*, Oxford: Rowland & Littlefield, p. 114.

13. SCSL Statute, art. 1(1).

14. ICC Statute, Preamble [4], arts 1, 5.

15. ICC Statute, arts 17, 53.

16. ICC-OTP (2003) "Paper on Some Policy Issues before the Office of the Prosecutor", The Hague: ICC-OTP, September, p. 7, available from http://www.icc-cpi.int/library/organs/otp/030905_Policy_Paper.pdf.

17. M. Bergsmo and P. Kruger (1999) "Article 54", in O. Triffterer, ed., *Commentary on the Rome Statute of the International Criminal Court* (Baden-Baden, Germany: Nomos-Verlagsgesellschaft).

18. Human Rights First *International Criminal Court Briefing Series* 1(1): 10–11.

19. International Committee of the Red Cross (1998) "Establishing an International Criminal Court: Towards the End of Impunity", available from http://www.icrc.org/Web/Eng/siteeng0.nsf/html/57JP2P; also see Amnesty International (1994) "Establishing a Just, Fair and Effective International Criminal Court", AI-Index IOR 40/005/1994, New York: Amnesty International, p. 27.

20. ICC Statute, art. 42(1).

21. ICTY Statute, art. 18(1); Statute of the International Criminal Tribunal for Rwanda (8 November 1994), S/RES/955, (ICTR Statute) art. 17(1).

22. G. Turone (2002) "Powers and Duties of the Prosecutor", in A. Cassese, P. Gaeta and J. R. W. D. Jones, eds, *The Rome Statute of the International Criminal Court: A Commentary*, Oxford: Oxford University Press, vol. 2, p. 1144.

23. ICC Statute, art. 13.

24. ICC Statute, arts 13(a), 14.

25. ICC Statute, art. 13(b).

26. ICC Statute, arts 13(c), 15.

27. Referrals by the Security Council may be processed more quickly due to the fact that the OTP does not have to notify states of its intention to investigate. See ICC Statute

art. 18. Commentators have suggested that this gives rise to "fast track" proceedings. See M. Bassiouni (1998) "Observations on the Structure of the (Zutphen) Consolidated Text", *Nouvelles Etudes Penales*, Pau, France: International Association of Penal Law, p. 13.

28. Bergsmo and Kruger, "Article 54", p. 705.
29. ICC Statute, art. 15(3).
30. Gurmendi (2001) "The Role of the Prosecutor", in M. Politi and G. Nesi, eds, *The Statute of the International Criminal Court: A Challenge to Impunity*, Burlington, Vt.: Ashgate Press, p. 56; International Law Commission (1994) "Report of the ILC on the Work of Its Forty-Sixth Session", UN Doc A/49/10, cited in P. Kirsch and D. Robinson (2002) "The Debates at the Rome Conference", in A. Cassese, ed., *The Rome Statute for an International Criminal Court: A Commentary*, Oxford: Oxford University Press, p. 661.
31. ICC-OTP (2003) "The Prosecutor on the Co-operation with Congo and Other States Regarding the Situation in Ituri, DRC", press release, The Hague: ICC-OTP, 26 September.
32. ICC-OTP (2004) "The Office of the Prosecutor of the International Criminal Court Opens Its First Investigation", press release, The Hague: ICC-OTP, 23 June.
33. ICTY Statute, art. 9; ICTR Statute, art. 8. For the surrender of Duško Tadić by Germany to the ICTY, see K. Kittichaisaree (2001) *International Criminal Law*, Oxford: Oxford University Press, p. 26.
34. SCSL Statute, art. 8.
35. ICC Statute, Preamble, arts 1, 17.
36. Except where a referral was made by the Security Council. ICC Statute, art. 18(2).
37. ICC Statute, arts 18(2), 19(2).
38. ICC Assembly of State Parties (2004) "Draft Programme Budget for 2005", ICC-ASP/3/2, available from http://iccnow.org/documents/asp/ungovdocs/3rdsession/ICC-ASP3-2_budget_English.pdf.
39. ICC-OTP (2003) "Measures Available to the International Criminal Court to Reduce the Length of Proceedings", informal expert paper, available from http://www.icc-cpi.int/library/organs/otp/length_of_proceedings.pdf.
40. ICC-OTP (2003) "The Principle of Complementarity in Practice", informal expert paper, available from http://www.icc-cpi.int/library/organs/otp/complementarity.pdf.
41. ICC Statute, art. 53(1).
42. ICC Statute, art. 53(1)(b).
43. ICC Statute, art. 15(2).
44. ICC Statute, art. 17.
45. ICC-OTP, "The Principle of Complementarity in Practice".
46. ICC Statute, arts 15(6), 18(3), 19(10).
47. The Rule of Law and Transitional Justice in Conflict and Post-Conflict Societies, Report of the Secretary-General, 23 August 2004, available from http://daccessdds.un.org/doc/UNDOC/GEN/N04/395/29/PDF/N0439529.pdf?OpenElement.
48. D. Zolo (2004) "Peace through Criminal Law?" *Journal of International Criminal Justice* 2: 727–734.
49. J. Duggard (2002) "Possible Conflict of Jurisdiction with Truth Commission", in A. Casesse, P. Gaeta and J. R. W. D. Jones, eds, *The Rome Statute of the International Criminal Court: A Commentary*, Oxford: Oxford University Press, vol. 1, pp. 693–704.
50. ICTY Statute, arts 1, 16.
51. Goldstone, quoted in Williams and Scharf, *Peace with Justice?* p. 114.
52. L. Arbour (2004) "The Crucial Years", *Journal of International Criminal Justice* 2: 396–402.

53. SCSL Statute, art. 1(1).
54. David Crane (2004) Prosecution Opening Statement, Trial of the CDF Accused, Free-town, Sierra Leone: SCSL, 5 July, available from http://www.sc-sl.org/Press/prosecutor-openingstatement070504a.pdf.
55. In passing the UN Security Council Resolution creating the ICTY, the Council stated "that it was convinced that in the particular circumstances of the former Yugoslavia, the establishment of an international tribunal would bring about the achievement of the aim of putting an end to such crimes and of taking effective measures to bring to justice the persons responsible for them, and would contribute to the restoration and maintenance of peace". United Nations General Assembly (1993) "Report of the Secretary General Pursuant to Paragraph 2 of Security Council Resolution 808 (1993)", UN Doc S/25704 [10], [26], New York: United Nations.
56. SCSL Statute, art. 1(1).
57. SCSL Statute, art. 15(5).
58. SCSL, "First Annual Report of the President of the Special Court for Sierra Leone for the Period 2 December 2002–1 December 2003", available from http://www.sc-sl.org/specialcourtannualreport2002-2003.pdf.
59. ICC Statute, art. 53.
60. United Nations (1990) "Guidelines on the Role of Prosecutors", UN Doc A/CONF.144/28/Rev.I, Eighth United Nations Congress on the Prevention of Crime and the Treatment of Offenders, Havana, Cuba, 27 August–7 September 1990.
61. ICC Statute, arts 53(1)(c), 53(2)(c), 54(1)(b).
62. ICC Statute, art. 68(3).
63. Victims may make representations to the Chamber in respect to jurisdiction or admissibility. ICC Statute, art. 19(3).
64. ICC RPE, rule 85.
65. United Nations, "Guidelines on the Role of Prosecutors".
66. International Court of Justice, *Case Concerning the Application of the Convention of 1902*.
67. ICC Statute, art. 53(1)(c).
68. ICC Statute, arts 53(1)(c), 53(2)(c).
69. M. Brubacher (2004) "Prosecutorial Discretion in Practice", *Journal of International Criminal Justice* 2(71); A. Cassese, P. Kirsch and B. Le Fraper Du Hellen (2001) "Round Table: Prospects for the Functioning of the International Criminal Court", in M. Politi and G. Nesi, eds, *The Rome Statute of the International Criminal Court: A Challenge to Impunity*, Burlington, Vt.: Ashgate, p. 300. The interests of peace and security have the additional relevance in that Article 16 allows the Security Council to defer ICC investigations if the Council deems the investigation to be a threat to international peace and security under Chapter 7 of the UN Charter.
70. Human Rights Watch (2005) *The Meaning of "The Interests of Justice" in Article 53 of the Rome Statute*, Policy Paper, New York: Human Rights Watch.
71. Para. 4 of the Preamble of the ICC Statute affirms that the most serious crimes of concern to the international community must not go unpunished; while the last paragraph states that the authors are resolved to guarantee lasting respect for the enforcement of international criminal justice.
72. The reference in Article 53(2)(c) of the ICC Statute to the role of the accused in the alleged crime combined with the gravity of the crime suggests that those in positions of authority will be most likely to be indicted.
73. The likelihood of the ICC investigating in ongoing armed conflicts is also due to the complementarity provision insofar as states in conflict are more likely unable and/or

unwilling to investigate the crimes themselves. There are previous experiences of international criminal courts intervening in ongoing armed conflicts, including the ICTY in Bosnia and Kosovo and the SCSL effect on the conflict in Liberia.

74. R. Wedgwood (1994) "War Crimes in the former Yugoslavia: Comments on the International War Crimes Tribunal", *Virginia Journal of International Law* 34: 267–274.

75. E. Wilmshurst (2001) "The International Criminal Court: The Role of the Security Council", in M. Politi and G. Nesi, eds, *The Rome Statute of the International Criminal Court: A Challenge to Impunity*, Burlington, Vt.: Ashgate, p. 40.

76. ICC Statute, art. 53(3), (4).

77. ICC Statute, art. 86.

78. ICTY (1997) *Blaskić Case (Judgment)*, IT-95-14, The Hague: ICTY, 29 October.

79. M. L. Volconsek (1997) "Supranational Courts in Political Contexts", in M. L. Volconsek, ed., *Law above Nations: Supranational Courts and the Legalization of Politics*, Gainsville, Fla.: University of Florida Press, p. 17.

80. ICC-OTP (2003) "Paper on Some Policy Issues before the Office of the Prosecutor", September, p. 2, available from http://www.icc-cpi.int/library/organs/otp/030905_Policy_Paper.pdf.

81. For a description of the functions of Jurisdiction, Cooperation and Complementarity Division, see ICC-OTP "Annex to the Paper on Some Policy Issues before the Office of the Prosecutor: Referrals and Communications", available from http://www.icc-cpi.int/library/organs/otp/policy_annex_final_210404.pdf.

82. The United States was the main donor to the SCSL, providing approximately 26 per cent of its budget.

83. The ICTY had the backing of the United States, without whom cooperation of relevant governments, the voluntary surrender of senior Croatian army officers and the arrest and transfer of Slobodan Milošević may not have been possible. R. Goldstone (2004) "A View from the Prosecution", *Journal of International Criminal Justice* 2: 380–383.

84. An application of power by the Court without an appreciation for its limitations may result in the misapplication of the rules it is attempting to promote, setting a negative precedent that may cause the rules to lose their legal character. See M. Byers (1999) *Custom, Power and the Power of Rules*, Cambridge: Cambridge University Press, p. 7.

85. Report of the Secretary-General (2004) "The Rule of Law and Transitional Justice in Conflict and Post-Conflict Societies", UN Doc S/2004/616, New York: United Nations.

86. D. Kennedy (2002) "The International Human Rights Movement: Part of the Problem?", *Harvard Human Rights Journal* 15: 101–117.

87. D. Horowitz (1985) *Ethnic Groups in Conflict*, Berkeley, Calif.: University of California Press; T. Sisk (1996) *Power Sharing and International Mediation in Ethnic Conflicts*, New York: Carnegie Commission on Preventing Deadly Conflict; D. Lake and D. Rothchild (1996) "Containing Fear: The Origins and Management of Ethnic Conflict", *International Security* 21: 41; T. Mak (1995) "The Case against an International War Crimes Tribunal for former Yugoslavia", *International Peacekeeping* 2: 536. Contrast with Williams and Scharf, *Peace with Justice?* p. 32.

88. S. Kirchner (2004) "The Human Rights Dimensions of International Peace and Security: Humanitarian Intervention after 9/11", *Journal of Humanitarian Assistance* 6, available from http://www.jha.ac/articles/a143.pdf.

89. M. Sapira (2003) "Review of *Peace with Justice? War Crimes Accountability in the former Yugoslavia*", *American Journal of International Law* 97: 1009–1011.

90. R. Goldstone (2000) "Reconstructing Peace in Fragmented Societies", in A. Wimmer, R. J. Goldstone, D. L. Horowitz, U. Joras and C. Schetter, eds, *Facing Ethnic Conflict*, Lanham, Md.: Rowman & Littlefield.

91. R. Goldstone (1996) "Justice as a Tool for Peace-Making: Truth Commissions and International Criminal Tribunals", *New York University Journal of International Law & Politics* 28: 485–486.

92. J. Stremlau (1998) "People in Peril: Human Rights, Humanitarian Action, and Preventing Deadly Conflict", *Journal of Humanitarian Assistance*, available from http://www.jha.ac/articles/a032.htm.

93. L. Arbour (1999) "The Status of the International Criminal Tribunal for former Yugoslavia and Rwanda: Goals and Results" in S. Tiefenbrun, ed., *Peace with Justice*, Hempsted, N.Y.: Hofstra Law & Policy Symposium, p. 41.

10

Alternatives to prosecution: The case of Rwanda

Gerald Gahima

What responses do and could lie between vengeance and forgiveness, if legal and cultural institutions offered other avenues for individuals and nations? For nations recovering from periods of mass atrocity, the stakes are high, the dangers enormous. Members of those societies need to ask not only what should count as good reason to forgive, and not only what are the appropriate limits to vengeance. They need to ask, what would it take, and what do our current or imagined institutions need to do, to come to terms with the past, to help heal the victims, the bystanders and even the perpetrators? What would promote reconstruction of a society devastated by atrocity? What could build a nation capable of preventing future massacres and incidents of regimes of torture?[1]

Dealing with the aftermath of a conflict in the course of which there have been widespread human rights violations presents very complex challenges. How should a society with a history of gross human rights abuses deal with the violence of its past? Should justice be sacrificed for the sake of peace? If there is to be accountability, what are the appropriate mechanisms? How far in time and scope should such a society go in seeking to bring perpetrators of human rights violations to justice? How does a society in transition balance the need to end impunity with the imperative to promote stability and reconciliation? Should "liberators", members of the regime that replaced the old order, account for their own crimes, regardless of the implications for national stability? What role should the international community play in the discourse relating to issues concerning human rights and democracy in transition societies? In particular,

Atrocities and international accountability: Beyond transitional justice, Hughes, Schabas and Thakur (eds), United Nations University Press, 2007, ISBN 978-92-808-1141-4

when is it appropriate to resort to international criminal justice rather than to rely solely on domestic mechanisms?

The end of the Cold War and the spread of democracy over the last decades provided an opportunity for some societies in transition to experiment with a variety of responses to their legacies of past violence. The horrors of genocide and other violations of international humanitarian and human rights law in Rwanda and Bosnia provided the critical impetus necessary for the creation of a more ambitious legal framework of accountability mechanisms for gross human rights abuses. A plethora of domestic and international mechanisms for bringing perpetrators of atrocity to justice has not only been created, but continues to evolve.

Criminal prosecution is considered by most to be the ideal mechanism of accountability for mass atrocity, not only because it ensures accountability, but also because it provides a fair hearing to the accused. The question that arises is whether criminal prosecutions are the only adequate or appropriate response to mass atrocity. What are the alternatives to prosecution; on what basis might they be adopted and what should the relationship between criminal proceedings and non-judicial responses to mass atrocity be?

There may be situations in which, for practical reasons or on the basis of sound policy, prosecution is inappropriate or inadequate and alternative non-judicial mechanisms to complement or replace criminal prosecutions are necessary. Societies in transition may opt to pursue non-judicial mechanisms of accountability because of a variety of reasons. When a society in transition seeks accountability for past atrocity through alternatives to criminal prosecutions, the choices of non-criminal mechanisms of accountability available include truth commissions, fact-finding commissions of inquiry, reparations and civil sanctions, including purges or bans from public office.

Description of the gacaca system

The case of Rwanda post-1994

Rwanda has a history of human rights violations orchestrated by the state dating back to 1959. The victims of this violence were largely but not exclusively the Tutsi minority. Faced with the prospect of losing political power and economic privilege as a result of reforms introduced by a peace agreement that the government had negotiated with a predominantly Tutsi rebel group (the Rwandan Patriotic Front, or RPF) in 1993, hardliners within the then-government decided to derail the peace agreement and democratization process by organizing a genocide of the Tutsi minority and massacres of moderate Hutu leaders.[2] The genocide went on concurrently with a civil war between the government and the RPF, as the RPF sought to end the genocide by taking over the country militarily.[3] The war and genocide together claimed more than a million lives.[4] It is generally accepted that the RPF army itself committed significant human rights violations during and after the genocide.[5] The extremists responsible for the genocide lost the military conflict and the RPF ascended to power.

In the aftermath of the genocide, there was unanimous agreement both in Rwanda and within the international community that there should be legal accountability for the genocide and other serious violations of human rights that had taken place. In 1995, the United Nations established the International Criminal Tribunal for Rwanda (ICTR), which is charged with prosecuting those who bore the greatest responsibility for the genocide.[6] Rwanda has also undertaken certain domestic initiatives. A major difference between the Rwanda genocide and other instances of mass atrocity was the unprecedented extent to which very large numbers of ordinary people participated in the commission of atrocity. The post-genocide government of Rwanda decided to deal with the genocide by a policy of investigating and prosecuting all perpetrators.[7] The initial domestic attempt at accountability was a 1996 law that sought to balance conflicting agendas for justice and stabilization of the country by prosecuting the perpetrators in ordinary criminal courts.[8] The law created Special Chambers within the existing court system to handle genocide cases[9] and divided suspects into four categories. The persons who bore the greatest responsibility, placed in the first category, would bear the full weight of the law. The rank-and-file perpetrators would receive more lenient treatment, depending on the degree of their cooperation with judicial and law enforcement agencies. The law excluded capital punishment as a possible penalty for all except offenders who bore the greatest responsibility for the offences that were committed, and sought to expedite trials and to establish the truth through a guilty plea and confession program.[10]

The large number of genocide suspects placed a strain on Rwanda's already struggling criminal justice system, as most of its professionals had either died during the genocide or fled to exile, and its infrastructure had been damaged or destroyed. The conditions of the detention centers were generally accepted to be inhumane. It soon became apparent that prosecution of the genocide through the ordinary criminal justice system was impossible. In 1999, the government decided to transfer the bulk of the genocide caseload to informal organs known as *gacaca* with the expectation that the gacaca courts would help reveal the truth about what happened in 1994, expedite the resolution of the genocide caseload, help promote the eradication of impunity, promote the unity and reconciliation of Rwandans and prove that Rwandan society had the capacity to settle its own problems through a system of justice based on Rwandan custom.[11] The new law transferring jurisdiction for genocide came into force in 2001.[12]

Organizational structure of gacaca courts

Gacaca courts are recognized as full-fledged judicial institutions under Rwandan law.[13] At their inception, they were organized in a hierarchy of four levels coinciding with the territorial organization of the country, namely the province, district, sector and cell.[14] This structure was still in force at the time of the Accountability for Atrocity conference held in Galway, Ireland, in July 2004. Gacaca courts at the district and provincial level have since been abolished.[15] There is one gacaca court at the cell level (the cell gacaca court) and two gacaca courts at the sector level, namely the sector gacaca court and the sector gacaca court of appeal.[16] The territorial organization of Rwanda has also been changed since 2004.[17] However, a law has been passed to preserve the gacaca courts established in accordance with the structure of territorial organization that existed before the recent reforms.[18] Each gacaca court, regardless of its status in the hierarchy, has three organs, namely a general assembly, a panel of judges and a coordinating committee.[19]

The assembly of a cell gacaca court is constituted by all residents of the cell who are 18 years or older, provided that the number of residents is not less than 200. The sector gacaca court and sector gacaca court of appeal have a common assembly, the General Assembly of the sector. The General Assembly of each sector is composed of all judges of the gacaca courts of the cells of the sector, the sector gacaca court and the sector gacaca court of appeal.[20]

Originally, each gacaca court had to have 19 judges but the large number of judges made gacaca courts unwieldy and inefficient and it was consequently reduced. Each gacaca court now has a panel of nine judges and five alternates.[21] The judges of gacaca courts are lay people without legal training. The judges of the cell gacaca courts are chosen by the respective cell Assembly from among its members and the judges of the sector gacaca court and the sector court of appeal are elected by the sector Assembly from among its membership.[22] Elections of gacaca judges are conducted by the National Election Commission in accordance with the modalities set out by a presidential decree.[23] The basic qualification for election as a gacaca court judge is being a person of integrity and being recognized as such by one's peers in the community.

The coordination committee of each gacaca court is constituted by a president, two vice presidents and two secretaries elected from among the judges of the court. The members of the coordination committee must be able to read and write Kinyarwanda.[24] Its functions are to convene and lead meetings and coordinate the activities of the panel; to register complaints, testimonies and evidence provided by the population; to receive dossiers of suspects whose cases are within the jurisdiction of the court; to register appeals decisions of gacaca courts; to transmit to the appellate gacaca court files of the cases whose decisions are appealed against; to register decisions made by organs of the court; and to collaborate with other state institutions in implementing decisions of the court.[25]

The regular prosecution service still has the power to investigate genocide and related crimes, but it is required to verify that the cases it is investigating have not already been heard or determined by any gacaca tribunal.[26] The prosecution must submit all dossiers it investigates to the relevant gacaca.

Jurisdiction

The jurisdiction of gacaca courts over genocide and related crimes is based on a system of categorization. Organic Law 16/2004 now organizes the prosecution of genocide, dividing suspects into three categories, as set out in Article 51.

Criminal participation that led to the death of victims renders the suspect liable to placement in the category of the most serious offenders, Category 1. Persons who took a lead in planning, organizing or inciting the genocide are automatically placed in Category 1, as well. Persons who were in leadership positions (whether in central government, local government, the military or the church) are also liable for placement in Category 1, as are persons accused of sexual offences (such as rape or torture involving sexual organs). Category 1 cases remain within the jurisdiction of the ordinary courts.[27]

Panels of cell gacaca courts have jurisdiction only over property offences and they are responsible for the classification of suspects into the various categories established by Organic Law 16/2004. Decisions of cell gacaca courts on issues relating to property claims are not subject to appeal.

Panels of sector gacaca courts have first-instance jurisdiction over charges brought against suspects who have been placed in Category 2 and over offences committed during proceedings before them, such as failure or refusal to provide evidence to the court, contempt of court or obstruction of justice in general.[28] They also have jurisdiction to hear appeals against decisions of sector gacaca court first-instance trials.

All panels of gacaca courts have the power to conduct follow-up investigations with respect to evidence received; to receive confessions, guilty pleas and communications of repentance and apology from persons who participated in genocide and related crimes; to decide upon applications for removal of one or more of their number from the panel; to hear and determine cases falling within their jurisdiction; and to hear appeals against the decisions of subordinate gacaca courts.

Procedure

Proceedings before gacaca courts are informal. The conduct of gacaca court proceedings is not subject to the normal criminal procedure law of Rwanda. Proceedings are conducted in three phases. The first stage in gacaca proceedings is the information-gathering stage, which is the responsibility of the Assembly of the cell gacaca court. In practice, the information-gathering process begins with *Nyumbakumi* leaders (heads of groupings of ten households) completing forms with the required information. Once this preliminary work has been completed, a meeting of the General Assembly of the cell gacaca court is convened. These lists are then read to a duly constituted meeting of the General Assembly and the General Assembly discusses the contents of the forms. It may add new accusations or delete unfounded allegations.[29]

The second stage of gacaca proceedings, which is also conducted by the cell, is the categorization of the suspects identified during the information-gathering phase. Upon completion of the categorization process, cases relating to suspects who have been placed in Category 1 are transmitted to the prosecution service.[30] Cases of Category 2 suspects are transmitted to the sector gacaca court.

The final stage of proceedings of gacaca courts is the trial phase, which is conducted by the panel of the gacaca court with jurisdiction to try the offences for which a suspect is accused. Any member of the cell has a right to provide evidence.

Gacaca courts enjoy the normal powers and privileges ordinarily accorded other courts.[31] Proceedings are open to the public, subject to certain restrictions on observers, researchers and journalists, who must have an official permit to observe the proceedings and present themselves to local government officials prior to the proceedings.[32] Gacaca hearings are public, unless they are hearings *in camera* that have been requested and granted for reasons of public order or good morals.[33]

Proceedings are lead by the presidents of the panels of judges.[34] The President first requests that the accused persons and the complainants identify themselves. The court thereafter informs accused persons of the charges against them and proceeds to consider the confession and guilty plea of the accused or to advise the accused of their rights under the guilty plea and confessions program. Should the accused choose not to join the guilty plea and confession program, the court summarizes the evidence against each defendant and each accused person is then given an opportunity to defend himself. Suspects in gacaca court proceedings are not allowed to be represented by legal counsel. Deliberations of the panels of judges are conducted in secrecy. Judgments are issued in open court and are in writing.[35] Gacaca courts are authorized to try suspects *in absentia* when the defendant's whereabouts cannot be determined.[36]

Penalties

The penalties to which suspects whose cases are handled by gacaca courts are subject depend on a variety of factors, including the nature of the offence, the category in which the accused person has been placed, whether the accused person has joined the guilty plea and confessions program and, if so, at what stage the offer to join the program was made, and any attenuating or aggravating circumstances that guide ordinary courts in matters relating to sentencing.[37] The current law on genocide trials permits all perpetrators, including Category 1 accused, to join the guilty plea and confessions program and be eligible for reductions of their sentence. Confessions must include a description of the offence, names of victims, witnesses and accomplices. It must also include an apology and offer to plead guilty.[38] One of the goals of the plea-bargaining program has always been to encourage reconciliation through establishing the truth about what happened. The guilty plea and confessions program also aims to expedite the process of adjudicating genocide trials and to ease the burden on the judicial system.

Individuals who were less than 14 years old at the time of their involvement in the 1994 atrocities are not liable to be prosecuted; those who were between 14 and 18 years of age at the time receive penalties of about half the maximum penalty for which adults guilty of the same offences are liable.[39] Defendants who committed offences relating to property are Category 3 suspects and are not liable to incur custodial sentences or other punishment and are required only to pay civil damages for the harm arising from their offences.[40]

In addition to penalties of imprisonment and community service, persons convicted of offences which place them in Categories 1 and 2 are liable to incur forfeiture of their civil rights, including the rights to vote in elections, contest public office, be witnesses in court proceedings, carry firearms or serve in the armed services, police or public service, or in the teaching and medical professions.[41]

A critical evaluation of gacaca

Positive aspects

Gacaca courts had barely begun their work at the time of the Galway conference in 2004. Indeed, the courts were able to start the trial phase of their work countrywide only in 2006. A comprehensive evaluation of the gacaca process will only be possible once the trial and appeals phases are over. Given the difficulties that even those involved in the operation of gacaca courts have previously had in predicting the schedule of the courts' activities, it is difficult to predict when gacaca trials will be completed. It is possible however to make some tentative observations about the gacaca process on the basis of the work of gacaca courts during the experimental phase (June 2002 to October 2004) and the information-gathering phase of the nationwide operation of the courts that began in January 2005.

On the basis of observations of the gacaca process at its current stage, some positive attributes of the gacaca system are evident. The gacaca process has compelled Rwandan society to confront the genocide more systematically than before. Gacaca localizes justice, ensuring that justice is visible to those who suffered.[42] Gacaca courts, even critics agree, are able to handle and dispose of more cases than the ordinary criminal justice system could ever have been able to handle. Investigations and trials conducted by gacaca courts are infinitely more expeditious than investigations and trials by the ordinary criminal justice process. Gacaca courts are thus more likely than ordinary courts to comply with the requirement to afford persons accused of genocide the right to trial without undue delay. The provisions of the guilty plea and confession program of the gacaca system have enabled the country to reduce the number of suspects in pre-trial detention and to improve the conditions of detention for the remaining suspects. This has led to financial savings that can be used to finance other necessary services provided by the state to the needy. The gacaca system has also enabled the public to play a wider role in the process of justice for genocide and enhanced public trust in the accountability process.[43]

Concerns raised by the gacaca system

Advocates of the gacaca system of courts argue that the process is an innovative and useful way to help Rwanda to heal. Despite the positive aspects indicated above, however, the gacaca system remains a controversial experiment. Critics of the gacaca process point to a number of shortcomings that, they argue, make it an inappropriate response to the genocide and mass atrocity that Rwanda experienced in 1994 and in the years that followed.

Scope

The gacaca system is a continuation of the Rwandan government's policy of dealing with the genocide by attempting to prosecute each and every perpetrator. Rwanda adopted this policy after the genocide and tried to apply it through the ordinary criminal justice system from 1996. The government, however, ultimately realized that the ordinary criminal justice system could not handle the genocide caseload and decided to explore alternatives to prosecutions through the ordinary criminal courts.

The results of the experimental phase of gacaca clearly indicate that even the gacaca system is not appropriate for dealing with a situation like Rwanda's, where a very large number of people have been involved in committing atrocities. The 751 gacaca courts involved in the initial phase alone identified more than 50,000 additional suspects. The National Service of Gacaca Jurisdictions has estimated that the total number of suspects who may have to be tried by gacaca courts may be at least 700,000,[44] approximately one-eighth of the country's population.

The scale of social participation in the Rwanda genocide makes it impossible for any system, including gacaca, to ensure the prosecution and punishment of every perpetrator in a manner that ensures due process and is believed by all the parties to be fair and impartial. Even if gacaca courts were able to investigate and try cases against all of the persons who participated in committing atrocities, it would still not be possible for the government to enforce the sentences. Most of the suspects who will not join the guilty plea and confessions program are subject to long terms of imprisonment.[45] Severe punishment of large numbers of genocide criminals would make the current government even more unpopular within the Hutu community and is unlikely to be attempted. The imprisonment of such a large number of perpetrators would enhance prospects for further conflict rather than promote reconciliation and stability.

The continued imprisonment of large numbers of citizens would also have certain adverse consequences for the country's economy and would be too costly for the government. Rwanda has been releasing detainees from custody over the past few years partly to reduce the prison population. The country can ill afford new arrests and detentions on the scale of the arrests that took place during the period just after the genocide. The growth of the prison population would take a substantial part of the adult population out of economic production and increase poverty for many households. It would also enhance hatred, mistrust and divisions between the ethnic groups at the community level.

On the other hand, failing to punish the perpetrators after they have been tried and convicted would be unacceptable to survivors. The policy of insisting on the prosecution and punishment of all perpetrators raises unrealistic expectations that all perpetrators of the genocide will be punished.

Non-compliance with internationally recognized fair trial standards

The gacaca system raises concerns about fair trial guarantees, particularly with respect to suspects who have not joined the guilty plea and confessions program and who face harsh penalties. The proceedings of gacaca are informal gatherings with few procedural rules or guarantees. The accused has no right to legal counsel. The situation is compounded by the fact that judges are lay people without any legal training or knowledge of the law. The ability of many of the gacaca judges to understand even the very law governing gacaca is open to question, as many of them cannot read or write. Amnesty International has reported that some pre-gacaca hearings have been marked by intimidation and haranguing by officials of defendants, defense witnesses and local populations.[46] The combination of these and other factors cannot but raise concern about the system's ability to ensure fair trials. The evident risk that gacaca proceedings may lead to widespread miscarriages of justice may adversely affect the credibility of the whole process.

The right to a fair trial is an integral part of the international human rights system, enshrined in several human rights treaties that Rwanda has ratified, especially the International Covenant on Civil and Political Rights and the African Charter on Human and Peoples' Rights. Furthermore, the Constitution of Rwanda guarantees the right of an accused person to be informed of the nature and cause of the charges the accused faces at all levels of judicial proceedings; the right to be tried by a competent court; the right to a public hearing; the right to a fair trial; the right to receive all necessary guarantees for defense; the prohibition against torture, physical abuse or cruel, inhumane or degrading treatment; and the right to presumption of innocence.[47]

The legal framework establishing gacaca courts and the non-statutory procedures governing the conduct of proceedings of gacaca courts violate both Rwandan law and international norms relating to the right to a fair trial.

The right to a fair hearing

The right to a fair hearing is a prerequisite for a fair trial under international as well as Rwandan law.[48] There are strong concerns that the gacaca system does not meet the requirements for compliance with the right to a fair hearing.

Gacaca judges play the roles of investigators, prosecutors, judges and jury at the same time and are likely to have formed opinions about the cases before them long before they come to the stage of weighing the evidence. Most gacaca judges lack the technical competence to fairly and competently judge many of the cases before them. The judges have no formal legal training or judicial experience. Many may indeed be completely illiterate and likely to find it difficult if not impossible to determine the law applicable to the cases they are trying. Observers agree that the training that gacaca judges have received is grossly inadequate, given the range, character and complexity of crimes that were committed during the genocide.[49] Some gacaca judges themselves readily acknowledge their own inadequacy to handle the genocide caseload.[50]

The most important criteria for evaluating compliance with the requirement for a fair hearing is respect for the right of equality of arms. Equality of arms means that each party should have an equal opportunity to present its case and that both parties are treated in a manner ensuring that they have a procedurally equal position during the trial.[51] Gacaca courts do not meet the requirement for equality of arms. The overwhelming resources of the state are used to support the investigation, prosecution and trial of the charges against the accused. Accused persons do not have comparable opportunity or resources to seek evidence exonerating them. Many of the accused persons are either illiterate or poorly educated and lack capacity to prepare an adequate defense for themselves. In any event, they do not have any opportunity to effectively prepare their own defense because they are in pre-trial detention. Without the assistance of counsel, they cannot effectively counter cases that have been prepared by state authorities with infinitely more resources at their disposal.[52]

There are also concerns that the general atmosphere in many gacaca proceedings does not afford an environment conducive to a fair hearing. Both Amnesty International and independent researchers have reported that some pre-gacaca hearings have been marked by tension, high emotions, intimidation and haranguing by officials of defendants, defense witnesses and local populations.[53] There are often attempts to manipulate the audience against some accused persons prior to hearings.[54] Some proceedings have reportedly become very emotional and confrontational.

All of the above conditions make it difficult for the right to a fair hearing to be respected in gacaca proceedings. The argument is not that all gacaca cases are unfair; it is that the gacaca system is an environment where widespread miscarriage of justice is not only possible but also very likely.

Judicial independence

An important safeguard of fair trial guarantees is the requirement for an independent tribunal. Article 7(1) of the African Charter on Human and Peoples' Rights refers only to a "competent" and "impartial" tribunal. However, Article 26 of the Charter imposes upon state parties a legal duty to guarantee the independence of courts. The constitution of Rwanda also guarantees the independence of the judiciary.[55] Practical safeguards for the independence of the judiciary include selection methods based on professional competence, which safeguard against appointment to judicial office for improper motives; the need for guaranteed tenure; the requirement for efficient, fair and independent disciplinary proceedings; and the duty of the state to provide enough resources (such as salaries and training) to enable judges to perform their functions properly, to mention but a few.[56]

The judiciary in Rwanda in general is prone to executive interference.[57] The large number of gacaca courts, their wide distribution across the country, the gravity of the offences the courts are trying, the low social and economic status of most of the judges, the lack of monetary compensation, and the absence of effective supervision mechanisms combine to make risks to the independence of gacaca courts very compelling.

Attempts at interference with the judicial process are likely to multiply as gacaca courts at the grass roots level take over the adjudication of genocide cases.[58] Corruption in judicial institutions was already an acknowledged fact before the introduction of gacaca courts. Indeed, the problem of corruption in the ordinary courts was cited as one of the reasons for moving the genocide caseload away from the classical courts to gacaca.[59] One of the causes of this corruption was identified as the poor pay of judges and prosecutors. Gacaca judges are for the most part ordinary peasants or other poor people and are not paid by the state for their services in spite of the substantial sacrifice they make to sit on the courts. Gacaca judges are compelled to work free of charge. Most of the judges are generally from the less well-to-do members of society and have no paid formal employment. Compulsory participation in gacaca proceedings occasions undue economic hardships on the rural poor. The gacaca judges are even more likely to be tempted to ask for or accept bribes than ordinary judicial officials. The omission of financial compensation for gacaca judges makes them vulnerable to manipulation and exposes them to corruption. Corruption within gacaca is already a problem.

At the local level, the forces that are likely to seek to interfere with gacaca courts are local government leaders such as mayors, police and security officials, sector leaders and other influential persons such as politicians, the business community and the clergy.[60] The state does not provide adequate resources to enable the gacaca courts to perform their work, nor do judges have security of tenure. The government can remove them at will because of its absolute control of the local government machinery. Some of the grounds for removal of gacaca judges go beyond the judges' professional competence and are political. Gacaca judges may, for example, be removed for reasons such as promoting divisionism, making sentimental decisions, lack of consensus spirit and behaviour incompatible with the objectives of gacaca courts.[61] These criteria are not defined by law and could easily be used to remove judges who either disagree with government policy or have personal misunderstandings with government officials or other community leaders.

Impartiality

Accused persons in criminal proceedings have the right to be tried by an impartial tribunal. The principle of impartiality, which applies to each individual case, demands that each of the decision makers, whether they are professionals or lay judges or juries, be unbiased.[62] The gacaca system presents very challenging difficulties as far as the right to trial by independent tribunals is concerned. This right may be compromised in many gacaca proceedings because many members of the organs of gacaca courts are likely to have some interest in the outcome of the cases before gacaca courts in their respective areas. The risk of a lack of impartiality arising from conflicts of interest on the part of some of the judges has been identified by some researchers as one of the risks facing the gacaca process.[63]

The architects of the Rwanda genocide succeeded in organizing the killing of many people because they were able to convince a large proportion of the Hutu population that it was in their political interest to exterminate the Tutsi population. Many members of gacaca institutions may have committed atrocities or may have identified with or supported the political ideologies of the organizers of the genocide, through membership in extremist political parties and militia groups that supported the genocide. Although some Hutu saved Tutsi and some even lost their lives in the process, a significant proportion of the Hutu shared the ideology of genocide. As a result, there is always a risk that some of the gacaca judges may themselves be responsible for atrocities. Many gacaca judges have been accused of having participated in committing atrocities and have had to be removed.[64] Many of the judges of gacaca courts may be personally connected to defendants by family relations or friendship ties. On the other hand, some of the judges of gacaca courts are genocide survivors who were themselves victims of violence. Tutsi survivors in general blame the entire Hutu population of their respective communities for the atrocities that claimed the lives of their relatives and the grave human rights violations to which they themselves were subjected.[65] Tutsi judges in gacaca courts judge persons accused of crimes of which they were targets. Given previous experiences where survivors' organizations have historically sought to influence judicial proceedings in some areas, it is legitimate for some Hutu to be apprehensive about the presence of survivors on the court panels. Hutu suspects are likely to fear the risk of victimization in certain areas, especially urban areas, where the Tutsi form a disproportionate percentage of gacaca judges.

The risk of the violation of the right to trial by an impartial tribunal is all the more grave because gacaca courts are unsupervised. There is no effective system for monitoring and supervision of gacaca courts to ensure their proper performance and to safeguard their impartiality. The compliance of ordinary courts with the law is ensured by the system of appeals and supervision by superior courts. Prior to reforms of gacaca that were introduced in 2004, gacaca courts were supervised by a department of the Supreme Court. At the time, decisions of gacaca courts that were deemed to constitute breaches of the law could also be referred to the Supreme Court for review. Since the 2004 reforms, gacaca courts are supervised by the National Service of Gacaca Jurisdictions, which does not have the legal power to interfere with decisions of gacaca courts. The re-organization of gacaca courts that was undertaken in 2004 and subsequent reforms of the public service have reduced even further the number of personnel responsible for the oversight and supervision of gacaca courts. The effective supervision of gacaca courts by the National Service of Gacaca Jurisdictions is less likely now than it was several years ago because the service has even fewer human resources for the task than the previous supervisory organ (the Gacaca Department of the Supreme Court) had. The possibility of overturning unlawful decisions of gacaca courts through the Supreme Court no longer exists. The alternative to judicial supervision is that the gacaca courts may be subject to supervision and control by the executive, which will in practice be the local government officials.

The divisions and mistrust that the genocide and surrounding events have created in Rwandan society make it difficult to find people who can be trusted by all sides to judge the genocide caseload impartially. Hutu and Tutsi alike are often apprehensive regarding the independence and impartiality of gacaca courts.[66] The level of mistrust between the two communities in many areas is such that there are legitimate grounds to fear that the right to be tried by an impartial tribunal is seriously at risk.

Legal representation

The right to legal representation is particularly crucial in gacaca proceedings because the judges themselves have no knowledge of the law and many of the defendants have little or no formal education. Defendants in the cases that will be judged by gacaca courts will not, however, have the benefit of legal representation. The gacaca system denies the right to legal representation even to persons who have their own financial resources to pay for counsel of their choice. Supporters of the gacaca process argue that lack of legal representation in gacaca proceedings is not fatal to having fair trials.

While it is true that Rwanda does not have the financial resources to provide legal representation for all defendants in genocide cases, it is also true that Rwanda would still not be able to assure legal representation to suspects even it had the financial resources to pay for legal representation, as the defense bar in Rwanda is still very small. These arguments are however not adequate to justify dispensing with the requirement to provide legal representation to defendants. Legal representation for persons accused of grave offences is necessary to avoid the risk of punishing suspects for offences they did not commit. The state should try only as many people as it is able to try fairly.

The state of Rwanda finds itself in a very difficult situation. It has a duty under international law and an obligation to its people to ensure accountability for the genocide and related crimes. The necessity of accountability should, however, be balanced with the obligation to guarantee the fair trial of the genocide caseload. Rwanda's judicial system cannot, in judging genocide cases, match basic international human rights norms. If the gacaca courts were to try the cases through meticulous investigation and trial as ordinary criminal courts ordinarily ought to exercise, the trials would take a very long time and the whole purpose of gacaca courts would be defeated. If, on the other hand, the government is to continue with the implementation of the gacaca process without regard for fair trial guarantees, and the trials before gacaca courts are rushed through just for the purpose of getting rid of the genocide caseload, it is inevitable that gacaca trials will involve widespread abuses of human rights and miscarriages of justice.

There are compelling reasons why the need for gacaca courts to comply with international norms relating to fair trials should be stressed far more frequently and forcefully than it has been until now. Rwanda's own laws demand respect of the fair trial guarantees. The state of Rwanda is a signatory to international treaties that oblige it to respect these human rights norms. Victimization of innocent people by gacaca and other judicial mechanisms only perpetuates hatred, mistrust and animosity between Rwanda's different communities and enhances rather than reduces prospects for future conflict. Unfair trials also undermine efforts to promote a culture of respect for human rights, establish the rule of law and promote national reconciliation.

Human rights abuses committed by the Rwandan Patriotic Army

One of the negative aspects of the gacaca process is the fact that it does not deal fairly with all violations of human rights that were committed by both sides during the Rwanda conflict. Gacaca proceedings are selective, partisan and discriminatory judicial processes. The gacaca system targets Hutu perpetrators of genocidal violence against the Tutsi but does not address the human rights violations committed by members of the Rwandan Patriotic Army (RPA) and some Tutsi civilians.

The RPA was responsible for very grave human rights violations during and after the genocide. The government of Rwanda denies responsibility for the offences but acknowledges that some members of the RPA did commit certain human rights abuses. The government's stand is that abuses by the RPA were neither widespread nor systematic and that they were committed by members of the RPA in their individual capacities rather than as RPA members. The government, in effect, disputes only the extent of RPA violations and the responsibility of commanders in the events. The government's position is that genocide and human rights violations by the RPA need to be distinguished from the genocide and that the proper forum for the investigation and prosecution of the alleged RPA human rights violations is in the military court justice system and not gacaca courts.

Survivors and relatives of the victims of RPA violence frequently express frustration over the failure of both the formal justice system and the gacaca courts to investigate and prosecute these offences. From the beginning of the pilot phase of gacaca courts, members of the public in different areas across the country raised the question as to how crimes committed against the Hutu would be dealt with. Many gacaca courts continue to receive complaints of atrocities committed by members of the RPA. The authorities have, however, instructed gacaca courts to respond to the complaints relating to human rights violations by members of the RPA by pleading lack of jurisdiction.

The exclusion of the offences that were committed by the RPA from the jurisdiction of gacaca courts would not by itself have been a problem if the government intended to address the allegations of RPA abuses in good faith by other means. That gacaca courts may not be an appropriate forum for trying military personnel may be a valid point. It would be unrealistic to expect the civilian peasants who sit on gacaca courts to confront members of a victorious army for its wartime human rights abuses. Gacaca courts would never be able to get the military to cooperate with investigations and prosecution of offences committed by its members. Only the formal civilian courts or military courts could have the ability to investigate and try such offences.

The problem is that under Rwandan law, offences committed by members of the military are investigated, prosecuted and tried exclusively by the military criminal justice system. Military courts try even civilian accomplices of military offenders. Rwanda's military court system is part and parcel of the RPA machinery. The majority of the judges, prosecutors and investigators of the military court system rose through the ranks of the RPA when it was still a rebel army. The RPA, including members of its justice system, is protective not only of its legacy but also of the reputation of the organization's members and especially of its leadership. It lacks the political will to ensure the investigation and prosecution of offences committed by its members. The military criminal justice system has investigated at least some of the major allegations of human rights abuses.[67] There has, however, been no serious effort to prosecute even the offences that have been investigated. There have been only a handful of indictments against members of the RPA for wartime offences and the sentences which have been passed in the few cases that have been prosecuted have been extremely lenient. The complaints that gacaca courts have received about RPA abuses are not followed up by the investigative, prosecutorial and judicial organs of the Rwanda military system.

The failure of the Rwandan government to establish credible, good-faith mechanisms for investigating and prosecuting violations of human rights abuses attributed to the RPA is one of the factors that most adversely affect the credibility of the gacaca process within Rwandan society.[68] The failure of the legal system of Rwanda to investigate offences committed by members of RPA discredits Rwanda's entire accountability regime, including gacaca, as victor's justice.[69]

Gacaca's potential for destabilization

One of the major objectives of the gacaca process was to promote reconciliation and social harmony nationally and at the community level. The thinking was that the collaboration of the members of each community in reconstructing the events of 1994, determining responsibility for the human rights violations that were committed and participating in determining penalties for the perpetrators would pave the way for reconciliation, healing and peaceful co-existence.

Unfortunately, the gacaca process has not in all places proceeded as the government had hoped. Many communities in Rwanda remain deeply divided along ethnic lines. Mistrust between the two major communities remains widespread and is manifested in every sphere of Rwandan national life, including justice. The government has undertaken some initiatives that are intended to heal ethnic divisions and to create a common national identity and has acknowledged the existence of these divisions, as it continues to warn that the ideology of genocide persists.[70]

The Hutu communities in Rwanda in general do not have much trust in the government. They trust the judicial system even less. Both gacaca and the genocide trials being conducted by the formal courts are largely perceived by the Hutu as one-sided victors' justice. The sympathies of many Hutu lie with the persons who stand accused of the genocide and who are reluctant to disclose the truth. On the other hand, many Tutsi question the genuineness of their Hutu neighbours' commitment to fully disclose all they know about the conduct of the genocide. The result is that in many communities survivors and the rest of the population are bitterly divided over accountability for crimes related to the 1994 war and genocide. In some places, the mistrust has given way to open acrimony between the two groups. Survivors of the genocide are few and isolated. Their role as witnesses exposes them to hatred and danger. Attacks against survivors and other witnesses have become a major national problem.

In this environment of intense polarization of society along ethnic lines, mechanisms of accountability for past human rights abuses are a potential source of new conflicts rather than an avenue for healing and reconciliation.[71] The gacaca courts are a battlefield on which communities are fighting an undeclared war over many issues of politics. The gacaca process has the potential to increase these divisions and conflicts across communities, rather than to promote healing, reconciliation and peace.

Reparations for victims of all violence

The provision of reparations to victims of past abuses is considered critical to the process of reconciliation and healing of societies that have experienced widespread human rights abuses. States have obligations under international law to provide victims of human rights abuses with adequate reparations.[72] Victims often also have rights to reparations under their own countries' laws and this is the case in Rwanda.[73] One of the most significant shortcomings of the gacaca process is its lack of a regime to provide adequate reparations to victims of the genocide and other crimes. Essentially, the victims of this violence fall into two categories, the Tutsi victims of genocide and Hutu who were killed by the organizers of the genocide as accomplices of the Tutsi, and Hutu victims of massacres at the hands of the RPA. Victims of genocide appreciate that the crimes that were committed against them have been recognized, condemned and, in some cases, punished but are unhappy that they have not received any monetary compensation. On the other hand, victims of RPA violations are not only unhappy about lack of compensation; they complain about the failure of the government to even acknowledge their suffering at all. Victims of RPA violations could not for a long time openly make any demand for compensation but they have in recent years complained about the failure of the state to recognize the abuses they were victims of and its failure or refusal to bring to justice the perpetrators of crimes that were directed at them.[74]

The government of Rwanda admitted its legal responsibility for the crimes directed against the victims of the genocide. However, even with regard to victims of the genocide, the government has until now refused to commit itself to providing any reparations. The government's reluctance to pay compensation to victims of the genocide is largely a result of financial constraints. The problem of compensation to victims has been complicated by the claims of Hutu victims for inclusion in whatever mechanisms of reparations are to be established. The government cannot agree to a system of reparations that entails acknowledgement of the responsibility of its forces for atrocities; on the other hand, establishing a compensation mechanism that discriminates between victims on the basis of ethnicity would aggravate existing divisions in Rwandan society and increase hostility of the majority of the population to both the regime and the Tutsi population.

In the absence of a settlement of the complex issue of reparations, the ability of the gacaca process to lead to reconciliation is undermined.

Conclusion

Accountability for mass atrocity is one of the major tools in the struggle to combat impunity and to enhance prospects for respect for human rights, particularly during times of conflict. The mechanism of accountability that a society attempting to reckon with a legacy of mass atrocity ultimately opts for is determined by many factors.[75]

In ideal circumstances, criminal prosecution should be the standard norm for accountability for atrocity, and alternatives to prosecution should be the exception. There is a growing consensus that prosecution should certainly be the sole acceptable mechanism of accountability for leaders for certain crimes and for persons who bear the greatest responsibility for atrocity. Prosecution by an independent international tribunal should be considered when there is no state able and willing to investigate in good faith those persons who bear the greatest responsibility for atrocity. With regard to accountability for the rank and file, whether the appropriate response to past abuses should be criminal prosecution or alternative mechanisms will depend on the circumstances of each society.

Rwanda's accountability mechanisms, like those of other post-conflict societies, have been shaped by the prevailing social and political environment. The adoption of the gacaca process, in particular, was a result of the constraints faced in prosecutions through the ordinary courts. The mechanisms of accountability that Rwanda has chosen have certainly had some positive effects. Rwandan society has been compelled to confront the dark legacy of the genocide. Gacaca courts have expedited the process of trying persons accused of involvement in the genocide. The truth about how the genocide was organized and carried out at the local level is emerging. Justice has been and is being rendered for some of the atrocities that were committed. A significant number of the perpetrators have admitted their wrongdoing and have asked the victims of their crimes for forgiveness. The acknowledgement by some perpetrators of the wrongs they committed has improved prospects for reconciliation. The trial and punishment of the genocide caseload may have a positive impact in sending the message that human rights violations against other citizens have legal consequences.

On the other hand, Rwanda's accountability mechanisms still have some fundamental shortcomings. Rwanda has not had any open debate about the violence of the past that addresses the grievances of all victims.[76] The government has unilaterally imposed its version of causes, process and consequences of the violence of the past as the official version. Rwanda's attempt to investigate and prosecute such a very large number of offences has been too ambitious in scope. The attempt to prosecute such a large number of cases has occasioned gross human rights abuses to suspects who have been kept in detention awaiting trail for up to a decade or more. The gacaca process entails significant risks of unfair trial. In any event, the value of Rwanda's accountability process is degraded by its selective, partisan and discriminatory character. Rwanda's judicial and law enforcement institutions have only investigated and prosecuted the genocide caseload and have overlooked human rights violations that were committed by the victorious side. The failure of the military leadership to investigate and punish RPA abuses not only hinders national reconciliation, but it also undermines efforts to establish the rule of law and respect for human rights. Not surprisingly, impunity still remains a problem of major concern in Rwandan society.

Rwanda's transitional justice process, like its transition to democracy, remains a work in progress. Rwanda's reckoning with the violence of its past raises fundamental concerns that still need to be addressed if the objectives that the processes of justice are intended to achieve are to ever be realized. Central to the issue of an appropriate response to Rwanda's past violence is the search for the complete truth. A nation's unity, José Zalaquett has noted, depends on a shared identity, which in turn depends upon a shared memory; the truth also brings a measure of social catharsis and prevents the past from recurring.[77] Rwanda's accountability process needs to be re-orientated to reflect the collective memory of all victims. The gacaca system may well not be the last chapter of Rwanda's attempts to reckon with the legacy of atrocities arising from the events of 1994 and the years that followed. It should not be. Whether, when or how Rwanda will address outstanding issues of concern can only be a matter of guesswork. What is certain is that the manner in which the country will deal with the shortcomings of its accountability mechanisms will have a very significant impact on its prospects for reconciliation, democracy and the rule of law and sustainable peace.

Notes

1. M. Minow (1998) *Between Vengeance and Forgiveness: Facing History after Genocide and Mass Violence*, Boston: Beacon Press, p. 21.

2. The RPF is a political organization that was established by Rwandan exiles in 1987. The original name of the organization was RANU (Rwandese Alliance for National Union). As part of a process of changing its policies and structures, RANU changed its name to RPF in 1987. The RPF launched an armed invasion of Rwanda from Uganda on 1 October 1990. The invasion led to the birth of the Rwandan Patriotic Army (RPA), the military or armed wing of the political organization. The RPA was initially made up mostly of Rwandan members of the Ugandan army. In theory, the RPA is subordinate to the political organs of the RPF. In practice, the RPA fully dominates and controls the political organs of the RPF.

3. Alison Des Forges (1999) *Leave None to Tell the Story: Genocide in Rwanda*, New York: Human Rights Watch.

4. Ministry of Local Administration, Information and Social Affairs (2002) *Dénombrement des Victimes du Genocide*, final report, Kigali, Rwanda: Republic of Rwanda.

5. Ibid., pp. 701–735; Gerard Prunier (1995) *The Rwanda Crisis: History of a Genocide*, Kampala, Uganda: Fountain Publishers.

6. Established by UN Security Council Resolution S/RES/955 (1994), 8 November 1994.

7. J. Sarkin (2001) "The Tension between Justice and Reconciliation in Rwanda: Politics, Human Rights, Due Process and the Role of Gacaca in Dealing with the Genocide", *Journal of African Law* 45(2): 143–146.

8. Organic Law No. 08/96 on the organization of prosecutions for offences constituting the crime of genocide or crimes against humanity committed since October 1, 1900.

9. Organic Law No. 16/2004, art. 19.

10. Organic Law No. 16/2004, art. 14 and arts 5–7.

11. National Service of Gacaca Jurisdictions, "The Objectives of the Gacaca Courts", available from http://www.inkiko-gacaca.gov.rw/En/EnObjectives.htm.

12. Organic Law No. 40/2000 establishing setting up Gacaca jurisdictions and organizing the prosecutions for offences constituting the crime of genocide or crimes against humanity committed between October 1, 1900 and December 31, 1994.

13. Constitution of the Republic of Rwanda, Article 143.

14. Rwanda is administratively divided into provinces, which are themselves divided into districts. Districts are divided into sectors and sectors, in turn, divided into cells, the cell being the lowest administrative organ in Rwanda. Before the recent re-organization, there were 10 provinces, 100 districts, 1,545 sectors and 9,011 cells and a corresponding number of gacaca courts at each level. Organic Law No. 40/2000, art. 3.

15. These changes were introduced by Organic Law No. 16/2004.

16. Organic Law No. 16/2004, art. 3.

17. The changes in the territorial organization (involving the re-organization of the country into 5 new provinces and only 30 districts) were effected by Organic Law No. 29/2005 of 31/12/2005 Determining the administrative entities of the Republic of Rwanda.

18. Organic Law No. 28/2006 Modifying and complementing Organic Law 16/2004 of 19/06/ 2004 Establishing setting up Gacaca jurisdictions and organizing the prosecutions for offences constituting the crime of genocide or crimes against humanity committed between October 1, 1900 and December 31, 1994.

19. Organic Law No. 16/2004, art. 5.

20. Organic Law No. 16/2004, art. 7.

21. Organic Law No. 16/2004, art. 8.

22. Organic Law No. 16/2004, art. 13.

23. Presidential Order No. 12/01 of 26/6/2001 Establishing modalities for organizing elections of members of "Gacaca Jurisdictions" organs.

24. Organic Law No. 16/2004, art. 11.

25. Organic Law No. 16/2004, art. 12.

26. Organic Law No. 16/2004, art. 46.
27. Organic Law No. 16/2004, art. 2.
28. Organic Law No. 16/2004, arts 29 and 30.
29. A. Megwalu (2006) "Looking Back, Moving Forward: The Gacaca Courts in Rwanda", unpublished thesis, Woodrow Wilson School of Public and International Affairs, Princeton University, p. 22.
30. Organic Law No. 16/2004, art. 34(10).
31. Organic Law No. 16/2004, art. 39.
32. Instruction No. 04/2005 of 16/02/2005 from the Executive Secretary of the National Service for Gacaca Courts Related to Conditions Required from Observers, Researchers and Journalists in the Gacaca Process.
33. Organic Law No. 16/2004, art. 21.
34. Organic Law No. 16/2004, arts 64, 65, 66 and 68.
35. Organic Law No. 16/2004, art. 70.
36. Organic Law No. 16/2004, art. 98.
37. Organic Law No. 16/2004, arts 72–81.
38. Organic Law No. 16/2004, art. 54.
39. Organic Law No. 16/2004, art. 78.
40. Organic Law No. 16/2004, art. 75.
41. Organic Law No. 16/2004, art. 76.
42. E. Daly (2002) "Between Punitive and Reconstructive Justice: The Gacaca Process in Rwanda", *New York University Journal of International Law & Politics* 34(2): 377.
43. Ibid., pp. 374.
44. Press interview with Domitilla Mukantangazwa (2006) *New Times*, Kigali, 15 July.
45. Rwanda is currently debating proposals to amend its laws so as to abolish the death penalty. The proposals are spearheaded by the RPF, the party that dominates all branches of the government, including the legislature. The passage of the proposals is virtually a foregone conclusion.
46. Amnesty International (2002) "Rwanda: Gacaca – Gambling with Justice", press release, London: Amnesty International, available from http://web.amnesty.org/library/index/ENGAFR470032002.
47. Constitution of the Republic of Rwanda, arts 18(2), 19(2), 19(1), 15(2), and 15(3).
48. Universal Declaration of Human Rights, arts 10 and 14; International Covenant on Civil and Political Rights, art. 14(1); African Charter on Human and Peoples' Rights, art. 60; Constitution of the Republic of Rwanda, art. 19.
49. Amnesty International (2002) *Gacaca: A Question of Justice*, AI Index AFR 47/007/2002, London: Amnesty International, p. 38.
50. Catherine Honeyman, Shakira Hudani, Alfa Tiruneh, Justina Hierta, Leila Chiraya, Andrew Iliff and Jens Meierhenrich (2004) "Establishing Collective Norms: Potentials for Participatory Justice in Rwanda", *Peace and Conflict: Journal of Peace Psychology* 10(1): 1–24, 15.
51. See European Court judgments in the cases of Ofrer and Hopfinger, Nos. 524/59 and 617/59, Dec. 19.12.60, Yearbook 6, pp. 680, 696.
52. Amnesty International, *Gacaca: A Question of Justice*, p. 35.
53. Honeyman et al., "Establishing Collective Norms", p. 18.
54. Amnesty International, *Gacaca: A Question of Justice*, pp. 36–37.
55. Constitution of the Republic of Rwanda, art. 140.
56. Basic Principles on the Independence of the Judiciary, principles 7, 10–12, and 17–20.
57. Amnesty International, *Gacaca: A Question of Justice*, p. 19.
58. Ibid.

59. Office of the President (1999) *Report on the Reflection Meetings Held in the Office of the President of the Republic from May 1998 to March 1999*, Kigali: Republic of Rwanda, paras 108–114.

60. Uvin (2002) *The Gacaca Tribunals of Rwanda*, IDEA case study, available from http:// www.idea.int/conflict/reconciliation/reconciliation_chap07cs-rwanda.pdf.

61. Instruction No. 06/2005 of 20/7/2005 of the Executive Secretary of the National Service of Gacaca Courts on Dismissal of the Judge Inyangamugayo from the Gacaca Court Bench, Dissolution of a Gacaca Bench and Replacement of the Judge Inyangamugayo, arts 3 and 10.

62. UN Human Rights Committee (1992) *Karttunen v. Finland* (387/1989) Report of the Human Rights Committee, vol. 2, (A/48/40), at 120, relating to lay judges; and UN Human Rights Committee (1991) *Collins v. Jamaica* (240/1987), Report of the Human Rights Committee, (A/47/40), at 236 para. 8.4, requiring jurors to be impartial.

63. See Africa Rights (2003) *Gacaca: A Shared Responsibility*, London: African Rights; and A. Corey and S. Joireman (2004) "Redistributive Justice: The Gacaca Courts in Rwanda", *African Affairs* 103: 73–85.

64. Some 1,226 gacaca judges were removed during the pilot phase of gacaca courts. Official Web site of the National Service of Gacaca Jurisdictions, available from http://www. inkiko-gacaca.com.

65. Personal interviews with genocide survivors during prosecutorial investigations, 1999– 2003.

66. Corey and Joireman, "Redistributive Justice".

67. Discussions with Chief Military Prosecutor, 2001–2003.

68. Honeyman et al., "Establishing Collective Norms", p. 11.

69. Corey and Joireman, "Redistributive Justice".

70. For an account of the way Rwandan society is deeply divided over justice relating to the war and genocide, see the reports of Penal Reform International, which has monitored the gacaca process since its inception, available from http//penalreform.org.

71. Amnesty International, *Gacaca: A Question of Justice*, p. 40.

72. J. Mendez (1997) "Accountability for Past Abuses", *Human Rights Quarterly*, 19: 255– 261.

73. S. Vandegiste (2003) "Victims of Genocide, Crimes against Humanity and War Crimes in Rwanda: The Legal and Institutional Framework of Their Right to Reparations", in J. Torpey, ed. *Politics and the Past: On Repairing Historical Injustices*, Lanham, Md.: Rowman & Littlefield.

74. The National Unity and Reconciliation Commission of Rwanda has produced a report, *Nation-wide Grassroots Consultations Report: Unity and Reconciliation Initiatives in Rwanda* (Kigali, Rwanda) which documents the deep-rooted frustrations of victims of RPA abuses over discrimination in access to state assistance and, indirectly, the refusal of the government to address the legacy of the crimes of which they were victims.

75. J. Sarkin (2001) "The Tension between Justice and Reconciliation in Rwanda: Politics, Human Rights, Due Process and the Role of Gacaca in Dealing with the Genocide", *Journal of African Law* 45(2): 143–172.

76. Ibid.

77. J. Zalaquett (1992) "The Dilemma of New Democracies Confronting Past Human Rights Abuses", *Hastings Law Journal* 43: 1425.

11

Independence and impartiality of the international judiciary: Some lessons learned, and some ignored

William A. Schabas

In principle, cautious, polite phrases are employed to describe defendants before the international criminal tribunals so as not to suggest that they are presumed guilty. But in practice, it is usually a foregone conclusion that they are responsible for terrible atrocities and will be convicted. Of course, there have been occasional acquittals. Three Nazi defendants were judged not guilty by the International Military Tribunal at Nuremberg.[1] It was never suggested that they were entirely innocent, however, and the trio was subsequently convicted by German courts for involvement in wartime atrocities. Only a handful of defendants at the ad hoc tribunals for the former Yugoslavia and for Rwanda have been discharged following trial or appeal. Two of the acquittals involved low-level government officials who were accused of crimes committed by others, on the basis of "superior responsibility".[2] The Prosecutor did not have enough evidence that the accused were actually "superiors" with command authority. At the International Criminal Tribunal for the former Yugoslavia (ICTY), Zejnil Delalić was acquitted of all charges because the Prosecutor did not establish that he exercised superior authority over the Celebici prison camp.[3] Delalić was alleged to have exercised authority over the Celebici prison camp in his role first as coordinator of the Bosnian Muslim and Bosnian Croat forces in the area, and later as Commander of the First Tactical Group of the Bosnian Army. Ignace Bagilishema, a *bourgmestre* or mayor, was acquitted by the International Criminal Tribunal for Rwanda (ICTR) because the Prosecutor failed to establish the exercise of real control over roving bands of

Atrocities and international accountability: Beyond transitional justice, Hughes, Schabas and Thakur (eds), United Nations University Press, 2007, ISBN 978-92-808-1141-4

killers.[4] The four other acquittals were all from one case, involving Croatians charged with attacking Bosnian Muslims in the village of Ahmici, in central Bosnia. Dragan Papić was acquitted by the Trial Chamber, which found the eyewitness evidence of one person too unreliable to sustain a conviction.[5] In the same case, the three Kupreškić brothers were initially convicted, but this was overturned by the Appeals Chamber for the same reason, namely, unreliable evidence from one eyewitness.[6] These cases are so isolated and unique as to confirm the general observation that once an individual is indicted, conviction is virtually inevitable. The Prosecutor obtains rates of conviction before the international tribunals comparable to those in Burma or in China, but that are unheard of in credible national justice systems.

To the likelihood of conviction, based simply on the statistical evidence, must be added the phenomenon of public condemnation and denunciation of alleged offenders by national and international political leaders, institutions and media. This is a serious violation of the presumption of innocence. In its General Comment on article 14 of the International Covenant on Civil and Political Rights, the UN Human Rights Committee explained that respect for the presumption of innocence imposes a duty on all public authorities to "refrain from prejudging the outcome of a trial".[7] According to the European Commission of Human Rights, in application of the equivalent provision in the European Convention on Human Rights,

> It is a fundamental principle embodied in [the presumption of innocence] which protects everybody against being treated by public officials as being guilty of an offence before this is established according to law by a competent court. Article 6, paragraph 2, therefore, may be violated by public officials if they declare that somebody is responsible for criminal acts without a court having found so. This does not mean, of course, that the authorities may not inform the public about criminal investigations. They do not violate Article 6, paragraph 2, if they state that a suspicion exists, that people have been arrested, that they have confessed, etc. What is excluded, however, is a formal declaration that somebody is guilty.[8]

The transposition of this principle to the international context leads to some interesting observations. The "authorities" on the international scene are such UN bodies as the Commission on Human Rights, the High Commissioner for Human Rights, the Security Council, the General Assembly and the Secretary-General. For example, in a resolution denouncing the atrocities in Srebrenica, the Security Council singled out for special mention the Bosnian Serb leaders Radovan Karadžić and Ratko Mladić, noting that they had been indicted by the International Criminal Tribunal for their responsibilities in the massacre.[9] The word "alleged" did not accompany the reference to their responsibilities. The resolution "condemn[ed] in particular in the strongest possible terms the violations of international humanitarian law and of human rights by Bosnian Serb and paramilitary forces in the areas of Srebrenica". The former Organization for Security and Cooperation in Europe High Representative for implementation of the Dayton Agreement, Carlos Westendorp, declared that the situation in Bosnia could not be "normalized" until Karadžić was brought before the International Tribunal;[10] such a statement could hardly be made if he were truly presumed innocent. And even the most reputable newspapers and other media indulge in public condemnation of persons accused before international tribunals in a manner that would be unthinkable in the context of national justice systems and "ordinary" crimes. The reproduction of the editorial cartoon on the front page of the distinguished French newspaper *Le Monde* following the initial appearance of Slobodan Milošević before the ICTY provides a good illustration (see Figure 11.1). And if this is the standard set by *Le Monde*, we can imagine the level of respect for the presumption

Figure 11.1 *Le Monde* editorial cartoon
Front page of *Le Monde* a few days after the transfer of Milošević to the Hague, in July 2001. The headline is "Milosevic Pleads 'Not Guilty'". Beneath it is an editorial cartoon showing Milošević as a bloody butcher saying, "Not guilty". (Paris, 4 July 2001.)

of innocence and the rights of the accused taken by less scrupulous newspapers.

The very high likelihood of conviction coupled with the very public denunciation and condemnation of accused persons by international organizations and major media organs provokes legitimate questions about the fairness of international criminal justice. The historic Nuremberg proceedings have always remained under just such a pall, condemned by one distinguished critic as a "high-grade lynching party"[11] and often labelled pejoratively as "victor's justice".[12] But the shortcomings of Nuremberg have also nourished the arguments of those who deny the Nazi war crimes,[13] and this runs at cross-purposes with the fundamental objectives of international justice. One of the best measures of fairness in the proceedings is therefore the independence and impartiality of the judges. Public confidence in the integrity of those meting out justice can do much to compensate for some of the evident and possibly inherent weaknesses in the system.

This chapter examines the question of independence and impartiality of the judiciary with respect to the four contemporary international criminal tribunals, the three ad hoc institutions that have been established by the United Nations for the former Yugoslavia, Rwanda and Sierra Leone, and the permanent International Criminal Court (ICC). The constitutive instruments of all four tribunals maintain, of course, that the judges are "independent". For example, the statutes of the three ad hoc tribunals declare that the Chambers are to be composed of "independent judges".[14] This seemingly gratuitous reference to "independent judges" is probably derived from article 2 of the Statute of the International Court of Justice. The Rome Statute of the International Criminal Court devotes a distinct provision to the subject:

Article 40. Independence of the judges

1. The judges shall be independent in the performance of their functions.
2. Judges shall not engage in any activity which is likely to interfere with their judicial functions or to affect confidence in their independence.
3. Judges required to serve on a full-time basis at the seat of the Court shall not engage in any other occupation of a professional nature.
4. Any question regarding the application of paragraphs 2 and 3 shall be decided by an absolute majority of the judges. Where any such question concerns an individual judge, that judge shall not take part in the decision.

The Statute of the Special Court for Sierra Leone (SCSL) also contains a specific text on this point, declaring that judges: "shall be independent in the performance of their functions, and shall not accept or seek instructions from any Government or any other source".[15] The statutes also impose a requirement of impartiality. The provision describing the qualifications of judges states that they "shall be persons of high moral character, impartiality and integrity".[16] Under the oath of office, ICTY judges declare that they will exercise their powers "honourably, faithfully, impartially and conscientiously".[17]

Interestingly, although the various fair trial provisions in the four statutes are derived from models in international human rights instruments, notably article 14 of the International Covenant on Civil and Political Rights,[18] they do not include the classic formulation of the right to be tried by an "independent and impartial tribunal" that first appeared in article 10 of the Universal Declaration of Human Rights: "Everyone is entitled in full equality to a fair and public hearing by an independent and impartial tribunal."[19] Perhaps it seemed inappropriate to recognize this right within a legal instrument establishing a tribunal, given that the statutes themselves were to ensure independence and impartiality. But there can be no question that impartiality as well as independence is a requirement imposed both upon the individual judges and the tribunals as a whole.

International human rights law distinguishes between "independence" and "impartiality". While independence is desirable in and of itself, its importance really lies in the fact that it creates the conditions for impartiality. The distinction was discussed by Judge Geoffrey Robertson of the SCSL in his separate opinion to a challenge to jurisdiction based upon a lack of judicial independence. Judge Robertson invoked the common law authorities rather than those of international human rights law, however:

> "Independence and impartiality" is an alliterative conjunction found in most human rights treaties, although the two concepts are in fact disparate and have different legal histories. "Independence" means putting judges in a position to act according to their conscience and the justice of the case, free from pressures from governments, funding bodies, armies, churches, newspapers or any other source of power and influence that may otherwise bear upon them. It was established in the common law by an enactment of the long parliament in 1641, as an early victory (to be defended subsequently by arms) in the struggle against "Stuart absolutism". "Impartiality", on the other hand, is generally regarded as the judicial characteristic of disinterest towards parties and their causes. The common law began to develop rules against bias in the nineteenth century, beginning with the disqualification of judges who held stock in companies which were parties in their court. There is, of course, an overlap: judges who are not independent of the state will be perceived (and may actually become) partial to the state when it is a party to litigation.[20]

The case law of international human rights bodies confirms that the discussion of judicial independence and impartiality involves two aspects, one objective and one subjective. As the old maxim goes, "justice must not only be done, it must be seen to be done".[21] An individual judge may be above reproach from the standpoint of impartiality, yet the conditions of appointment, remuneration and tenure may lead a "reasonable person" to suspect that justice cannot be done. According to the European Court of Human Rights:

> Under the objective test, it must be determined whether, quite apart from the judge's personal conduct, there are ascertainable facts which may raise doubts as to his impartiality. In this respect, even appearances may be of a certain importance. What is at stake is the confidence which the courts in a democratic society must inspire in the public and above all, as far as criminal proceedings are concerned, in the accused. Accordingly, any judge in respect of whom there is a legitimate reason to fear a lack of impartiality must withdraw. This implies that in deciding whether in a given case there is a legitimate reason to fear that a particular judge lacks impartiality, the stand-point of the accused is important but not decisive. What is decisive is whether this fear can be held to be objectively justified.[22]

A judge who lacks the appropriate trappings of independence is potentially vulnerable to manipulation. The ICTY Appeals Chamber has described judicial impartiality in this manner:

> A Judge should not only be subjectively free from bias, but also ... there should be nothing in the surrounding circumstances that objectively gives rise to an appearance of bias. On this basis, the Appeals Chamber considers that the following principles should direct it in interpreting and applying the impartiality requirement of the Statute:
>
> A. A Judge is not impartial if it is shown that actual bias exists.
> B. There is an unacceptable appearance of bias if:
>   (i) a Judge is a party to the case, or has a financial or proprietary interest in the outcome of a case, or if the Judge's decision will lead to the promotion of a cause in which he or she is involved, together with one of the parties. Under these circumstances, a Judge's disqualification from the case is automatic; or
>   (ii) the circumstances would lead a reasonable observer, properly informed, to reasonably apprehend bias.[23]

To the extent that the judge is even concerned about such interference, his or her judgment may be clouded by improper factors. Obviously this must go beyond mere speculation. Judge Robertson has warned about misreading the "reasonable observer" concept:

> There is always the risk, of course, that hypothetical "reasonable observers" will be accredited with such extensive knowledge about the law and its traditions that they will be turned into lawyers, or indeed judges – a temptation that judges must guard against. What is required of the "reasonable observer" is a fairly hard-nosed appreciation both of how institutional pressures and "old boy networks" can operate, and a feet-on-the-ground ability to exclude far-fetched or theoretical risks. The standpoint of an experienced journalist or human rights researcher may not be inappropriate. Among the qualities of "reasonableness" would include a recognition of the importance of efficient and expeditious prosecution of international crimes.[24]

Judges benefit from a presumption of impartiality, which can be rebutted only on the basis of adequate and reliable evidence.[25] But a judge who is worried about improper influence, and who may compensate accordingly for this, is not an impartial judge. For this reason, it is simply not enough to respond to concerns about independence and impartiality by pointing to the impeccable integrity of those who hold international judicial office. In *Giraklar v. Turkey*, the European Court of Human Rights observed that to "establish whether a tribunal could be considered independent (for the purpose of article 6(1) [of the European Convention on Human Rights]), regard must be made inter alia, to the manner of appointment of its members and their term of office, the existence of safeguards against outside pressures and the question whether it presents an appearance of independence".[26]

Of course, in specific cases there may well be evidence suggesting that a particular individual in specific circumstances lacks impartiality.[27] This possibility is specifically contemplated by the Rules of Procedure and Evidence of the four tribunals, which call for disqualification in such cases.[28] In some cases, defendants have argued on appeal that the behaviour of members of the bench at trial indicated a lack of impartiality.[29]

Over the years, the Human Rights Committee, the regional human rights bodies and national constitutional courts have established a certain number of principles to be considered in analysing whether a person has been tried before an independent and impartial tribunal. There are also important decisions of leading constitutional courts.[30] Guidelines on independence and impartiality have also been provided in specialized international instruments, the most important of them being the "Basic Principles on the Independence of the Judiciary", which was adopted in 1985 by the Seventh United Nations Congress on the Prevention of Crime and the Treatment of Offenders and subsequently endorsed by

General Assembly resolutions.[31] After some introductory provisions dealing with general issues, the Basic Principles consider the subject under
four broad sub-headings: qualifications, selection and training; conditions
of service and tenure; professional secrecy and immunity; and discipline,
suspension and removal. The Basic Principles provide a convenient
framework for a more detailed consideration of the components of judicial independence and impartiality in light of the law applicable to the
international criminal tribunals.

Qualifications, selection and training

Only one provision of the Basic Principles is devoted to "qualifications,
selection and training":

> 10. Persons selected for judicial office shall be individuals of integrity and abil-
> ity with appropriate training or qualifications in law. Any method of judicial
> selection shall safeguard against judicial appointments for improper motives.
> In the selection of judges, there shall be no discrimination against a person on
> the grounds of race, colour, sex, religion, political or other opinion, national or
> social origin, property, birth or status, except that a requirement, that a candi-
> date for judicial office must be a national of the country concerned, shall not be
> considered discriminatory.

The four statutes of the international criminal tribunals affirm that judges
must be persons of "high moral character, impartiality and integrity".[32]
In addition, judges of the international criminal tribunals must "possess
the qualifications required in their respective countries for appointment
to the highest judicial offices".[33] This language is borrowed from Article
2 of the Statute of the International Court of Justice. A variety of requirements is also imposed with respect to nationality,[34] expertise in
public international law and criminal law,[35] fluency in the official languages of the institution,[36] and even expertise concerning violence
against women and children[37] and in juvenile justice,[38] although these
are not particularly relevant to a discussion of independence and impartiality.

The Basic Principles speak of "selection" and do not favour any particular method for designating judges, no doubt reflecting the very wide
range of approaches taken by national justice systems from around the
world. Three of the international tribunals designate judges by election,
and one designates them by appointment.

Judges of the ICTY and ICTR are elected by majority vote of the
General Assembly of the United Nations. The Secretary-General invites

nominations from Member States of the United Nations, as well as from non-member States maintaining permanent observer missions at United Nations Headquarters. Each State is entitled to nominate up to two candidates, although they may not be of the same nationality. The Secretary-General forwards the nominations to the Security Council, which establishes a list of not less than 22 and not more than 33 candidates. In preparing its list for the General Assembly, the Security Council is to take "due account of the adequate representation of the principal legal systems of the world".[39] Although there are no egregious examples of abuse, the system is fraught with the potential for manipulation and political influence at every stage. As Ruth Mackenzie and Philippe Sands have pointed out,

> A state nominates or appoints individuals to international judicial office knowing that the judge may be involved in deciding a contentious case that implicates its national interests. It would be unreasonable to expect that a nominating or appointing state would not put forward as a candidate a person who shares (in general terms) the value systems of the nominating state. But how far is a state entitled to go in ensuring the nomination of a "safe pair of hands"? At what point should a prior relationship between a potential judge and the nominating state preclude appointment?[40]

Concerns about the appointment process at the ICTY and the ICTR led the drafters of the Rome Statute to effect some important refinements in the process. Judges of the ICC are elected by the Assembly of States Parties. By comparison with the ICTY and the ICTR, where a state's right to propose candidates is unfettered, the Rome Statute accords an important degree of attention to the integrity of the nomination process. Two methods are envisaged. Judges may be nominated according to the procedure for the nomination of candidates for appointment to the highest judicial offices in the state in question.[41] There is an implicit assumption that pursuant to the internal law of many States, this nomination procedure is accompanied by various safeguards designed to ensure independence and impartiality. In the United Kingdom, for example, nomination of its candidate involved advertising the position of ICC judge within the national media and inviting persons qualified for senior judicial office in the country to submit their applications. Alternatively, judges may be nominated by the procedure provided for the nomination of candidates for the International Court of Justice in the Statute of that court.[42]

An elaborate and controversial procedure was developed by the Assembly of States Parties for the election of ICC judges.[43] The principal concern was to ensure gender balance on the bench and, to a lesser extent, regional diversity. Because the Rome Statute also imposes quotas with respect to the number of judges claiming expertise in either criminal law or public international law, the electoral process also had to take this into account.[44] These complex criteria were met by requiring, as a condition of validity of a ballot, that Member States include six names from each gender, as well as three candidates from each of the five regional groups that make up the international system. The voting was apparently a nasty business, with an especially high proportion of states, even by United Nations standards, making promises to support certain candidates that they did not in fact honour. Many States made more promises than they had votes to cast. Although rancour may have been an unintended by-product, the system did result in the election of a record number of women judges to an international tribunal. It also achieved a degree of regional balance, although one constrained by the fact that membership in the Court itself does not accurately reflect the regions of the world.

These improvements in the selection process, which made it considerably more transparent and professional, served only to highlight the weaknesses of the system in place for the ICTY and the ICTR. How surprising it was, then, that the most recent of the judicial institutions to be created, the SCSL, has the most primitive scheme of them all. There is no real nomination procedure, and no election. Judges are appointed, five of them by the Secretary-General of the United Nations, and three of them by the government of Sierra Leone.[45] Those appointed by the Secretary-General are drawn from nominations forwarded by states, and in particular the member states of the Economic Community of West African States and the Commonwealth.[46]

Designation by the Secretary-General following a process that lacks real transparency is nowhere near an ideal situation. Some small improvements could easily have been introduced without undue hardship. For example, the conditions of nomination by states that appear in the Rome Statute might well have been incorporated. Still, it is unlikely that the proverbial "reasonable person" would be overly perturbed by the situation. The Secretary-General is a person of great integrity who, moreover, appears to have no particular interest except that justice of the highest quality be done. Would that the same could be said of the government of Sierra Leone, which is responsible for designating three of the judges. When the President of Sierra Leone initiated efforts to establish the Tribunal, in June 2000, he demonstrated his bias by calling for an institution whose mandate it would be to prosecute members of the Revolutionary United Front, that is to say, his enemies.[47] Members of the government of Sierra Leone, including the President, participated in the conflict over which the Special Court has jurisdiction, and are suspects themselves. In fact, one of those currently accused and standing trial, Sam Hinga Norman, was a minister in the government at the time the judges were initially appointed, in July 2002, as well as at the time of his arrest, in March 2003. Without in any way impugning the actual impartiality of the individual judges appointed by the government of Sierra Leone, a "reasonable person" might well be uncomfortable with such a process. In the practice of the Court, the only judge to be disqualified was a government of Sierra Leone appointee. The Appeals Chamber considered it improper for him to sit in trials with Revolutionary United Front (RUF) suspects because in a widely circulated book – which was in print at the time of his appointment – he had expressed views on the responsibility of the RUF and of its leaders for various atrocities.[48] The views expressed in the book largely corresponded, of course, to the narrative of the conflict espoused by the government of Sierra Leone.[49]

Issues concerning the selection of judges also arise in the case of vacancies, where special measures are envisaged. Vacancies may result from illness, death or resignation of a member of one of the tribunals. In the case of the ICTY and ICTR, the Statutes allow the Secretary-General to appoint a judge for the remainder of the term, after consulting with the presidents of the Security Council and the General Assembly.[50] In practice, the Secretary-General invites the State that nominated the judge responsible for the vacancy to designate his or her successor. Such a solution is a nod of deference to the highly politicized environment of judicial election within the United Nations, and an unpleasant reminder that more is involved than simply finding the best person for the job. In effect, states make deals with other states concerning the balloting that may have little or nothing to do with the qualifications of the various candidates. Once victorious, they are not willing to lose "their" judge because of an inconvenient departure.[51] This practice follows that of the International Court of Justice. But while the idea of a national judge may at least be somewhat understandable in the context of an international court that deals with the rights and obligations of states, the situation is entirely different for a criminal tribunal charged with determining the guilt or innocence of individuals.[52] The practice by which states essentially appoint judges to serve the balance of a vacant term at the ICTY and the ICTR is hard to reconcile with international standards of judicial independence and impartiality concerning the selection of judges.

The SCSL instruments make no special provision for vacancies. Given that judges are appointed in the first place, their replacement, even before the expiration of the term of office, raises no special issues. The flaws in the appointment process, discussed above, are merely replicated in the case of vacancies.

Once again, the International Criminal Court offers the best approach. Under the Rome Statute, if a judicial position becomes vacant, it is filled by election. However, the new judge only completes the term of office in question. If the remaining period is three years or less, then the new judge may stand for re-election.[53] This is similar to the approach at the International Court of Justice.[54] In practice, vacancies at the International Court of Justice, as well as at the ICTY and ICTR, are filled by judges of the same nationality as the departing judge, although there are a few exceptions. Because there have as yet been no vacancies, it remains to be seen whether the states parties to the International Criminal Court will follow the same tradition.

In 2001, following various proposals aimed at expediting trials,[55] the Security Council authorized the establishment of a new category of judge, known as the *ad litem* judge.[56] The ICTY Statute was duly amended to authorize the election of judges who would sit in trials on a case-by-case basis. The maximum term was set at three years, thereby ensuring that they would not become eligible for United Nations pensions. A pool of ad litem judges was elected, from which could be designated judges to join specific trial chambers. As a general rule, priority was given to those who had obtained the highest number of votes in the General Assembly elections. Two years later, after entreaties from the President of the ICTR,[57] a similar pool of ad litem judges was elected for that Tribunal.[58] The ad litem judges sit as full members of a Trial Chamber, but they do not have the same powers as "permanent judges"[59] with respect to pre-trial matters and administrative issues, such as amendment of the Rules of Procedure and Evidence (RPE).[60]

Conditions of service and tenure

Four provisions of the Basic Principles concern conditions of service and tenure, an indication as to the importance these issues play in the protection of judicial independence and impartiality.

11. The term of office of judges, their independence, security, adequate remuneration, conditions of service, pensions and the age of retirement shall be adequately secured by law.
12. Judges, whether appointed or elected, shall have guaranteed tenure until a mandatory retirement age or the expiry of their term of office, where such exists.
13. Promotion of judges, wherever such a system exists, should be based on objective factors, in particular ability, integrity and experience.
14. The assignment of cases to judges within the court to which they belong is an internal matter of judicial administration.

The third of these provisions, article 13, is of no relevance to the international tribunals. Article 14 is reflected in various provisions of the applicable law of the international tribunals.[61] The only issue here concerns the assignment of cases to ad litem judges at the ICTY and ICTR, when such "assignment" is also, in fact, an appointment to serve.

Ad litem judges are employed essentially on a contractual basis. Once formally appointed, they work only when the President of the Tribunal assigns them to the Trial Chambers.[62] To this extent they are, in a sense, designated three times. First, they must be elected to the roster, second, they must actually be assigned to the Tribunal from the roster and third, they must be given an actual case. The President's discretion with respect to the assignment of a case would seem to be unlimited. While there have been no suggestions of impropriety, does it never cross the mind of an ad litem judge, in considering whether or not to make an unpopular decision, whether this might compromise his or her chances of being assigned to another case? It is not difficult to conceive of issues that might make an ad litem judge fall from favour, for example, a ruling that might have as a consequence a considerable addition to the length of the proceedings. The uncertainty of re-assignment does not appear to have been raised in any litigation before the Trial Chambers. A simple solution to this difficulty would be a rule by which ad litem judges can sit in only one case. But the tendency has been to move in the other direction. A recent amendment to the ICTY Statute allows ad litem judges to stand for re-election for another term, compounding their vulnerability to improper considerations.[63]

Judges of the tribunals are remunerated at high international levels, and there can be few complaints in this area. For judges from developed countries, the salaries are certainly competitive with judicial remuneration at the national level. For judges from developing countries, the international salaries are by and large well above the norm for national judges.

Remuneration for the ICTY and ICTR judges is drawn from the general funds of the United Nations, and is relatively secure. Remuneration for SCSL judges is dependent upon the resources of the SCSL itself, which are in fact somewhat precarious. The SCSL is funded by voluntary contributions from Member States. When the Court was being established, the Secretary-General was reluctant to proceed until funds had been raised for at least three years of operations, but he later compromised. This situation was challenged unsuccessfully by one of the defendants at the SCSL in a preliminary motion. The SCSL Appeals Chamber said, "mere complaint about funding arrangements of a Court cannot by itself be a ground for imputing a real likelihood of bias to a judge. What is material and has to be established is that such funding arrangements are capable of creating a real and reasonable apprehension in the mind of an average person that the judge is not likely to be able to decide fairly."[64] The Appeals Chamber pointed out that the judges had secure contracts of three years, and that the SCSL was liable for the amount. It described the challenge as "far-fetched" and lacking any "factual basis".[65] In an individual and concurring opinion, Judge Robertson examined the funding arrangements in some detail, noting the concern by the Secretary-General about the uncertainty of funding. He cited the agreement establishing the Court, which said that in the event voluntary contributions were insufficient, the Secretary-General and the Security Council would "explore alternate means of financing the Court", taking this as an "assurance that the Security Council accepts continuing responsibility for the Court and will make up the balance should voluntary contributions prove inadequate".[66]

The Rome Statute of the International Criminal Court contains the following provision:

Article 49. Salaries, allowances and expenses
The judges, the Prosecutor, the Deputy Prosecutors, the Registrar and the Deputy Registrar shall receive such salaries, allowances and expenses as may be decided upon by the Assembly of States Parties. These salaries and allowances shall not be reduced during their terms of office.

As is the case at the other treaty-based court, the Special Court for Sierra Leone, judges are dependant upon the ongoing commitment of States to fund the tribunal. In contrast with the SCSL, States parties to the Rome Statute are under a treaty obligation to fund the institution, in accordance with their assessed contribution. At the SCSL, all contributions are voluntary.

Judges at the ICTY and ICTR are eligible for pensions as employees of the United Nations. The ad litem judges at the ICTY and ICTR have no pensions; the maximum three-year term was set by the Security Council quite intentionally so as to avoid these judges becoming eligible for United Nations pensions under the general rules of the organization. The SCSL judges have no pensions either. Judges at the ICC are entitled to a pension similar to that applicable to judges of the International Court of Justice.[67]

The prospect of re-election or re-appointment at the conclusion of a judge's term is inherently troublesome. No sitting judge should ever be concerned with pleasing members of the Security Council, or members of the General Assembly, or even the Secretary-General or, above all, the government of Sierra Leone, so as to improve his or her chances of a second term. One SCSL judge has said that in the interests of independence, "judges on contracts should not have them renewed more than once".[68] Obviously, the judge understood the problem, and his observation is a useful one. But why doesn't it apply to re-appointment (and re-election) altogether?

It is precisely for this reason that the drafters of the Rome Statute rejected the idea of re-election. Instead, they opted for relatively long terms, of nine years, and a single mandate.[69] There are two minor exceptions to this general principle. In order to obtain a rotation of the eighteen ICC judges, with elections of six judges being held every three years, only six of the first group of judges elected were designated to serve nine-year terms. Six others were given a six-year term, and six a three-year term. The three-year term judges are allowed to stand for re-election to a second term, which will run for nine years.[70] As has already been mentioned, a judge elected to complete the mandate of a vacant judge may also stand for re-election, to the extent that the vacancy period is three years or less.

Though a marked improvement on the ad hoc tribunals, even the ICC is not without shortcomings in this area. In most justice systems, a judge will be given job security for his or her entire career. The problem with international judges who work for a term, even a relatively lengthy one of nine years, is that they need to consider future job prospects. These may involve a judicial appointment in their state of origin, or some important position in national government or an international organization. This situation is not likely to promote the independence and impartiality of a judge called upon to make unpopular decisions. It is worth recalling that the subject matter of international tribunals is inherently political, and that both governments and international organizations have clear interests in the outcomes of the international judicial process.

All three ad hoc tribunals have increased the number of judges originally provided for. Nothing in the applicable law of the three institutions determines whether the Security Council, in the case of the ICTY and ICTR, or the two parties to the Agreement, the United Nations and the government of Sierra Leone, in the case of the SCSL, could also reduce the number of judges. Presumably, they have the power to do so. But there is no provision preventing this from taking place in such a way as to jeopardize the term of office of a judge. That this is a live issue is confirmed in the ICC Statute, which allows for a reduction in the number of judges if this is dictated by a decreased workload. However, the Assembly of States Parties can do this only by attrition, that is, by waiting until the end of an individual judge's term before shrinking the size of the Court.[71]

Professional secrecy and immunity

Two provisions of the Basic Principles concern professional secrecy and immunity:

15. The judiciary shall be bound by professional secrecy with regard to their deliberations and to confidential information acquired in the course of their duties other than in public proceedings, and shall not be compelled to testify on such matters.

16. Without prejudice to any disciplinary procedure or to any right of appeal or to compensation from the State, in accordance with national law, judges should enjoy personal immunity from civil suits for monetary damages for improper acts or omissions in the exercise of their judicial functions.

These principles are not easily transposable to an international context. It is relatively straightforward for national legislation to protect professional secrecy and to ensure immunity from civil suit where judges of the same national legal system are concerned. But international judges do not belong to any distinct and coherent legal system.

The statutes of the ad hoc tribunals for the former Yugoslavia and Rwanda contain a provision concerning immunities:

The status, privileges and immunities of the International Tribunal

1. The Convention on the Privileges and Immunities of the United Nations of 13 February 1946 shall apply to the International Tribunal, the judges, the Prosecutor and his staff, and the Registrar and his staff.

2. The judges, the Prosecutor and the Registrar shall enjoy the privileges and immunities, exemptions and facilities accorded to diplomatic envoys, in accordance with international law.[72]

Because the Statute is annexed to a resolution of the Security Council, it may be argued that these provisions are mandatory with respect to all Member States of the United Nations. Nevertheless, most states would require implementing legislation to give effect to such provisions, and it is doubtful that effective measures have been taken by most of them in this respect. Most States have no particular legal provisions protecting judges at the international tribunals from the threat of being compelled to testify about matters that should remain secret. Within the host states of the two tribunals, of course, specific arrangements govern to ensure appropriate protection. These establish the inviolability of the archives of the institutions, and treatment equivalent to that of diplomats with respect to confidential correspondence, immunity from legal process and similar matters.[73]

The Special Court for Sierra Leone is in a less enviable position, because it is unlikely that the participation of the United Nations and the involvement of the Security Council are enough to make the provisions of its Statute binding upon third states. In any event, the privileges and immunities provision found in the ICTY and ICTR Statutes is not reproduced in the SCSL Statute, so even if the Statute were to be mandatory on United Nations Member States, there is no relevant provision to be enforced. Of course, Sierra Leone has a host state agreement that is broadly equivalent to those of the ICTY and ICTR.[74]

The ICC Statute requires states parties to ensure to its judges "when engaged on or with respect to the business of the Court" privileges and immunities equivalent to those accorded to heads of diplomatic missions. Moreover, after the expiry of their terms of office, they continue to be accorded immunity from legal process of every kind in respect of words spoken or written and acts performed by them in their official capacity.[75] More elaborate and generous provisions are set out in the Agreement on the Privileges and Immunities of the International Criminal Court.[76]

With respect to secrecy, provisions in the RPE of the ad hoc tribunals and in the ICC Statute establish that the deliberations are secret.[77] A notable addition to the oath of office for ICC judges that does not appear in the comparable text for the ICTY or ICTR is the pledge to "respect the confidentiality of investigations and prosecutions and the secrecy of deliberations".[78] There is authority for the proposition that judicial deliberations and observations in relation to matters upon which the judges of the tribunals are required to adjudicate may not be the subject of compelled evidence before the tribunals themselves. The ICTY Appeals Chamber has noted that those persons cannot be subpoenaed to testify as witnesses in the matter at issue since their work, which is integral to the operation of the Tribunal, must be protected by confidentiality.[79]

Discipline, suspension and removal

Although financial security is vital to judicial independence and impartiality, an assurance that judges cannot be dismissed is probably the most important dimension of this question. The Basic Principles contain four provisions dealing with discipline, suspension and removal:

17. A charge or complaint made against a judge in his/her judicial and professional capacity shall be processed expeditiously and fairly under an appropriate procedure. The judge shall have the right to a fair hearing. The examination of the matter at its initial stage shall be kept confidential, unless otherwise requested by the judge.
18. Judges shall be subject to suspension or removal only for reasons of incapacity or behaviour that renders them unfit to discharge their duties.
19. All disciplinary, suspension or removal proceedings shall be determined in accordance with established standards of judicial conduct.
20. Decisions in disciplinary, suspension or removal proceedings should be subject to an independent review. This principle may not apply to the

decisions of the highest court and those of the legislature in impeachment or similar proceedings.

Only one of the four international criminal tribunals under consideration, the International Criminal Court, has any applicable provision in its Statute concerning excusing and disqualification of judges. This is a very serious shortcoming.

The Rome Statute authorizes removal of a judge for serious misconduct or serious breach of duties, or when a judge is unable to exercise his or her functions.[80] Elaborate definitions of "serious misconduct" and "serious breach of duties" are provided in the Rules of Procedure and Evidence.[81] The RPE also set out a procedure for the handling of a complaint directed against a judge that might lead to dismissal.[82] A decision to remove a judge from office must be made by a two-thirds majority of the states parties, in a secret ballot, acting upon a recommendation adopted by a two-thirds majority of the other judges.[83] This is a high threshold; the requirement of a recommendation by the other judges ensures that the power of removal will not be exercised capriciously.

None of the three statutes of the ad hoc tribunals address the issue of dismissal or removal of judges in any way. The RPE of the three tribunals contain provisions dealing with disqualification of judges in specific cases, but this is not at all the same thing as dismissal or removal. Proceeding from the hypothesis that a judge at one of the tribunals actually became unfit but refused to resign, who would be responsible for dismissal? Moreover, there is nothing to indicate what grounds for dismissal might consist of. The importance of some detailed provision in this respect is evidenced by the texts in the Rome Statute and the ICC RPE on this subject. Lack of any clarity on these points in the law applicable to the ICTY, ICTR and SCSL is, in itself, a serious shortcoming and a threat to judicial impendence and impartiality. It is important for a judge to know what might constitute sufficient grounds for removal from office.

The issue of dismissal of judges has been raised before the ICTY, but not decided. In a challenge, the defence argued that the Security Council, a political body, had the authority to dismiss judges. The defence claimed that this meant the independence and impartiality of the judges was compromised. The Bureau replied that there was nothing in the ICTY Statute to give this responsibility to either the Security Council or the General Assembly. According to Judge Mohamed Shahabuddeen, an argument that the Tribunal is a subsidiary organ of the Security Council and that the latter could therefore act even without authorization from the Statute of the Tribunal and without first amending it would collide with the nature of the Tribunal: the latter was obviously intended to be "established, not as an advisory organ or a mere subordinate committee

... but as an independent and truly judicial body".[84] Judge Shaha-buddeen doubted whether the Plenary would have the power to remove a judge.[85]

It is probably a general principle of law that where no mechanism is established to remove an office-holder, the authority for removal resides with the body that appointed the office-holder. In the case of the ICTY and ICTR, that body is surely the United Nations General Assembly. In the case of the SCSL, five judges are appointed by the Secretary-General of the United Nations, and three by the government of Sierra Leone. Removal of ICTY and ICTR judges by the United Nations General Assembly, and removal of SCSL judges by the Secretary-General, would probably not shock the "ordinary person". The same cannot be said about the three SCSL judges who are appointed by the government of Sierra Leone. It is entirely unacceptable that judges appointed by the government of Sierra Leone have no clear idea of the conditions that might justify dismissal, especially given the fact that it would appear this lies within the sole prerogative of the government of Sierra Leone. One of the nine individuals standing trial was a minister in that government at the time of his arrest, in March 2003. Any attempt by the government to dismiss a judge would be politically disastrous, but this cannot justify the uncertainties and ambiguities of the position of judges at the Special Court for Sierra Leone.

A similar situation obtains with respect to discipline of judges. Again, the applicable law of the ICC provides a good model, with detailed provisions on the subject, while in the case of the three ad hoc tribunals there is the same disturbing silence. Disciplinary matters concerning ICC judges are dealt with in the Rules of Procedure of Evidence, in accordance with article 47 of the Rome Statute.[86] The statutes and RPE of the ad hoc tribunals are mute on the question of judicial discipline. Silence on this subject is obviously incompatible with the Basic Principles.

Nothing in the public record suggests that any issues concerning discipline of the judges have arisen before the four courts.

Conclusions

At the ad hoc tribunals, there have been several challenges to individual judges aimed at recusing them from specific cases. Defendants have also invoked, on appeal, an alleged lack of impartiality manifested in the behaviour of the trial judges.

Structural weaknesses in the system with respect to judicial independence and impartiality have not generated much litigation. One challenge before the SCSL was dismissed by the Appeals Chamber. On the other hand, the evident flaws in the assignment of ad litem judges have never been challenged. The reluctance of defence counsel (or, for that matter, the Prosecutor) to raise these problems is disappointing, and difficult to understand. That lawyers hesitate before confronting individual judges is understandable; if the challenge fails, they must complete the case before someone they have accused of not being impartial. But when the contestation concerns the working conditions of the judges, one would expect a friendly reception from the bench. This is generally how such litigation has operated at the national level, and there is no reason why the same will not take place before international tribunals.

The major legal instruments of the ad hoc tribunals do a poor job of ensuring judicial independence and impartiality. It was dissatisfaction with this situation that to some extent provoked greater attention and more detailed provisions in the Rome Statute. The relatively prolix provisions of the Rome Statute may also be explained by the fact that the drafters considered that nationals of their own states might find themselves before the Court, and for this reason they insisted on greater safeguards for an independent judiciary. Considering that it was adopted after the Rome Statute, when the elements of this discussion about independence and impartiality were well known, the Statute of the Special Court for Sierra Leone seems a considerable setback. The SCSL has been held up as a "lean" version of the ad hocs, and a cost-efficient alternative to their cumbersome structure and procedure. This is true to an extent, but it is also clear that corners have been cut in the interests of economies and political compromise. The judges of the SCSL are particularly vulnerable to manipulation by the very states that have specific political interests in the outcome of the trials. Hopefully the individual integrity of the members of the Court will ensure that these objective factors concerning their appointment, their tenure and the security of their salaries will not have any real effect on their good judgment.

But the real lesson is that judicial independence and impartiality has been better protected by the International Criminal Court than by the ad hoc tribunals. Not only did the ICC improve on the situation prevailing at those ad hoc tribunals existing when it was established, it shines in comparison with "ad hoc light", the post-Rome model of the Special Court for Sierra Leone. In February and March 2005, the Security Council debated whether to refer the Darfur situation to the ICC, in accordance with the recommendations of the Commission of Inquiry it had set up months earlier.[87] There were competing proposals, notably from the United States, which favoured an ad hoc institution modelled on the SCSL. Ultimately, the Security Council opted for the ICC.[88] There were many good reasons for it to have done so. The far superior guarantees of judicial independence and impartiality at the ICC when compared with an SCSL-type tribunal should certainly have figured in the debate.

International criminal tribunals are created by states. States are driven by a range of competing interests. For the sake of discussion, it may be assumed that the altruistic delivery of impartial justice for international crimes is one of these. It cannot be gainsaid that states also participate in the creation of international criminal tribunals to promote their own interests, to ensure that their adversaries are defeated and to secure their political positions within various regions of the world. The most candid example is provided by the letter of Sierra Leonean President Ahmed Tejan Kabbah to the Security Council in June 2000, asking for the establishment of an international tribunal to prosecute his enemies in the Revolutionary United Front. Generally, states will be careful not to manifest the political goals that they seek in participating in the establishment of international criminal courts. But these essentially political objectives are present, nevertheless, and it is naive to expect states not to attempt to steer international justice in such a way as to fulfil such objectives. This helps to explain the flaws in the institutions with respect to their independence and impartiality. It is a fact that many States seek to influence the direction of international justice, and that they will resist efforts to strengthen the independence and impartiality of the judiciary because this threatens their ability to fulfil such an agenda. The fact is, they do not want a court that is entirely beyond their control.

Independence and impartiality comes at a high cost. Ensuring secure salaries and pensions and the other accoutrements recognized in international law, including the Basic Principles, places important financial demands upon states. The states parties to the Rome Statute understand the important commitments they have made. The share in financing the institution is significant, and it is a recurrent expense, to be paid year after year. Although the burden may be shared more broadly as more States join the Court, the costs will also increase to the extent that the ICC proves it can work effectively. Success will engender expansion, with additional judges and related staff. Low cost has been held out as one of the advantages of the Special Court for Sierra Leone. It has operated on a shoestring budget, by comparison with its senior cousins in the Hague and Arusha. Important economies were obtained by limiting dramatically the number of cases the Court could prosecute. Money was also saved by limiting the judges to very short mandates, and denying them pensions. Hiring judges on short-term contracts certainly helps reduce the bottom line of the tribunal, but it also compromises fundamental principles relating to independence and impartiality. Independence and impartiality have a price. As with many things in life, it seems that in this area, you get what you pay for.

Notes

1. *France et al. v. Göring et al.* (1946) 22 IMT 203, 13 ILR 203, *American Journal of International Law* 41: 172.
2. In accordance with art. 7(3) of the *Statute of the International Criminal Tribunal for the former Yugoslavia*, UN Doc. S/RES/827 (1993), annex (hereinafter ICTY Statute), and art. 6(3) of the *Statute of the International Criminal Tribunal for Rwanda*, UN Doc. S/RES/955 (1994), annex (hereinafter ICTR Statute).
3. *Prosecutor v. Delalić et al.* (Case No. IT-96-21-T), Judgment, 16 November 1998, paras 1046, 1071, 1124, 1144.
4. *Prosecutor v. Bagilishema* (Case No. ICTR-95-1A-T), Judgment, 7 June 2001.
5. *Prosecutor v. Kupreškić et al.* (Case No. IT-95-16-T), Judgment, 14 January 2000, paras 767–768.
6. *Prosecutor v. Kupreškić et al.* (Case No. IT-95-16-A), Appeal Judgment, 23 October 2001.
7. General Comment No. 13 (21), para. 7.
8. *Krause v. Switzerland* (1978) (App. No. 7986/77) 13 DR 73. Also, from the Court: *Allenet de Ribemont v. France*, Series A, No. 308, 10 February 1995, paras 37, 41.
9. UN Security Council (1995) "Former Yugoslavia", UN Doc. S/RES/1034.
10. Press briefing of 27 July 1998.
11. These are the words of United States Chief Justice Harlan Fiske Stone, cited in A. T. Mason (1956) *Harlan Fiske Stone: Pillar of the Law*, New York: Viking Press, pp. 715–716. Stone wrote: "So far as the Nuremberg trial is an attempt to justify the application of the power of the victor to the vanquished because the vanquished made aggressive war ... I dislike extremely to see it dressed up with a false facade of legality. The best that can be said for it is that it is a political act of the victorious States which may be morally right.... It would not disturb me greatly ... if that power were openly and frankly used to punish the German leaders for being a bad lot, but it disturbs me some to have it dressed up in the habiliments of the common law and the Constitutional safeguards to those charged with crime. Jackson is away conducting his high-grade lynching party in Nuremberg.... I don't mind what he does to the Nazis, but I hate to see the pretense that he is running a court and proceeding according to common law. This is a little too sanctimonious a fraud to meet my old-fashioned ideas."
12. For an example, see S. de Bertodano (2002) "Judicial Independence in the International Criminal Court", *Leiden Journal of International Law* 15: 409–412.
13. See, for example, D. Irving (1996) *Nuremberg: The Last Battle*, London: Focal Point.
14. ICTY Statute, art. 12; ICTR Statute, art. 11; Statute of the Special Court for Sierra Leone (hereinafter SCSL Statute), art. 12(1).
15. SCSL Statute, art. 13(1).
16. ICTY Statute, art. 13(1); ICTR Statute, art. 12(1); SCSL Statute, art. 13(1); ICC Statute, art. 36(3)(a).
17. Rules of Procedure and Evidence [of the ICTY], IT/32 (hereinafter ICTY RPE), Rule 14(A); Rules of Procedure and Evidence [of the ICTR] (hereinafter ICTR RPE), Rule 14(A); Rules of Procedure and Evidence [of the ICC], ICC-ASP/1/3, pp. 10–107

(hereinafter ICC RPE), Rule 5(1)(a); Rules of Procedure and Evidence [of the SCSL] (hereinafter SCSL RPE), Rule 14(A).

18. ICTY Statute, art. 21; ICTR Statute, art. 20; ICC Statute, art. 67; SCSL Statute, art. 17.

19. UN General Assembly (1948) "Universal Declaration of Human Rights", Res. 217 A (III), UN Doc. A/810.

20. The distinction between independence and impartiality is discussed at some length in *Prosecutor v. Norman* (SCSL-2004-14-AR72(E)), Separate Opinion of Justice Geoffrey Robertson, 13 March 2004, para. 2.

21. *R. v. Sussex Justices, Ex Parte* McCarthy (1924) 1 KB 256.

22. *Hauschildt v. Denmark*, 27 May 1981, Series A, No. 43, para. 52.

23. *Prosecutor v. Furundžija* (Case No. IT-95-17/1-A), Judgment, 21 July 2000, para. 189.

24. *Prosecutor v. Norman*, para. 18.

25. *Prosecutor v. Akayesu* (ICTR-96-4-A), Judgment, 1 June 2001, para. 91.

26. European Court of Human Rights (1998) App. No. 19601/92, 28 October.

27. See, for example, *Prosecutor v. Sesay* (SCSL-2004-15-AR15), Decision on Defence Motion Seeking the Disqualification of Justice Robertson from the Appeals Chamber, 13 March 2004. Most such challenges before the international tribunals have been dismissed, often with harsh words from the Chambers: *Prosecutor v. Karemera et al.* (ICTR-98-44-T), Decision on Motion by Nzirorera for Disqualification of Trial Judges, 17 May 2004; *Prosecutor v. Furundžija* (IT-95-17/1-A), Judgment, 21 July 2000, paras 189–190; *Prosecutor v. Delalić et al.* (IT-96-21-A), Judgment, 20 February 2001, paras 697–699, 707; *Prosecutor v. Norman* (SCSL-2004-04-14-PT), Decision on the Motion to Recuse Judge Winter from the Deliberation in the Preliminary Motion on the Recruitment of Child Soldiers, 28 May 2004; *Prosecutor v. Šešelj* (Case No. IT-03-67-PT), Decision on Motion for Disqualification, 10 June 2003. See also J. Cockayne (2004) "Special Court for Sierra Leone: Decisions on the Recusal of Judges Robertson and Winter", *Journal of International Criminal Justice*: 1154.

28. ICTY RPE, Rule 15(A); ICTR RPE, Rule 15(A); SCSL RPE, Rule 15(A); ICC RPE, Rule 34. See also ICC Statute, art. 41(2)(a); H. Morrison (2001) "Judicial Independence: Impartiality and Disqualification", in Richard May, David Tolbert, John Hocking, Ken Roberts, Bing Bing Jia, Daryl Mundis and Gabriël Oosthuizen, eds, *Essays on ICTY Procedure and Evidence in Honour of Gabrielle Kirk McDonald*, The Hague: Kluwer Law International, pp. 111–120.

29. For example, Jean-Paul Akayesu charged that Judge Pillay had asked a witness about sexual violence committed at Taba ("Any report of incidence of rape that you have heard?"), although nothing of the sort had been alleged in the indictment. He said this showed she was not impartial with regard to the specific issue of sexual violence committed at Taba. The ICTR Appeals Chamber noted that the "question was asked in a neutral tone, just like all the other questions that Judge Pillay asked", and dismissed the argument. *Prosecutor v. Akayesu* (Case No. ICTR-96-4-A), Judgment, 1 June 2001, paras 197–200. Judge Kama interrupted Akayesu's counsel, during cross-examination of a rape victim: "Is that important? ... She was raped so frequently that she can no longer remember how often it was; 4, 5, 6, 7 times." Akayesu's counsel argued that this indicated he believed the witness, and sought to protect her from questions that might have embarrassed her. The Appeals Chamber considered that, in the context of the entire cross-examination, Judge Kama was merely exercising the normal functions of a presiding judge. Ibid., paras 203–207.

30. See, for example, *Reference Re Remuneration of Judge of the Provincial Court of Prince Edward Island* [1997] 3 SCR 3 (Supreme Court of Canada); *Bow Street Metropolitan Stipendiary Magistrate and others, ex parte Pinochet Ugarte (No 2)* [1999] 1 All

ER 577 (House of Lords, United Kingdom). See also M. L. Friedland (1996) "Judicial Independence and Accountability: A Canadian Perspective", *Criminal Law Forum* 7: 605.

31. UN General Assembly Res. 40/32, GA Res. 40/146.
32. ICTY Statute, art. 13(1); ICTR Statute, art. 12(1); SCSL Statute, art. 13(1); ICC Statute, art. 36(3)(a).
33. Ibid.
34. ICTY Statute, art. 13(2)(b), (d); ICTR Statute, art. 12(2)(b), (d); ICC Statute, art. 36(4)(b), 36(7).
35. ICTY Statute, art. 13(1); ICTR Statute, art. 12(1); SCSL Statute, art. 13(1); ICC Statute, art. 36(3)(b).
36. ICC Statute, art. 36(3)(c).
37. ICC Statute, art. 36(8)(b).
38. SCSL Statute, art. 13(2).
39. ICTY Statute, art. 13; ICTR Statute, art. 12.
40. R. Mackenzie and P. Sands (2003) "International Courts and Tribunals and the Independence of the International Judges", *Harvard Journal of International Law* 44: 271–278.
41. ICC Statute, art. 36(4)(a)(i).
42. ICC Statute, art. 36(4)(a)(ii).
43. International Criminal Court (2002) "Procedure for the election of the judges for the International Criminal Court", Resolution ICC-ASP/1/Res.3. See also International Criminal Court (2002) "Procedure for the nomination and election of judges, the Prosecutor and Deputy Prosecutors of the International Criminal Court", Resolution ICC-ASP/1/Res.2, arts 1–23.
44. This aspect of the appointment process is not examined in this paper, which concerns independence and impartiality rather than competence. A judge of marginal competence or expertise may still be independent and impartial, just as an experienced and knowledgeable magistrate may be unacceptably biased.
45. SCSL Statute, art. 12(1).
46. SCSL Agreement, art. 2(2).
47. "Letter of 12 June 2000 from the President of Sierra Leone to the Secretary-General and the Suggested Framework Attached to It", UN Doc. S/2000/786, annex.
48. *Prosecutor v. Sesay* (Case No. SCSL-2004-15-AR15), Decision on Defence Motion Seeking the Disqualification of Justice Robertson from the Appeals Chamber, 13 March 2004.
49. G. Robertson (2002) *Crimes against Humanity: The Struggle for Global Justice*, 2nd ed., London: Penguin Books.
50. ICTY Statute, art. 13(3); ICTR Statute, art. 12(3).
51. For example, shortly after election in 1993, the French judge Le Foyer de Costil resigned because of ill health. He was replaced by another French judge, Claude Jorda. In 1995, the Egyptian Georges Abi-Saab resigned and was replaced by another Egyptian, Fouad Abdel-Moneim Riad. Rustam Sidhwa of Pakistan resigned in July 1996 and was replaced the following month by Saad Saood Jan, also of Pakistan. Similarly, in 1999, Gabrielle Kirk McDonald of the United States of America was replaced by Patricia Wald, an American, Antonio Cassese of Italy was replaced by another Italian, Fausto Pocar, and Wang Tieya of China was replaced by another Chinese, Liu Daqun. In 2004, Richard May of the United Kingdom was replaced by Iain Bonomy, also of the United Kingdom. There have been only a few exceptions to the appointment by the Secretary-General of nationals to replace "their" judge. In 1996, Jules Deschênes of

Canada was replaced by Mohamed Shahabuddeen, of Guyana. When Dionysios Kondylis of Greece resigned less than two weeks after taking his oath of office, in 1999, he was replaced by Asoka de Zoysa Gunawardana of Sri Lanka.

52. At Nuremberg and Tokyo, it was the "victim" states that appointed the judges. The four judges at the International Military Tribunal represented the four "great powers" who had defeated the Nazis (*Agreement for the Prosecution and Punishment of Major War Criminals of the European Axis, and Establishing the Charter of the International Military Tribunal (IMT)* (1951) 82 UNTS 279, art. 2). The eleven judges at the International Military Tribunal for the Far East were drawn from the nine signatories to the instrument of Japanese surrender, plus India and the Philippines (International Military Tribunal for the Far East, TIAS No. 1589, Annex, Charter of the International Military Tribunal for the Far East, art. 2).

53. ICC Statute, art. 37.

54. Statute of the International Court of Justice, arts 14–15.

55. D. A. Mundis (2000) "Improving the Operation and Functioning of the International Criminal Tribunals", *American Journal of International Law* 94: 759, 767–773.

56. UN Doc. S/RES/1329 (2000), para. 1.

57. *Seventh Annual Report of the ICTR*, UN Doc. A/57/163-S/2002/733, annex, paras 19–20.

58. UN Doc. S/RES/1431 (2002). See also UN Doc. S/RES/1512 (2003).

59. This terminology was adopted when ad litem judgeships were created, although it seems odd to describe those who serve four-year terms as "permanent".

60. UN Doc. S/RES/1481 (2003), which added art. 13 *quater* to the ICTY Statute; UN Doc. S/RES/1512 (2003), which added art. 12 *quater* to the ICTR Statute.

61. ICTY Statute, art. 14(3); ICTR Statute, arts 13(3), 14(5); ICTY RPE, Rules 15(A), 15(B), 15*bis* (C), 15*bis* (D), 27(C), 28(A); ICTR Statute, arts 13(3), 14(5); ICTR RPE, Rules 15(A), 15(B), 15*bis* (C), 15*bis* (D), 27(C), 28; ICC Statute, art. 39; ICC RPE, Rules 4(I)(b). Under the SCSL Statute, the assignment to the various chambers is made at the time of appointment: SCSL Statute, art. 12.

62. ICTY Statute, art. 14(3), (5).

63. UN Doc. S/RES/1597 (2005), amending art. 13 *ter* (1)(e) of the ICTY Statute.

64. *Prosecutor v. Norman*, para. 30.

65. Ibid., para. 37.

66. *Prosecutor v. Norman*, para. 6.

67. Conditions of service and compensation of the judges of the International Criminal Court, ICC-ASP/1/3, Annex 6, p. 320.

68. *Prosecutor v. Norman*, para. 12.

69. ICC Statute, art. 36(9).

70. ICC Statute, art. 36(9)(c).

71. ICC Statute, art. 36(2)(c)(ii).

72. ICTY Statute, art. 30; ICTR Statute, art. 29 (with minor differences of a technical nature).

73. "Agreement between the United Nations and the Kingdom of the Netherlands Concerning the Headquarters of the International Tribunal for the Prosecution of Persons Responsible for Serious Violations of International Humanitarian Law Committed in the Territory of the former Yugoslavia", UN Doc. S/1994/848, annex, art. 14; "Agreement between the United Nations and the United Republic of Tanzania Concerning the Headquarters of the International Tribunal for Rwanda", UN Doc. A/51/399-S/1996/778, annex, art. 14.

74. Headquarters Agreement between the Republic of Sierra Leone and the Special Court for Sierra Leone, 21 October 2003, arts. 3, 14.

75. ICC Statute, art. 48(2).

76. ICC-ASP/1/3, pp. 215–232, art. 15.

77. ICTY RPE, Rule 29; ICTR RPE, Rule 29; SCSL RPE, Rule 29; ICC Statute, art. 74(4).

78. ICC RPE, Rule 5(1)(a).

79. *Prosecutor v. Delalić et al.* (Case No. IT-96-21-A), Decision on Motion to Preserve and Provide Evidence, 22 April 1999.

80. ICC Statute, art. 46(1).

81. ICC RPE, Rule 24.

82. ICC RPE, Rule 26.

83. ICC Statute, art. 46(2). See also ICC RPE, Rule 29; Rules of Procedure of the Assembly of States Parties, ICC-ASP/1/3, pp. 156–179, Rules 81, 82.

84. *Prosecutor v. Delalić et al.* (Case No. IT-96-21-A), Declaration of Judge Shahabuddeen, 25 October 1999 (Judge Shahabuddeen cited the *Effect of Awards of Compensation Made by the United Nations Administrative Tribunal, Advisory Opinion*, [1954] International Court of Justice Reports, 53).

85. *Prosecutor v. Delalić et al.* (Case No. IT-96-21-A), Decision of the Bureau on Motion to Disqualify Judges Pursuant to Rule 15 or in the Alternative that Certain Judges Recuse Themselves, 25 October 1999.

86. ICC RPE, Rules 27, 32.

87. UN Security Council (2005) *Report of the International Commission of Inquiry on Violations of International Humanitarian Law and Human Rights Law in Darfur*, UN Doc. S/2005/60.

88. UN Doc. S/RES/1593 (2005).

12

Impartiality deficit and international criminal judging

Diane Marie Amann

It is a testament of sorts to human ingenuity that laudable ends at times have worked to justify dubious means.[1] "Civilization" once proved a watchword for myriad instances of colonial subjugation. Today that role may be played by "human rights": rights claimed center stage, for example, in the second inaugural speech of the US President whose first term had been marked by the invasion of a sovereign state outside the framework of the UN Charter and by a policy of prolonged and harsh detention. The embrace of rhetoric common in human rights circles by a leader proud of such a record underscores the great caution owed any project said to promote human rights.

Among such projects is international criminal justice; that is, the global effort to punish committers of atrocity. Fallow for decades after Nuremberg, the project yielded much fruit at century's turn. Two-thirds of the world's countries voted for a permanent International Criminal Court, even as two ad hoc international criminal tribunals adjudicated offenses arising out of Balkan wars and Rwandan genocide. Mixed or hybrid tribunals, which combined national and international laws and judges, operated in East Timor, Kosovo and Sierra Leone; negotiators worked to set up a counterpart in Cambodia. In pursuit of former Chilean dictator Augusto Pinochet and others, individual states took it upon themselves to prosecute crimes occurring outside their own territory. These developments surely had salutary results – though not uniformly so. On the one hand, prosecutors tried perpetrators who otherwise would have remained in power. Victims received the vindication of seeing persecutors in the

Atrocities and international accountability: Beyond transitional justice, Hughes, Schabas and Thakur (eds), United Nations University Press, 2007, ISBN 978-92-808-1141-4

dock. Public opinion was transformed, so that human rights is now a subject of debate on matters as disparate as the pedigree of African diamonds and the entry of China into the World Trade Organization. On the other hand, corruption and malfeasance tarnished some tribunals. Prime suspects not infrequently evaded capture. Outreach often fell short of stated goals like national reconciliation or restoration and maintenance of international peace and security.

Revival of the international criminal justice project produced another, less noted effect: tribunals' construction and operation sometimes bore the marks of compulsion to convict and inattention to the rights of the accused. This article focuses on how that tendency – called here "impartiality deficit" – has affected international judging.

Impartiality deficit

"Impartiality deficit" is coined, of course, from "democracy deficit". The latter describes a central objection to interstate integration, in Europe and elsewhere. Critics complain that the burgeoning strength of multilateral institutions strips the ordinary citizen of any power to hold decision makers accountable. Accountability frequently is linked to elections; governance by unelected officials thus is said to render institutions undemocratic.[2] Particularly in the United States, scholars and politicians apply this critique to international criminal justice; most notably, to the International Criminal Court.[3] Who, they ask, or what entity, may initiate an investigation? Who has the power to imprison? For what reasons? On what authority? To what extent are such decisions the product of a public, transparent process? Can the decisions, and those who made them, be challenged, and by whom?

Such questions, though not irrelevant, are peripheral to impartiality deficit. Its core critique is that in aiming at punishment, international criminal justice has lost sight of individuals on whom suspicion settled. Demands for "fairness" and "justice" – invoked on behalf of defendants during the rights revolution of the twentieth century – have referred in this new era almost exclusively to victims. A 2004 communiqué from the International Federation of Human Rights, France's leading human rights organization, thus began: "*Garantir les droits des victimes avant tout!*"; that is, "Guarantee victims' rights before all!" That slogan ought to disturb. Placing victims' rights before all other considerations upsets the balance of competing goals that contemporary criminal justice systems must serve. It cannot be forgotten that to fight impunity via criminal justice mechanisms is to expand repressive powers. Nor can it be denied that states have been known to abuse those powers. Persons have been charged and convicted, imprisoned or executed, based on false or unreliable evidence admitted with little adversarial challenge and credited with little judicial scrutiny. In a system that truly values human rights, the risk of such abuse is no less grave a matter than flawed accountability.

A justice system free from impartiality deficit would owe much to the architecture of its founding charter. Not only judicial, prosecutorial and administrative functions, but also the defence function would appear in that charter as equals in status, resources and respect. The rights of the accused would be robust and set out in full detail. As for day-to-day operations, court officers would neither act nor speak in a manner that eroded a suspect's fundamental right to be presumed innocent unless and until proved guilty. That measure of respect would help to convey to the media and to affected communities the essential message that a criminal justice system cannot fulfil its objectives – retribution and deterrence, to be sure, but also stigmatization and reconciliation – unless its processes are fair and its record-making accurate.

Unfortunately, these mileposts of impartiality have not always been evident at the sundry sites where international criminal justice operated. With the notable exception of the ICC Statute, tribunals' founding statutes typically target "persons responsible" rather than "persons alleged to be responsible" for certain crimes.[4] Each statute does list some defence rights, so that an accused must: receive a fair, public and speedy trial before a competent tribunal; be presumed innocent unless and until proved guilty at trial; be informed of charges; have the assistance of an interpreter; have adequate time and resources to prepare a defence; be permitted to cross-examine adverse witnesses and to compel testimony from favorable witnesses; be permitted to remain silent; be allowed to appeal conviction; and be free from double jeopardy.[5] But the contours of such rights remain unclear and subject to curtailment in the interests of victims and witnesses. No statute founding a tribunal established a defence organ on equal footing with Chambers, the Prosecutor and the Registry, although the Special Court for Sierra Leone eventually added a Defence Unit charged to coordinate representation of the accused.[6] Elsewhere defendants had to vie with others – including the very persons whom they are supposed to have harmed – for the attention of administrators. This has not always been easy. A law professor who represented an ICTY defendant contended that he was treated with hostility, kept out of tribunal offices and denied the military transport given prosecutors on fact-finding missions. Of a conversation with "the chief Registrar", he wrote: "When I said rather firmly that I regarded myself as an officer of the court and that my role was to help see that justice was done, all she said was that she didn't ask me to take this job, and if I didn't like it, I could go back to Chicago."[7] Ill feelings about defendants were not contained within the walls of the tribunal, either; to the contrary, some prosecutors reviled indictees in public statements duly reported by the media. There seemed at times to be little care about whether an accused was treated justly; to the contrary, in the words of one barrister, the "tendency is to expect convictions" rather than fair trials.[8] Few top lawyers stepped up to represent the accused. Significant segments of affected communities, in countries as disparate as Bosnia and Sierra Leone, dismissed the tribunals as biased.[9]

Judicial independence as guarantor of impartiality

Bias – partiality – may taint any system of justice. Systems that value human rights endeavor to reduce the risk of bias in part by relying on an independent judiciary. This article thus considers, first, what constitutes judicial independence and, second, whether judges in today's international criminal justice systems are sufficiently independent to counteract the impartiality deficit.

Liberal tradition places the duty to dispel bias, to ensure impartiality, on the judiciary. James Madison, one of the framers of the US Constitution, declared that judges ought to "consider themselves in a peculiar manner the guardians" of individual rights.[10] For those framers – and for Montesquieu before them – discharge of this duty hinged on the degree to which the judiciary enjoyed independence. Two centuries later, judges from many nation-states determined in the 2002 Bangalore Principles of Judicial Conduct that "the importance of a competent, independent and impartial judiciary to the protection of human rights is given emphasis by the fact that the implementation of all the other rights ultimately depends upon the proper administration of justice".[11] This view is incorporated in international human rights and humanitarian law. "In the determination of any criminal charge against him", states the International Covenant on Civil and Political Rights, "everyone shall be entitled to a fair and public hearing by a competent, independent and impartial tribunal established by law".[12] A protocol to the Geneva Conventions likewise provides: "No sentence shall be passed and no penalty shall be executed on a person found guilty of an offense except pursuant to a conviction pronounced by a court offering the essential guarantees of independence and impartiality."[13] Similar language appears in the Universal Declaration of Human Rights, in African, European and inter-American human rights instruments and in statutes establishing international or mixed criminal tribunals.[14]

At first blush, "independence" and "impartiality" seem synonyms without much distinct meaning, not unlike the legal phrases "null and void" and "cease and desist". But that is not the case.

The term "independence" refers chiefly to institutional design; that is, to what has been called "structural independence" from other governmental entities, to "freedom from interference".[15] It encompasses matters such as judges' financial and job security. One hallmark of judicial independence is a guarantee that a judge will enjoy a long tenure and may not be removed unless she is shown to have engaged in specified misconduct. Judicial independence further guarantees that no judge need fear reduction in salary or resources should she issue an unpopular decision. Such guarantees first made an appearance in Article III of the US Constitution, which states: "The Judges, both of the supreme and inferior Courts, shall hold their Offices during good Behaviour, and shall, at stated Times, receive for their Services, a Compensation, which shall not be diminished during their Continuance in Office." The guarantees were endorsed at a 1985 conference that the United Nations sponsored in Milan; the Basic Principles on the Independence of the Judiciary adopted at that conference thus require that matters such as judicial "term of office" and "remuneration ... shall be adequately secured by law", and that judges "shall have guaranteed tenure until ... expiry of their term".[16]

As explained in those 1985 Basic Principles, judicial independence also entails a duty to adhere to procedure. Principle 6 thus states: "The principle of the independence of the judiciary entitles and requires the judiciary to ensure that judicial proceedings are conducted fairly and that the rights of the parties are respected." A judge will best be able to satisfy this requirement if she has a firm grasp of the law and experience with the task of adjudication. Accordingly, another hallmark of judicial independence is adoption of a method for selecting the best and brightest out of a pool of candidates with prescribed qualifications. The United Nations' 1985 Basic Principles thus recommend, as a key means to promote judicial independence, attention to "selection" and "training", and they further require that "any method of judicial selection shall safeguard against judicial appointments for improper motives".[17]

The concept of impartiality is distinct from that of independence. The latter will enhance the former, but cannot guarantee it. Conversely, a judge may choose to act impartially even absent a structure that encourages him to do so. "Impartiality", in the words of one commentator, "is the subjective characteristic by which the international decision-maker achieves a reputation for consistency".[18] In its 1985 decision in *Valente v. The Queen*, Canada's Supreme Court similarly referred to impartiality as "a state of mind or attitudes of the tribunal in relation to the issues and the parties in a particular case".[19] Put simply, an impartial judge must act without bias and, as other commentators have noted, "prior involvement of a judge either with a party before the court or an issue before the court might give rise to challenge on the ground of bias or the appearance of bias".[20] A judge who acts without bias complies with a primary mandate of the United Nations' 1985 Basic Principles, set forth in Principle 2: "The judiciary shall decide matters before them impartially, on the basis of facts and in accordance with the law, without any restrictions, improper influences, inducements, pressures, threats, or interferences, direct or indirect, from any quarter or for any reason."

At the same time, the judge cannot be what has been called "preneutral",[21] devoid of prior thoughts about issues that come before the bench, for a justice system cannot thrive unless its judges have expertise on the law regarding those issues. An impartial judge of course will share with other humans a revulsion to atrocity and a desire to punish its perpetrators; nevertheless, on donning the judge's robe he will decide each defendant's fate according to law and based on evidence adduced within, not on prejudices developed outside, the courtroom. It was with this distinction between impartiality and preneutrality in mind that the ICTY Appeals Chamber in *Prosecutor v. Furundzija*, a rape case, denied a motion to disqualify a judge who had served on the UN Commission on the Status of Women. The Appeals Chamber reasoned that even if it were shown that the judge favored promotion of women's rights, "that inclination, being of a general nature, is distinguishable from an inclination to implement those goals and objectives as a Judge in a particular case".[22]

Independence, impartiality and international criminal justice

There is room to improve judicial independence and impartiality in international criminal justice.

Perhaps more than in other kinds of litigation, interest in the tragic human issues that underlie international criminal cases may invite judicial bias. This insight prompted the British House of Lords in 2000 to vacate its first judgment against Pinochet for the reason that one judge was a director of a charity affiliated with an intervener, the human rights organization Amnesty International. In voting to disqualify, one Law Lord wrote, "that in any case where the impartiality of a judge is in question the appearance of the matter is just as important as the reality".[23] Ethicists' emphasis on the appearance, and not just on the reality, is longstanding. That emphasis reflects the epistemic truth that one can never know a judge's actual or subjective motivation, but that one can identify objective factors that give an appearance of bias. And it serves the basic institutional goal of legitimacy: a tribunal eager to earn the esteem of affected communities simply cannot afford to render decisions that appear, rightly or wrongly, the result of improper motive. The 2002 Bangalore Principles thus state: "The behaviour and conduct of a judge must reaffirm the people's faith in the integrity of the judiciary. Justice must not merely be done but must also be seen to be done."[24] Given the particular readiness with which opponents of international criminal justice label disliked decisions biased or political, this project in particular ought to aspire, like Caesar's wife, to be above reproach.

Structural weaknesses impede that aspiration, and so have contributed to instances of international judicial conduct that appeared less than fully impartial. In many tribunals Chambers and the Prosecutor are placed, figuratively and literally, in closer quarters than a strict separation of powers would seem to recommend. Founding documents typically define a tribunal as comprising three organs, Chambers, Prosecutor and a Registry. The ICTY Statute underscores that the Registry is engaged in "servicing both" Chambers and the Prosecutor; one critic has noted that these three organs all had offices in the same building, on floors from which he and other defence counsel were excluded.[25] Moreover, the chief judge, or President, of such tribunals typically is duty-bound to act on behalf not only of the bench but also of the tribunal as a whole. Statutes for the ad hoc tribunals, for example, authorize the President inter alia to consult with the UN Secretary-General in choosing a Registrar for the tribunal.[26] Article 38 of the ICC Statute mandates that the Presidency "shall be responsible for ... proper administration of the Court, with the exception of the Office of the Prosecutor", and also for "other functions conferred upon it in accordance with this Statute"; with the Prosecutor, the Presidency is to "coordinate and seek concurrence on all matters of mutual concern".

At times these presidential duties have prompted conduct seemingly inconsistent with desiderata of judicial detachment. Judges of some tribunals appeared in joint press conferences with the Prosecutor in efforts to prod the international community to expend financial and enforcement resources. One reporter wrote of a "public outburst" by "the normally discreet" first ICTY President, Antonio Cassese, that failures to arrest suspected war criminals would send this message: "Go ahead! Kill, torture, maim! Commit acts of genocide! ... You may enjoy impunity!"[27] One critic labeled such incidents a judicial "foray into the province of the Prosecutor".[28] Succeeding Presidents at times promoted their tribunals to degrees not often seen in judiciaries that enjoy long acceptance in the communities they serve.

This is not to say that tribunals ought not to aim to open the judicial process to public scrutiny. Transparency helps to assure that decisions will be both fair and seen as fair. Tribunal statutes advance this goal not only by inviting dissenters to publish their disagreement, but also by imposing on each panel the duty to give reasoned explanations for its decision. The ICC Statute thus requires:

> The decision shall be in writing and shall contain a full and reasoned statement of the Trial Chamber's findings on the evidence and conclusions. The Trial Chamber shall issue one decision. When there is no unanimity, the Trial Chamber's decision shall contain the views of the majority and the minority. The decision or a summary thereof shall be delivered in open court.[29]

The ICTY Appeals Chamber has demonstrated the force of this injunction: in *Prosecutor v. Kupreškić*, a 2001 judgment that stands as a landmark in the rights of the internationally accused, it freed two brothers, in jail for four years, on the ground that the Trial Chamber had failed to give sufficient reasons justifying conviction.[30]

Other structural safeguards are less than secure. International judges are compensated for their work. But tribunals have faced budgetary shortfalls, and at times donor states have wielded the power of their purses to convey displeasure with tribunal operations.[31] In line with concerns that already had been raised by the UN Secretary-General and by Human Rights Watch, defendants argued in *Prosecutor v. Norman* that the funding and management scheme of the Special Court for Sierra Leone placed undue influence in the hands of a few states, and thus impinged on judicial independence. In that case, the Special Court disagreed.[32] Yet the critique resurfaced in Cambodia.[33] It seems evident in any event that circumstances of precarious finances create a danger of encroachment on the independence of any chambers.

Tribunal statutes provide for terms of office that are as long as nine years, for ICC judges, yet, for judges of Sierra Leone's Special Court, as short as three years.[34] All tribunal statutes specify qualifications, a component essential to establishing a learned judiciary free from outside interference: Judges typically must be "persons of high moral character, impartiality and integrity who possess the qualifications required in their respective countries for appointment to the highest judicial offices".[35] The ICC Statute goes further, mandating in Article 36(3)(b) that prospective judges possess "established competence" either in "criminal law and procedure" or in "relevant areas of international law". Other tribunal statutes ask only that "in the overall composition of the Chambers and sections of the Trial Chambers, due account shall be taken of the experience of the judges in criminal law, international law, including international humanitarian law and human rights law"[36] – phrasing that would seem to permit appointment of individuals who fail to meet any of these criteria.

The risk that candidates might not satisfy baseline standards would seem a special risk in hybrid tribunals, in which national and international officials share appointment of judges and have no formal power to veto the others' choices. Of the three Trial Chamber judges at the Special Court for Sierra Leone, for example, two are to be appointed by the Secretary-General of the United Nations and one by the government of Sierra Leone; of five Appeals Chamber judges, two are to be appointed by Sierra Leone and three by the Secretary-General.[37] Ultimate selection of judges for the Cambodia tribunal is, moreover, delegated to the "Supreme Council of the Magistracy"; the Cambodia agreement gave the state not only the power to select national judges, but also the final choice on international judges, from a list supplied by the UN Secretary-General.[38]

Selection processes have tended to be less than fully transparent, a fact that has been acknowledged by former ICTY Judge Patricia M. Wald, among other commentators.[39] There long has been worry that in international tribunals, state-selected international judges might not rule impartially in matters of interest to their own state.[40] And yet the ICC Statute, to cite one instance, fails to eliminate this concern: although it properly prescribes a process and qualifications that promise a bench diverse in gender, geography and expertise, and further requires detailed submissions on "how the candidate fulfils the requirements", the statute opts for selection not by a merit commission, as some advocated, but rather by states parties.[41] Election of the first ICC judges was swift, but then things bogged down. The last of the 18 judges was not elected until the thirty-third ballot, cast on the fourth day.[42] This succession of ballots invited suspicion that as time passed, states' votes reflected factors other than candidates' relative merits.

A second instance in which less-than-transparent judicial selection may give rise to concern is the mixed or hybrid tribunal. Appointment procedures for these tribunals operate so that each member of the bench will know the precise identity of her patron. It is true that hybrid statutes often have given to international judges the final say on whether to convict. At the Special Court for Sierra Leone, a majority of judges in either Chamber must be UN appointees, and any "judgement" requires the vote of a majority of judges in a given Chamber.[43] The agreement establishing the Cambodia tribunal urges unanimity and likewise requires "decisions" – an undefined term – to be made by supermajorities that must include the international judge.[44] Drafters of such statutes assumed such mechanisms would avoid partiality for the reason that the "international" interest is more likely than the "national" interest to be fair. That premise may not always prove true. In any event, the voting mechanisms do not always cabin other judicial determinations, such as whether to admit evidence that may dispose of a case as surely as any verdict. Unless the tribunal statute fully insulates the judge from unwarranted removal, a judge thus yet may feel pressure to please the person to whom she owes her job.

Impartiality deficit in action

Risks associated with impartiality deficit came to unfortunate fruition in the early days of the Special Court for Sierra Leone. Atrocities – including forced recruitment of child soldiers and the cutting off of innocents' hands – had been commonplace during the civil war that plagued Sierra Leone in the 1990s. In order to try persons believed most responsible, a 2000 agreement between the Sierra Leone government and the United Nations established the Special Court. Considerable attention has been paid this mixed tribunal. Its first Prosecutor acted with audacity, indicting not only members of the rebel Revolutionary United Front, but also the incumbent deputy defence minister of Sierra Leone, Sam Hinga Norman, and the then-President of Liberia, Charles Taylor. Such moves drew a mix of comments from Western journalists and academics and from a segment of Sierra Leonean society.[45] Some commentators pointed to this tribunal as a model international criminal justice mechanism – even as allegations of partiality dogged the Special Court.

In a letter written to the United Nations months before initial appointments to the Special Court were made, the non-governmental organization Human Rights Watch emphasized the need to select impartial judges who were independent of all the states or factions that had held an interest in the Sierra Leone conflict.[46] And yet opening day at the new courthouse found the Special Court thrown "into disarray", to quote one reporter.[47] At issue on that day in 2004 was the impartiality *vel non* of President Geoffrey Robertson QC, a British human rights lawyer and author of *Crimes against Humanity: The Struggle for Global Justice*. The book's second paperback edition, published in 2002, included numerous passages on Sierra Leone. Among other things, the book advanced opinions on what ought to be the rulings on issues that were likely to come before the Special Court. On whether, despite doubts that had been raised in a 2000 Secretary-General's report, international custom barred recruitment of child soldiers, Robertson wrote that it was "crucial for customary international law to recognize their recruitment as a war crime entailing individual responsibility".[48] On another key issue – whether the amnesty granted RUF leader Foday Sankoh and his rebels in a UN-brokered peace accord should be honored – Robertson wrote:

> Just as genocide and torture are repugnant to international law to such an extent that no circumstances can justify them (hence these convention obligations are non-derogable), so amnesties given to perpetrators of such deeds by frightened or blackmailed governments cannot be upheld by international law, even when agreed by international diplomats. For this reason, the UN was justified in reinterpreting the amnesty given to the despicable Foday Sankoh: it pardoned him only for crimes committed under Sierra Leone law, not international law.[49]

Of Sankoh himself, Robertson wrote in like vein:

> Those who order atrocities believe at the time that their power will always enable them to bargain with any new government to let bygones be bygones, and history since Nuremberg has tended to prove them correct – most bizarrely in Sierra Leone, when by the Lome Agreement in July 1999 the UN not only amnestied Foday Sankoh, the nation's butcher, but rewarded his pathological brutality by making him deputy leader of the government and giving him control of the diamond mines.[50]

Sankoh would die before his Special Court trial began. Yet the book's descriptions of other indictees were equally vivid. The RUF was said to have been "programmed to kill and pillage and mutilate", to be "guilty of atrocities on a scale that amounts to a crime against humanity".[51] Taylor was labeled a "vicious warlord":

> Charles Taylor, the popular president of Liberia, is said by The Times to gourmandize on the body parts of dissidents, who have been arrested, dissected and cooked by a special unit of cannibal police. It is absurd to kow-tow to people like this, who run governments which claim an "immunity" from justice on the basis of a dignity they entirely lack.[52]

Just weeks after penning the preface to this edition, Robertson was named President of the Special Court – the only non-Sierra Leonean among the three "national" judges chosen by the government of Sierra Leone.[53]

A defendant alleged to have been an RUF commander moved for Robertson's disqualification, attaching to the filing several pages of the book.[54] The prosecution agreed that certain passages "could lead a reasonable observer, properly informed, to apprehend bias".[55] Robertson refused to recuse himself. Consequently, the Special Court colleagues adopted a rules amendment that operated to end his term as President and issued an order barring him from hearing adjudicating cases "involving the RUF".[56] The RUF was, of course, a key force behind the civil war. The Special Court's order thus meant that a sizable number of cases would be decided without any participation by one of its five Appeals Chamber judges.

As a result of the RUF disqualification order Robertson did not participate in the Special Court decision that held – in keeping with an assertion Robertson had made in his book – that the 1999 amnesty did not apply to prevent prosecution of RUF defendants.[57] But he joined the affirmation of this holding in a case involving a defendant alleged to have waged war on behalf of the government.[58]

On at least one matter quoted above – whether customary international law forbade child recruitment – Robertson's judicial decision was at odds with the import of his published statement. When presented with the question in *Prosecutor v. Norman*, a majority of the Appeals Chamber concluded that "the norm prohibiting child recruitment ... entered customary law well before 1996", the beginning date for the Special Court's temporal jurisdiction.[59] Robertson dissented on the ground that customary international law criteria were not met "as of 1996 in relation to the prohibition on child enlistment".[60]

Actual decisions do not obviate that Sierra Leone–related passages in a book by a member of the Special Court had raised in reasonable minds appearances both of prejudgment of legal disputes and of prejudice against opponents of the very government to which that member owed his appointment. The disqualification order thus was correct. It would have been better if the Special Court never had been forced to the decision; if, that is, the statute had required vetting of candidates' impartiality and had allowed either of the two appointing authorities to object to the other's selections. As one reporter put it days after the disqualification order: "It has yet to be explained how the tribunal failed to note the explosive nature of Mr Robertson's book."[61] An absence of safeguards against partiality thus had helped to embroil the Special Court in an unwanted controversy that even the Prosecutor said "ultimately" was bound "to reflect upon the credibility of the Special Court for Sierra Leone and the integrity of its proceedings".[62]

The controversy also invited other defendants to challenge the integrity of another judge. A motion filed within days of the issuance of the order disqualifying Robertson sought to recuse Appeals Chamber Justice Renate Winter from deliberating on a defence challenge to the validity of the statutory proscription against recruiting child soldiers. Winter had been a youth court judge in Austria and an international judge in a Kosovo mixed tribunal.[63] In 2002 she was among 50 experts who commented on, but did not write, a report by UNICEF; that agency subsequently had filed with the Special Court a brief *amicus curiae* opposing the child recruitment motion. In this instance, neither the Prosecutor nor the Special Court agreed with the defence assertion that there was "an unacceptable appearance of bias".[64] The Special Court concluded that Winter's expertise was evidence not of bias, but rather of her qualifications to be a judge.[65] The decision effectively recognized that appointment of a learned individual, able to draw on her background in rendering fair decisions free from the taint of predetermination, is preferable to selection of a person who has never thought about issues central to the task before her. Yet there is inherent tension in the search for expertise, on the one hand, and impartiality, on the other. Reinforcement of structural safeguards of judicial independence is essential lest that tension list in favor of the impartiality deficit.

Conclusion

"Perfection is the enemy of justice", wrote one human rights activist frustrated with criticism of the plan to try alleged architects of the 1970s reign of terror that left 1.7 million dead in Cambodia.[66] There is truth in his statement. Every criminal justice system suffers from flaws, but seldom does it cease operation on that account. In societies that truly value human rights, rather, prosecutions proceed alongside efforts to confront and correct errors. That parallel process ought to apply as well to the international criminal justice project. Of course its salutary achievements deserve recognition. But so do its negative effects, such as the impartiality deficit that at times renders treatment of the internationally accused less than optimally fair. That deficit is especially visible when international judges appear to lack independence or impartiality. As two commentators have written: "Challenges to judicial process based on alleged lack of independence or impartiality" often are to be welcomed as "a sign of the maturation of the international judicial system, as the system begins to exhibit the traits and adhere to the same standards of fairness and impartiality of domestic systems".[67] Though an unrealistic demand of perfection well may be an enemy of international criminal justice, so too is undue resignation to imperfection.

Notes

1. Aspects of this article were presented in July 2004 at "Accountability for Atrocity", a conference in Galway, Ireland, sponsored by the Irish Centre for Human Rights and the United Nations University, and in February 2005 at International Law Weekend –

West in California and at a colloquium at the University of Houston Law Center. Thanks to NaTasha Ralston for research assistance.

2. J. H. H. Weiler (1991) "The Transformation of Europe", *Yale Law Journal* 100: 2403, 2417–2419, 2429–2431, 2465–74; Douglas Lee Donoho (2003) "Democratic Legitimacy in Human Rights: The Future of International Decision-Making", *Wisconsin International Law Journal* 21(1): 5–29; Andrew T. Guzman (2004) "Global Governance and the WTO", *Harvard International Law Journal* 45: 303, 336–38.

3. Madeline Morris (2002) "The Democratic Dilemma of the International Criminal Court", *Buffalo Criminal Law Review* 5: 591–592; but see Diane Marie Amann (2004) "The International Criminal Court and the Sovereign State", in Ige F. Dekker and Wouter G. Werner, eds, *Global Governance and International Legal Theory*, Leiden, the Netherlands: Martinus Nijhoff Publishers, esp. pp. 190–194; David Golove (2003) "The New Confederalism: Treaty Delegations of Legislative, Executive, and Judicial Authority", *Stanford Law Review* 55: 1697–1699.

4. Compare Rome Statute of the International Criminal Court, art. 1, UN Doc. No. A/CONF.183/9 (July 17, 1998) [hereinafter ICC Statute] with Statute of the International Criminal Tribunal for Rwanda, art. 1, SC Res. 955, UN SCOR, 49th Sess., 3453d mtg., Annex, UN Doc. S/RES/955 (1994) [hereinafter ICTR Statute]; Statute of the International Criminal Tribunal for the former Yugoslavia, art. 1, SC Res. 827, UN SCOR, 48th Sess., 3217th mtg., Annex, UN Doc. S/RES/827 (1993) [hereinafter ICTY Statute]; Statute of the Special Court for Sierra Leone, art. 1(1), available from http://www.sc-sl.org/scsl-statute.html (visited 26 November 2006) [hereinafter SCSL Statute].

5. ICC Statute, art. 67; ICTR Statute, art. 20; ICTY Statute, art. 21; SCSL Statute, art. 17.

6. Defence Office, Rule 45, Special Court for Sierra Leone, Rules of Procedure and Evidence, available from http://www.sc-sl.org/scsl-procedure.html (visited 26 November 2006).

7. Anthony D'Amato (2003) "Trying Saddam: The Iraqi Special Tribunal for Crimes against Humanity", *Jurist*, 15 December, available from http://jurist.law.pitt.edu/forum/forumnew132.php (visited 26 November 2006).

8. Sylvia de Bertodano (2002) "Judicial Independence in the International Criminal Court", *Leiden Journal of International Law* 15: 409–410.

9. Human Rights Center & International Human Rights Law Clinic, University of California, Berkeley, and Centre for Human Rights, University of Sarajevo (2000) "Justice, Accountability and Social Reconstruction: An Interview Study of Bosnian Judges and Prosecutors", *Berkeley Journal of International Law* 15: 102–104; Mike Butscher (2004) "Sierra Leone: Special Court in Bribery Scandal", *New African*, 1 August.

10. James Madison (1789) Speech to House of Representatives, June 8, quoted in Maeva Marcus (1992) "The Adoption of the Bill of Rights", *William & Mary Bill of Rights Journal* 1: 115–119.

11. Bangalore Principles of Judicial Conduct, adopted by the Judicial Group on Strengthening Judicial Integrity, as revised at the Round Table Meeting of Chief Justices held at the Peace Palace, the Hague, 25–26 November 2002, fourth preambular para., available from http://www.unodc.org/pdf/crime/corruption/judicial_group/_principles.pdf (visited 29 April 2005) [hereinafter Bangalore Principles].

12. International Covenant on Civil and Political Rights, art. 14(1), Dec. 16, 1966, GA Res. 2200, UN GAOR, 21st Sess., Supp. No. 16, at 49, UN Doc. A/6316 (1967).

13. Protocol Additional to the Geneva Conventions of 12 August 1949, and Relating to the Protection of Victims of Non-International Armed Conflicts (Protocol II), art. 6, 8 June 1977, 1125 UNTS 609.

14. Universal Declaration of Human Rights, art. 10, Dec. 10, 1948, GA Res. 217 A, UN GAOR, 3d Sess., UN Doc. A/810, at 71 (1948); African Charter on Human and Peoples'

Rights, art. 7(1)(d), June 26, 1981, OAU Doc. CAB/LEG/67/3 Rev. 5; Convention for the Protection of Human Rights and Fundamental Freedoms, art. 6(1), Nov. 4, 1950, 213 UNTS 221; American Convention on Human Rights, art. 8(1), Nov. 22, 1969, OAS Treaty Ser. No. 36, Organization of American States, OAS Off. Rec. OEA/Ser. K/XVI/ 1.1 doc. 65 rev. 1 corr. 2 (1979), 1144 UNTS 123; ICC Statute, art. 36(3); ICTR Statute, art. 12; ICTY Statute, art. 13; SCSL Statute, art. 13.

15. "The Independence of Judges and Lawyers: U.N. Standard Setting and the Siracusa Draft Principles on the Independence of the Judiciary", *American Society of International Law Proceedings* 76: 326–339 (1982).

16. Principle Nos. 11 & 12, Basic Principles on the Independence of the Judiciary, Seventh UN Congress on the Prevention of Crime and the Treatment of Offenders, Milan, 26 August–6 September 1985, UN Doc. A/CONF.121/22/Rev.1 at 59 (1985), available from http://www1.umn.edu/humanrts/instree/i5bpij.htm (visited 26 November 2006).

17. Ibid., Ninth preambular para. and Principle No. 10; Ruth Mackenzie and Philippe Sands (2003) "International Courts and Tribunals and the Independence of the International Judge", *Harvard International Law Journal* 44: 271–276.

18. Thomas B. Moorhead (1969) "Book Review", University of Pennsylvania Law Review 117: 926–927 (reviewing Thomas M. Franck (1968) *The Structure of Impartiality*, New York: Macmillan).

19. *Valente v. The Queen* [1985] 2 SCR 673–685, quoted in Office of the High Commissioner for Human Rights in Cooperation with the International Bar Association, *Human Rights in the Administration of Justice*, ch. 4, § 4.3, available from http://www1.umn.edu/humanrts/monitoring/adminchap4.html (visited 26 November 2006).

20. Mackenzie & Sands, "International Courts and Tribunals", 280–281.

21. Moorhead, "Book Review", 927 n. 5 (citing Charles DeVisscher (1957) *Theory and Reality in Public International Law*, Princeton, N.J.: Princeton University Press, pp. 306–307).

22. *Prosecutor v. Furundzija*, Case No. IT-95-17-1-A, Appeals Chamber Judgment, para. 200 (21 July 2000).

23. *R. v. Bow Street Metropolitan Stipendiary Magistrate, Ex parte Pinochet* (No. 2) [2000] 1 AC 119, 139 (Opinion of Lord Nolan).

24. Bangalore Principles, Value 3.2.

25. ICTY Statute, art. 11; D'Amato,"Trying Saddam". See ICTR Statute, art. 10; SCSL Statute, art. 11; ICC Statute, art. 34.

26. ICTR Statute, art. 16(3); ICTY Statute, art. 17(3).

27. Marlise Simons (1996) "Italian Issues a Warning at War Crimes Tribunal", *New York Times*, 26 July; see Jon Swain (1996) "Serb War Criminals Flaunt Their Freedom", *Sunday Times*, London, 23 June.

28. de Bertodano, "Judicial Independence", 417.

29. ICC Statute, art. 74(5); see also ICTR Statute, art. 22(2); ICTY Statute, art. 23(2); SCSL Statute, art. 18. Cf. John Jackson and Sean Doran (1996) *Judge without Jury*, Oxford: Oxford University Press, pp. 252, 265, 274–285 (discussing duty); John H. Langbein (1981) "Mixed Court and Jury Court: Could the Continental Alternative Fill the American Need", *American Bar Foundation Research Journal* 1: 195–214 (same).

30. *Prosecutor v. Kupreškić*, Case No. IT-95-16-A, Appeals Chamber Judgement (Oct. 23, 2001), discussed in Diane Marie Amann (2002) "International Decisions: *Prosecutor v. Kupreškić*", *American Journal of International Law* 96: 439.

31. Ben Barber (2002) "U.S. Calls U.N. Tribunals Wasteful, Wants Them Closed", *Washington Times*, Washington, D.C., 1 March; Betsy Pisik (2003) "War-Crimes Tribunals Forced to Borrow Cash: U.N. Nations behind on Payments", *Washington Times*, Washington, D.C., 24 November.

32. *Prosecutor v. Norman*, Case No. SCSL-04-14-AR72(E), Appeals Chamber Decision on Preliminary Motion Based on Lack of Jurisdiction (Judicial Independence) (13 March 2004), available from http://www.sc-sl.org/CDF-decisions.html (visited 26 November 2006). See Diane Marie Amann (2001) "Calling Children to Account: The Proposal for a Juvenile Chamber in the Special Court for Sierra Leone", *Pepperdine Law Review*, 29: 167–175, n. 53; Peter Takirambudde and Richard Dicker (2002) "Recommendations for the Sierra Leone Special Court: Letter to Legal Advisors of UN Security Council Member States and Interested States", New York: Human Rights Watch, 7 March, available from http://hrw.org/press/2002/03/sleone0307-ltr.htm (visited 26 November 2006) [hereinafter HRW Letter].

33. Erik Wasson (2006) "NGO: Khmer Rouge Tribunal Budget Inadequate", *Cambodia Daily*, 10 October, available from http://www.justiceinitiative.org/db/resource2?res_id= 103452 (visited 26 November 2006).

34. ICC Statute, art. 36(9)(a); SCSL Statute, art. 13(3). Judges at the ad hoc tribunals serve four years. ICTR Statute, arts 12*bis*(3), 12*ter*(1)(e); ICTY Statute, arts 13*bis*(3), 13*ter*(1)(e).

35. ICTR Statute, art. 12; ICTY Statute, art. 13; SCSL Statute, art. 13(1). See ICC Statute, art. 36(3)(a).

36. ICTR Statute, art. 12; ICTY Statute, art. 13. Similar language may be found in SCSL Statute, art. 13(2) (adding experience in juvenile justice), and in the Draft Agreement between the United Nations and the Royal Government of Cambodia Concerning the Prosecution under Cambodian Law of Crimes Committed during the Period of Democratic Kampuchea, art. 3(4), UN GAOR 3d Comm., 57th Sess., Annex, Agenda Item 109(b), UN Doc. A/57/806 (2003) [hereinafter Cambodia Agreement].

37. SCSL Statute, art. 12(1).

38. Cambodia Agreement, art. 3(1), (5).

39. Patricia M. Wald (2004) "Reflections on Judging: At Home and Abroad", University of Pennsylvania Journal of Constitutional Law 7: 219–228; see Mackenzie and Sands, "International Courts and Tribunals", at pp. 277–279.

40. Stephen M. Schwebel (1999) "National Judges and Judges Ad Hoc of the International Court of Justice", *International and Comparative Law Quarterly* 48: 889–893.

41. ICC Statute, art. 36(4); de Bertodano, "Judicial Independence", 421–422 (criticizing rejection of proposal for merit committee).

42. Edith M. Lederer (2003) "World's First Permanent War Crimes Tribunal Elected", AP Worldstream, 8 February; see Joshua Rozenberg (2003) "Canadian Elected Judge of International Court: Political Correctness Weighs against Western Candidates", *National Post*, Canada, 7 February.

43. SCSL Statute, arts 12(1), 18.

44. Cambodia Agreement, art. 4. See Sophie Cheang (2006) "Leading Khmer Rouge Figure Defends Role as Cambodian Genocide Judges Sworn In", Associated Press Alert – Crime, July 3.

45. See W. Michael Reisman (2004) "Why Regime Change Is (Almost Always) a Bad Idea", *American Journal of International Law* 98: 516–517; Douglas Farah (2005) "A Protected Friend of Terrorism", *Washington Post*, 25 April; Brima Kebble (2004) "When Heroes Fall, All Hope Seems Gone", AllAfrica.com, June 4; Joseph Kamanda (2003) "Is the Special Court Truly Independent and Impartial?" *Concord Times*, Sierra Leone, 11 December.

46. HRW Letter, § A(4).

47. Rory Carroll (2004) "War Crimes QC under Pressure to Quit after Bias Claims", *Guardian*, London, 10 March.

48. Geoffrey Robertson (2002) *Crimes against Humanity: The Struggle for Global Justice*, 2d ed., London: Penguin Books, p. 469; see Report of the Secretary-General on the

Establishment of a Special Court for Sierra Leone, paras 17–18, at 4, UN SCOR, 52d Sess., UN Doc. S/2000/915 (2000), discussed in Amann, "Calling Children to Account", p. 175, n. 54.

49. Robertson, *Crimes against Humanity*, p. 277. See William A. Schabas (2004) "Amnesty, the Sierra Leone Truth and Reconciliation Commission and the Special Court for Sierra Leone", *University of California Davis Journal of International Law and Policy* 11: 145–169.

50. Robertson, *Crimes against Humanity*, p. 220; see also p. 467.

51. Ibid., pp. 467, 469.

52. Ibid., pp. 466, 425. A footnote cites Michael Dynes (1999) "Liberia's Gruesome Top 20 Killers", *Times*, London, 2 November.

53. "Appointments to Sierra Leone Special Court", M2 Presswire, 29 July 2002.

54. *Prosecutor v. Sesay*, Case No. SCSL-2003-05-PT, Defence Motion Seeking the Disqualification of Justice Robertson from the Appeals Chamber (27 February 2004) (on file with author).

55. *Prosecutor v. Sesay*, Case No. SCSL-2004-15-PT, Prosecution Response to the Defence "Motion Seeking Disqualification of Justice Robertson from the Appeals Chamber", para. 2, at 2 (1 March 2004) (on file with author) [hereinafter Prosecution Response].

56. *Prosecutor v. Sesay*, Case No. SCSL-2004-15-AR15, Appeals Chamber Decision on Defence Motion Seeking the Disqualification of Justice Robertson from the Appeals Chamber, para. 18, at 8 (13 March 2004), available from http://www.sc-sl.org/Documents/SCSL-04-15-PT-058.pdf (visited 27 November 2006); see "Sierra Leone War Crimes Court Replaces President", Agence France Presse English Wire, 17 March 2004.

57. *Prosecutor v. Kallon*, Case No. SCSL-04-15-AR72(E), Appeals Chamber Decision on Challenge to Jurisdiction: Lomé Accord Amnesty (13 March 2004), available from http://www.sc-sl.org/Documents/SCSL-04-15-PT-060-I.pdf (visited 27 November 2006); see text accompanying note 49.

58. *Prosecutor v. Kondewa*, Case No. SCSL-2004-14-AR72(E), Appeals Chamber Decision on Lack of Jurisdiction/Abuse of Process, Amnesty Provided by the Lomé Accord (25 May 2004), Separate Opinion of Justice Robertson, at 3-31, available from http://www.sc-sl.org/CDF-decisions.html (visited 27 November 2006).

59. *Prosecutor v. Norman*, Case No. SCSL-2004-14-AR72(E), Appeals Chamber Decision on Preliminary Motion Based on Lack of Jurisdiction (Child Recruitment), para. 20, at 14 (31 May 2004), available from http://www.sc-sl.org/CDF-decisions.html (visited 27 November 2006).

60. Ibid., Dissenting Opinion of Justice Robertson, para. 22, at 18.

61. Hugh Davies (2004) "War Crimes Tribunal Bars Its Judge", *Daily Telegraph*, London, 15 March.

62. Prosecution Response, *Prosecutor v. Sesay*, Case No. SCSL-2004-15-PT, para. 4, at 2.

63. See Chambers, http://www.sc-sl.org/chambers.html (visited 27 November 2006).

64. *Prosecutor v. Norman*, Case No. SCSL-2004-14, Appeals Chamber Decision on the Motion to Recuse Judge Winter from the Deliberation on the Preliminary Motion on the Recruitment of Child Soldiers, para. 23, at 8 (28 May 2004), available from http://www.sc-sl.org/Documents/SCSL-04-14-PT-112.pdf (visited 27 November 2006) (quoting *Prosecutor v. Furundzija*, Case No. IT-95-17-1-A, para. 189).

65. Ibid., para. 30, at 11.

66. Gregory H. Stanton (2003) "Perfection Is the Enemy of Justice: A Response to Amnesty International's Critique of the Draft Agreement between the U.N. and Cambodia", 19 May, available from http://www.hawaii.edu/powerkills/COMM.5.24.03.HTM (visited 27 November 2006).

67. Mackenzie and Sands, "International Courts and Tribunals", p. 275.

13

The effect of amnesties before domestic and international tribunals: Morality, law and politics

Leila Nadya Sadat

Before the US invasion of Iraq, Saddam Hussein was offered the opportunity to leave Iraq to save his country.[1] Later that year, Charles Taylor, President of Liberia, succumbed to American pressure to accept exile in Nigeria.[2] Haiti's President Jean Bertrand Aristide was subsequently deposed (arguably in part due to US pressure) and took up residence in South Africa.[3] Thus one wonders: Have exile and amnesty become a legitimate tool of US foreign policy?

Although the practice of exile and the granting of amnesties were widespread prior to World War II, during the second half of the twentieth century offering exile or amnesty to individuals accused of human rights atrocities collided with the erection of a new system of international criminal justice. While exile might still be an option for individuals accused of general venality – tax fraud, corruption or embezzlement – the notion of allowing the perpetrators of human rights atrocities to go unpunished appears to have become normatively unacceptable. Fuelled by the horrors of the Second World War, inspired by the relative success of the Nuremberg trial and nourished by the aspirations of democratization and the new rhetoric of international human rights that followed the establishment of the United Nations, the "impunity" paradigm came to be replaced by calls for accountability and a demand for the investigation and criminal prosecution of those who ordered or committed human rights atrocities. Indeed, requiring accountability for past crimes has been posited by both scholars and practitioners as a remedy to impunity, as well as a necessary, if not sufficient, predicate for the re-establishment

Atrocities and international accountability: Beyond transitional justice, Hughes, Schabas and Thakur (eds), United Nations University Press, 2007, ISBN 978-92-808-1141-4

of peace. Accordingly, the establishment of the International Criminal Tribunals for Rwanda (ICTR) and the former Yugoslavia (ICTY), the Special Court for Sierra Leone (SCSL) and the Special War Crimes Panels for East Timor was conceived of by the international community, and perhaps particularly by the United States,[4] as a means (although not *the* means) to re-establish peace and stability, foster a transition to democratic principles of government, and establish general principles of international law to deter future atrocities. The negotiation and establishment of the International Criminal Court (ICC) treaty in 1998 drew heavily from this emerging practice, and seemed to offer the imprimatur of permanence to a then-experimental concept.

Even as the ad hoc tribunals have continued their work and the ICC has commenced its activities, however, many challenges to international criminal accountability remain. Some are practical in nature: the desire to trade peace for justice in order to end a conflict more quickly, even if temporarily; the overwhelming task of bringing cases against hundreds or even thousands of individuals implicated in the commission of genocide or other mass atrocities; and even the passage of time, which may cause authorities to hesitate in pursuing justice or extinguish otherwise valid cases through the application of statutes of limitations. Others question the entire international criminal justice endeavour itself, arguing that criminal trials may be counterproductive in fostering reconciliation, or that justice, to be effective, must be local, rather than international, in character.[5] Finally, the fledgling international justice system has also encountered political and ideological objections from those concerned with its constraint of State power. The US objections to the International Criminal Court (ICC) fall into this category, predicated as they are on the argument that international norms on accountability (particularly as embodied in the ICC Treaty) are problematic insofar as they might affect the conduct of US foreign affairs, or impinge upon US citizens' ability to travel abroad with impunity.[6]

These challenges notwithstanding, there is substantial countervailing evidence that the notion of accountability has gained considerable traction in international and domestic state practice, as this chapter makes clear. The Special Court for Sierra Leone, for example, declared in 2004 that the Lomé accord, which granted amnesty to the perpetrators of crimes committed during the conflict in Sierra Leone, could not deprive the SCSL of jurisdiction, given that the crimes within the Special Court's statute were crimes subject to universal jurisdiction.[7] Similarly, the amnesties granted in Chile during Pinochet's regime and in Argentina during Argentina's "dirty war" have been recently set aside, both by courts and legislatures in those countries, as well as by courts asked to consider them abroad.[8] Even governments advocating exile initially, such as the

Bush administration's offer to Saddam Hussein, have subsequently sought accountability in the form of criminal trials or other redress.[9] Most recently, the Sudanese government, many of whose members have been accused of serious crimes under international law, has not argued that accountability is a poor idea; instead, the government has argued that it should be able to bring prosecutions itself, rather than having the Darfur situation referred to the International Criminal Court.

This chapter challenges the conventional wisdom that "swapping justice for peace" is morally and practically acceptable. Instead, I argue that international negotiators offering exile are neither morally nor legally justified in doing so. Indeed, although it is beguiling to imagine that offering exile to Saddam Hussein would save thousands of lives, or that the Lord's Resistance Army of Uganda would have laid down its weapons in return for automatic immunity,[10] the evidence suggests the contrary: that warlords and political leaders capable of committing human rights atrocities are not deterred by the amnesties obtained, but emboldened. Indeed, the cases of Sierra Leone, the former Yugoslavia and Haiti suggest that amnesties imposed from above or negotiated at gunpoint do not lead to the establishment of peace – but at best create a temporary lull in the fighting. Indeed, amnesty deals typically foster a culture of impunity in which violence becomes the norm, rather than the exception.

Additionally, this chapter addresses the status of domestic, transnational and international amnesties before national and international courts. In this connection, it should be noted that this work confines itself to addressing the problem of amnesties for the commission of *jus cogens* crimes[11] – crimes covered by peremptory, non-derogable norms of international law[12] – which may not be set aside by conflicting municipal laws. This is why the question of amnesties is problematic, especially before international courts.[13] Indeed, I argue that the legal effect of any particular grant of amnesty or exile will be determined, in part, by the forum before which the amnesty is invoked. In particular, the treatment of amnesties before international courts and tribunals is quite different from their effect before domestic or municipal courts. Thus, in my analysis, I distinguish between "domestic" (granted as a matter of municipal law by the territorial state) and "transnational" amnesties (generally de facto amnesty received by individuals upon the condition that they leave the territorial state and take up residence elsewhere).[14] In each case, the question raised is whether a particular amnesty is effective in the territorial state (where the offences were committed), in a custodial state (where the "accused" may be found), or before an international court or tribunal. While both theory and practice dovetail nicely on the consideration of domestic and transnational amnesties before both state and international courts, the question of whether the international community itself, whether by treaty or an act of the Security Council, may amnesty crimes so that even the territorial state is deprived of jurisdiction is a very difficult one, a complete treatment of which is beyond the scope of this essay, but which is briefly considered below.

This question has become of particular importance given the recent practice of the Security Council in exempting US nationals, in particular, from the jurisdiction of the ICC as well as the territorial jurisdiction of states receiving UN missions. With regard to domestic amnesties, although effective in the state where granted, their effectiveness clearly diminishes with time. As regards a custodial state, I propose that courts in that jurisdiction should treat the amnesty as presumptively invalid; a presumption that can be overcome if the state granting the amnesty in question did so pursuant to a process that did not undermine the quest for accountability as a whole.[15] The same is true in reverse for transnational amnesties, which have no effect in the territorial state, but may at least temporarily protect an accused so long as he remains in exile. Any third state, however, would not be bound by the grant of asylum in the state of exile.

This chapter concludes that the limited and recent efforts to revive the practice of exile are inconsistent with crystallizing or already existent international law norms, as opposed to evidence of a change in state practice as regards the ultimate legality of amnesties.[16] Even where amnesties or exile appear initially to have taken effect successfully, that effect appears to wane with time, leading to calls for prosecution years, or even decades, after the initial crimes were committed. This, in turn, suggests that whatever practical effect the initial grants of exile or amnesties may have, delayed litigation and prosecution appear to be the norm, not the exception. Perhaps, even more importantly, they appear to collide with evolving social and political norms that condemn the grant of impunity for the commission of atrocities as unacceptable. It is important, however, to emphasize that the international community and states tend to differentiate between the grant of amnesties to those most responsible for the commission of atrocities, who are held most responsible, and lower level perpetrators. Creative solutions, such as those adopted in South Africa and Rwanda may be necessary to avoid an "impunity gap" whereby senior leadership may be prosecuted and lower level perpetrators left untouched.

Finally, and perhaps controversially, this chapter contends that although international criminal justice is currently tainted by a lack of even-handedness that has a certain imperialist tinge, the unfairness is largely manifested by the failure of Western governments to submit themselves and their leaders to the rule of law rather than the decision to pursue justice and accountability in particular cases. Moreover, the as-

sumption that international negotiators have a moral or legal right to negotiate away the rights of victims and survivors by exchanging justice for
peace is deeply problematic, particularly in light of the unacceptable nature such a trade off would represent if the victims were their own citizens. Although respect for indigenous processes through the principles
of complementarity and subsidiarity is vital if the international justice
system is to retain its credibility, accountability imposed in a sensitive,
situation-specific and principled manner remains a fundamental cornerstone of transitional justice.

Amnesty and imperialism

The critique is sometimes offered that the notion of an international
criminal justice system is a Western one, insensitive to Eastern, Islamic
or other non-Western sensibilities. However, modern writers on the subject correctly point to Chinese, Islamic and Hindu traditions that under-
score the universal values enshrined in the prohibition of *jus cogens*
crimes that shock the conscience of humankind.[17] Unlike human rights
law, which has a comprehensive agenda, international criminal law (at
least as regards *jus cogens* crimes) limits its concern, for the most part,
to "the most serious crimes of concern to the international community
as a whole",[18] avoiding perhaps some of the difficulties human rights
lawyers face when they argue universality in the face of national legal
rules challenging the international standards asserted.

What *is* probably a fair critique, however, is that the *enforcement* of
international criminal law depends upon a combination of force and political power, and is often influenced by the foreign policy agenda of powerful states. Just as rich and powerful citizens may dominate a national
legal system, wealthy and powerful countries such as the United States
may not only influence which cases are brought but, perhaps even more
problematically, may refuse to permit the application of international
criminal law to themselves and their nationals, even when insisting it
should be applied to others. This is evinced by the Statute of the Iraqi
Special Tribunal, which permits an Iraqi Court (originally established
under US occupation) to exercise jurisdiction over Saddam Hussein and
his associates for violations of international humanitarian law and gross
violations of human rights, but deprives it of jurisdiction over US soldiers
or civilians accused of mistreating Iraqi detainees in Iraqi prisons such as
Abu Ghraib.[19] Clearly, the imperialism evinced by this double standard
in the application of legal rules decreases the legitimacy of the entire endeavour; but it would be a mistake to confuse the *tu quoque* defence with
a principle of justice. As Justice Robert Jackson argued in his opening

statement at Nuremberg, those credibly accused of the commission of human rights atrocities may be "hard pressed" if called to account before the bar of justice, but they are certainly not "ill-used".[20]

Similarly, imperialism often taints the argument that one should "trade justice for peace" in order to end a conflict quickly. While it may be correct that in some highly exceptional cases, exile or amnesty will serve both the long- and short-term interests of peace, the exception easily becomes the rule, with highly corrosive effects on the rule of law, as well as international peace and security.

Take the Saddam Hussein example, invoked above. Implicit in the challenge to those who insist on bringing Hussein to justice are three assumptions: first, that the departure of Hussein from Iraq would have stopped a US invasion of Iraq, a proposition that seems completely unlikely (and even extraordinarily cynical) given the US insistence on removing Iraq's alleged weapons of mass destruction; second, the idea that once out of the country, Hussein would cease his criminal activities and lead a quiet life, posing no danger to anyone; and, finally, that US negotiators are morally, legally and practically justified in determining whether or not thousands of Iraqis are killed in a war launched by the United States itself.

Regarding the last point, particularly in respect of any moral claim that the US might make in trading Iraqi justice for a US peace, imagine if General Pervez Musharraf of Pakistan offered Osama bin Laden amnesty in exchange for a promise that he would cease and desist his terrorist activities – would the families of those killed in the terrorist attacks of 11 September feel that General Musharraf had any moral or legal right to trade their justice for peace? Even if by doing so, it could be argued that future lives would be saved once bin Laden had stopped his terrorist activities? Two different challenges, at least, might be raised to such a proposition, the first being that we would not trust Osama to honour the agreement; the second that such an agreement could embolden other would-be terrorists by setting an example of impunity. Indeed, if amnesty is generally an unacceptable proposition in cases of *jus cogens* crimes committed against US nationals (although, once again, it might be important to distinguish between lower level perpetrators and their leaders), it is not clear why it would be acceptable for amnesties to be granted to individuals who have "merely" victimized their own countrymen and -women, unless, of course the country in question decided upon remedies uniquely suited to its particular circumstances.

The Saddam Hussein example invoked in this chapter, is, of course, atypical. The more usual scenario is one in which warlords or political leaders insist upon amnesty as a condition of ceasing their criminal behaviour. Yet only South Africa can be evoked as an example of a successful transition to democratic and peaceful rule accompanied by the grant of amnesties, and, in fact, this appears to be because of the unique leadership, historical circumstances and ultimately the particularized consideration of individual cases that accompanied the truth and reconciliation commission process.[21] That is not to say that truth commissions are not appropriate vehicles for transitional justice in many cases; only that for at least the most culpable perpetrators, simply acknowledging the crimes committed seems insufficient.

One reason that the criminal law has been invoked in such cases is because the behaviour is seen as pathological,[22] with all that implies, and the deaths and human rights abuses carried out are seen not as incidental to a particular political strategy, but as the intentional commission of terrible acts of cruelty.[23] Blanket amnesties, particularly when issued by leaders who have presided over the commission of atrocities to themselves and their followers, are, for the most part, simply self-serving declarations by government officials exempting themselves from the reach of the law. They represent an attempt to trump the application of rules of law, and as such constitute a threat to both the legitimacy and the fairness of the rules.[24] In the poignant words of one Rwandan lawyer:

> We are in the process of falling into the trap that these murderers have set for us. This genocide is distinguished by the fact that a maximum number of people have been implicated in the killings – there is talk of a million killers. The Hutu extremists estimated that no court in the world could judge that many criminals, and they bet that they were going to get off. Are we going to say that they're right?[25]

As I have suggested elsewhere, perhaps in cases of mass atrocities criminal trials, particularly international criminal trials, should be required for the leaders, while other mechanisms of accountability, including the use of conditional amnesties, truth commissions, lustration laws, reparations, counselling and other measures, may be appropriate for lower-level perpetrators.[26]

The effect of amnesties for *jus cogens* crimes

The effect of domestic amnesties for jus cogens crimes

Before national courts

Recent jurisprudence of the International Court of Justice and the Special Court for Sierra Leone suggests that a domestic amnesty is valid in the state where granted, unless that state decides otherwise (through a regime change or otherwise).[27] Whether or not those courts are correct as a matter of law and state practice, clearly the situation before a court in a third state is quite different. States seeking to exercise universal jurisdiction over perpetrators do so pursuant to internal legislation adapted to that end. If faced with claims of a defendant's immunity, granted by domestic amnesty provisions, how should the state in question (the forum state) respond?

With respect to amnesties or immunities granted by municipal law, the first question to be answered is, What law applies? Public international law has not yet developed a system of conflicts of laws to address this question, because it is largely operating under the *Lotus* paradigm: every state being an independent sovereign, every state may apply its law to a problem unless there is some rule prohibiting it from doing so.[28] Moreover, many states refuse to enforce foreign public law, and would consider criminal proceedings as well as amnesty laws "public", applying what one writer has dubbed the "public law taboo".[29] Yet to the extent that national courts are using universal jurisdiction as the bases for the trial of perpetrators that otherwise have no connection to the forum,[30] they are already applying, through the medium of international law, an exception to the rule that penal jurisdiction is generally territorial in character. Thus, the national court exercising universal jurisdiction has a dual role: to apply and interpret national law, and to effectively sit as a court of the international community, applying international legal norms. Thus, in considering what effect a national amnesty should have before a foreign court, it is appropriate to consider whether the applicable law should be the law of the forum state, the law of the state granting the defendant immunity, the law of the state of the defendant's nationality, the law of the state upon whose territory the crimes were committed (the territorial state) or international law to resolve the question.

While a full treatment of this subject is beyond the scope of this chapter, I will nonetheless suggest some general parameters that may be of use. To begin with, surely, it would be paradoxical for the forum state to use the law of the state granting immunity as the measure of its own exercise of universal jurisdiction. First, as most of these crimes are committed in internal conflicts by regimes in power, the state granting immunity will typically be the state of the defendant's nationality as well as the territorial state. Since the defendant will presumably have violated clear norms of international law, there can be no issue relating to *nullum crimen, nullum poena sine lege* – no punishment without law – if an amnesty granted after the crime's commission is ultimately ineffective if the defendant travels abroad.[31] Moreover, many immunities are granted by regimes to themselves just before they step down, or are extracted from a successor regime with threats of rebellion and violence. The former situation is a classic example of law that is blatantly self-interested and prob- ably illegitimate. The second situation, while involving amnesties granted by a presumably legitimate government, could appear to be an illegal contract, void *ab initio*, if the beneficiary seeks to enforce it, as against public policy and extracted by duress.[32] Indeed, both the SCSL and, more recently, the Supreme Court of Mexico both came to the conclusion that a domestic amnesty granted as regards a *jus cogens*[33] crime cannot affect the jurisdiction of a third state.

Assuming then that it is not a state other than the forum state whose law should govern the question whether the amnesty or other immunity is valid, the choices remaining are the law of the forum and international law. I discuss the last possibility first. The international law criminalizing gross abuses of human rights has developed considerably since World War II. The explicit thesis of this chapter is that the substantive norms, whether initially established by treaty or by custom, are well-established norms of customary international law, and indeed, *jus cogens* norms that are non-derogable in nature.[34] This position appears to be confirmed by most recent state court decisions, and was reaffirmed during the Rome Diplomatic Conference to establish the ICC, where most governments were comfortable codifying these norms and applying them universally in the event the Security Council referred a particular case to the Court. A state investigating a non-national for one of these crimes pursuant to an exercise of universal jurisdiction is thus applying, through the medium of its national law, international law. What is not clear is whether the state is bound, in the absence of a specific treaty obligation, to apply in- ternational rules *related to* the substantive norm. The most that can be said is that there is at least some evidence that a state is required to do so, at least as to certain rules.

First, the Charter and judgment of the International Military Tribunal at Nuremberg clearly affirmed the primacy of international law over na- tional law, at least insofar as crimes against peace, war crimes and crimes against humanity were concerned.[35] The Charter essentially abolished the defence of superior orders, and was explicit in rejecting municipal law as a defence to an international crime. The Nuremberg principles were adopted in a resolution by the United Nations General Assembly in 1946,[36] and have not been seriously questioned since. It would seem odd for international law to prime national law, only for national law to extinguish the legal obligation imposed either through the application of a statute of limitations, amnesty or some other form of domestic immu- nity. Although there was some doubt as to whether a rule concerning the statute of limitations existed in customary international law,[37] that doubt would seem to be laid to rest after the widespread adoption of the Rome Statute, which provides that the crimes therein do not expire.[38]

Moreover, recently some jurisdictions have been adopting provisions abolishing the Statute of Limitations as regards at least certain *jus cogens* crimes.[39] Similarly, the issue of superior orders is clearly addressed in the Rome Statute, and its widespread adoption by states will presumably create clear legal rules on those issues. Thus, although the manner in which international law is applied by states is generally a question of national law, given that these particular rules of international law appear to be inextricably intertwined with the application of a *jus cogens* norm of fundamental importance, the better rule would be that national legal systems are bound, as a matter of international law, to apply international, and not national, rules regarding superior orders and statutes of limitation.[40]

Head of state immunity presents a slightly different problem,[41] for if international law abolishes head of state immunity as regards the *international* prosecution of current, as well as former, heads of state, national prosecutions of current leaders (unlike their predecessors) might unduly strain the international legal system, which is still premised largely on the sovereign equality of states. The International Court of Justice took this view in its recent decision in *Congo v. Belgium* and the decision on the immunity of Charles Taylor of the Special Court for Sierra Leone appears compatible with these views.[42]

I turn now to the last issue, the difficult question of amnesty, either de facto or de jure. International law (by treaty) appears to reject the possibility of amnesties for genocide, grave breaches of the 1949 Geneva Conventions, torture and perhaps other serious crimes committed in international armed conflict.[43] However, with respect to crimes against humanity and other war crimes, the law may be less clear. If we reject the law of the State granting the amnesty as a source of law to apply (for the reasons given above or through a simple refusal to accord the amnesty any extraterritorial effect), we must assume the relevant law to be the national law of the forum state.[44] Of course, it is quite likely, however, that the forum state may not have any law on the question, for its legislature probably has not considered the problem. Thus, the remainder of this section proposes some policy considerations that a court in the forum state might use in evaluating a foreign amnesty, keeping in mind that it will need to balance the international community's interest in pursuing justice against concerns of comity and the importance of respecting the difficult choices a particular jurisdiction has made as to how it will treat the perpetrators of past atrocities.

Courts in the forum state should keep in mind that amnesties are disfavoured, perhaps even illegal, in international law. Moreover, to permit national amnesties to extinguish obligations imposed by international law would seem contrary to the foundational principles of international criminal law, and stand in opposition to the clear weight of authority and much of the state and international practice emerging in this field. This should create a presumption that the forum state should refuse to accept the amnesty. This presumption would be rebuttable, however, in specific cases. First, even the ICC Statute does not prohibit amnesties per se. Instead, as noted earlier, it leaves open the possibility that some amnesties might serve the interests of justice. Assuming the decision is made in good faith, national fora presumably may do the same. Their courts may already be overburdened, the defendant may have already been placed "in jeopardy" of criminal prosecution elsewhere, or comity may require that the forum state abstain from prosecution in a specific case, particularly with respect to conditional amnesties that have resulted from a carefully negotiated and potentially fragile agreement entered into as part of a transition to democracy. Of course, a state may use other filtering mechanisms in evaluating the viability of a particular exercise of universal jurisdiction, such as the "subsidiarity principle" suggested by the Spanish courts in their recent jurisprudence,[45] or the exercise of prosecutorial discretion, as Belgium's universal jurisdiction law provides.[46] In the United States, US conflicts principles or the doctrine of comity may be employed to determine when and under what circumstances a US court should entertain a prosecution of a foreign national if that individual invokes a foreign amnesty.[47] Indeed, assuming the decision of the forum state is made without the influence of political pressure, and pursuant to sound jurisprudential reasoning, a case-by-case approach to the problem of amnesties serves the interest of justice more than a per se rule.

Before concluding this section, it is worth noting that the conundrum posited by the application of international law by national legal systems is not new. All legal systems involving multiple and overlapping courts must address this problem, and it is a particularly interesting feature of both horizontal and vertical transjudicial process. This is evidenced by the *Erie* doctrine elaborated by the United States Supreme Court to govern the application of state law by federal courts, and by the European Court of Justice (ECJ) regarding the application of European law by national courts (the reverse situation). Indeed, faced with the disparate application of EU law by national courts, the ECJ has developed doctrines that require national courts to apply EU law, but allow them a certain degree of discretion in how they do so. A central point in the ECJ's jurisprudence, however, which US law also underscores, is that a national court's application of procedural rules to an EU cause of action may not discriminate against the application of Community law, or completely vitiate the substantive right, or render the right impossible to exercise in practice.[48]

The relationship between EU courts and national courts, and between federal and state courts in the United States, are of course quite different from the diffuse and relatively informal links that characterize the relationship of national courts to each other, to other international tribunals such as the ICTY and ICTR and to the International Criminal Court and the International Court of Justice. The treaties establishing the European Communities and the European Union form a nascent constitution constraining the member states, the communities and the European Union in a much more formal and legal relationship than exists in the international arena. Similarly, the balance between the federal and state courts in the United States is governed by a written constitution. Nevertheless, as the international legal system matures, and takes on its own constitutional form, it may be instructive to consider case law elaborated in two well-developed two-tier legal systems as a guide to doctrines that might ultimately be useful to international criminal law.

Before international courts and tribunals

The international jurisprudence on the subject appears uniform on this point: domestic amnesties, whatever their legality *ab initio*, cannot immunize an accused faced with prosecution before an international court. It is interesting to note that the Courts so opining have yet to provide much in the way of a *ratio decidendi* for their holdings;[49] however, it is this author's contention that national amnesties have no play before international courts for at least two reasons. First, the problem of frictions between sovereigns in a horizontal relationship of full equality simply does not exist in the international context. Second, given the primacy and hierarchical status of the norms as *jus cogens*, it has been true since the Nuremberg trials that international courts exercising (international) universal jurisdiction[50] have not been bound by municipal law that would serve as an obstacle to prosecution. That is, the holdings of the International Court of Justice and the Special Court for Sierra Leone, as well as the many national court decisions and commentaries to the same effect, rest on an understanding of the international legal order as autonomous from and existing in a vertical relationship to (at least for these purposes) sovereign states. Thus, the status of amnesties for *jus cogens* crimes, while seemingly banal, raises fundamental questions concerning the structure and function of the global constitutional order.

The effect of transnational amnesties (exile) for jus cogens crimes

The question posed by this section is a simple one: what is the legal status of an individual accused of a *jus cogens* crime, who has sought and been given refuge in a third state? This is not so much a question of international law but of common sense: the short answer appears to be that the individual may benefit from the grant of asylum within the state of refuge under the constitutional system in place there, but presumably could not travel with his immune status, for it would cease to have any effect outside the territory of the state of refuge. Given that criminal laws are generally laws of territorial application, surely it cannot be that by granting immunity to Charles Taylor in Nigeria, for example, or to Idi Amin in Saudi Arabia, the prescriptive jurisdiction of the territorial state has been in any way affected. Thus, the effect of a transnational amnesty (exile) in the territorial state (or presumably any third state as well), would appear to be null. Similarly, as is the case with domestic amnesties before international courts, presumably any grant of exile has no legal effect before an international court (as the Special Court for Sierra Leone held by implication in the Charles Taylor case).[51]

The effect of international amnesties for jus cogens crimes

The question arises whether individual responsibility for the commission of international crimes can be abrogated by treaty or even by the Security Council itself. As regards the effect of an "amnesty treaty" in national courts, some interesting questions arise. Although there is some contention on this point, it is currently the practice of the United Nations to reject amnesty for crimes against humanity and genocide (and presumably serious violations of international humanitarian law, as well).[52] We have, of course, already seen that amnesty is disfavoured in state practice and by international courts. Moreover, most international criminal law treaties, particularly the Rome Statute, the Genocide Convention, the Torture Convention, the Grave Breaches provisions of the Geneva Conventions and many anti-terrorism treaties, arguably prohibit amnesties by their requirement that offenders must be punished. Thus, presumably this problem will not surface extensively. However, if immunity is granted pursuant to a treaty to which the forum state is not a party, it is difficult to see why it should or would apply. Indeed, implicit in the amnesty opinion of the SCSL is a holding that the agreement is binding upon the parties – just not upon the Special Court. Thus, in principle it seems possible that states could bind themselves by an international agreement to that effect, not to engage in criminal prosecutions of each others nationals, even for the commission of *jus cogens* crimes. On the other hand, given that the crimes are covered by peremptory norms of international law, and that most international instruments either defining them or creating adjudicatory mechanisms state that a duty to prosecute such crimes exists, it may be that such a treaty is against international public policy and would be as void as a treaty permitting the commission of those crimes in the first place. As we saw above, in such case, although the amnesties might be enforceable in the territorial state, presumably they would have no effect in a third state or before an international court or tribunal.

If we suppose, however, that the Security Council has in some way countenanced the grant of exile, or, acting pursuant to its Chapter 7 powers, ordered an amnesty, the question becomes more difficult. If the Resolution is adopted pursuant to Chapter 7 of the Charter and directed to all Member States, pursuant to Article 25 of the Charter, all states would be required to comply with the amnesty agreement.[53] The question remains whether such a resolution would be *ultra vires*. (And, of course, even if it were beyond the Council's powers, would any remedy be available to a state wishing to contest the Council's actions?) This possibility appears much more probable than an "amnesty treaty" because the recent practice of the Security Council has been to accept (at least in some cases), language in Council resolutions that may immunize nationals of certain countries from prosecution for the commission of *jus cogens* crimes. Indeed, frustrated with its inability to obtain immunity under customary international law and before the ICC, the US has turned to the Security Council as a vehicle to immunize US nationals from the reach of international criminal law. The most recent example is Resolution 1593, which grants contributing states exclusive jurisdiction over their nationals for all "alleged acts or omissions arising out of or related to operations in Sudan".[54] In this case, the territorial state (Sudan) is deprived of jurisdiction, even if the contributing state declines to investigate allegations of war crimes.

When acting under Chapter 7, the Security Council is limited to the powers granted it pursuant to the UN Charter, and the International Court of Justice has suggested that its actions are not above the law.[55] On the other hand, the ICJ has never invalidated a Security Council Resolution.[56] Moreover, Article 16 of the ICC's Statute appears to grant the Council a role in criminal prosecutions in conjunction with its mandate to promote international peace. Article 16 provides that the Council may stop a prosecution from proceeding (for one year) by affirmatively voting to do so.[57] This may suggest that the granting of an amnesty is somehow perceived by the international community as properly within the ambit of the Council's powers; or, given how narrowly it constrains the Council, it could be seen as only a small concession to the Council granted to cover an emergency situation. Certainly, a territorial State might wish to challenge such a Security Council Resolution; as to the amnesty's status before an international court, it is unclear how the ICC, for example, would treat an amnesty imposed pursuant to Security Council Resolution, although the Court would presumably think hard before disregarding it out of hand.[58]

Conclusion

Societies in transition are messy places, in which delivering justice is a difficult, laborious and often frustrating process. Large numbers of perpetrators, overwhelmed institutions, poverty and weak social cohesion may make the process of bringing perpetrators to book extraordinarily difficult, even impossible, particularly in the most ideal forum, the country in which the crimes were perpetrated. In such a case, international assistance, and probably international prosecutions, will be a vital component of restoring peace and combating impunity. Indeed, international law may take on a pivotal role, offering an "alternate construction of law that, despite substantial political change, is continuous and enduring".[59]

Yet international criminal justice is not and should not be a "one size fits all" proposition, nor is it a panacea for the world's ills. The South African experience suggests that although the criminal law is an important tool, where a society is able to come together in a democratic process and engage in deliberation concerning the fate of perpetrators of atrocities under a former regime, some of which may be prosecuted, others not, that decision should be respected. Yet the exception must not be taken for the rule: both state and international practice now suggest that exile and amnesty is a largely unacceptable response to the commission of *jus cogens* crimes.

Although it may be, as the Special Court for Sierra Leone has held, that amnesties, even for the commission of *jus cogens* crimes, are lawful in the territorial state, a conclusion that at least some courts and commentators have challenged, the cases to date have unanimously concluded that the amnesties cannot "travel" with efficacy to other jurisdictions, and, in particular, are without force before international courts and tribunals. Indeed, whether that practice has crystallized as an absolute *legal* prohibition almost seems of decreasing importance, given the transnational legal process of norm construction that increasingly renders it politically and socially unacceptable (even if not illegal per se) in virtually all cases to promote impunity. The current practice of some governments, and particularly the United States, to reject accountability in certain circumstances thus appears either opportunistic or maybe even cynical, representing not so much a real challenge to this emerging norm of international law and politics, but an assertion of raw power. As such, offers of asylum to Saddam Hussein and Charles Taylor, for example, do not suggest the emergence of a new paradigm but instead embody probably unacceptable exceptions to the rule.[60]

Individuals, as well as societies, appear to seek justice just as intently as they seek peace. Survivors pursue their tormentors across long periods of space and time, often waiting years until conditions permit their cause to be heard. As a result, the efforts by international negotiators to swap amnesty for peace appear to offer little more than a temporary respite for international criminals, and have little staying power outside the country where negotiated. Moreover, what longitudinal case studies we have suggest that our intuitions about amnesties are correct – that they promote a culture of impunity in which violence remains the norm rather than the exception. In light of these practical realities, arguments that amnesties may contribute to or be necessary for peace seem to have little moral or persuasive force.

Notes

1. On the evening of 17 March 2003, President Bush declared, "Saddam Hussein and his sons must leave Iraq within 48 hours", or war would result. W. A. Ross and A. Langley (2003) "White House Still Hopes Saddam Hussein Will Choose Exile", US Mission to the European Union, available from http://www.useu.be/Categories/GlobalAffairs/Iraq/Mar1803USSaddamExile.html (last visited 17 February 2005). Donald Rumsfeld, US Secretary of Defense, suggested that the "senior leadership" in Iraq and their families should be afforded safe haven in some other country to avoid the prospect of war. *Lateline* (2003) "US Offers Exile to Saddam Hussein", Australian Broadcasting Corporation, 20 February, available from http://www.abc.net.au/lateline/s789392.html (last visited 20 January 2004).

2. Taylor arrived in Calabar, Nigeria, with his wife, daughters and a large entourage in August 2003. According to news reports, the US government supported Taylor's exile, believing that it would save lives (BBC News (2003) "U.S. Denies Charles Taylor Bounty", 13 November, available from http://newsvote.bbc.co.uk/mpapps/pagetools/print/news.bbc.co.uk/1/hi/world/africa/326607), and opposed Congressional efforts to offer a US$2 million bounty for his capture, and to force Nigeria to extradite Taylor to the Special Court for Sierra Leone pursuant to an indictment issued by that court. CBSNews.com (2003) "Taylor: Fugitive, or Exile?", 14 November, available from http://www.cbsnews.com/stories/2003/11/14/world/printable583572. Taylor was ultimately rendered to the Special Court for Sierra Leone, and his trial will begin summer 2007.

3. G. Marx (2004) "Haitians in a Vise of Nature, Politics: Weeks after Floods Killed at least 1,900 in Gonaives, Relief Efforts Have Faltered in a Climate of Violence Over Who Should Rule", *Chicago Tribune*, 25 November.

4. Although the US administration currently opposes the International Criminal Court (see, for example, L. N. Sadat (2003) "Summer in Rome, Spring in the Hague, Winter in Washington?: U.S. Policy Towards the International Criminal Court", *Wisconsin International Law Journal* 21: 557), US leadership was critical to the establishment of the ICTY and ICTR, the SCSL and even, arguably, in bringing the Sudan situation to the UN Security Council. W. Hoge (2005) "U.N. Will Refer Darfur Crimes to Court in Hague", *International Herald Tribune*, 2–3 April.

5. J. Alvarez (1999) "Crimes of State/Crimes of Hate: Lessons from Rwanda", *Yale Journal of International Law* 24: 385; M. A. Drumbl (2005) "Collective Violence and Individual Punishment: The Criminality of Mass Atrocity", *Northwestern University Law Review* 99: 539; D. Wippman (1999) "Atrocities, Deterrence, and the Limits of International Justice", *Fordham International Law Journal* 23: 473. See also E. Bradley (1998)

"In Search for Justice: A Truth in Reconciliation [sic] Commission for Rwanda", *Journal of International Law and Practice* 7: 129.

6. See, for example, Sadat, "Summer in Rome".

7. It did not, however, find the amnesty invalid per se. *Prosecutor v. Kallon & Kamara, Decision on Challenge to Jurisdiction: Lomé Accord Amnesty*, Case Nos. SCSL-2004-15-AR72(E), SCSL-2004-16-AR72(E), paras 87–89 (SCSL App. Ch., Mar. 13, 2004). This decision followed the opinion of the ICTY in *Furundzija* to the same effect, *Prosecutor v. Anto Furundzija, Judgment*, Case No. IT-95-17/1-T, (T. Ch. II, Dec. 10, 1998) [hereinafter *Furundzija*], and was cited with approval by a recent United Nations report on impunity. UN Commission on Human Rights (2004) *Promotion and Protection of Human Rights: Impunity*, UN Doc. C/CN.4/2004/88 (Feb. 27, 2004) (Advance Edited Version) (Professor Diane Orentlicher, Rapporteur) [hereinafter Orentlicher Impunity Study].

8. In March 2001, an Argentinean judge declared Argentina's amnesty laws unconstitutional and in violation of international law, a decision confirmed in August 2003, when both houses of Argentina's Congress voted by a large majority to annul those laws. Human Rights Watch (2003) "Argentina: Holding Rights Abusers Accountable", press release, 14 August, available from http://www.hrw.org/press/2003/08/argentina081403.htm (last visited 14 July 2004). The Supreme Court of Argentina recently affirmed this decision. See Supreme Court of Argentina (2005) *Case of Julio Héctor Simon* (decision declaring Argentina's Amnesty Laws unconstitutional), 14 June. Similarly, courts in Chile have sidestepped Pinochet's self-granted amnesty, permitting Pinochet and others to be indicted and, in the case of some individuals, convicted of crimes committed during the Pinochet regime. See generally R. Aldana (2004) "Steps Closer to Justice for Past Crimes in Argentina and Chile: A Story of Judicial Boldness", *War Crimes Research Portal*, Frederick K. Cox International Law Center, available from http://law.case.edu/war-crimes-research-portal/instant_analysis.asp?id=12 (last visited 17 February 2005). Another Chilean judge recently held that Pinochet was competent to stand trial for abuses during his tenure in office, L. Rohter (2004) "Chilean Judge Says Pinochet Is Fit for Trial", *New York Times*, 14 December. The decision was rendered by Judge Juan Guzmán Tapia on 13 December 2004 and, according to press reports, rendered Pinochet mentally fit to "undergo criminal investigation in Chile in all of its stages", including depositions and "face to face interrogations" about his role in the perpetration of crimes against political opponents in the 1970s while head of state. Ibid.

9. The United States is currently supporting the trial of Saddam Hussein and other former Baath party leaders in Iraq both financially and logistically.

10. In fact, an amnesty was issued in Uganda four years ago for the members of the Lord's Resistance Army and others; it is estimated that between 10 and 14 thousand rebels received it. "Official Tells Xinhua Over 14,000 Ugandan Rebels Got Amnesty", World News Connection (Newswire), 2 March 2005; nonetheless, the situation in Uganda is still so bad that the Ugandan government asked the ICC Prosecutor to open an investigation into the commission of atrocities there.

11. I have specifically eschewed the somewhat cumbersome terminology – "serious crimes under international law", Princeton Principles on Universal Jurisdiction, Principle 2 (2001) [hereinafter Princeton Principles] – often employed to describe the subset of (international) crimes over which universal jurisdiction may presumptively be exercised by states. Because this chapter addresses not only the question of amnesties in connection with the exercise of criminal jurisdiction by states, but before international tribunals as well, it is simpler and more consistent with the purport of the definition to be clear that these are *jus cogens* crimes covered by peremptory norms of international law.

12. This idea is codified in article 53 of the Vienna Convention on the Law of Treaties, which provides that a "peremptory norm of general international law is a norm accepted and recognised by the international community of states as a whole as a norm from which no derogation is permitted and which can be modified only by a subsequent norm of general international law having the same character". Vienna Convention on the Law of Treaties, art. 53.

13. I must emphasize that it is problematic *only* as regards *jus cogens* crimes. Corruption, looting, tax fraud, general venality or criminality are clearly crimes not within this category.

14. It may be objected that exiling a leader and his retinue is not tantamount to issuing a domestic amnesty – for in many instances, no legal action has led to the individual's removal from his country of residence to his home in exile. While this is true, nonetheless, just as an amnesty may place the individual *juridically* outside the purview of the law, even if he continues to reside in his country of origin, exile places him *physically* outside the reach of the law. That is why, for purposes of evaluating its effect, exile granted to a leader that is accused of committing *jus cogens* offences can be considered as a "transnational" amnesty.

15. The South African Truth and Reconciliation Commission comes to mind.

16. *Nicaragua v. United States of America* (Military and Paramilitary Activities in and against Nicaragua) (1986) International Court of Justice 15, available from http://www.icj-cij.org/icjwww/icases/inus/inus_ijudgment/inus_ijudgment_19860627.pdf (last visited 15 February 2005).

17. See, for example, M. C. Bassiouni (2003) *Introduction to International Criminal Law*, Ardsley, N.Y.: Transnational Publishers, pp. 21–55.

18. See, for example, *Rome Statute of the International Criminal Court*, United Nations Diplomatic Conference of Plenipotentiaries on the Establishment of an International Criminal Court, July 17, 1998, Annex II, UN Doc. A/CONF. 183/9 (1998), Preamble [hereinafter Rome Statute].

19. See, for example, L. N. Sadat (2004) "International Legal Issues Surrounding the Mistreatment of Iraqi Detainees by American Forces", available from http://www.asil.org/insights, May. Another example is presented by the Security Council's Resolution referring the Darfur situation in the Sudan to the International Criminal Court, which, although referring the nationals of Sudan, a non-party state, to the ICC, contains language exempting persons from other non-party states from the Court's jurisdiction. UN Security Council Res. 1593, para. 6 (Mar. 31, 2005).

20. R. H. Jackson (1971) *The Nürnberg Case*, New York: Cooper Square Publishers, p. 34.

21. In addition to the constitutional challenges brought against the amnesty laws, the families of many of those who were tortured and killed have objected to amnesty proceedings for the perpetrators of those who victimized their loved ones. J. Dugard (1998) "Reconciliation and Justice: The South African Experience", *Transnational Law and Contemporary Problems* 8: 286–301.

22. For the view that human violence is "normal", not pathological, see P. Seabright (2004) *The Company of Strangers*, Princeton, N.J.: Princeton University Press.

23. Others label them morally unjust. K. Greenawalt (2000) "Amnesty's Justice", in R. I. Rotberg and D. Thompson, eds, *Truth v. Justice: The Morality of Truth Commissions*, Princeton, N.J.: Princeton University Press, p. 189.

24. Cf. T. M. Franck (1995) *Fairness in International Law and Institutions*, Oxford: Oxford University Press, p. 16. See also R. J. Goldstone (2000) *For Humanity: Reflections of a War Crimes Investigator*, New Haven, Conn.: Yale University Press, p. 122.

25. L. Bijard (1996) "Can Justice Be Done? Massacred: 1,000,000: Tried 0", *World Press Review* 7, June (quoting Rwandan lawyer Frederic Mutagwera), cited in Bradley, "In Search for Justice", p. 139.

26. L. N. Sadat (2006) "Exile, Amnesty and International Law", *Notre Dame Law Review* 3: 955.

27. *Congo v. Belgium*, Case Concerning the Arrest Warrant of 11 April 2000, International Court of Justice, Feb. 14, 2002. *Prosecutor v. Kallon & Kamara*.

28. *France v. Turkey*, Case Concerning the S.S. Lotus, 1927 Permanent Court of International Justice, Ser. A, no. 10.

29. W. S. Dodge (2002) "Breaking the Public Law Taboo", *Harvard International Law Journal* 43: 161, quoting A. Lowenfeld (1979) "Public Law in the International Arena: Conflict of Laws, International Law, and Some Suggestions for their Interaction", *Recueil Des Cours* 163: 311–326.

30. The *Pinochet* case provides an excellent example. In 1998, the Spanish National Court, the *Audiencia Nacional*, held that the Spanish courts could exercise jurisdiction over genocide, torture and terrorism alleged to have been committed in Chile under Spain's universal jurisdiction law, subject to a caveat (known as the subsidiarity principle) that if a court in the territorial state had exercised its jurisdiction, then the Spanish courts would defer to that court, at least as to charges of genocide. See Order of the Criminal Chamber of the Spanish *Audiencia Nacional* affirming Spain's Jurisdiction, Appeal 173/98, 1st Section, Criminal Investigation 1/98 (Nov. 5, 1998), unofficial translation in R. Brody and M. Ratner, eds (2000) *The Pinochet Papers: The Case of Augusto Pinochet in Spain and Britain*, The Hague: Kluwer Law International, p. 95 [hereinafter 1998 Spanish AN Decision].

31. This may be less true, however, in the case of conditional amnesties, where the defendant has voluntarily come forward and placed him or herself in jeopardy of prosecution by confessing the crime. In this case, the better rule may be that the forum state should examine the particular proceeding to see if the principle of *ne bis in idem* should attach and immunize the particular defendant from subsequent prosecutions. Again, the issue arises whether the forum uses its own rules or an international rule of *ne bis in idem*. The practical response of most fora will most likely be to use some combination of the two, due to the fact that the international law on the subject is not well-codified, and the need to balance the competing interests involved.

32. As between the state of nationality and the territorial state, if the two were to differ, it would seem logical to look first to the territorial state, the application of the criminal law generally being territorial in nature.

33. Decision on the Extradition of Ricardo Miguel Cavallo, Supreme Court of Mexico (June 10, 2003), 42 ILM 888 (2003).

34. M. C. Bassiouni (2000) "Combating Impunity for International Crimes", *University of Colorado Law Review* 71: 409.

35. Charter of the International Military Tribunal [Nuremberg Charter] of 8 August 1945.

36. 1 UN GAOR (Part II) at 188, UN Doc. A/61/Add.1 (1946).

37. There are two treaties on the subject, but they have not been widely adopted. United Nations Convention on the Non-Applicability of Statutory Limitations to War Crimes and Crimes against Humanity, Nov. 26, 1968, 754 UNTS 75. The Convention came into force on 11 November 1970 and, according to the United Nation's web site, currently has only 10 signatories and 44 parties, available from http://untreaty.un.org. Shortly thereafter, the Council of Europe adopted a similar Convention. European Convention on the Non-Applicability of Statutory Limitation to Crimes against Humanity and War Crimes, Jan. 25, 1974, ETS No. 82, reprinted in (1974) 13 ILM 540. The European Convention was ratified by only two states and never entered into force. Interestingly, both conventions were largely a response to German statutes of limitation that would have caused Nazi crimes to prescribe, and prevented prosecution. This result, which was apparently perceived as desirable in Germany, was viewed as unacceptable by many other

countries. See L. Sadat Wexler (1994) "The Interpretation of the Nuremberg Principles by the French Court of Cassation: From Touvier to Barbie and Back Again", *Columbia Journal of Transnational Law* 32: 318–21.

38. Rome Statute, art. 29 ("The crimes within the jurisdiction of the Court shall not be subject to any statute of limitations").
39. Orentlicher Impunity Study.
40. This appears to be the view taken by the Special Court for Sierra Leone. See *Prosecutor v. Kallon & Kamara*.
41. The British House of Lords recognized this in the *Pinochet* case. In 1998, Pinochet was arrested in London (after leaving the "safety" of Chile) on a request for extradition from the Spanish investigating judge, Balthazar Garzón. Pinochet ultimately appealed to the House of Lords. The Lords (six out of seven) ultimately could only agree that Pinochet could stand trial for acts charged that occurred after 29 September 1988, when the British courts would have had jurisdiction over the Spanish claims. See *Regina v. Bartle and the Commissioner of Police for the Metropolis and Others (Ex Parte Pinochet)* (British House of Lords, 24 March 1999), 38 ILM 581 (1999).
42. *Congo v. Belgium*, Case Concerning the Arrest Warrant of 11 April 2000 International Court of Justice, Feb. 14, 2002, 41 ILM 536 (2002).
43. Pardons and conditional amnesties may be distinguishable, for both involve the use of judicial or quasi judicial proceedings and involve particularized consideration of a defendant's guilt or innocence in a particular case. Assuming the proceedings are not a sham, even where amnesties are generally prohibited, pardons and conditional amnesties may be acceptable, or even required by the legality principle, if the defendant has been "put in jeopardy" of criminal proceedings.
44. "Pure" cases of universal jurisdiction appear to be quite rare. Rather, there generally appears to be some connection between the defendant and the forum State, in most instances, again suggesting the appropriateness of the forum applying its law to the question.
45. See note 30. See also Decision of the Supreme Court Concerning the Guatemala Genocide Case, Dec. No. 327/2003 (Feb. 25, 2003, Spanish Supreme Court), reprinted in (2003) 42 ILM 686 (unofficial English translation).
46. Loi du 16 juin 1993 relative à la répression des infractions graves aux Conventions internationales de Genève du 12 août 1949 et aux Protocols I et II du 8 juin 1977, additionels à ces Conventions, *Moniteur Belge*, 5 août 1993 [hereinafter 1993 Belgium Law]. The 1993 Belgian Law, which covered only war crimes, was amended in 1999 to include the possibility of universal jurisdiction over genocide and crimes against humanity. A translation, in English, of the 1999 law can be found at 38 ILM 918.
47. Cf. *Hartford Fire Insurance v. California* (US 1993); *Timberlane Lumber Co. v. Bank of America*, 549 F.2d 597 (9th Cir. 1976).
48. P. Craig and G. de Burca (1998) *EU Law: Text, Cases, and Materials*, 2d ed., Oxford: Oxford University Press, pp. 214–215.
49. More may be coming soon from the International Court of Justice in the case of *Congo v. France*.
50. I refer to the exercise of jurisdiction over *jus cogens* crimes as universal international jurisdiction to distinguish it from cases involving the exercise of universal jurisdiction by states. See L. N. Sadat and S. R. Carden (2000) "The New International Criminal Court: An Uneasy Revolution", *Georgetown Law Journal* 88: 381.
51. *Prosecutor v. Charles Ghankay Taylor*, Case No. SCSL-2003-01-1, Decision on Immunity from Jurisdiction (SCSL App. Ch., May 1, 2004).
52. D. Robinson (2003) "Serving the Interests of Justice: Amnesties, Truth Commissions and the International Criminal Court", *European Journal of International Law* 14: 481.

53. UN Charter, art. 25.
54. Resolution 1593, para. 6. Earlier resolutions include Resolution 1497, adopted by the Council on 1 August 2003, to address the threat to peace and security in Liberia, operative paragraph 7 of which is substantially identical to Resolution 1593. See SC Res. 1497, UN SCOR (4803rd mtg), UN Doc. S/RES/1497 (2003), and Resolution 1422.
55. *Libyan Jamahiriya v. UK*, Order with Regard to Request for Indication of Provisional Measures in the Case Concerning Questions of Interpretation and Application of the 1971 Montreal Convention Arising from the Aerial Incident at Lockerbie, 1992 ICJ 3 (Apr. 14); *Libyan Jamahiriya v. US*, 1992 ICJ 114 (Apr. 14).
56. The ICJ has however affirmed its competence to decide whether UN organs have acted in conformity with the Charter when the issue arises in the normal course of its judicial functions. See, for example, Legal Consequences for States of the Continued Presence of South Africa in Namibia Notwithstanding Security Council Resolution 276 (1971), 1971 ICJ 16, 45 (Jun. 21), para. 53 [hereinafter South West Africa Case].
57. This provision was relied upon by the US to bring about the adoption of Resolution 1422 (renewing the UN peacekeeping mission in Bosnia) on 12 July 2002, which provided that no personnel from a state not party to the Rome Statute could be brought before the ICC for a 12-month period, pursuant to article 16 of the ICC Statute. SC Res. 1422, UN SCOR (4572nd mts), UN Doc. S/RES/1422 (2002). M. El Zeidy (2002) "The United States Dropped the Atomic Bomb of Article 16 on the ICC Statute: Security Council Power of Deferrals and Resolution 1422", *Vanderbilt Journal of Transnational Law* 35: 1503. It was renewed over the objections of several states one year later as Resolution 1487, and in 2003, following the Abu Ghraib prison scandal, when other members of the Council voiced determined opposition, the Resolution was withdrawn.
58. See M. P. Scharf (1999) "The Amnesty Exception to the Jurisdiction of the International Criminal Court", *Cornell International Law Journal* 32: 509, 522–524.
59. R. Teitel (1997) "Transitional Jurisprudence: The Role of Law in Political Transformation", *Yale Law Journal*, 105: 2028.
60. Exceptions that not even the United States has seriously maintained, given that Saddam Hussein has been turned over to the Iraqi Special Tribunal for trial, and the US government has come under increasing pressure to do something about bringing Charles Taylor before the SCSL. "Bush Is Pressed on Status of Warlord" (2005) *Associated Press*, 10 April.

14

Trading justice for peace: The contemporary law and policy debate

Michael P. Scharf

During the 2006 trial of Saddam Hussein before the Iraqi High Tribunal, his lawyer, Khalil al-Dulaimi, gave an interview to the *New York Times* in which he described the unusual defence strategy. Al-Dulaimi noted that the defence was convinced that Saddam would be found guilty and that his best chance was therefore to use the proceedings to inflame the insurgency and prolong the trial, so that in the end the United States would agree to set Saddam free in return for his help in restoring peace to Iraq.[1] This idea was not completely far-fetched, considering that three years earlier, on the eve of the 2003 invasion of Iraq, President George W. Bush had offered to call off the attack if Saddam Hussein and his top lieutenants would agree to relinquish power and go into exile.[2] Working through President Hosni Mubarak of Egypt, the United States had actively pursued the matter with several Middle East countries, ultimately persuading Bahrain to agree to provide sanctuary to Hussein if he accepted the deal.[3] When Hussein rejected the proposal, Bush promised that the Iraqi leader would be forced from power and prosecuted as a war criminal.[4]

Admittedly, thousands of lives could have been spared if Hussein had accepted the 2003 deal, and perhaps such a deal at the end of his trial in 2006 would also have had the potential to save lives. But, at the risk of being accused of blindly embracing Kant's prescription that "justice must be done even should the heavens fall",[5] this essay argues that it was inappropriate for the Bush Administration even to make the 2003 offer,

Atrocities and international accountability: Beyond transitional justice, Hughes, Schabas and Thakur (eds), United Nations University Press, 2007, ISBN 978-92-808-1141-4

and that if implemented an exile-for-peace deal involving Saddam Hussein would have seriously undermined the Geneva Conventions and the Genocide Convention, which require prosecution of alleged offenders without exception.

A few months after the 2003 invasion of Iraq, US officials helped broker a deal whereby Liberian President Charles Taylor, who had been indicted for crimes against humanity by the Special Court for Sierra Leone, agreed to give up power and was allowed to flee to Nigeria, where he received asylum.[6] At the time, forces opposed to Taylor, which had taken over most of the country, were on the verge of attacking the capital city Monrovia, and tens of thousands of civilian casualties were forecast. The exile deal averted the crisis and set the stage for insertion of a UN peacekeeping mission that stabilized the country and set it on a path to peace and democracy.[7] In contrast to the Hussein case, the Taylor arrangement did not in any way violate international law. This essay explains why international law should treat the two situations differently, prohibiting exile and asylum for Saddam Hussein while permitting such a justice-for-peace exchange in the case of Charles Taylor.

This is one of the first scholarly pieces in recent years to focus on the significant issue of exile. Scholarship on the analogous issue of amnesty has been written largely from the point of view of aggressive advocates of international justice, whose writing is based on the assumption that the widespread state practice favouring amnesties constitutes a violation of, rather than a reflection of, international law in this area.[8] Before analysing the relevant legal principles, the essay begins with an examination of the practical considerations that counsel for and against the practice of "trading justice for peace." Next, using the Saddam Hussein and Charles Taylor cases as a focal point, the essay analyses the relevant international instruments that require prosecution under limited circumstances. This is followed by a critique of the popular view that customary international law and the principle of *jus cogens* broadly prohibit actions that prevent prosecution of crimes under international law. The essay establishes that there does not yet exist a customary international law rule requiring prosecution of war crimes in internal armed conflict or crimes against humanity, but that there is a duty to prosecute in the case of grave breaches of the Geneva Conventions, the crime of genocide and torture. Where the duty to prosecute does apply, it is important that states and international organizations honour it, lest they signal disrespect for the important treaties from which the duty arises, potentially putting their own citizens at risk and generally undermining the rule of law.

Practical considerations

Interests favouring exile, asylum and amnesty

Notwithstanding the popular catch phrase of the 1990s – "no peace without justice" – achieving peace and obtaining justice are sometimes incompatible goals – at least in the short term. In order to end an international or internal conflict, negotiations often must be held with the very leaders who are responsible for war crimes and crimes against humanity. When this is the case, insisting on criminal prosecutions can prolong the conflict, resulting in more deaths, destruction and human suffering.[9]

Reflecting this reality, during the past 30 years Angola, Argentina, Brazil, Cambodia, Chile, El Salvador, Guatemala, Haiti, Honduras, Ivory Coast, Nicaragua, Peru, Sierra Leone, South Africa, Togo and Uruguay have each, as part of a peace arrangement, granted amnesty to members of the former regime that committed international crimes within their respective borders.[10] With respect to five of these countries – Cambodia, El Salvador, Haiti, Sierra Leone and South Africa – "the United Nations itself pushed for, helped negotiate, or endorsed the granting of amnesty as a means of restoring peace and democratic government".[11]

In addition to amnesty (which immunizes the perpetrator from domestic prosecution), exile and asylum in a foreign country (which puts the perpetrator out of the jurisdictional reach of domestic prosecution)[12] is often used to induce regime change, with the blessing and involvement of significant states and the United Nations. Peace negotiators call this the "Napoleonic Option", in reference to the treatment of French emperor Napoleon Bonaparte who, after his defeat at Waterloo in 1815, was exiled to St Helena rather than face trial or execution.[13] More recently, a number of dictators have been granted sanctuary abroad in return for relinquishing power. Thus, for example, Ferdinand Marcos fled the Philippines for Hawaii; Jean-Claude "Baby Doc" Duvalier fled Haiti for France; Mengisthu Haile Miriam fled Ethiopia for Zimbabwe; Idi Amin fled Uganda for Saudi Arabia; General Raoul Cédras fled Haiti for Panama; and Charles Taylor fled Liberia for exile in Nigeria – a deal negotiated by the United States and UN envoy Jacques Klein.[14]

As Payam Akhavan, then Legal Adviser to the Office of the Prosecutor of the International Criminal Tribunal for the former Yugoslavia, observed a decade ago: "It is not unusual in the political stage to see the metamorphosis of yesterday's war monger into today's peace broker."[15] This is because, unless the international community is willing to use force to topple a rogue regime, cooperation of the leaders is needed to bring about peaceful regime change and put an end to violations of international humanitarian law. Yet, it is not realistic to expect them to agree to a peace settlement if, directly following the agreement, they would find themselves or their close associates facing potential life imprisonment.

In brokering the Charles Taylor exile deal, the United States and United Nations were particularly encouraged by the success of similar amnesty/exile for peace arrangements relating to Haiti and South Africa in the 1990s. From 1990 to 1994, Haiti was ruled by a military regime headed by General Raoul Cédras and Brigadier General Philippe Biamby, which executed over 3,000 civilian political opponents and tortured scores of others.[16] The United Nations mediated negotiations at Governors Island in New York Harbor, in which the military leaders agreed to relinquish power and permit the return of the democratically elected President (Jean-Bertrand Aristide) in return for a full amnesty for the members of the regime and a lifting of the economic sanctions imposed by the UN Security Council.[17] Under pressure from the United Nations mediators, Aristide agreed to the amnesty clause of the Governors Island Agreement.[18] The Security Council immediately "declared [its] readiness to give the fullest possible support to the Agreement signed on Governors Island",[19] which it later said constitutes "the only valid framework for the resolution of the crisis in Haiti".[20] When the military leaders initially failed to comply with the Governors Island Agreement, on 31 July 1994, the Security Council took the extreme step of authorizing an invasion of Haiti by a multinational force.[21] On the eve of the invasion on 18 September 1994, a deal was struck, whereby General Cédras agreed to retire his command and accept exile in response to a general amnesty voted into law by the Haitian parliament and an offer by Panama to provide him asylum.[22]

The amnesty deal had its desired effect: The democratically elected Aristide was permitted to return to Haiti and reinstate a civilian government, the military leaders left the country for sanctuary in Panama, much of the military surrendered their arms, and most of the human rights abuses promptly ended – all with practically no bloodshed or resistance.[23] Although the situation in Haiti has once again deteriorated, with a wave of violent protests and strikes erupting in 2004, the more recent problems were due largely to President Aristide's mismanagement and corruption, not the fact that the military leaders escaped punishment ten years earlier.[24]

South Africa stands as another success story, indicating the potential value of trading justice for peace. From 1960 to 1994, thousands of black South Africans were persecuted and mistreated under that country's apartheid system. With the prospect of a bloody civil war looming over negotiations, "the outgoing leaders made some form of amnesty for those responsible for the regime a condition for the peaceful transfer to a fully democratic society".[25] The leaders of the majority black population

decided that the commitment to afford amnesty was a fair price for a relatively peaceful transition to full democracy.[26] In accordance with the negotiated settlement between the major parties, on 19 July 1995, the South
African Parliament created a Truth and Reconciliation Commission, con-
sisting of a Committee on Human Rights Violations, a Committee on
Amnesty and a Committee on Reparation and Rehabilitation.[27] Under
this process, amnesty would be available only to individuals who personally applied for it and who disclosed fully the facts of their apartheid
crimes. After conducting 140 public hearings and considering 20,000 written and oral submissions, the South African Truth Commission published
a 2,739-page report of its findings on 29 October 1998.[28] Most observers
believe the amnesty in South Africa headed off increasing tensions and a
potential civil war.

It is a common misconception that trading amnesty or exile for peace is
equivalent to the absence of accountability and redress.[29] As in the Haitian and South African situations described above, amnesties can be tied
to accountability mechanisms that are less invasive than domestic or international prosecution. Ever more frequently in the aftermath of an
amnesty- or exile-for-peace deal, the concerned governments have made
monetary reparations to the victims and their families, established truth
commissions to document the abuses (and sometimes identify perpetrators by name) and instituted employment bans and purges (referred to as
"lustration") that keep such perpetrators from positions of public trust.[30]
While not the same as criminal prosecution, these mechanisms do encompass much of what justice is intended to accomplish: prevention, deterrence, punishment and rehabilitation. Indeed, some experts believe that
these mechanisms do not just constitute "a second best approach" when
prosecution is impracticable, but that in many situations they may be better suited to achieving the aims of justice.[31]

Factors favouring prosecution

Although providing amnesty and exile to perpetrators may be an effective way to induce regime change without having to resort to force, there
are several important countervailing considerations favouring prosecution that suggest amnesty/exile should be a bargaining tool of last resort
reserved only for extreme situations. In particular, prosecuting leaders
responsible for violations of international humanitarian law is necessary
to discourage future human rights abuses, deter vigilante justice and reinforce respect for law and the new democratic government.

While prosecutions might initially provoke resistance, many analysts
believe that national reconciliation cannot take place as long as justice is

foreclosed. As Professor Cherif Bassiouni, then Chairman of the UN Investigative Commission for Yugoslavia, stated in 1996, "if peace is not intended to be a brief interlude between conflicts", then it must be accompanied by justice.[32]

Failure to prosecute leaders responsible for human rights abuses breeds contempt for the law and encourages future violations. The UN Commission on Human Rights and its Sub-Commission on Prevention of Discrimination and Protection of Minorities have concluded that impunity is one of the main reasons for the continuation of grave violations of human rights throughout the world.[33] Fact-finding reports on Chile and El Salvador indicate that the granting of amnesty or de facto impunity has led to an increase in abuses in those countries.[34]

Further, history teaches that former leaders given amnesty or exile are prone to recidivism, resorting to corruption and violence and becoming a disruptive influence on the peace process. From his seaside villa in Calabar, Nigeria, for example, Charles Taylor orchestrated a failed assassination plot in 2005 against President Lansana Conte of Guinea, a neighbouring country that had backed the rebel movement that forced Taylor from power.[35]

What a new or reinstated democracy needs most is legitimacy, which requires a fair, credible and transparent account of what took place and who was responsible. Criminal trials (especially those involving proof of widespread and systematic abuses) can generate a comprehensive record of the nature and extent of violations, how they were planned and executed, the fate of individual victims, who gave the orders and who carried them out. While there are various means to develop the historic record of such abuses, the most authoritative rendering of the truth is possible only through the crucible of a trial that accords full due process. US Supreme Court Justice Robert Jackson, the Chief Prosecutor at Nuremberg, underscored the logic of this proposition when he reported that the most important legacy of the Nuremberg trials was the documentation of Nazi atrocities "with such authenticity and in such detail that there can be no responsible denial of these crimes in the future".[36] According to Jackson, the establishment of an authoritative record of abuses that would endure the test of time and withstand the challenge of revisionism required proof of "incredible events by credible evidence".[37]

In addition to truth, there is a responsibility to provide justice. While a state may appropriately forgive crimes against itself, such as treason or sedition, serious crimes against persons, such as rape and murder, are an altogether different matter. Holding the violators accountable for their acts is a moral duty owed to the victims and their families. Prosecuting and punishing the violators would give significance to the victims' suffering and serve as a partial remedy for their injuries. Moreover, prosecutions help restore victims' dignity and prevent private acts of revenge by those who, in the absence of justice, would take it into their own hands.[38]

While prosecution and punishment can reinforce the value of law by displacing personal revenge, failure to punish former leaders responsible for widespread human rights abuses encourages cynicism about the rule of law and distrust toward the political system. To the victims of human rights crimes, amnesty or exile represents the ultimate in hypocrisy: While they struggle to put their suffering behind them, those responsible are allowed to enjoy a comfortable retirement. When those with power are seen to be above the law, the ordinary citizen will never come to believe in the principle of the rule of law as a fundamental necessity in a society transitioning to democracy.

Finally, where the United Nations or major countries give their imprimatur to an amnesty or exile deal, there is a risk that leaders in other parts of the world will be encouraged to engage in gross abuses. For example, history records that the international amnesty given to the Turkish officials responsible for the massacre of over 1 million Armenians during World War I encouraged Adolf Hitler some 20 years later to conclude that Germany could pursue his genocidal policies with impunity. In a 1939 speech to his reluctant General Staff, Hitler remarked, "Who after all is today speaking about the destruction of the Armenians?"[39] Richard Goldstone, the former Prosecutor of the International Criminal Tribunal for the former Yugoslavia, has concluded that "the failure of the international community to prosecute Pol Pot, Idi Amin, Saddam Hussein and Mohammed Aidid, among others, encouraged the Serbs to launch their policy of ethnic cleansing in the former Yugoslavia with the expectation that they would not be held accountable for their international crimes".[40] When the international community encourages or endorses an amnesty or exile deal, it sends a signal to other rogue regimes that they have nothing to lose by instituting repressive measures; if things start going badly, they can always bargain away their responsibility for crimes by agreeing to peace.

The limited international legal obligation to prosecute

In a few narrowly defined situations (described below) there is an international legal obligation to prosecute regardless of the underlying practical considerations. Where this is the case, failure to prosecute can amount to an international breach. An amnesty or asylum given to the members of the former regime could be invalidated in a proceeding before either the state's domestic courts[41] or an international forum.[42] International support for such an amnesty or asylum deal would undermine international respect for and adherence to the treaties that require prosecution. Finally, it would be inappropriate for an international criminal court to defer to a national amnesty or asylum in a situation where the amnesty or asylum violates obligations contained in the very international conventions that make up the court's subject matter jurisdiction.

Crimes defined in international conventions

The prerogative of states to issue an amnesty or grant asylum for an offence can be circumscribed by treaties to which the states are party. There are several international conventions that clearly provide for a duty to prosecute the humanitarian or human rights crimes defined therein, including in particular the grave breaches provisions of the 1949 Geneva Conventions,[43] the Genocide Convention[44] and the Torture Convention.[45] When these Conventions are applicable, the granting of amnesty or asylum to persons responsible for committing the crimes defined therein would constitute a breach of a treaty obligation for which there can be no excuse or exception. It is noteworthy, however, that these Conventions were negotiated in the context of the Cold War and by design apply only to a narrow range of situations, as such limitations were necessary to ensure widespread adoption.

The 1949 Geneva Conventions

The four Geneva Conventions were negotiated in 1949 to codify, inter alia, the international rules relating to the treatment of prisoners of war and civilians during armed conflict and in occupied territory after a war. Almost every country of the world is party to these conventions. Each of the Geneva Conventions contains a specific enumeration of "grave breaches", which are war crimes under international law for which there is individual criminal liability and for which states have a corresponding duty to prosecute or extradite. Grave breaches include wilful killing, torture or inhuman treatment, wilfully causing great suffering or serious injury to body or health, extensive destruction of property not justified by military necessity, wilfully depriving a civilian of the rights of fair and regular trial and unlawful confinement of a civilian.[46]

Parties to the Geneva Conventions have an obligation to search for, prosecute and punish perpetrators of grave breaches of the Geneva Conventions, or to hand over such persons for trial by another state party. The Commentary to the Geneva Conventions, which is the official history of the negotiations leading to the adoption of these treaties, confirms that the obligation to prosecute grave breaches is "absolute", meaning, inter alia, that state parties can under no circumstances grant perpetrators immunity or amnesty from prosecution for grave breaches of the Conventions.[47]

It is important to recognize that while states or international tribunals may prosecute persons who commit war crimes in internal armed conflicts, the duty to prosecute grave breaches under the Geneva Conventions is limited to the context of international armed conflict. Furthermore, there is a high threshold of violence necessary to constitute a genuine armed conflict, as distinct from lower level disturbances such as riots, isolated and sporadic acts of fighting or unilateral abuses committed by a government in the absence of widespread armed resistance by the target population.[48] Moreover, to be an international armed conflict, the situation must constitute an armed conflict involving two or more states, or a partial or total occupation of the territory of one state by another.[49]

In contrast to the duty to prosecute grave breaches occurring in an international armed conflict, with respect to internal armed conflict amnesties are not only permitted, but are encouraged by Article 6(5) of Additional Protocol II[50] – a point the South African Constitutional Court stressed in finding that the amnesties granted by the Truth and Reconciliation Commission did not violate international law.[51] The rationale for this provision is to encourage reconciliation, which is of greater importance in non-international armed conflicts where patrolable international borders do not exist between former enemies. Thus, the Commentary on the Protocol, prepared by the International Committee of the Red Cross, states: "The object of this sub-paragraph is to encourage gestures of reconciliation which can contribute to reestablishing normal relations in the life of a nation which has been divided."[52]

The Geneva Conventions, then, would require prosecution of Saddam Hussein for acts committed during the international armed conflicts involving Iran, Kuwait and the 1991 Persian Gulf War. They would not, however, require prosecution of Charles Taylor, who is accused only of complicity in war crimes during the internal armed conflict in Sierra Leone.

The Genocide Convention

Most of the countries of the world are party to the Genocide Convention, which entered into force on 12 January 1952, and the International Court of Justice has determined that the substantive provisions of the Convention constitute customary international law binding on all states.[53] Like the Geneva Conventions, the Genocide Convention provides an absolute obligation to prosecute persons responsible for genocide as defined in the Convention.[54]

The Genocide Convention defines genocide as committing atrocities "with intent to destroy, in whole or in part, a national, ethnical, racial or religious group, as such".[55]

There are several important limitations inherent in this definition. First, to constitute genocide, there must be proof that abuses were committed with the specific intent required by the Genocide Convention. It is not enough that abuses were intended to repress opposition; the intent must be literally to destroy a group of people. Second, and even more importantly, the victims of such abuses must constitute a group of one of the four specific types enumerated in the Genocide Convention, namely, national, ethnic, racial or religious. In this respect, it is noteworthy that the drafters of the Genocide Convention deliberately excluded acts directed against "political groups" from the Convention's definition of genocide.[56]

The Genocide Convention would require prosecution of Saddam Hussein, who has been accused of ordering attacks aimed at destroying the Northern Iraqi Kurds and the Southern Iraqi Marsh Arabs as a people, resulting in hundreds of thousands of casualties. Charles Taylor, in contrast, has not been accused of acts of genocide.

The Torture Convention

The Torture Convention entered into force on 26 June 1987, and currently has 138 parties.[57] The Convention defines "torture" as

> any act by which severe pain or suffering, whether physical or mental, is intentionally inflicted on a person for such purposes as obtaining from him or a third person information or a confession, punishing him for an act he or a third person has committed or is suspected of having committed, or intimidating or coercing him or a third person, or for any reason based on discrimination of any kind, when such pain or suffering is inflicted by or at the instigation of or with the consent or acquiescence of a public official or other person acting in an official capacity. It does not include pain or suffering arising only from, inherent in or incidental to lawful sanctions.[58]

The Torture Convention requires each state party to ensure that all acts of torture are offences under its internal law[59] and to establish its jurisdiction over such offences in cases where the accused is found in its territory,[60] and if such a state does not extradite the alleged offender, the Convention requires it to submit the case to its competent authorities for the purpose of prosecution.[61] Persons convicted of torture are to be subjected to harsh sentences proportionate to the grave nature of the offence.[62]

The Special Court for Sierra Leone charged Charles Taylor with committing crimes against humanity in Sierra Leone, including complicity in widespread and systematic acts of torture, from 1991 to 1999.[63] Notably, however, none of Sierra Leone (the state where the acts of torture occurred), Liberia (the state of nationality of the accused) and Nigeria (the state where Charles Taylor was given asylum) were parties to the Torture Convention when the acts of torture in Sierra Leone were committed.[64] And although the United States, which helped broker the exile-for-peace deal, was a party to the Torture Convention during that time, the requirements of the convention are not applicable to the United States in this case because the acts of torture did not occur in US territory, the offender was not a national of the United States and the offender was not present in US territory.[65] Under the Vienna Convention on the Law of Treaties, the provisions of a treaty "do not bind a party in relation to any act or fact which took place ... before the date of the entry into force of the treaty with respect to that party".[66] Consistent with the Vienna Convention as well as the reasoning of the British High Court in the *Pinochet* case, the obligations to prosecute and to refrain from taking actions that would frustrate prosecution contained in the Torture Convention were not applicable to the case of Charles Taylor because his alleged involvement in acts of torture pre-dated the ratification of the Convention by the relevant states.[67]

Still, some might argue that the Torture Convention is relevant to the situation involving Charles Taylor based on the Committee against Torture's 1990 decision concerning the Argentinean amnesty laws. In that case, the Committee against Torture, which is the treaty body created by the Torture Convention to facilitate its implementation, decided that communications submitted by Argentinean citizens on behalf of their relatives who had been tortured by Argentinean military authorities were inadmissible because Argentina had ratified the Convention only after the amnesty laws had been enacted.[68] However, in dictum, the Committee stated, "Even before the entry into force of the Convention against Torture, there existed a general rule of international law which should oblige all states to take effective measures to prevent torture and to punish acts of torture".[69]

The Committee's statement should not be mistakenly construed as suggesting that amnesties/asylum for persons who commit torture is invalid under customary international law. By using the word "should", the Committee indicated that its statement was aspirational rather than a declaration of binding law. On the basis of its decision, the Committee *urged* Argentina to provide remedies for the victims of torture and their surviving relatives; it did not suggest that international law *required* that Argentina do so.[70] Nor did it specify that the remedy should be prosecution of those responsible, rather than some other appropriate remedy such as compensation. The Committee's decision, therefore, should not be read as indicating that the Torture Convention required Nigeria, Liberia or Sierra Leone to prosecute those whose acts of torture pre-dated their ratification of the Convention.

General human rights conventions

General human rights conventions include the International Covenant on Civil and Political Rights[71] and the similarly worded European Convention for the Protection of Human Rights and Fundamental Freedoms[72] and American Convention on Human Rights.[73] Although these treaties do not expressly require states to prosecute violators, they do obligate states to "ensure" the rights enumerated therein. There is growing recognition in the jurisprudence of the treaty bodies responsible for monitoring enforcement of these conventions and the writings of respected commentators that the duty to ensure rights implies a duty to hold specific violators accountable.[74]

Yet, a careful examination of the jurisprudence of these bodies suggests that methods of obtaining specific accountability other than criminal prosecutions would meet the requirement of "ensuring rights".[75] This jurisprudence indicates that a state must fulfil five obligations in confronting gross violations of human rights committed by a previous regime: (1) investigate the identity, fate and whereabouts of victims; (2) investigate the identity of major perpetrators; (3) provide reparation or compensation to victims; (4) take affirmative steps to ensure that human rights abuse does not recur; and (5) punish those guilty of human rights abuse. Punishment can take many non-criminal forms, including imposition of fines, removal from office, reduction of rank, forfeiture of government or military pensions, and exile.

Crimes against humanity

Definition

As developed in the jurisprudence of the Nuremberg Tribunal and codified in the Statutes of the International Criminal Tribunal for the former Yugoslavia,[76] the International Criminal Tribunal for Rwanda,[77] the Special Court for Sierra Leone[78] and the Rome Statute for the International Criminal Court,[79] crimes against humanity are defined as inhumane acts committed during a widespread or systematic attack against a civilian population.[80]

States are required to prosecute grave breaches of the Geneva Conventions and the crime of genocide, but there exists no treaty requiring prosecution of crimes against humanity (except for torture where the state is party to the Torture Convention at the time the crime is committed); crimes against humanity are purely a creature of customary international law.[81] Traditionally, those who committed crimes against humanity were treated like pirates, as *hostis humani generis* (an enemy of all humankind), and any state, including their own, could punish them through its domestic courts.[82] In the absence of a treaty containing the *aut dedere aut judicare* (extradite or prosecute) principle, this so-called "universal jurisdiction" is generally thought to be permissive, not mandatory. Yet several commentators and human rights groups have recently taken the position that customary international law (and the notion of *jus cogens* – meaning peremptory norms) not only establishes permissive jurisdiction over perpetrators of crimes against humanity, but also requires their prosecution and conversely prohibits the granting of amnesty or asylum to such persons.[83]

Customary international law

Notwithstanding the chimerical conclusions of some scholars, there is scant evidence that a rule prohibiting amnesty or asylum in cases of crimes against humanity has ripened into a compulsory norm of customary international law. Customary international law, which is just as binding upon states as treaty law, arises from "a general and consistent practice of states followed by them from a sense of legal obligation" referred to as *opinio juris*.[84] Under traditional notions of customary international law, "deeds were what counted, not just words".[85] Yet those who argue that customary international law precludes amnesty/exile for crimes against humanity base their position on non-binding General Assembly resolutions,[86] hortative declarations of international conferences[87] and international conventions that are not widely ratified,[88] rather than on any extensive state practice consistent with such a rule.

Commentators often cite the 1967 UN Declaration on Territorial Asylum[89] as the earliest international recognition of a legal obligation to prosecute perpetrators of crimes against humanity. The Declaration provides that "the right to seek and enjoy asylum may not be invoked by any person with respect to whom there are serious reasons for considering that he has committed a ... crime against humanity".[90] Yet according to the historic record of this resolution, "the majority of members stressed that the draft declaration under consideration was not intended to propound legal norms or to change existing rules of international law, but to lay down broad humanitarian and moral principles upon which States might rely in seeking to unify their practices relating to asylum".[91] This provides evidence that, from the outset, the General Assembly resolutions concerning the prosecution of crimes against humanity were aspirational only, and not intended to create any binding duties.

In addition to this contrary legislative history, the trouble with an approach to proving the existence of customary international law that focuses so heavily on words is "that it is grown like a flower in a hot-house and that it is anything but sure that such creatures will survive in the much rougher climate of actual state practice".[92] Indeed, to the extent any state practice in this area is widespread, it is the practice of granting amnesties or asylum to those who commit crimes against humanity.[93] That the United Nations itself has felt free of legal constraints in endorsing recent amnesty and exile-for-peace deals in situations involving crimes against humanity suggests that customary international law has not yet crystallized in this area. The Special Court for Sierra Leone confirmed this when it recently held that domestic amnesties for crimes against humanity and war crimes committed in an internal armed conflict were not unlawful under international law.[94]

Commentators may point to the Secretary General's August 2004 Report to the Security Council on the Rule of Law and Transitional Justice as an indication that the United Nations has recently altered its position on the acceptability of amnesty/exile-for-peace deals. In that report, the Secretary-General of the United Nations said that peace agreements and Security Council resolutions and mandates should "reject any endorsement of amnesty for genocide, war crimes, or crimes against humanity, including those relating to ethnic, gender and sexually based international crimes, [and] ensure that no such amnesty previously granted is a bar to prosecution before any United Nations–created or –assisted court".[95] It is more significant, however, that in the Security Council's debate on the Secretary-General's Report, there was no consensus on this particularly controversial recommendation (only two of the fifteen members of the Council – Brazil and Costa Rica – spoke in favour of it while several opposed it), and the statement approved by the Council at the end of the debate made no reference to the issue of amnesty.[96]

Jus cogens

The concept of *jus cogens* – meaning "peremptory norms" – is said to be among the "most ambiguous and theoretically problematic of the doctrines of international law".[97] Since the inception of the modern state system three and a half centuries ago,[98] international law has been based on notions of consent. Under this concept of *jus dispositivium* (positive law), states were bound only to treaties to which they had acceded and to those rules of customary international law to which they had acquiesced. The concept of *jus cogens*, in contrast, is based in part on natural law principles that "prevail over and invalidate international agreements and other rules of international law in conflict with them".[99]

Though the term itself was not employed, the *jus cogens* concept was first applied by the US Military Tribunal at Nuremberg, which declared that the treaty between Germany and Vichy France approving the use of French prisoners of war in the German armaments industry was void under international law as *contra bonus mores* (contrary to fundamental morals).[100] The debates within the UN International Law Commission, which codified the *jus cogens* concept in the 1969 Vienna Convention on the Law of Treaties,[101] reflect the view that the phenomenon of Nazi Germany rendered the purely contractual conception of international law insufficient for the modern era.[102] Consequently, the International Law Commission opined that a treaty designed to promote slavery or genocide, or to prepare for aggression, ought to be declared void.[103]

Thus, pursuant to the *jus cogens* concept, states are prohibited from committing crimes against humanity and an international agreement between states to facilitate commission of such crimes would be void *ab initio*. Moreover, there is growing recognition that universal jurisdiction exists such that all states have a right to prosecute or entertain civil suits against the perpetrators of *jus cogens* crimes.[104] From this, some commentators take what they view as the next logical step and argue that the concept also prohibits states from undertaking any action that would frustrate prosecution, such as granting amnesty or asylum to those who have committed crimes against humanity.[105]

Such scholars fail, however, to take into consideration the fact that although *jus cogens* has natural law underpinnings, the concept is also related to customary law. A rule will qualify as *jus cogens* only if it is "accepted by the international community of States as a whole as a norm from which no derogation is permitted".[106] Thus, *jus cogens* norms have been described by one court as "a select and narrow subset of the norms recognized as customary international law".[107] As with ordinary customary international law, *jus cogens* norms are formed through widespread state practice and recognition,[108] but unlike ordinary customary international law, a state cannot avoid application of a *jus cogens* norm by being a persistent objector during its formation.

Though there is no question that the international community has accepted that the prohibition against committing crimes against humanity qualifies as a *jus cogens* norm,[109] this does not mean that the associated duty to prosecute has simultaneously attained an equivalent status. In fact, all evidence is to the contrary. Not only have there been numerous instances of states providing amnesty and asylum to leaders accused of crimes against humanity, but, even more telling, there have been no protests from states when such amnesty or asylum has been offered. Moreover, there has been widespread judicial recognition that the *jus cogens* nature of crimes against humanity does not prevent accused perpetrators from successfully asserting head of state immunity or sovereign immunity to avoid criminal or civil liability in foreign courts.[110] Because *jus cogens*, as a peremptory norm, would by definition supersede the customary international law doctrine of head of state immunity where the two come into conflict, the only way to reconcile these rulings is to conclude that the duty to prosecute has not attained *jus cogens* status.

Conclusion

This essay has described how, under the present state of international law, the international procedural law imposing a duty to prosecute is far more limited than the substantive law establishing international offences.[111] The reason for this is historical: With respect to all but the most notorious of international crimes, it was easier for states to agree to recognize permissive jurisdiction than to undertake a duty to prosecute. And where states did recognize a duty to prosecute, it was only through the carefully negotiated provisions of a treaty – such as the Geneva Conventions, Genocide Convention or Torture Convention – that would narrowly define the applicable circumstances and perhaps – like the Rome Statute establishing the International Criminal Court – provide escape clauses permitting states to disregard the obligation to prosecute when strict enforcement would frustrate greater interests of international peace and justice.[112]

But where the duty to prosecute does apply, it is critical that states and international organizations honour it, lest they express contempt for the important treaties from which the duty arises, potentially putting their own citizens at risk pursuant to the international law principle of reciprocity.

This is not to suggest, however, that states must rush to prosecute all persons involved in offences under these treaties. Selective prosecution and use of "exemplary trials" is acceptable as long as the criteria used reflect appropriate distinctions based upon degrees of culpability and sufficiency of evidence.[113] Moreover, while the provisions of the treaties requiring prosecution are non-derogable even in time of public emergency that threatens the life of the nation, the doctrine of *force majeure* can warrant temporary postponement of prosecutions for a reasonable amount of time until a new government is secure enough to take such action against members of the former regime or until a new government has the judicial resources to undertake fair and effective prosecutions.[114]

In the case of Saddam Hussein, the United States had accused the Iraqi leader of grave breaches of the Geneva Conventions and violations of the Genocide Convention. Both the United States and Iraq were parties to these treaties, which contain an absolute obligation to prosecute offenders. By offering to permit exile and perpetual sanctuary in Bahrain in lieu of invasion and prosecution, the Bush administration signalled that the provisions of these treaties are inconsequential, thereby undermining the rule of law in a critical area of global affairs. This must be viewed also in light of other US actions involving application of the Geneva Conventions to the conflict in Iraq, most notably the infamous White House memos authored by now–Attorney General Alberto Gonzales. The memos refer to the Geneva Conventions as "obsolete" and "quaint",[115] and wrongly opine that the Torture Convention permits mild forms of torture,[116] thereby creating a climate of disdain toward international humanitarian law and opening the door to the abuses committed at Abu Ghraib prison in Iraq. In a statement before the Senate Judiciary Committee, Admiral John Hutson, Judge Advocate General of the US Navy from 1997 to 2000, urged the Bush administration to officially and unequivocally repudiate Gonzales's erroneous position. In doing so, Hutson stressed that:

Since World War II and looking into the foreseeable future, United States armed forces are more forward-deployed both in terms of numbers of deployments and numbers of troops than all other nations combined. What this means in practical terms is that adherence to the Geneva Conventions is more important to us than to any other nation. We should be the nation demanding adherence under any and all circumstances because we will benefit the most.[117]

Because Hussein did not accept the 2003 exile-for-peace offer, the damage to the rule of law in this instance was negligible. Would greater damage to the rule of law have nevertheless been acceptable if it succeeded in averting a war that has resulted in tens of thousands of casualties on both sides since 2003? This essay has described the policy reasons generally favouring prosecution, including the fact that former leaders who have resorted to war crimes and crimes against humanity tend to be recidivists. Saddam Hussein himself launched a coup and initiated his policy of terror after he was released from prison through a domestic amnesty in 1968. It is not hard to imagine the dangers Hussein could present to the Iraqi democratic transition from exile in nearby Bahrain. Moreover, the people of Iraq have insisted on Hussein's trial before the Iraqi Special Tribunal.[118] Morally, what right would American negotiators have to trade away the ability of thousands of Hussein's victims to see the dictator brought to justice? Finally, it is worth stressing that the duty to prosecute Hussein arising from these treaties did not require or even justify the invasion of Iraq. Rather, it merely prohibited actions that are manifestly incompatible with the prosecution of Hussein, such as arranging for exile and sanctuary in Bahrain.

The situation involving Charles Taylor is distinguishable. Taylor has been charged by the Special Court for Sierra Leone with complicity in crimes against humanity and war crimes in an internal armed conflict. As the Special Court itself has recognized, since there is no treaty-based or customary international law duty to prosecute crimes against humanity or war crimes in an internal conflict, an amnesty or exile-for-peace deal would not constitute a violation of international law.[119]

The distinction reflects the fact that, notwithstanding the natural law rhetoric of *jus cogens* employed by proponents of a broad duty to prosecute, the international legal order is still governed by principles of positive law under the 357-year-old Westphalian concept of sovereignty.[120] State practice belies the existence of a customary international law duty (based on the positive law notion of state acquiescence to rules over time) to prosecute outside of the treaty framework. Consequently, the obligation to prosecute and the corresponding duty to refrain from frustrating prosecution through amnesty or exile applies only to certain treaty-based crimes where the treaty sets forth such an obligation and the affected states are party to the treaty at the time of the acts in question. This conclusion is analogous to that of the House of Lords in the *Pinochet* case, in which the British High Court held that the head of state immunity doctrine prevented the United Kingdom from extraditing to Spain former Chilean President Augusto Pinochet for crimes against humanity, with the exception of crimes of torture committed after the United Kingdom, Chile and Spain had all ratified the Torture Convention.[121] Thus, while there was a treaty-based duty to prosecute Saddam Hussein under the Geneva Conventions and Genocide Convention, no such duty existed in the case of Charles Taylor, who was accused of crimes against humanity.

This did not mean, however, that the Special Court for Sierra Leone was bound to honour the Charles Taylor exile-for-peace deal. The Special Court made clear that amnesty and exile arrangements are only binding within the state(s) granting them. They do not apply to other states or to international tribunals such as the Special Court. Moreover, it is important to recognize that amnesty, exile and sanctuary arrangements are often temporary in nature. They are not a permanent right of the recipient, but a privilege bestowed by the territorial state, which can be revoked by a subsequent government or administration. The trend in recent years is to use amnesty and exile as a transitional step toward eventual justice, not as an enduring bar to justice.[122] As a US Department of State official explained in 2003 with respect to Charles Taylor, "First we'll get him out of Liberia, then we'll get him to the Court."[123] Three years later, on 29 March 2006, Nigeria revoked Taylor's asylum and surrendered him to the Special Court for Sierra Leone for trial.[124]

Notes

1. See Michael P. Scharf and Gregory S. McNeal (2006) *Saddam on Trial: Understanding and Debating the Iraqi High Tribunal*, North Carolina: Carolina Academic Press, p. 162.
2. Julian Borger (2003) "Diplomacy Dies, Now It's War: Bush Gives Saddam and His Sons 48 Hours to Leave Iraq or Face Massive Military Onslaught", *Guardian* (London), 18 March (describing President Bush's exile offer).
3. Emily Wax (2003) "Arab Leaders Fail in Last Minute Efforts: Mubarak Blames Iraq, Cautions Coalition: Bahrain Signals that It Would Give Hussein Sanctuary", *Washington Post*, 20 March.
4. Richard W. Stevenson (2003) "Threats and Responses: The President; Bush Gives Hussein 48 Hours, and Vows to Act", *New York Times*, 18 March.
5. Immanuel Kant (1991, 1785) *The Metaphysics of Morals*, Mary Gregor, trans., Cambridge: Cambridge University Press, p. 141.
6. Ryan Lizza (2005) "Charles at Large", *New Republic*, 25 April, p. 10.
7. Ibid.
8. M. Cherif Bassiouni (1992) *Crimes against Humanity in International Criminal Law*, Dordrecht, the Netherlands: Martinus Nijhoff Publishers, pp. 492, 500–501 (arguing that there is an international duty to prosecute or extradite those who commit crimes against humanity); Leila Nadya Sadat (2003) "Universal Jurisdiction, National Amnesties, and Truth Commissions: Reconciling the Irreconcilable", in Stephen Macedo, ed., *Universal Jurisdiction: National Courts and the Prosecution of Serious Crimes under International Law*, Pennsylvania: University of Pennsylvania Press, pp. 194–201 (arguing that amnesties create a "culture of impunity" incompatible with international justice); M. Cherif Bassiouni (1996) "International Crimes: Jus Cogens and Obligatio Erga Omnes", *Law and Contemporary Problems* 59: 63 (arguing that states have an obligation to prosecute *jus cogens* crimes); Carla Edelenbos (1994) "Human Rights Violations: A Duty to Prosecute?" *Leiden Journal of International Law* 7: 5–14 (noting the United Nation's affirmation of duty to prosecute war crimes); Diane F. Orentlicher (1991) "Settling Account: The Duty to Prosecute Human Rights Violations of a Prior Regime", *Yale Law Journal* 100: 2537–2593 (explaining that analysts interpret law generated by the Nuremberg trials, and UN actions ratifying that law, to "require punishment of crimes against humanity"); Naomi Roht-Arriaza (1990) "State Responsibility to Investigate and Prosecute Grave Human Rights Violations in International Law", *California Law Review* 78: 451–461 (urging the necessity of an international duty to investigate grave human rights violations).
9. As an anonymous government official stated in an oft-quoted article: "The quest for justice for yesterday's victims of atrocities should not be pursued in such a manner that it makes today's living the dead of tomorrow." Anonymous (1996) "Human Rights in Peace Negotiations", *Human Rights Quarterly* 18: 249–258.
10. Steven Ratner (1999) "New Democracies, Old Atrocities: An Inquiry in International Law", *Georgetown Law Journal* 87: 707–723 (mentioning the governments in transitional democracies that have passed amnesty laws); Roht-Arriaza, "State Responsibility to Investigate", p. 461 (noting grants of amnesty in Argentina, Chile, Uruguay, Guatemala and El Salvador); Michael P. Scharf (1996) "The Letter of the Law: The Scope of the International Legal Obligation to Prosecute Human Rights Crimes", *Law and Contemporary Problems* 59: 41 (discussing these countries' amnesty programs).
11. Scharf, "The Letter of the Law", p. 41.
12. In cases of exile, the state where the offence occurred (the territorial state) cannot commence proceedings because it does not have physical custody over the accused,

and the sanctuary state may be prevented from prosecuting or extraditing by the doctrine of head of state immunity. See, for example, *Regina v. Bow St. Metro. Stipendiary Magistrate, ex parte Pinochet Ugarte* (No. 3), [2000] 1 AC 147, 242 (HL 1999) (UK) (noting that the doctrine "protects all acts which the head of state has performed in the exercise of the functions of government").

13. Michael P. Scharf (1997) *Balkan Justice: The Story Behind the First International War Crimes Trial Since Nuremberg*, North Carolina: Carolina Academic Press, p. 5.
14. Dave Gilson (2003) "The Exile Files, 2003", available from http://www.globalpolicy.org/intljustice/general/2003/0826exile.htm (discussing the exile arrangements of more than a dozen individuals).
15. Payam Akhavan (1996) "The Yugoslav Tribunal at a Crossroads: The Dayton Peace Agreement and Beyond", *Human Rights Quarterly* 8: 259–271.
16. Michael P. Scharf (1996) "Swapping Amnesty for Peace: Was There a Duty to Prosecute International Crimes in Haiti?" *Texas International Law Journal* 31: 1–5 (describing human rights violations documented by the US Department of State and various human rights groups).
17. The Secretary-General (1993) *The Situation of Democracy and Human Rights in Haiti*, UN Doc. S/26063, A/47/975, 12 July (reproducing the text of the Governors Island Agreement). The Governors Island Agreement was supplemented by a document known as the New York Pact, which was signed by the two sides on 16 July 1993. Paragraph 4 of the New York Pact provides that "the political forces and parliamentary blocs undertake to ensure that the following laws are passed, on the bases of an emergency procedure: ... (ii) Act concerning the amnesty". The Secretary-General (1993) *The Situation of Democracy and Human Rights in Haiti* annex, para. 4, UN Doc. S/26297, A/47/1000, 13 August.
18. Irwin P. Stotzky (1995) "Haiti: Searching for Alternatives", in Naomi Roht-Arriaza, ed., *Impunity and Human Rights in International Law and Practice*, Oxford: Oxford University Press, p. 188.
19. Letter from the President of the Security Council to the Secretary-General, UN SCOR, 48th Sess. at 120, UN Doc. S/INF/49 (15 July 1993).
20. Statement of the President of the Security Council, UN SCOR, 48th Sess., 3298th mtg. at 126, UN Doc. S/INF/49 (25 October 1993).
21. SC Res. 940, para. 4, UN Doc. S/RES/940 (31 July 1994).
22. "Haitian Lawmakers Pass Partial Amnesty to Pressure Cedras", *Commercial Appeal* (Memphis, Tenn.), 8 October 1994.
23. Maggie O'Kane (1995) "After the Yanks Have Gone", *Guardian* (London), 18 February (describing Aristide's generally peaceful return to power).
24. International Crisis Group (2004) "A New Chance for Haiti?" International Crisis Group Report No. 10, pp. 7–11.
25. Martha Minow (1998) *Between Vengeance and Forgiveness*, Boston: Beacon Press, p. 52.
26. Ibid., p. 55.
27. National Unity and Reconciliation Act 34 of 1995 §§ 2, 12, 16, and 23.
28. The text of the South African Truth Commission's Report is available from http://www.info.gov.za/otherdocs/2003/trc.
29. William W. Burke-White (2001) "Reframing Impunity: Applying Liberal International Law Theory to an Analysis of Amnesty Legislation", *Harvard International Law Journal* 42: 467–482.
30. Naomi Roht-Arriaza (1995) *Impunity and Human Rights in International Law and Practice*, Oxford: Oxford University Press, pp. 282–291.

31. Minow, *Between Vengeance and Forgiveness*, p. 9 (contending that prosecutions "are slow, partial, and narrow").

32. M. Cherif Bassiouni (1996) "Searching for Peace and Achieving Justice: The Need for Accountability", *Law and Contemporary Problems* 59: 9–13.

33. UN Economic and Social Council, Commission on Human Rights, Working Group on Enforced or Involuntary Disappearances (1990) *Report on the Consequences of Impunity*, para. 344, U.N. Doc. E/CN.4/1990/13, reprinted in N. Kritz, ed. (1995) *Transitional Justice: How Emerging Democracies Reckon with Former Regimes*, Washington, D.C.: United States Institute of Peace Press, pp. 18–19.

34. UN Economic and Social Council (1983) "Protection of Human Rights in Chile", para. 341, UN Doc. A/38/385.

35. Lizza, "Charles at Large", p. 10 (citing an intelligence report prepared by investigators for the Special Court for Sierra Leone). In response, the UN Security Council adopted Resolution 1532, which required all states to freeze Charles Taylor's assets in order to prevent him from further engaging "in activities that undermine peace and stability in Liberia and the region", SC Res. 1532, preamble, UN Doc. S/RES/1532, 12 March 2004.

36. Robert H. Jackson (1946) "Report from Justice Robert H. Jackson, Chief of Counsel for the United States in the Prosecution of Axis War Criminals, to the President (Oct. 7, 1946)", *Temple Law Quarterly* 20: 338–343.

37. Robert H. Jackson (1945) "Report from Justice Robert H. Jackson, Chief of Counsel for the United States in the Prosecution of Axis War Criminals, to the President (June 7, 1945)", *American Journal of International Law* 39: 178–184, supp.

38. Haitian citizens, for example, have committed acts of violence against the former members of the brutal military regime who were given amnesty for their abuses. Gary Borg (1995) "Former Haitian General Is Gunned Down in Street", *Chicago Tribune*, 4 October.

39. Adolf Hitler (1939) Speech to Chief Commanders and Commanding Generals, 22 August, quoted in M. Cherif Bassiouni, *Crimes against Humanity in International Criminal Law*, p. 176, n. 96.

40. Interview with Richard Goldstone, Chief Prosecutor, International Criminal Tribunal for the Former Yugoslavia, in Brussels, Belgium (July 20, 1996) (on file with author).

41. When the South African amnesty scheme was challenged on the grounds that it violated the rights of families to seek judicial redress for the murders of their loved ones, the newly created Constitutional Court rejected the claim on the ground that neither the South African Constitution nor any applicable treaty prevented granting amnesty in exchange for truth. *Azanian Peoples Org. v. President of S. Afr.* (1996) (4) SA 671 (CC), para. 50 (S. Afr.), available from http://www.constitutionalcourt.org.za/Archimages/2529.PDF ("The epilogue to the Constitution authorised and contemplated an 'amnesty' in its most comprehensive and generous meaning"). A challenge to the Argentinean amnesty law fared better. In March 2001, an Argentinean judge declared the amnesty law unconstitutional and in violation of international law, a decision confirmed in August 2003 when Argentina's Parliament voted to annul the amnesty law. Debora Rey (2003) "Argentina Approves Ending Laws on Amnesty", *Washington Post*, 22 August. At the time of writing, a lawsuit was winding its way through the courts of Nigeria, seeking to strike down the asylum granted to Charles Taylor on the ground that it violated Nigeria's obligations under international and domestic law to prosecute and deny asylum to perpetrators of war crimes and crimes against humanity. James A. Goldston (2005) "Some Quiet Victories for Human Rights", *International Herald Tribune*, 22 December.

42. "Challenges to amnesty laws enacted in Argentina, El Salvador, Suriname, and Uruguay have been lodged with the Inter-American Commission on Human Rights of the Organization of American States." Diane F. Orentlicher (1991) "Settling Accounts: The Duty to Prosecute Human Rights Violations of a Prior Regime", *Yale Law Journal* 100: 2537–2540, n. 5.

43. Geneva Convention for the Amelioration of the Condition of the Wounded and Sick in Armed Forces in the Field, art. 49, 12 August 1949, 6 UST 3114, 75 UNTS 31 [hereinafter Geneva Convention I]; Geneva Convention for the Amelioration of the Condition of the Wounded, Sick and Shipwrecked Members of Armed Forces at Sea, art. 50, 12 August 1949, 6 UST 3217, 75 UNTS 85 [hereinafter Geneva Convention II]; Geneva Convention Relative to the Treatment of Prisoners of War, art. 129, 12 August 1949, 6 UST 3316, 75 UNTS 135 [hereinafter Geneva Convention III]; and Geneva Convention Relative to the Protection of Civilian Persons in Time of War, art. 146, 12 August 1949, 6 UST 3516, 75 UNTS 287 [hereinafter Geneva Convention IV].

44. Convention on the Prevention and Punishment of the Crime of Genocide, art. IV, 9 December 1948, 78 UNTS 277 [hereinafter Genocide Convention].

45. Convention against Torture and Other Cruel, Inhuman or Degrading Treatment or Punishment, art. 7, opened for signature 4 February 1985, S. Treaty Doc. No. 100-20 (1988), 1465 UNTS 113, reprinted in 23 ILM 1027 (1984), as modified, 24 ILM 535 (1984) (entered into 26 force June 1987) [hereinafter Torture Convention].

46. Geneva Convention I, art. 50; Geneva Convention II, art. 51; Geneva Convention III, art. 130; Geneva Convention IV, art. 147.

47. Virginia Morris and Michael P. Scharf (1995) *An Insider's Guide to the International Criminal Court for the former Yugoslavia*, New York: Transnational Publishers, pp. 114–115 and 341, n. 356 (quoting J. Pictet, ed. (1952) *Geneva Convention for the Amelioration of the Condition of the Wounded and Sick in Armed Forces in the Field: Commentary*, Geneva: International Committee of the Red Cross, p. 373, commentary to article 51); see also Theodor Meron (1989) *Human Rights and Humanitarian Norms as Customary Law*, Oxford: Clarendon Press, p. 210 (noting that the universality principle of jurisdiction, on which the grave breaches clauses of the Geneva Conventions are based, requires states to prosecute or extradite those charged with committing grave breaches).

48. Protocol Additional to the Geneva Conventions of 12 Aug. 1949, and Relating to the Protection of Victims of Non-International Armed Conflicts (Protocol II) art. 1(2), 8 June 1977, 1125 UNTS 609 [hereinafter Additional Protocol II] (stating that the Protocol "shall not apply to situations of internal disturbances and tensions, such as riots [and] isolated and sporadic acts of violence"). But see Michael P. Scharf (2004) "Defining Terrorism as the Peacetime Equivalent of War Crimes: Problems and Prospects", *Case Western Reserve Journal of International Law* 36: 359–367 (citing the Inter-American Commission on Human Rights' 1997 decision in *Juan Carlos Abella v. Argentina*, Case 11.137, Inter-Am. CHR, Report No. 55/97, OEA/Ser.L/V/II.98, doc. 6 rev., paras 155–156, and the United States response to the 11 September attacks as developments that have sought to lower the armed conflict threshold).

49. Geneva Conventions I, II, III and IV, art. 2.

50. Additional Protocol II, art. 6(5) ("At the end of hostilities, the authorities in power shall endeavor to grant the broadest possible amnesty to persons who have participated in the armed conflict, or those deprived of their liberty for reasons related to the armed conflict, whether they are interned or detained").

51. *Azanian Peoples Org. v. President of S. Afr.* (1996) (4) SA 671 (CC), para. 30 (S. Afr.).

52. Claude Pilloud, Jean de Preux, Bruno Zimmermann, Philippe Eberlin, Hans-Peter Gasser and Claude Wenger (1987) *Commentary on the Additional Protocols of 8 June*

1977 to the Geneva Conventions of 12 August 1949, Geneva: International Committee of the Red Cross, p. 1402.

53. Reservations to the Convention on the Prevention and Punishment of the Crime of Genocide, Advisory Opinion, 1951 ICJ 15, 23 (stating that the Convention's principles are binding on states, "even without any conventional obligation").

54. Article IV of the Genocide Convention states: "Persons committing genocide or any of the acts enumerated in article III shall be punished, whether they are constitutionally responsible rulers, public officials or private individuals." Genocide Convention, art. IV. Article V of the Genocide Convention requires states to "provide effective penalties" for persons guilty of genocide. Article VI of the Genocide Convention requires prosecution by the state in whose territory genocide occurs or in an international court established for this purpose. Article VI suggests that only the territorial state and state parties to an international criminal court have an obligation to prosecute the crime of genocide, other states would still be bound to extradite an individual accused of genocide if they are not able to prosecute. Therefore amnesty or exile/sanctuary for peace deals would be manifestly inconsistent with the obligations of the Genocide Convention.

55. Genocide Convention, art. II; Rome Statute for the International Criminal Court art. 6, 17 July 1998, 2187 UNTS 90 [hereinafter Rome Statute], available from http://www.un.org/law/icc/statute/english/rome_statute(e).pdf.

56. The exclusion of "political groups" was due in large part to the fact that the Convention was negotiated during the Cold War, during which the Soviet Union and other totalitarian governments feared that they would face interference in their internal affairs if genocide were defined to include acts committed to destroy political groups. According to Leo Kuper, "One may fairly say that the delegates, after all, represented governments in power, and that many of these governments wished to retain an unrestricted freedom to suppress political opposition." L. Kuper (1982) *Genocide*, New Haven, Conn.: Yale University Press, p. 30.

57. Office of the United Nations High Commissioner for Human Rights, Status of the Ratification of the Convention against Torture, available from http://www.ohchr.org/english/law/cat-ratify.htm (last visited 22 November 2005) [hereinafter Torture Convention Ratification Status].

58. Torture Convention, art. 1.

59. Ibid., art. 4. Article 4 also requires parties to criminalize acts that "constitute complicity or participation in torture".

60. Ibid., art. 5.

61. Ibid., art. 7.

62. According to the negotiating record of the Torture Convention, "In applying article 4 [which requires states to make torture "punishable by appropriate penalties which take into account their grave nature"], it seems reasonable to require ... that the punishment for torture should be close to the penalties applied to the most serious offenses under the domestic legal system". J. Burgers and H. Danelius (1988) *The United Nations Convention against Torture*, Dordrecht, the Netherlands: Martinus Nijhoff Publishers, p. 129.

63. *Prosecutor v. Charles Ghankay Taylor*, Case No. SCSL-2003-01-I, Indictment, paras 29–31, 7 March 2003), available from http://www.sc-sl.org/Documents/SCSC-03-01-I-001.pdf.

64. The acts of torture alleged in the Special Court for Sierra Leone's indictment of Charles Taylor occurred from 1991 to 1999. Sierra Leone ratified the Torture Convention on 25 April 2001; Nigeria ratified the Convention on 28 July 2001; Liberia ratified the Convention on 22 September 2004; and the United States ratified the Convention

on 21 October 1994. See Torture Convention Ratification Status (listing ratifying states).

65. Torture Convention, art. 5 (setting forth conditions under which a state must take action in response to Convention violations).

66. Vienna Convention on the Law of Treaties, art. 28, 23 May 1969, 112 Stat. 2681-822, 1155 UNTS 331 [hereinafter Vienna Convention]; cf. Rome Statute, art. 24 (recognizing that the International Criminal Court has no retroactive jurisdiction and that obligations under the Rome Statute do not apply to crimes committed prior to the ICC's entry into force in July 2002).

67. Regina v. Bow St. Metro. Stipendiary Magistrate, ex parte Pinochet Ugarte (No. 3), [2000] 1 AC 147, 148-149 (HL 1999) (UK) (holding that head of state immunity prevented prosecution or extradition of former Chilean President Augusto Pinochet for acts that predated the ratification of the Torture Convention by Chile, Spain and the United Kingdom).

68. UN Committee against Torture, Decision on Admissibility, annex VI, at 109–113, UN Doc. A/45/44, 21 June 1990.

69. Ibid.

70. Ibid., 111.

71. International Covenant on Civil and Political Rights, opened for signature 16 December 1966, 6 ILM 368, 999 UNTS 171. The International Covenant currently has 154 parties, including both Liberia and Nigeria. Office of the United Nations High Commissioner for Human Rights, "Ratifications and Reservations: International Covenant on Civil and Political Rights", available from http://www.ohchr.org/english/countries/ratification/4.htm (last visited 18 December 2005).

72. European Convention for the Protection of Human Rights and Fundamental Freedoms, 4 November 1950, 213 UNTS 221.

73. Organization of American States, American Convention on Human Rights, adopted 22 November 1969, OAS TS No. 36, 1144 UNTS 123.

74. Yoram Dinstein (1981) "The Right to Life, Physical Integrity, and Liberty", in Louis Henkin, ed., The International Bill of Rights, New York: Columbia University Press, pp. 114, 119 (arguing that parties to the International Covenant on Civil and Political Rights arguably must exercise due diligence to prevent intentional deprivation of life by individuals, "as well as to apprehend murderers and to prosecute them in order to deter future takings of life"); Orentlicher, "Settling Account", 2568 (arguing that states have a duty to bring torturers to justice); Thomas Buergenthal (1981) "To Respect and To Ensure: State Obligations and Permissible Derogations", in Louis Henkin, ed., The International Bill of Rights, New York: Columbia University Press, pp. 72, 77 ("[The] obligation to 'ensure' rights creates affirmative obligations on the state – for example, to discipline its officials").

75. Scharf, "The Letter of the Law", pp. 49–51 (criticizing the conclusion that decisions of the Inter-American Court and Commission establish criminal prosecution as the only permissible remedy for violations of the American Convention); Velásquez Rodríguez Case, 1988 Inter-Am. Ct. HR (ser. C) No. 4, Judgment, paras 164, 194 (29 July 1988) (reaching disposition of case without ordering criminal prosecution); Hermosilla v. Chile, Case 10.843, Inter-Am. CHR, Report. No. 36/96, OEA/Ser.L/V/II.95, doc. 7 rev., paras 57, 63, 66, 77 (1996) (finding that Chile's grant of amnesty and failure to investigate related disappearances violated American Convention because they foreclosed victims' families' rights to pursue their own criminal and civil remedies); Orayece v. Chile, Case 11.505 et al., Inter-Am. CHR, Report No. 25/98, OEA/ser.L/V/II.98, doc. 6 rev., paras 60–71 (1998) (making similar findings regarding Chile's violation of duty to investigate and to provide victims and families with judicial remedies);

Espinoza v. Chile, Case 11.725, Inter-Am. CHR, Report No. 133/99, OEA/Ser.L/V/ II.106, doc. 3 rev., paras 79–107 (2000) (making similar findings). For a summary of several relevant decisions of international and regional human rights bodies, see UN Economic and Social Council, Sub-Committee on Prevention of Discrimination and Protection of Minorities (1993) "Study Concerning the Right to Restitution, Compensation and Rehabilitation for Victims of Gross Violations of Human Rights and Fundamental Freedoms", paras 50–92, UN Doc. E/CN.4/SUB.2/1993/8 (submitted by Theo van Boyen), reprinted in Law and Contemporary Problems 59 (1996): 284–324.

76. The Secretary-General (1993) "Report of the Secretary-General Pursuant to Paragraph 2 of Security Council Resolution 808, annex, delivered to the Security Council", UN Doc. S/25704.

77. SC Res. 955, annex art. 3, UN Doc. S/RES/955 (Nov. 8, 1994).

78. Statute of the Special Court for Sierra Leone, art. 2, available from http://www.sc-sl. org/scsl-statute.html (last visited 13 November 2005).

79. Rome Statute, art. 7.

80. See, for example, ibid.

81. The Charter of the Nuremberg War Crimes Tribunal was the first international instrument in which crimes against humanity were codified. Charter of the International Military Tribunal annexed to the Agreement for the Prosecution and Punishment of Major War Criminals of the European Axis, 8 August 1945, 59 Stat. 1544, 82 UNTS 279, as amended by Berlin Protocol of 6 October 1945, reproduced in Virginia Morris and Michael P. Scharf (1998) *The International Criminal Tribunal for Rwanda*, New York: Transnational Publishers, vol. 2, 473–480.

82. Naomi Roht-Arriaza (1995) "Sources in International Treaties of an Obligation to Investigate, Prosecute and Provide Redress", in N. Roht-Arriaza, ed., *Impunity and Human Rights in International Law and Practice*, Oxford: Oxford University Press, p. 25.

83. See note 8 (collecting sources).

84. Restatement (Third) of the Foreign Relations Law of the United States § 102(2) (1987); see also Statute of the International Court of Justice, art. 38(1)(b), 26 June 1945, 59 Stat. 1031, 1051, available from http://www.icj-cij.org/icjwww/ibasicdocuments.htm (providing that sources of international law applied by the court include "international custom, as evidence of a general practice accepted as law").

85. Bruno Simma (1995) "International Human Rights and General International Law: A Comparative Analysis", in *Collected Courses of the Academy of European Law*, Trier: Academy of European Law, vol. 4, pp. 153–216.

86. See, for example, Declaration on Territorial Asylum, GA Res. 2312 (XXII), art. 4, UN GAOR, 22d Sess., Supp. No. 16, UN Doc. A/6716 (1 December 1967) (stating that the right to asylum may not be invoked for crimes contrary to the purposes and principles of the United Nations); Question of the Punishment of War Criminals and of Persons Who Have Committed Crimes against Humanity, GA Res. 2712 (XXV), para. 3, UN GAOR, 25th Sess., Supp. No. 28, UN Doc. A/8028 (15 December 1970) (adopted 55-4 with 33 abstentions) (condemning crimes against humanity and calling "upon the States concerned to bring to trial persons guilty of such crimes"); Question of the Punishment of War Criminals and of Persons Who Have Committed Crimes against Humanity, GA Res. 2840 (XXVI), para. 4, UN GAOR, 26th Sess., Supp. No. 29, UN Doc. A/8429 (18 December 1971) (adopted 71-0 with 42 abstentions) (affirming that a state's refusal "to cooperate in the arrest, extradition, trial and punishment" of persons accused or convicted of crimes against humanity is "contrary to the United Nations Charter and to generally recognized norms of international law"); Principles of International Cooperation in the Detection, Arrest, Extradition, and Punishment of Persons

Guilty of War Crimes and Crimes against Humanity, GA Res. 3074 (XXVIII), para. 1, UN GAOR, 28th Sess., Supp. No. 30, UN Doc. A/9030 (3 December 1973) (adopted 94-0 with 29 abstentions) (providing that crimes against humanity "shall be subject to investigation and the persons against whom there is evidence that they have committed such crimes shall be subject to tracing, arrest, trials and, if found guilty, to punishment"); Declaration on the Protection of All Persons from Enforced Disappearances, GA Res. 47/133 preamble, art. 14, UN Doc. A/47/49, at 207, 209 (18 December 1992) (equating disappearances to a crime against humanity and requiring states to try any person suspected of having perpetrated an act of enforced disappearance); see also Principles on the Effective Prevention and Investigation of Extra-Legal, Arbitrary and Summary Executions, ESC Res. 1989/65 annex, para. 18, UN Doc. E/1989/89, at 53 (24 May 1989) (resolving that states shall bring to justice those accused of having participated in extra-legal, arbitrary or summary executions). It is noteworthy that large numbers of countries abstained during voting on the above-listed resolutions, and thereby did not manifest their acceptance of the principles enumerated therein.

87. The final Declaration and Programme of Action of the 1993 World Conference on Human Rights affirms that "states should abrogate legislation leading to impunity for those responsible for grave violations of human rights such as torture and prosecute such violations, thereby providing a firm basis for the rule of law". World Conference on Human Rights, 14–25 June 1993, "Vienna Declaration and Programme of Action", para. 60, UN Doc. A/Conf.157/23 (25 June 1993).

88. See, for example, Convention on the Non-Applicability of Statutory Limitations to War Crimes and Crimes against Humanity, art. 1(b), done Nov. 26, 1968, 754 UNTS 73 (entered into force 11 November 1970) (providing that no statutory limitation shall apply to crimes against humanity, irrespective of the date of their commission). Only 39 states have ratified the Convention. Even if the Convention were more widely ratified, the prohibition on applying a statute of limitations to crimes against humanity is not the equivalent of a duty to prosecute such crimes.

89. Declaration on Territorial Asylum, GA Res. 2312 (XXII), art. 1(2), UN GAOR, Sess. 24, Supp. No. 16, UN Doc. A/6716, 14 December 1967.

90. Ibid. at 81. Even if the Declaration were binding, the prohibition on granting asylum is not the equivalent of a duty to prosecute, and informal sanctuary can be accorded without a formal grant of asylum.

91. "Declaration of Territorial Asylum", 1967 UNYB 758, 759, UN Sales No. E.68.I.1.

92. Simma, "International Human Rights and General International Law", p. 217.

93. Scharf, "The Letter of the Law", pp. 57–58 (citing numerous examples).

94. *Prosecutor v. Kallon & Kambara*, Case Nos. SCSL-2004-15-AR72(E), SCSL-2004-16-AR72(E), Decision on Challenge to Jurisdiction: Lomé Accord Amnesty, para. 7 (13 March 2004), available from http://www.sc-sl.org/Documents/SCSL-04-15-PT-060-I.pdf and http://www.sc-sl.org/SCSL-04-15-PT-060-II.pdf (holding that there was no "general obligation for States to refrain from amnesty laws on these crimes ... [and that] consequently, if a State passes any such law, it does not breach a customary rule", quoting Antonio Cassese (2003) *International Criminal Law*, Oxford: Oxford University Press, p. 315).

95. The Secretary-General (2004) "Report of the Secretary-General on the Rule of Law and Transitional Justice in Conflict and Post-Conflict Societies" para. 64, UN Doc. S/2004/616. See also UN SCOR, 59th Sess., 5052nd mtg. at 5, UN Doc. S/PV.5052 (6 October 2004), for the Secretary-General's remarks to the Security Council.

96. UN SCOR, 59th Sess., 5052nd mtg. at 14, UN Doc. S/PV.5052 (6 October 2004); UN SCOR, 59th Sess., 5052nd mtg., Resumption 1 at 26, 37–38, UN Doc. S/PV.5052 (Resumption 1) (6 October 2004).

97. Christopher A. Ford (1994) "Adjudicating *Jus Cogens*", Wisconsin International Law Journal 13: 145; see also Anthony D'Amato (1990) "It's a Bird, It's a Plane, It's *Jus Cogens*", *Connecticut Journal of International Law* 6: 1, (discussing the broad array of norms lumped under the heading *jus cogens*).

98. The state system, characterized as an association of sovereign states governed by positive law rules to which they must consent before they are bound, is widely believed to have originated with the Peace of Westphalia, which ended the Thirty Years War in 1648. Stephane Beaulac (2000) "The Westphalian Legal Orthodoxy: Myth or Reality?" Journal of the History of International Law 2: 148. For the full text of the Peace of Westphalia (Osnabrück and Münster) Treaties, in both their Latin and English versions, see Clive Parry, ed. (1969) *Consolidated Treaty Series*, New York: Oceana Publications, vol. 1, pp. 119–270.

99. Restatement (Third) of the Foreign Relations Law of the United States § 102 cmt. (1987).

100. *United States v. Krupp*, 9 Trials of War Criminals Before the Nierenberg Military Tribunals Under Control Council Law No. 10, at 1395 (1950).

101. Article 53 of the Vienna Convention provides:

> A treaty is void if, at the time of its conclusion, it conflicts with a peremptory norm of general international law. For the purposes of the present Convention, a peremptory norm of general international law is a norm accepted and recognized by the international community of States as a whole as a norm from which no derogation is permitted and which can be modified only by a subsequent norm of general international law having the same character.

> Vienna Convention, at 344.

102. Remarks of Antonio de Luna (Spain) in Summary Records of the 15th Session, 684th Meeting [1963] Year Book of the International Legal Commission 1(72), para. 61, UN Doc. A/CN.4/156 and Addenda.

103. Ibid.

104. Michael P. Scharf (2001) "The ICC's Jurisdiction over the Nationals of Non-Party States: A Critique of the U.S. Position", *Law and Contemporary Problems* 64: 67–90 ("It is now widely accepted that crimes against humanity are subject to universal jurisdiction."); *Demjanjuk v. Petrovsky*, 776 F.2d 571, 582 (6th Cir. 1985) (observing that "international law recognizes 'universal jurisdiction' over certain offenses", including crimes against humanity and genocide).

105. See note 8 (collecting sources).

106. Vienna Convention, at 344.

107. *Princz v. Federal Republic of Germany*, 26 F.3d 1166, 1180 (D.C. Cir. 1994) (Wald, J., dissenting) (citing *Comm. of U.S. Citizens Living in Nicar. v. Reagan*, 859 F.2d 929, 940 (D.C. Cir. 1988)).

108. As Judge Patricia Wald noted in *Princz*:

> To ascertain customary international law, judges resort to "the customs and usages of civilized nations, and, as evidence of these, to the works of jurists and commentators." These same tools are used to determine whether a norm of customary international law has attained the special status of a *jus cogens* norm.

> Ibid. (quoting *The Paquete Habana*, 175 US 677, 700 (1900)).

109. See *Siderman de Blake v. Argentina*, 965 F.2d 699, 715 (9th Cir. 1992) ("The universal and fundamental rights of human beings identified by Nuremberg – rights against

genocide, enslavement, and other inhumane acts – are the direct ancestors of the universal and fundamental norms recognized as jus cogens." (citation omitted)); *Demjanjuk*, 776 F.2d at 582 (stating that "international law recognizes 'universal jurisdiction' over certain offenses", including crimes against humanity and genocide); *Hirsh v. Israel*, 962 F. Supp. 377, 381 (SDNY 1997), aff'd 133 F.3d 907 (2d Cir. 1997) ("A foreign state violates *jus cogens* when it participates in such blatant violations of fundamental human rights as 'genocide, slavery, murder, torture, prolonged arbitrary detention, and racial discrimination.'" (quoting *Comm. of U.S. Citizens Living in Nicar. v. Reagan*, 859 F.2d 929, 941 (D.C. Cir. 1988)); Barcelona Traction, Light & Power Co. (*Belg. v. Spain*), 1970 ICJ 3, 32 (5 February) (distinguishing between rights of protection that have entered into the body of general international law and those that are conferred by international instruments); Reservations to the Convention on the Prevention and Punishment of the Crime of Genocide, Advisory Opinion, 1951 ICJ 15, 23 (28 May) ("The principles underlying the Convention are recognised by civilised nations as binding on States even without any conventional obligation."); Theodor Meron (1995) "International Criminalization of Internal Atrocities", *American Journal of International Law* 89: 554–558 ("The core prohibitions of crimes against humanity and the crime of genocide constitute *jus cogens* norms.").

110. See *Wei v. Jiang*, 383 F.3d 620, 627 (7th Cir. 2004) (concluding that violation of *jus cogens* is not an implied waiver of head of state immunity); *Smith v. Socialist People's Libyan Arab Jamahiriya*, 101 F.3d 239, 244 (2d Cir. 1996) (same); *Princz v. Federal Republic of Germany*, 26 F.3d 1166, 1173 (D.C. Cir. 1994) (same); *Siderman de Blake v. Argentina*, 965 F.2d 699, 719 (9th Cir. 1992) (determining whether sovereign immunity under US law applies to *jus cogens* violations); *Regina v. Bow St. Metro.* Stipendiary Magistrate, *ex parte* Pinochet Ugarte (No. 3), [2000] 1 AC 147 (HL 1999) (UK) (allowing head of state immunity defence for crimes committed prior to ratification of Torture Convention); Case Concerning the Arrest Warrant of 11 April 2000 (*Dem. Rep. Congo v. Belg.*), 2002 ICJ 21–22 (14 February), available from http://www.icj-cij.org/icjwww/idocket/iCOBE/iCOBEframe.htm (denying exception to head of state immunity for war crimes); *Al-Adsani v. United Kingdom*, No. 35763/97, § 61, Eur. Ct. HR (2001) (affirming state immunity from international civil suits).

111. Cf. Ratner, "New Democracies, Old Atrocities", 714 (characterizing the procedural requirement to prosecute as "accountability norms" and the substantive law establishing offenses as "liability norms"); Mark A. Summers (2003) "The International Court of Justice's Decision in *Congo v. Belgium*: How Has It Affected the Development of a Principle of Universal Jurisdiction that Would Obligate All States to Prosecute War Criminals?", *Boston University International Law Journal* 21: 63–95 (characterizing the procedural requirement to prosecute as "obligatory universal jurisdiction", and distinguishing it from "voluntary universal jurisdiction").

112. Michael P. Scharf (1999) "The Amnesty Exception to the Jurisdiction of the International Criminal Court", *Cornell International Law Journal* 32: 507–527; Darryl Robinson (2003) "Serving the Interests of Justice: Amnesties, Truth Commissions and the International Criminal Court", *European Journal of International Law* 14: 482, n. 5.

113. Michael P. Scharf and Nigel Rodley (2002) "International Law Principles on Accountability", in M. Cherif Bassiouni, ed., *Post-Conflict Justice*, New York: Transnational Publishers, pp. 89–95.

114. Ibid., p. 96.

115. Memorandum from Alberto R. Gonzales, Counsel to the President, to President George W. Bush, 25 January 2002, at 2, available from http://www.humanrightsfirst.org/us_law/etn/gonzales/memos_dir/memo_20020125_Gonz_Bush.pdf. In a dissenting memo, Secretary of State Colin Powell argued that Gonzales's position "reverse[s]

over a century of U.S. policy and practice in supporting the Geneva Conventions and undermine[s] the protections of the law of war for our troops, both in this specific conflict and in general". Memorandum from Colin L. Powell, US Secretary of State, to Alberto R. Gonzales, Counsel to the President, and Condoleezza Rice, Assistant to the President for National Security Affairs, 26 January 2002, at 2, available from http://www.humanrightsfirst.org/us_law/etn/gonzales/memos_dir/memo_20020126 _Powell_WH%20.pdf.

116. Memorandum from US Department of Justice, Office of Legal Counsel, to Alberto R. Gonzales, Counsel to the President, 1 August 2002, at 1, available from http://www. humanrightsfirst.org/us_law/etn/gonzales/memos_dir/memo_20020801_JD_%20Gonz_. pdf.

117. Confirmation Hearing on the Nomination of Alberto R. Gonzales to be Attorney General of the United States: Hearing Before S. Comm. on the Judiciary, 109th Cong. 507 (2005) (testimony of John D. Hutson, Dean and President of Franklin Pierce Law Center).

118. Scharf and McNeal, *Saddam on Trial*.

119. See note 94 and accompanying text.

120. Beaulac, "The Westphalian Legal Orthodoxy", p. 148 (describing the origins of the state system in the Peace of Westphalia, which ended the Thirty Years War in 1648).

121. *Regina v. Bow St. Metro*. Stipendiary Magistrate, *ex parte* Pinochet Ugarte (No. 3), [2000] 1 AC 147, 148–149 (HL 1999) (UK).

122. Peter A. Barcroft (2005) "The Slow Demise of Impunity in Argentina and Chile", available from http://www.asil.org/insights/2005/01/insight050107.htm (reporting that Chile has revoked Pinochet's immunity and initiated criminal proceedings against him) (on file with *Washington and Lee Law Review*).

123. Lizza, "Charles at Large", p. 10. The European Parliament advocated the adoption of a UN Security Council Resolution that would require Nigeria to surrender Taylor to the Special Court for Sierra Leone for prosecution. Bruce Zagaris (2005) "European Parliament Passes Resolution Calling for Action to Ensure Taylor's Court Appearance", International Enforcement Law Report 21: 200. On 11 November 2005, the UN Security Council unanimously adopted Resolution 1638, which expanded the mandate of the UN force in Liberia to include apprehending Charles Taylor in the event that he returns to Liberia and to transfer him to the Special Court for Sierra Leone for prosecution. Although the resolution did not require Nigeria to revoke Taylor's asylum, it did pointedly refer to Taylor's asylum as a "temporary stay" in Nigeria. SC Res. 1638, preamble, para. 1, UN Doc. S/RES/1638 (11 November 2005).

124. "Nigeria; Taylor Deported, Now in S-Leone", *Africa News*, 30 March 2006.

15

Concluding remarks:
The questions that still remain

William A. Schabas and Ramesh Thakur

Not very long ago, the issues that make up the subject matter of this volume barely concerned the international community. Certainly, the idea of international prosecution and other forms of accountability was not novel, and there were important precedents. After both of the world wars, the victorious allies experimented with judging the vanquished. That these initiatives were considerably more successful after the Second World War than after the First might suggest some progressive development. And indeed, Nuremberg and the related proceedings were followed by a brief period of dynamism, manifested in efforts to codify principles of accountability in international law.

The post–Second World War developments included efforts at definition of international crimes. Both "genocide" and a category of war crimes known as "grave breaches" were codified in the late 1940s by well-accepted treaties. But the central concept of crimes against humanity remained relatively impotent, emasculated at Nuremberg by a requirement that they be committed in association with armed conflict.[1] The law of international crimes then remained relatively static for several decades until a period of spectacular development in the 1990s that was associated with the establishment of the ad hoc international criminal tribunals for the former Yugoslavia and Rwanda, and the adoption of the Rome Statute of the International Criminal Court.

In the post–Second World War period, there was great uncertainty about where these crimes could be prosecuted. Universal jurisdiction had some precedents, but with regard to crimes like piracy, where all or many

Atrocities and international accountability: Beyond transitional justice, Hughes, Schabas and Thakur (eds), United Nations University Press, 2007, ISBN 978-92-808-1141-4

states had some collective self-interest in repression of acts committed on the high seas. But there was much resistance to applying the concept to crimes where the perpetrators were associated with the state itself. The original draft resolution on genocide presented to the United Nations General Assembly in late 1946 said: "*Whereas* the punishment of the very serious crime of genocide when committed in time of peace lies within the exclusive territorial jurisdiction of the judiciary of every State concerned, while crimes of a relatively lesser importance such as piracy, trade in women, children, drugs, obscene publications are declared as international crimes and have been made matters of international concern".[2] But the reference to universal jurisdiction was dropped in the final version of the resolution, adopted in December 1946, nor was the idea endorsed in the 1948 Genocide Convention.

This was largely a consequence of the Cold War context. States were extremely reluctant to allow for crimes committed on their territory to be punished elsewhere, out of concern this become a vehicle for political mischief and manipulation. Thus, while the 1949 Geneva Conventions set out a duty to investigate and either prosecute or extradite persons suspected of committing grave breaches no matter where they were committed,[3] the 1948 Genocide Convention contented itself with an obligation to prosecute crimes committed on the territory of the state where the crime was committed.[4] It was a recipe for impotence, as many critics at the time insisted.

By the early 1960s, the courts of Israel, relying upon "customary international law", had enlarged the jurisdictional scope of prosecution for genocide. Despite terms of the 1948 Genocide Convention, which directed prosecution of Nazi war criminal Adolf Eichmann before the courts of Germany or Poland, they authorized his trial in Jerusalem to proceed.[5] But while significant in a theoretical sense, states remained extremely reluctant to appoint themselves as the enforcers of international law in the absence of some important national interest. The Eichmann trial stands in relative isolation as one of the rare episodes of the exercise of universal jurisdiction prior to the 1990s.

In the past, transitional periods were often accompanied by blanket amnesties. Sometimes this was predicated on a well-intentioned belief that it was best to forgive and forget. Often, though, the motivation was more cynical, a deal cut with former tyrants in return for their graceful (and peaceful) departure. The wisdom of amnesty seemed confirmed in international law, the most relevant provision being article 6(5) of the Additional Protocol to the Geneva Conventions concerning non-international armed conflict, which was adopted in 1977: "At the end of hostilities, the authorities in power shall endeavour to grant the broadest possible amnesty to persons who have participated in the armed conflict, or those deprived of their liberty for reasons related to the armed conflict, whether they are interned or detained."[6] In a general sense, this provision crystallized an approach to transitional justice or post-conflict justice that set peace and reconciliation as the fundamental objective.

The important legal developments of the 1990s that form the backdrop for the discussions in this volume can trace their immediate origins to changes in the law and philosophy of international human rights. In the 1980s, a rights-based approach began to emerge that took the standpoint of victims of atrocities. The human rights movement had not always been so eager to combat impunity. In an earlier time, it tended to view the criminal justice system not as a tool for the enforcement of human rights but rather as an instrument of repression by evil regimes. Human rights activists took sides, as a general rule, with the defendant and with the prisoner, and held an undisguised contempt for prosecutors and jailers. One of the defining moments in the transformation of the human rights movement was the *Velásquez-Rodríguez* case of the Inter-American Court of Human Rights, one of that institution's very first contentious decisions. Manfredo Velásquez was "disappeared" by a paramilitary group widely believed to be associated with the authorities. Faced with the difficulty in proving any direct link between the killers and the state, the Inter-American court turned to the suspicious failure of police and judicial officials in Honduras to properly investigate the crime and to bring the perpetrators to justice.[7]

Henceforth, this "horizontal" dimension of human rights law became increasingly predominant. Again and again, in rulings of the European and Inter-American Courts of Human Rights, the European and African Commissions,[8] and the treaty bodies or committees established under the relevant United Nations instruments for the protection of human rights,[9] it was held that the State had a positive duty to investigate crimes and to bring those responsible to justice. In March 2001, the European Court of Human Rights affirmed that the *European Convention on Human Rights* "implies a primary duty to secure the right to life by putting in place effective criminal-law provisions to deter the commission of offences which endanger life, backed up by law-enforcement machinery for the prevention, suppression and sanctioning of breaches of such provisions".[10]

Some have also argued that accountability for atrocities is dictated by the very needs of a peace process or a transition. They argue that societies that do not address the crimes of the past are in a sense fatally compromised, doomed to return to conflict and violence as cycles of revenge reassert themselves in subsequent generations. There is anecdotal evidence to suggest this is the case, but in the last resort it remains a matter of conjecture, an unproven hypothesis. Some transitions fail and some societies return to violence, but this may be explained by many factors, and not solely because justice was not delivered. Furthermore, there is no shortage of examples of societies that have transited from periods of conflict to those of peace and social stability without any accountability process. Spain is a recent example that is often cited in this respect.

Thus, although the peacebuilding rationale for transitional justice may have some place in the discourse, it is nevertheless not the most compelling justification. Lawyers, in particular, seem much more comfortable addressing these issues where the raison d'être is a rights-based legal imperative rather than a utilitarian measure to be employed on a case by case basis, depending on the anticipated needs of a particular society. The victim-based philosophical underpinnings reflected in the judgments of the international human rights courts has become the basis of the claim that accountability for atrocity is not only desirable in some cases, but it must be delivered in *all* cases, regardless of the consequences on a peace process.

But at least two recent cases involving the interaction of transitional justice and peace negotiations, those of Liberia and Uganda, suggest that too absolute an approach to the matter is not without troublesome consequences.

In March 2003, the Special Court for Sierra Leone issued an indictment directed against the sitting president of neighbouring Liberia, Charles Taylor.[11] One of Africa's more notorious tyrants, he was charged with manipulating rebel forces during the Sierra Leone conflict and, under evolving principles of individual criminal liability, was deemed an accomplice in various atrocities although he may not have ordered them or ever set foot in the territory himself. Some months later, in June 2003, when Taylor travelled to Ghana for peace negotiations related to his own country's civil war, the indictment was made public and the Court called upon Ghana to arrest him. Ghana demurred, allowing Taylor to return to Liberia. But the peace talks were disrupted and the war continued.

In August 2003, negotiations in Monrovia succeeded in bringing peace to Liberia. Nigerian president Olusegun Obosanjo cut the Gordian knot, granting Taylor asylum as an inducement enabling him to relinquish power. Since then, Liberia has enjoyed a dynamic peacebuilding process. Democratic elections in 2005 brought the first woman head of state in Africa to power. As a symbol of its evolving democratic culture, Liberia abolished capital punishment and ratified the Second Optional Protocol to the International Covenant on Civil and Political Rights.

It would be difficult to argue that in dealing with the Charles Taylor indictment in 2003, the Special Court for Sierra Leone held the Liberian peace process uppermost in its considerations. Nor, many would argue, should it. There is a strong argument that justice should be blind to such considerations. Richard Goldstone, who was the first operational prosecutor of the International Criminal Tribunal for the former Yugoslavia, recounts in his memoirs the aftermath of the indictment of Bosnian Serb leaders Karadžić and Mladić, in July 1995, as the peace process in that war was maturing. UN Secretary-General Boutros Boutros-Ghali complained at not being consulted prior to Goldstone's decision to indict Karadžić and Mladić. Boutros-Ghali left Goldstone with the impression that his advice would have been to forestall indictment until peace negotiations had been completed. "The point is", wrote Goldstone, "that prosecutors cannot expect to be briefed fully on the politics of a situation, and politicians cannot expect to be briefed on the knowledge of the prosecutor."[12]

Liberia provides an example of peace without justice, yet one whose success cannot be gainsaid. A truth and reconciliation commission has been established, but there is no momentum for prosecutions of the old regime. Eventually, in 2006, bowing to enormous international pressure, Nigerian president Obosanjo relinquished Taylor to the Special Court for Sierra Leone. According to the Secretary-General, although some Liberians wanted Taylor to be brought to justice (for crimes committed in Sierra Leone), "others argued that he should have been left in Nigeria as his trial would be disruptive to the Liberian reconciliation process and could destabilize Liberia and the subregion".[13] The Security Council gave its imprimatur to the transfer of Taylor to the Hague, where he is to stand trial in a courtroom loaned to the Special Court for Sierra Leone by the International Criminal Court. The Council declared that "the continued presence of former President Taylor in the subregion is an impediment to stability and a threat to the peace of Liberia and of Sierra Leone and to international peace and security in the region".[14] It said that trial of Charles Taylor before the Special Court for Sierra Leone would "contribute to achieving truth and reconciliation in Liberia and the wider subregion", but made no mention of possible accountability for crimes Taylor may have committed in Liberia.[15]

During the negotiations leading to the adoption of the Rome Statute of the International Criminal Court, the South African delegation regularly took the floor to raise the question of how the Court might handle a potential conflict between a domestic peace process and the imperatives of international prosecution. At the time, South Africa was in the midst of the work of its celebrated Truth and Reconciliation Commission. The Commission was part of a transitional process that had essentially renounced the idea of criminal accountability of those responsible for the racist apartheid regime that had prevailed in South Africa for many decades. If the International Criminal Court requires prosecution for such crimes, the South Africans asked, how will it react when domestic peacemakers, in their own wisdom, conclude that prosecution is not only not desirable but plainly counterproductive?

The question was never answered. The conundrum was left unresolved. The Rome Statute says "it is the duty of every State to exercise its criminal jurisdiction over those responsible for international crimes". The Prosecutor has a degree of discretion, under article 53, and may decide not to proceed if this does not "serve the interests of justice". The exercise of this discretion is considered in the essay in this volume by Matthew Brubacher. The Court, in the exercise of judicial rather than prosecutorial discretion, may itself also decline a case that "is not of sufficient gravity".

The South Africans proved to be clairvoyant in their insistence that the issue be addressed. That the Court may not be a vehicle for peace but rather an obstacle to it moved from a theoretical possibility to a genuine problem with its first "situation", the prosecution of five leaders of the Lord's Resistance Army of northern Uganda. In late 2003, Prosecutor Luis Moreno-Ocampo instigated Ugandan President Yoveri Museveni to refer the situation in northern Uganda to the Court, in accordance with article 14 of the Rome Statute.[16] Probably, Museveni saw the Court as a mechanism that could bring the rebels to heel, and help resolve the civil war that had wracked the country for nearly two decades. But as the peace process in Uganda ripened, the five arrest warrants directed at the Lord's Resistance Army commanders became an important issue in negotiations. In contrast with the situation of a decade earlier, in South Africa, when Nelson Mandela could promise F. W. De Klerk there would be no prosecutions as a quid pro quo for democratic transition, Museveni could no longer negotiate on the same basis. The trump card of immunity from prosecution had been taken from his hand. Or rather, it had been played, with the ratification of the Rome Statute of the International Criminal Court.

It is increasingly obvious that we are now in a brave new world where, for the first time in history, the negotiators of an agreement to end war and conflict can no longer barter justice for peace. More and more governments have their hands tied by the Rome Statute. There is the likelihood that in the future the International Criminal Court may contribute to the prolongation of conflict rather than its resolution. For many activists, experts and observers, this is a welcome development, as it enhances the campaign against impunity. But at the very least, it immensely complicates the task of the peacemakers.

The problem received inadequate attention when the Rome Statute was being drafted, not because of neglect but because the views on the subject were too diverse. It had not arisen in the same way with the ad hoc tribunals because they remained under the dominance of the Security Council. If criminal justice ever threatened the prerogatives of the Security Council in its search for international peace and security, there was a mechanism to address the difficulty. This Scylla and Charybdis of peace and justice, far from being resolved by the Rome Statute and the growing commitment to accountability, seems destined to emerge as one of the great challenges of the future.

When Boutros Boutros-Ghali asked Richard Goldstone why he had not taken "political" advice before indicting Bosnian Serb leaders, out of concern this might compromise peace negotiations, he struck at the heart of the problem. Should the prosecutor of an international court even contemplate such matters? Common sense suggests that peace and justice are related, that they interact. But as we continue to experiment in our quest for accountability for atrocity, a final answer eludes us.

Criminal justice is not, of course, the only form of accountability for atrocity. The internationalization of prosecution in recent years, whether it be through the vehicle of genuinely international courts, or through national courts, on the basis of universal jurisdiction, or so-called hybrid tribunals that blend international and domestic features, has been accompanied by another genre of mechanism labelled generically as a "truth commission". The South African Truth and Reconciliation Commission is the paradigm, at least in the popular mind, although it had some quite unique features. There have been many other truth commissions, each with its own distinctions, in post-conflict situations.[17] They are now a virtually ubiquitous part of the transitional justice landscape. In a few cases, lawmakers have rejected the approach entirely, such as in Rwanda. But these are the exceptions that prove the rule.

Truth commissions typically involve an intense research phase in which reports and data are gathered about violations of human rights and international humanitarian law, by interviewing both victims and perpetrators. A period of public hearings follows, with testimony about the atrocities themselves, as well as a more thematic or expert analysis of the conflict. It is dangerous here to generalize too much, because no two commissions are the same, but they normally seek to clarify the truth about atrocities and then promote some form of reconciliation for those who were involved.

The idiosyncrasies of the South African model have distorted many discussions of truth commissions in general. It was empowered to grant amnesty to perpetrators in exchange for their testimony. In effect, criminal justice could be avoided in exchange for a contribution to the truth-telling process. But very few truth commissions have operated on this basis. In Sierra Leone, for example, where a truth commission operated from 2002 to 2004, there was no issue of granting amnesty. Perpetrators had already escaped justice as a result of an amnesty contained within the

1999 Lomé Peace Agreement. Yet, perpetrators testified before the Sierra Leone Truth and Reconciliation Commission at a rate that was more or less comparable to that of the South African body, suggesting that the promise of amnesty for truth may be less significant than many believe. In any event, a perceptive South African could see easily enough that there was little likelihood of prosecution, even without an amnesty.

Like criminal prosecution, the truth commission is also inspired and driven by a logic derived from human rights law and practice. Victims are entitled to justice, but they are also entitled to truth. In one of the early United Nations studies dealing with impunity and accountability, prepared for the Sub-Commission on the Prevention and Promotion of Human Rights, French magistrate Louis Joinet wrote of the "inalienable right to truth": "Every people has the inalienable right to know the truth about past events and about the circumstances and reasons which led, through the consistent pattern of gross violations of human rights, to the perpetration of aberrant crimes. Full and effective exercise of the right to the truth is essential to avoid any recurrence of such acts in the future."[18]

Truth commissions are generally predicated on the inability of criminal justice to address all forms of criminal behaviour associated with a civil war or with a period of tyrannical rule. They are widely perceived as alternatives to criminal prosecution. Again, the South African approach has been terribly influential here, with its suggestion that a truth commission operates in a kind of tension with criminal prosecution. The two were set up as rivals, a bit like the classic scenario of the "good cop/bad cop" interrogation.

It may be more accurate to say that truth commissions fill the gaps left by criminal prosecution, which is generally inadequate to deal with the accountability issues that follow periods of mass atrocity. Besides being politically daunting to bring all perpetrators to justice, this may also be impossible because of resource issues alone. Justice is expensive, if it is done properly, and few poor countries have the wherewithal to meet its demands. And choices are to be made. Making criminal justice the imperative could mean neglecting other important pieces of post-conflict reconstruction, such as schools, hospitals and other infrastructure, of necessary support.

The Rwandan example is particularly instructive here, as Gerald Gahima's paper in this volume suggests. Rwanda is probably the most uncompromising in its insistence that all perpetrators be brought to trial. It has attempted to innovate, with a form of criminal prosecution that combines some elements of the truth commission process, at least in its South African variant. Perpetrators receive an incentive, in the form of a reduced sentence, as a quid pro quo for public confession. The process was aimed at a socially untenable situation where a significant proportion

of the country's population had been in detention for many years following the 1994 genocide. But when the new trials before traditional courts
known as *gacaca* began in earnest, the confessions led to denunciations,
and the case load skyrocketed. From perhaps 100,000 suspects who were
to be addressed by the gacaca courts, the number soon climbed to about
1 million. But dealing with 1 million alleged perpetrators of atrocity in a
country with a population of less than 8 million poses a challenge to accountability that seems beyond contemplation.

It is probably better to view truth commissions and similar mechanisms
as complementary to rather than competitive with criminal justice. Increasingly, countries will opt for a combination of approaches to accountability. The experience in Sierra Leone, where the Special Court for
Sierra Leone worked alongside the Truth and Reconciliation Commission,
has shown that this is feasible. For two years the institutions operated in
parallel, from premises that were even located in geographic proximity
within Freetown. There were a few points of tension, but this tended to
confirm the general compatibility of the two institutions. Similar positive
reports of constructive relationships between courts and truth commissions emerge from Argentina, Peru and East Timor.[19]

Some observers reported that ordinary Sierra Leoneans were sometimes confused about the distinction between the Special Court and the
Truth Commission. This was said to be a problem requiring various sen-
sitization campaigns in order to improve public awareness. But perhaps it
was too ambitious to expect them to understand clearly the differences
between the two bodies. It would be unusual for ordinary citizens in
other countries to provide a sophisticated description of the applicable
justice system. That does not mean they do not understand that if crimes
are committed, they will be punished. And so it is with post-conflict justice environments.

If Sierra Leoneans with limited education and literacy were confused
about the differences between the Special Court and the Truth Commission, this same fact proves that they grasped some of the fundamentals:
atrocities would not be forgotten, and institutions would stigmatize the
perpetrators. Moreover, in the fog of their alleged confusion they appear
to have discerned a fundamental commonality of the two mechanisms.
There is a spectrum of approaches to dealing with the horrors of the
past. Not only should we expect countries to experiment with various options, their choices may evolve over time, as the Rwandan experience has
demonstrated.

If nothing else, the papers in this volume manifest the diversity of recent experience in post-conflict justice. Decades of silence have been
followed by an increasingly robust international commitment to ensure
accountability for atrocity. No formula exists to determine the correct

proportions, as this is dependent upon too many variables, and the particularities of each country, its culture and its history. Out of all of this, new insights emerge.

The term "accountability" implies a focus on the past. Its association with such concepts as a "right to truth" or "historical memory" seems to confirm this retrospective vision. But there is a dialectic at work here. We deal with the past in order to address the future. It is easy to confirm that accountability "works" if we are indifferent to whether it prevents atrocity and not only commemorates it. Whether or not accountability deters future cycles of violence and persecution is in the realm of speculation. There is no proof of effectiveness. Our confidence is intuitive, at best. Nevertheless, to the extent that accountability, whatever form it may take, is utilitarian and not only retributive, it seems worth all of the efforts that are underway, and more.

Notes

1. *Agreement for the Prosecution and Punishment of Major War Criminals of the European Axis, and Establishing the Charter of the International Military Tribunal (I.M.T.)*, (1951) 82 UNTS 279, art. 7(c).
2. UN Doc. A/BUR/50, preamble.
3. *Convention for the Amelioration of the Condition of the Wounded and Sick in Armed Forces in the Field* (1949) 75 UNTS 31, art. 49; *Convention for the Amelioration of the Condition of Wounded, Sick and Shipwrecked Members of Armed Forces at Sea* (1950) 75 UNTS 85, art. 50; *Convention Relative to the Treatment of Prisoners of War* (1950) 75 UNTS 135, art. 129; *Convention Relative to the Protection of Civilian Persons in Time of War* (1950) 75 UNTS 287, art. 146.
4. *Convention on the Prevention and Punishment of the Crime of Genocide* (1951) 78 UNTS 277, art. 6.
5. *A.-G. Israel* v. *Eichmann* (1968) 36 I.L.R. 5 (District Court, Jerusalem), paras 20–38; *A.-G. Israel* v. *Eichmann* (1968) 36 I.L.R. 277 (Israel Supreme Court), para. 12.
6. *Protocol Additional to the 1949 Geneva Conventions and Relating to the Protection of Victims of Non-International Armed Conflicts* (1979) 1125 UNTS 609, art. 6(5).
7. *Velásquez Rodríguez* v. *Honduras*, 29 July 1988, Series C, No. 4.
8. Douglass Cassel (2001) "International Human Rights Law in Practice: Does International Human Rights Law Make a Difference?" *Chicago Journal of International Law*, 2: 121.
9. For example: *Bautista de Arellana* v. *Colombia* (no. 563/1993), UN Doc. CCPR/C/55/D/563/1993, paras 8, 3, 10; *Laureano* v. *Peru* (no. 540/1993), UN Doc. CCPR/C/56/D/540/1993, para. 10.
10. *Streletz, Kessler and Krenz* v. *Germany*, European Court of Human Rights, 22 March 2001, para. 86. Also: *Akkoç* v. *Turkey*, European Court of Human Rights, 10 October 2000, para. 77.
11. *Prosecutor* v. *Taylor* (Case No. SCSL-2003-01-I), Indictment, 7 March 2003; *Prosecutor* v. *Taylor* (Case No. SCSL-2003-01-I), Decision Approving the Indictment and Order for Non-Disclosure, 7 March 2003.

12. R. J. Goldstone (2000) *For Humanity: Reflections of a War Crimes Investigator*, New Haven, Conn.: Yale University Press.
13. "Eleventh Progress Report of the Secretary-General on the United Nations Mission in Liberia", UN Doc. S/2006/376, para. 3.
14. UN Doc. S/RES/1688 (2006), preamble. Also: *Prosecutor v. Taylor* (Case No. SCSL-2003-01), Order Changing Venue of Proceedings, 19 June 2006.
15. UN Doc. S/RES/1688 (2006), preamble.
16. M. El Zeidy (2005) "The Ugandan Government Triggers the First Test of the Complementarity Principle: An Assessment of the First State's Party Referral to the ICC", *International Criminal Law Review* 5: 5.
17. For the authoritative study, see P. Hayner (2002) *Unspeakable Truths: Facing the Challenge of Truth Commissions*, 2d ed., New York: Routledge.
18. "Question of the Impunity of Perpetrators of Human Rights Violations (Civil and Political), Final Report Prepared by Mr. Joinet Pursuant to Sub-Commission Decision 1996/119", UN Doc. E/CN.4/Sub.2/1997/20.
19. "The Rule of Law and Transitional Justice in Conflict and Post-Conflict Societies, Report of the Secretary-General", UN Doc. S/2004/616, para. 26.

Index